The Absent Dialogue

MODERN SOUTH ASIA

The Other One Percent
Sanjoy Chakravorty, Devesh Kapur, and Nirvikar Singh

Social Justice through Inclusion
Francesca R. Jensenius

Dispossession without Development
Michael Levien

The Man Who Remade India
Vinay Sitapati

Business and Politics in India
Edited by Christophe Jaffrelot, Atul Kohli, and Kanta Murali

Mobilizing the Marginalized
Amit Ahuja

Clients and Constituents
Jennifer Bussell

Gambling with Violence
Yelena Biberman

The Absent Dialogue
Anit Mukherjee

The Absent Dialogue

Politicians, Bureaucrats, and the Military in India

ANIT MUKHERJEE

OXFORD
UNIVERSITY PRESS

OXFORD
UNIVERSITY PRESS

Oxford University Press is a department of the University of Oxford. It furthers
the University's objective of excellence in research, scholarship, and education
by publishing worldwide. Oxford is a registered trade mark of Oxford University
Press in the UK and certain other countries.

Published in the United States of America by Oxford University Press
198 Madison Avenue, New York, NY 10016, United States of America.

© Oxford University Press 2020

Library of Congress Cataloging-in-Publication Data
Names: Mukherjee, Anit, author.
Title: The absent dialogue : politicians, bureaucrats, and the military in India / by Anit Mukherjee.
Description: [New York] : [Oxford University Press], [2019] | Includes bibliographical references. |
Summary: "Civilian control over the military is widely hailed as among the biggest successes of India's
democracy. This is a rarity, especially among post-colonial states, and is rightfully celebrated. But has this
come at a cost? In The Absent Dialogue, Anit Mukherjee argues that the pattern of civil-military relations in
India has hampered its military effectiveness. Indian politicians and bureaucrats have long been content with
the formal and ritualistic exercise of civilian control, while the military continues to operate in institutional
silos, with little substantive engagement between the two. In making this claim, the book closely examines
the variables most closely associated with military effectiveness—weapons procurement, jointness (the
ability of separate military services to   operate together), officer education, promotion policies, and
defense planning. India's pattern of civil-military relations—best characterized as an absent dialogue—
adversely affects each of these processes. Theoretically, the book adopts the 'unequal dialogue' framework
proposed by Eliot Cohen but also argues that, under some conditions, patterns of civil-military relations
maybe more closely resemble an 'absent dialogue.' Informed by more than a hundred and fifty interviews
and recently available archival material, the book represents a deep dive into understanding the power and
the limitations of the Indian military. It sheds new light on India's military history and is essential reading for
understanding contemporary civil-military relations and recurring problems therein. While the book focuses
on India, it also highlights the importance of civilian expertise and institutional design in enhancing civilian
control and military effectiveness in other democracies"—Provided by publisher.
Identifiers: LCCN 2019017422 | ISBN 9780190905903 (hardback) | ISBN 9780190905927 (epub) |
ISBN 9780190905910 (updf)
Subjects: LCSH: Civil-military relations—India. | India—History, Military. |
India—Politics and government.
Classification: LCC JQ220.C58 M86 2019 | DDC 322/.50954—dc23
LC record available at https://lccn.loc.gov/2019017422

1 3 5 7 9 8 6 4 2

Printed by Integrated Books International, United States of America

For
Shyamoli and Pulak Mukherjee

CONTENTS

ACKNOWLEDGMENTS

As is not uncommon, this book began much before I began my graduate education in 2003. Looking back, I think the questions about military effectiveness started during my second stint in Kashmir, when the insurgency was militarily at its most violent phase. As junior officers are wont to do, I remember anguished and angry conversations complaining about the state of our weapons, night vision devices, and radio sets. When queried, most senior officers had one stock answer—the problems we faced were created by the faceless but all-powerful civilians sitting in Delhi. Later, in 2001–2002 during Operation Parakram, the border mobilization crisis with Pakistan, I was to hear similar refrains. The leitmotif within the Indian military was clear—it was paying the price, often in blood, for weaknesses on the civilian side. Critically examining this narrative formed the core of my doctoral dissertation. Like with all intellectual journeys, my answer, however, took me in a different direction; and I realized that it is a bit more complicated than that. There are constraints on India's military effectiveness to be sure, but these stem from problems on both the civilian *and* the military sides.

From the army to academia has been a long journey, and I owe a debt of thanks to lots of people and institutions. First, the Indian Army, the National Defence Academy, and 19 Armoured Regiment, where I was commissioned, have all played a role in shaping my identity—one that I am very proud of. I still count on my association with all of them and hope they see this book for what it is—a labor of love and not just one of unbridled criticism.

Second, upon leaving the army, I was very lucky to find an academic home at the Paul H. Nitze School of Advanced International Studies (SAIS), Johns Hopkins University. The university provided a perfect environment for learning and for friendships. I owe a debt of gratitude to my committee and advisers: Walter Andersen, Eliot Cohen, Stephen Cohen, Sunil Khilnani, Thomas Mahnken, and Ashley Tellis. They all played a role in both challenging and encouraging me, and this book owes a lot to them. SAIS was also great for the friends I made, among the faculty and fellow students; and I would like to especially acknowledge Tuong Do, Jennifer Gulbrandson, Selina Ho, Claudio Lilienfeld, Khalid Nadiri, Oriana Scherr, Samit Shah, Levi Tilleman, Benedikt Wahler, and Jennifer Wethey, among many others.

Third, I had many institutional homes during my dissertation—the Brookings Institution (first as a research assistant and later as a non-resident fellow at Brookings India), the RAND Corporation (as a summer associate), and the Foreign Policy Research Institute. From 2010 to 2012, I was also fortunate to work as a research fellow at the Institute for Defence Studies and Analysis (IDSA), in New Delhi. This was a perfect home and a very congenial place (especially the Military Affairs Centre) to engage with and learn from the Indian strategic community, and I am grateful to successive directors—Narendra Sisodia and Arvind Gupta. In 2012, I got an opportunity as a postdoctoral fellow at the Centre for the Advanced Study of India, University of Pennsylvania. For this I am grateful to Devesh Kapur, who not only taught me how to build a community but also that scholarship should be grounded in humility. I continue to cherish the association and friendship I built up there, and thanks so much to Juliana Di Giustini, Aparna Wilder, Apoova Jadhav, Georgette Rochlin, and Alan Atchison.

The S. Rajaratnam School of International Studies (RSIS), Nanyang Technological University in Singapore, has now been my home since 2013; and I have enjoyed teaching and researching at this institution. I would like to thank Ong Keng Yong, Barry Desker, Rajesh Basrur, Joseph Liow, Ralf Emmers, Tan See Seng, Ang Cheng Guan, Bhubhindar Singh, Sinderpal Singh, Sumitha Narayan Kutty, Evan Resnick, and other members of the staff and students. I would especially like to acknowledge Pascal Vennesson, who encouraged me to present sections of this book at the RSIS Luncheon Seminar Series. I would also like to thank two wonderful research assistants, Shivani Bagdai and Joseph Matten.

Research for this book has benefited from a number of different sources. I would like to thank the staff at the Hartley Library, University of Southampton, Teen Murti Memorial and Library, the United Services Institution of India, the IDSA library (especially Mukesh Kumar), and Chong Yee Ming and Jean Lai Foong Yee at the RSIS library. I also learned a lot from the community of journalists—many of whom have been reporting fearlessly, and without favor, for decades. Thanks especially to Rahul Bedi, Indrani Bagchi, Pramit Pal Chaudhuri, Natasha Israni, Saurabh Joshi, Maya Mirchandani, Dinakar Peri, Ajai Shukla, Seema Sirohi, Sushant Singh, Josy Joseph, and Sandeep Unnithan. Among the most satisfying aspects of this book were the more than one hundred and fifty interviews, many of them repeated, with high-ranking officials. Those interviewed are listed at the end of this book—and I would like to thank each one of them.

In addition, I conducted around fifty interviews with serving officials who requested anonymity. All of these interviews were extremely educative, and I am grateful to all of them for their time. I take full responsibility for the views in this book and would like to apologize to my interviewees in case they feel that I was not able to accurately convey their perspectives.

Fifth, despite popular characterization, I found academia and the think-tank world to be a surprisingly social place and must consider myself fortunate to have a community of scholars. From a different generation, I would like to thank Kanti Bajpai, Nayan Chanda, Sumit Ganguly, Tim Hoyt, C. Raja Mohan, T. V. Paul, Stephen Rosen, and Steven Wilkinson. There is also an entire community which is closer to my age—although most are not really all that close. I would like to thank: Cara Abercrombie, Amit Ahuja, Bilal Baloch, Nicolas Blarel, Rudra Chaudhuri, Amit Chanda, Ian Hall, Ho Shu Huang, Dhruva Jaishankar, Gaurav Kampani, Shashank Joshi, Sharad Joshi, Yogesh Joshi, Mara Karlin, Walter Ladwig, Sameer Lalwani, Manjeet Pardesi, Samir Puri, Tanvi Madan, Oriana Skylar Mastro, Manjari Chatterjee Miller, Siddharth Mohandas, Rani Mullen, Rohan Mukherjee, Srinath Raghavan, Ayesha Ray, Rahul Sagar, Vance Serchuk, Zorawar Daulet Singh, Paul Staniland, Caitlin Talmadge, Arzan Tarapore (especially for sharing his as yet unpublished dissertation), Milan Vaishnav, Urmila Venugopalan, Joshua White, and Constantino Xavier. Chris Clary and Vipin Narang deserve special mention for helping me reshape the book when it was required.

While I was turning the dissertation into this book, I published a version of two of the chapters as journal articles. The first, titled "Fighting Separately: Jointness and Civil–Military Relations in India," was published by the *Journal of Strategic Studies* and I was lucky to be awarded the Amos Perlmutter Prize in 2017 by the journal. The second, titled "Educating the Professional Military: Civil–Military Relations and Professional Military Education in India," was published in *Armed Forces & Society*, I thank both journals for letting me republish parts of these articles in this book.

This book owes a lot to the Modern South Asia series editors Pradeep Chibber and Ashustosh Varshney. Also, my editor, David McBride, helped me tremendously and ably steered me to the finish line. In addition, I would like to thank Niko Pfund, Emily Mackenzie, and Barun Sarkar.

I am also fortunate to have friends, some of them for a lifetime, who supported me in this long journey: Suranya Aiyar, Yamini Aiyar, Prashant Bahadur, Cassandra Berman, Arul Chib, Brin Desai, Santanu De, Amit Kapur, Adarsh Kumar, Raimund Magis, Azad Oomen, Rajat Pratap, Rishi Shehrawat, Manohar Thyagaraj, and so many others. In addition, I would also like to thank Lillian Jamin for the domestic support she has given our family over the last six years.

Among the other benefits of my education in America was that it allowed me to spend time with my brother, Romit, and his family Vrinda, Rohan, and Aanya. They generously welcomed me into their lives, and I am very grateful for the memories. My wife, Malobi, took on more than her share, allowing me to complete this book, and typically, just pointed out that this is probably the longest acknowledgment she read in her whole life. She has been a source of constant joy and a wonderful mother to our two boys, Ayan and Aayush. They suffered, not always silently; and I hope they forgive me for not being there as much. Finally, I would like to thank my parents—who have been a constant source of love and support; my dreamlike journey would not have been possible without them. It is to them that I dedicate this book.

ABBREVIATIONS

AAP	Annual Acquisition Plans
ACR	Annual Confidential Reports
ACC	Appointment Committee of the Cabinet
AFSPA	Armed Forces Special Powers Act
ARTRAC	Army Training Command
BJP	Bhartiya Janata Party
BRO	Border Roads Organization
BSF	Border Security Force
CDS	Chief of Defence Staff
COSC	Chiefs of Staff Committee
CDM	College of Defence Management
COSTIND	Commission for Science, Technology and Industry for National Defense
CORTOS	Committee for the Review of Training of Officers for the Services
CDP	Committee on Defense Planning
CONDU	Committee to Recommend the Outline for a National Defense University
CAG	Comptroller and Auditor General
CII	Confederation of Indian Industries
CIJW	Counter Insurgency and Jungle Warfare
DPSU	Defence Public Sector Undertakings
DSSC	Defence Services Staff College
DAC	Defense Acquisition Council
DMC	Defense Ministers Committee
DOPMA	Defense Officer Personnel Management Act
DPC	Defense Planning Committee
DPS	Defense Planning Staff

DPSUs	Defense Public Sector Units
DRDO	Defense Research and Development Organization
DGA	Director General of Armaments
FOST	Flag Officer Sea Training
FDI	Foreign Direct Investment
FAC	Forward Air Controllers
GSQRs, often called QRs	General Staff Qualitative Requirements
GEC	Grievances Examination Committee
GoM	Group of Ministers
IAS	Indian Administrative Services
IDAS	Indian Defense Accounts Services
INDU	Indian National Defense University
IPKF	Indian Peace Keeping Force
IDS	Integrated Defence Staff
IB	Intelligence Bureau
JAAOC	Joint Army Air Operation Center
JSCSC	Joint Services Command and Staff College
LTTE	Liberation Tigers of Tamil Eelam
LCA	Light Combat Aircraft
LoC	Line of Control
LTIPP	Long Term Integrated Perspective Plan
MGO	Master General of Ordnance
MMRCA	Medium Multi-Role Combat Aircraft
MS	Military Secretary
DMA	Ministerial Delegation for Armament
MEA	Ministry of External Affairs
MoF	Ministry of Finance
NDA	National Defence Academy
NDC	National Defence College
NSAB	National Security Advisory Board
NSCS	National Security Council Secretariat
NSG	National Security Guard
NTRO	National Technical Research Organisation
OSD	Office of the Secretary of Defense
OROP	One Rank, One Pay
OROP	One Rank, One Pension
OF	Ordnance Factories
called HQ OFC	Overall Forces Headquarters
PAF	Pakistan Air Force
PLA	People's Liberation Army
PCOSC	Permanent Chairman Chiefs of Staff Committee

PMO	Prime Minister's Office
PME	Professional Military Education
RFP	Request for Proposal
RAW	Research and Analysis Wing
RTI	Right to Information
SLAWS	School of Land and Air Warfare
SA	Scientific Adviser
SCAP	Service Capital Acquisition Plan
SME	Small Medium Enterprises
TAC	Tactical Air Center
TRADOC	Training Command
UN	United Nations

ABOUT THE COMPANION WEBSITE

http://global.oup.com/us/companion.websites/9780190900656/

Oxford has created a website to accompany the titles in the Modern South Asia series. Material that cannot be made available in a book, namely series editor information and submission guidelines, are provided here. Readers are encouraged to consult this resource if they would like to find out more about the books in this series.

Introduction

How does a developing country create an effective military that is not a threat to its democracy? Can a state exercise civilian control and, at the same time, maximize the effectiveness of its military? Or is this a zero-sum game where one comes at the cost of the other? This book addresses these questions and argues that the prevailing norm and the structure of civil–military relations in India have had an adverse impact on the effectiveness of its military.

The success of India's democracy, in the face of formidable challenges, has attracted much scholarly attention. However, the effect of this on the Indian military—more than a million strong and involved in numerous external wars and internal counterinsurgencies—has not fetched as much interest.[1] Direct military intervention in politics, the bane of democracy in many developing countries, is fortunately not a major concern in India. Despite external threats and significant deployment in internal security missions, the military has not posed a serious threat to the country's polity, coup rumors notwithstanding. This is one of the bigger achievements of India's democracy, to the credit of its politicians and the military. As such, India is a mature democracy, defined as one "where civilian control has historically been strong and military establishments have focused on external defense."[2] In fact, there is a counternarrative, very popular within the military, that civilians have too much control. Stephen Cohen, one of the foremost experts on the Indian military, argued that "not only does India have civilian control; it has an almost crushing civilian dominance over

---

[1] Some notable exceptions are Stephen P. Cohen, *The Indian Army: Its Contribution to the Development of a Nation* (New Delhi: Oxford University Press, 1990); Stephen P. Rosen, *Societies and Military Power: India and Its Armies* (Ithaca, NY: Cornell University Press, 1996); and Steven I. Wilkinson, *Army and Nation: The Military and Indian Democracy since Independence* (Cambridge, MA: Harvard University Press, 2015).

[2] Richard Kohn, "How Democracies Control the Military," *Journal of Democracy* 8, no. 4 (1997): 141. For a similar conceptual approach, see Douglas Bland, "Patterns in Liberal Democratic Civil–Military Relations," *Armed Forces and Society* 27, no. 4 (2001): 525–40.

a very powerful and large military."[3] More recent accounts support this notion and, according to one commonly held view, "India's biggest curse, where defense preparedness goes, is the excessive civilian dominance over military planning."[4] There is an element of truth to this characterization, but it overstates the case. To borrow from Samuel Huntington's seminal work *The Soldier and the State*, the problem in India is "not armed revolt but the relation of the expert to the politician."[5] Civilians, for instance, have very little input in defense and operational planning, and the military enjoys significant autonomy on this and other issues. In effect, civilians and the military operate in silos, and there is thus an absence of a well-informed dialogue between the two, which is detrimental to military effectiveness.

This chapter begins by relating some vignettes of contemporary civil–military relations in India, which give us an insight and convey a sense of the disquiet and the recurring crises in this field.[6] Next, it describes the conditions of the "absent dialogue," which I argue best captures the nature of India's civil–military relations. Thereafter, it explains why these conditions persist. It then highlights the relevance of this book. The penultimate section describes the sources and methodology, and I conclude by providing an overview of the book.

It may be noted that this book does not focus on the relationship between the Indian military and society. While this is an important yet understudied subject, it requires a substantially different research approach. Rather, the focus of this book is on the interaction between politicians, bureaucrats, and the military.

"A Dysfunctional Equilibrium": Crises in India's Civil–Military Relations

On the night of January 16, 2012, an Indian mechanized infantry battalion moved from Hisar, its home station, toward New Delhi, just about 150 kilometers away. Around the same time, a parachute battalion also moved

---

[3] Stephen Cohen, "Civilian Control of the Military in India," in *Civilian Control of the Military*, ed. Claude E. Welch Jr., 47 (Albany: State University of New York Press, 1976).

[4] Ravi Vellor, *India Rising: Fresh Hope New Fears* (New Delhi: Konark Publishers, 2016), 202.

[5] Samuel Huntington, *The Soldier and the State: The Theory and Politics of Civil–Military Relations* (Cambridge, MA: Harvard University Press, 1957), 20.

[6] Anit Mukherjee, "The Crisis in Civil–Military Relations," *Hindu Business Line*, September 26, 2012.

from Agra toward the capital. These movements were unexpected and not reported to civilian officials in the Ministry of Defence (MoD). According to one account, these units moved directly on orders from army headquarters and without the knowledge of the field commanders, in this case the western and central army commanders, respectively.[7] This happened on the same day when Chief of Army Staff General V. K. Singh, in an unprecedented step, made a personal representation against the government in the Supreme Court.[8] Indian intelligence agencies detected the movement of these military units and a "bemused establishment raised an alert of sorts."[9] According to one version, they deliberately issued a false warning of an impending terrorist strike, to slow down the army convoys—as the highway traffic was now subject to security checks—while the MoD and the security establishment, right up to the prime minister, tried to understand the intentions underlying these movements. Eventually, after a meeting between senior civil and military officials, the army convoys returned to their home station. *The Indian Express*, a well-regarded newspaper, first reported this story on April 5, 2012; and it immediately created a media storm. Top political leaders, including Prime Minister Manmohan Singh and Defence Minister A. K. Antony, denied the story; but clearly, there was a considerable mistrust between civilians and the military. A couple of years later this story was confirmed by the former director general of military operations, Lieutenant General A. K. Choudhary, when he admitted that he had been called in by a "worried" defense secretary and asked to explain these movements.[10]

This instance of civil–military distrust is not unique. In 2008, in a controversy over a report by the Sixth Pay Commission, the three service chiefs—of the army, navy, and air force—refused to notify a cabinet order as they were unhappy with its recommendations. This action led a leading columnist to argue, "for the first time, these incumbents [service chiefs] have stood in defiance of civil authority as no military chiefs have ever done in India's history."[11]

---

[7] Interview with a senior official who served in the Ministry of Defence at that time, Singapore, February 16, 2015. To speak frankly, the official requested anonymity.

[8] The army chief was embroiled in a dispute about his date of birth, see "Army Chief Takes Govt. to Supreme Court over Age Issue," *The Indian Express*, January 20, 2012.

[9] This account of the incident relies on Shekhar Gupta, Ritu Sarin, and Pranab Dhal Samanta, "The January Night Raisina Hill Was Spooked: Two Key Army Units Moved Towards Delhi Without Notifying Govt.," *Indian Express*, April 5, 2012.

[10] Manu Pubby, "Lt-Gen A K Choudhary: 'Troop Movement Should've Been Avoided if They Knew (V K Singh's) Court Date,'" *Indian Express*, February 21, 2014.

[11] Shekhar Gupta, "Chain of Command, Demand," *Indian Express*, September 7, 2011, http://archive.indianexpress.com/news/chain-of-command-demand/369248/0.

Allegations that the military was "out of control" also emerged when in 2013 Home Minister P. Chidambaram expressed his helplessness at amending a controversial law, the Armed Forces Special Powers Act (AFSPA), "as the army has taken a strong stand."[12] However, there is a counternarrative that ignorant politicians and a callous bureaucracy were undermining the military's concerns and denying it an institutional role in deliberating upon matters pertaining to national security. These concerns came to public attention in a dramatic manner when, in an unprecedented gesture, on February 26, 2014, the chief of naval staff, Admiral D. K. Joshi, resigned from service. The first service chief to do so, in his resignation letter he accepted "moral responsibility" for a series of naval accidents. This set off a fresh bout of speculation and allegations of mismanagement of defense leading to "strains and eruptions in civil–military relations like never before."[13] A few months after leaving office Admiral Joshi, in a hard-hitting interview, called attention to the "dysfunctional and inefficient" pattern of administration "wherein professional competence, domain expertise, accountability, responsibility and authority, these all reside in separate silos."[14]

According to some, these problems were primarily due to political mishandling by the Congress government, so when Narendra Modi came to power in 2014, his early speeches in support of defense reforms raised high expectations. However, within a couple of years, he came under attack for not delivering on his promises and, in fact, even for general inattention to the MoD.[15] Modi was unable to overcome the structural problems in India's civil–military relations. These problems arise from what I term the "absent dialogue."

---

[12] See Sandeep Joshi, "Army's Stand Makes It Hard to Amend AFSPA: Chidambaram," *The Hindu*, February 7, 2013; also see Sanjoy Hazarika, "An Abomination Called AFSPA," *The Hindu*, February 12, 2013.

[13] Vishal Thapar, "Undermined Chiefs Unhappy with Antony," *Sunday Guardian*, March 2, 2014; also see C. Uday Bhaskar, "Civil–Military Relation in India Need Holistic Review," *Salute: To the Indian Soldier*, February–March 2014; and Rajat Pandit and V. Narayan, "Indian Navy Chief Admiral D.K. Joshi Resigns over Warship Accidents," *Times of India*, February 26, 2014.

[14] Nitin A. Gokhale, "'Vested Interests Have Stalled Reforms,' Former Navy Chief Admiral DK Joshi Tells NDTV: Full Transcript," NDTV.com, October 15, 2014. The website was subsequently pulled down, but a transcript of the interview is available here: https://aamjanata.com/politics/media/vested-interests-have-stalled-reforms-former-navy-chief-admiral-dk-joshi-tells-ndtv-full-transcript/.

[15] D. S. Hooda, "Civil–Military Relations: Let's Not Weaken the Corporate Character of Our Force," News18.com, http://www.news18.com/news/india/opinion-civil-military-relations-lets-not-weaken-the-corporate-character-of-our-forces-1563541.html; Srinath Raghavan, "Decoding OROP and the Politics at Play," NDTV, June 2, 2015; and Purnima S. Tripathi, "United Against Pay Panel Award," *Frontline*, 33, no. 20, October 14, 2016.

The Absent Dialogue

The central claim advanced in this book is that the pattern of civil–military relations in India compromises the effectiveness of the military. This pattern, which I term an "absent dialogue," consists of the following: (1) lack of civilian expertise on military issues at both the bureaucratic and political levels, (2) an institutional design wherein the military is under strong bureaucratic control, and (3) considerable military autonomy over activities that it considers to be within its own domain. In practical terms, the MoD is almost exclusively staffed by civilians, whereas military officers work out of the services. These factors are a cause of much discord between civilians and the military.

In making this claim I examine the variables associated with military effectiveness—weapons procurement, jointness (the ability of the army, air force, and navy to operate together), professional military education, promotion policies, and defense planning. To be sure, there are other factors shaping military effectiveness, and it is incorrect to imagine it as monocausal.[16] However, as discussed in Chapter 1, most studies attribute military effectiveness to these five inputs. At the same time, I do not explicitly link these inputs with military effectiveness. This is not only because it is a difficult exercise (for instance, to show how officer promotion and education policies in democracies shape military effectiveness), but it would also require a different methodological approach, which is beyond the scope of this book. Instead, I study the variables associated with military effectiveness. Moreover, this study does not focus on the output end of military effectiveness, which would be to examine combat operations at the tactical or operational level. Such an approach requires access to battlefield data and operational records, which are still largely unavailable and can even be unreliable.[17]

As we shall see later in the book and I readily acknowledge, elements of the absent dialogue do not always apply. For instance, civilians play a negligible role in shaping military education. This finding is at variance with popular perceptions of "stifling civilian control."[18] Therefore, such insights about the nature of civilian control in India are in themselves valuable. In addition, it is important to note that the structure of civil–military relations is not static and that

---

[16] For a good discussion on this, see Fillipo Andreatta, "Conclusion: The Complexity of Military Effectiveness," in *The Sword's Other Edge: Trade-offs in the Pursuit of Military Effectiveness*, ed. Dan Reiter, 254–67 (Cambridge: Cambridge University Press, 2017).

[17] For instance, there is a discrepancy in battlefield casualty data in the records of the Indian Army. See Anit Mukherjee, "Name upon a Grave," *The Caravan*, February 2014, 22–24.

[18] Rahul Bedi, "Why Are India's Army and Government at Loggerheads?," BBC News, April 6, 2012, https://www.bbc.com/news/world-asia-india-17635618.

certain reforms have brought about systemic changes. Despite these changes, as Verghese Koithara evocatively put it, civil–military relations in India still reflect a "pattern of depthless interaction."[19]

Why Does This Pattern of Civil–Military Relations Persist?

Over the past decade or so, perhaps because of the numerous controversies, there has been a renewed interest in civil–military relations in India. It is widely accepted that there are major fissures in civil–military relations and that this has adversely affected its military effectiveness. According to the defense analyst Air Commodore Jasjit Singh, India has an "ossified system of defense management" and the "structure of the ministry is a major factor for its inefficiency."[20] Others have made similar arguments.[21] It is not as if those within the government do not recognize these weaknesses. For example, the term "defense preparedness," arguably a corollary of military effectiveness, has been used extensively in numerous reports by the Indian Parliament's standing committee on defence and by the press.[22] Weaknesses in defense preparedness were also highlighted in reports of the comptroller and auditor general on ammunition shortages and by Vice Chief of Army Staff Lieutenant General Sarath Chand before the standing committee on defense.[23]

[19] Verghese Koithara, *Managing India's Nuclear Forces* (Washington, DC: Brookings Institution Press, 2012), 184.

[20] Jasjit Singh, "Higher Defence Management: Principles and Practice in India," *CLAWS Journal* (Summer 2013): 9–10. For a discussion of "shortcomings" in national security, see Arun Prakash, "Civil–Military Dissonance: The Bane of India's National Security," *Maritime Affairs* 10, no. 1 (2014): 1–19.

[21] For two thoughtful critiques written by former defense secretaries, see Shekhar Dutt, "The Conundrum of Indian Defense and Civil–Military Relationship," in *Core Concerns in Indian Defence and the Imperatives for Reforms*, ed. Vinod Misra, 9–18 (New Delhi: Pentagon Press, 2015); and N. N. Vohra, "Civil–Military Relations: Opportunities and Challenges," *Air Power Journal* 8, no. 4 (2013): 1–17.

[22] See, for instance, Standing Committee on Defense, *Demand for Grants: First Report* (New Delhi: Lok Sabha Secretariat, August 2004), 20, and "PM Briefed upon India's Defense Preparedness," *Outlook India*, December 26, 2008.

[23] See the following: "Indian Army Ammunition Won't Even Last 10 Days in Event of a War, Suggests CAG Reports," *The Indian Express*, May 9, 2015; Vishnu Som, "70% Equipment Vintage": Army Officer Says Defence Budget Dashed Hopes," NDTV News, March 14, 2018, https://www.ndtv.com/india-news/70-of-armys-equipment-is-vintage-army-officer-to-parliament-panel-1823474; and Standing Committee for Defense, *Forty Second Report: Capital Outlay on Defense Services, Procurement Policy and Defense Planning* (New Delhi: Lok Sabha Secretariat, March 2018).

Why, then, does India continue with this pattern of civil–military relations despite its widely acknowledged drawbacks? I delineate three independent factors to explain this: lack of existential threat, low salience in electoral politics, and a reluctance to change the status quo.

Civilian leaders believe that India does not face an existential threat and that, therefore, the current model of civil–military relations is efficient enough to deal with existing threats. Moreover, there has been a historical fear among both politicians and bureaucrats of the possibility of a coup or of a politically empowered military.[24] Members of the Indian military may cry themselves hoarse about their apolitical nature and their commitment to civilian control; however, politicians are wary of the potential threat that the military poses to the democratic order. Also, civilians are reluctant to alter the current structure as they are afraid that in a policy dispute the military's view will prevail more easily. According to Ashley Tellis,

> the weaknesses of this [civilian] control system are widely recognized in India, but being content with the protection afforded by the country's great size and inherent strength relative to its adversaries, Indian security managers—historically—have consciously refrained from altering the structure of strict civilian control no matter what benefits in increased military efficiency might accrue as a result.[25]

Second, there is little electoral incentive for the political elite as, short of defeat in battle, military issues do not resonate with most voters. "Defense management," Vipin Narang and Paul Staniland point out, "has almost always been both low salience and low clarity, with complex, long-term projects that evade simple responsibility for outcomes or the knowledge and interest of the general public."[26] As a result, few politicians are willing to put in the effort to gain familiarity with this subject. Interestingly though, in states with a large veteran community, like Punjab, Himachal Pradesh, and Haryana, politicians are responsive but mainly on matters pertaining to the welfare or status of soldiers and veterans. Specialist topics like defense reforms and structure of civilian control have not yet received attention. In light of recent events, including what is claimed to be

---

[24] Steven Wilkinson's excellent book captures these fears and describes some of the "coup-proofing" measures undertaken to prevent such a possibility, see Wilkinson, *Army and Nation*.

[25] Ashley Tellis, *India's Emerging Nuclear Posture: Between Recessed Deterrent and Ready Arsenal* (Santa Monica, CA: Rand, 2001), 285.

[26] Vipin Narang and Paul Staniland, "Democratic Accountability and Foreign Security Policy: Theory and Evidence from India," *Security Studies* 27, no. 3 (2018): 427.

the first national security elections in India in the summer of 2019, we shall revisit this assertion at the end of the book.

Third, despite occasional protests from some reformists, all stakeholders prefer to continue with the status quo. As far as the military is concerned, it is comfortable with the existing structure of civil–military relations as it gives the military considerable autonomy over what it sees as its domain. The military prefers that civilians not interfere or ask well-informed questions—necessarily born out of expertise—on professional matters. Civilians are also content with the existing structure as they enjoy power with limited accountability. Thus, there is very little impetus for change—unless perhaps there is a military crisis that ends badly. As highlighted by the Kargil Review Committee, set up after the 1999 war with Pakistan, it is difficult to usher in reforms as the "political, bureaucratic, military and intelligence establishments appear to have developed a vested interest in the status quo."[27]

Relevance of the Book

This study of civil–military relations and military effectiveness in India is important for a number of reasons. First, this book is the single most detailed study of civil–military relations in the world's largest democracy, which faces military threats across all ends of the spectrum—terrorist attacks on military bases, low-intensity warfare (across the Line of Control with Pakistan), counterinsurgency, limited and large-scale conventional warfare, and potential nuclear war. The Indian military is an exception as despite being a large standing army with significant internal and external roles, conditions ordinarily considered ripe for intervention, it has not displayed praetorian tendencies. This should be instructive for those countries struggling with civilian control. Among the major insights is the critical role of the MoD and the military's desire to be apolitical. It also highlights India's successes and challenges and the manner in which it exercises civilian control. India's story in this regard, like in many other fields, is both an exemplary and a cautionary one.

Second, this book contributes to the current "renaissance" in the study of civil–military relations.[28] Perhaps due to the involvement of Western militaries in wars abroad, there is renewed interest in the exercise of military power. The effect

---

[27] Kargil Review Committee, *From Surprise to Reckoning: The Kargil Review Committee Report* (New Delhi: Sage Publications, 2000), 252.

[28] Peter Feaver, "Civil–Military Relations and Policy: A Sampling of a New Wave of Scholarship," *Journal of Strategic Studies* 40, no. 1–2 (2017): 17.

of civil–military relations on military effectiveness, however, is understudied, with calls for making it "a priority for future research."[29] Most studies so far have examined either non-democracies or the effects of "coup-proofing" on military effectiveness.[30] By examining military effectiveness in a democracy through the prism of civil–military relations, this book advances a less examined conceptual approach.[31] It sheds new light on the issue of civilian control in democracies and provides a fresh perspective on concepts like military autonomy, institutional design, and civilian expertise.

Third, this study helps contextualize some of the current controversies pertaining to Indian politics and defense policy. For example, to a degree not seen before, in recent times, Indian television audiences are subjected to former soldiers arguing, often indignantly, usually about some alleged civilian malfeasance. These complaints, more fully explored in Chapter 8, pertain to different issues—pay and allowances, status, rank equivalence, etc. It might be tempting to dismiss their views as a stereotype, but it is important to understand that their (real and imaginary) grievances have historical roots. Some of their views, seamlessly transmitted through social media, are downright strident and portend unhealthy civil–military relations.

Finally, apart from India's defense policy, there are larger implications of this study. Based on the central premise of the book, it can be argued that similar administrative, procedural, and governing norms should lead to similar outcomes. Hence, if the generalist civil service, administrative procedures, denial of information, and lack of expertise adversely impact the effectiveness of the Indian military, then these should have a similar effect on other governmental organizations. I argue that at a macro level there are problems with the effectiveness of *every* ministry and government department in India. Admittedly, such a sweeping generalization requires further research but resonates with current

---

[29] Peter Feaver, "Civil–Military Relations," *Annual Review of Political Science* 2 (June 1999): 234.

[30] Caitlin Talmadge, *The Dictator's Army: Battlefield Effectiveness in Authoritarian Regimes* (Ithaca, NY: Cornell University Press, 2015); Timothy Hoyt, "Social Structure, Ethnicity, and Military Effectiveness: Iraq, 1980–2004," in *Creating Military Power: The Sources of Military Effectiveness*, Risa Brooks and Elizabeth Stanley, 55–79 (Stanford, CA: Stanford University Press, 2007); James T. Quinlivan, "Coup-Proofing: Its Practice and Consequences in the Middle East," *International Security* 24, no. 2 (1999): 131–65; and Ulrich Pilster and Tobias Bohmelt, "Coup-Proofing and Military Effectiveness in Interstate Wars, 1967–99," *Conflict Management and Peace Science* 28, no. 4 (2011): 331–50.

[31] For notable exceptions, see Hew Strachan, "Making Strategy: Civil–Military Relations after Iraq," *Survival* 48, no. 3 (2006): 66–72; and Suzanne C. Nielsen, "Civil–Military Relations Theory and Military Effectiveness," *Public Administration and Management* 10, no. 2 (2005): 61–84.

debates regarding administrative reforms, state capacity, and institutional effectiveness in the country.[32]

Sources and Methodology

Research for this book is a combination of archival research, fieldwork, and a reinterpretation of secondary sources. I conducted archival research in New Delhi, London, and Southampton. The papers and collections accessed are listed in Appendix A. I also learned a great deal from interacting with a number of defense journalists—some of whom have reported fearlessly on stories even at the risk of offending powerful bureaucracies and lobbies. A few were also kind enough to share less widely circulated government documents. The list of these and other government documents is provided in Appendix B. One of the most enjoyable and educative aspects of this book was the field research, which consisted of over a hundred and fifty interviews; many of them repeated, with senior politicians, civil servants, and military officers. The names of those interviewed are given in Appendix C. In addition, there were over fifty interviews with serving and recently retired officials, who chose to remain unidentified.

A major research limitation has been the absence of declassification procedures in the Indian military. Therefore, it is difficult to access primary documents pertaining to military procedures and processes. As a result, the research has benefited from what has "slipped through"—in either the collection of personal papers or observations by foreign observers. In order to obtain access to primary material, I invoked the Right to Information (RTI)— the Indian equivalent of the Freedom of Information Act—and specifically requested six historical documents. However, responding to the RTI, the MoD simply stated that five of the six documents "were not available."[33] This indicated that historical documents were either untraceable or, worse, even destroyed.[34] This callous approach of the MoD and the armed forces to this issue severely inhibits the development of strategic studies in India and ought to be urgently remedied.

---

[32] For instance, see Devesh Kapur and Pratap Bhanu Mehta, eds., *Public Institutions in India: Performance and Design* (New Delhi: Oxford University Press, 2005); and S. K. Das, *Building a World-Class Civil Service for Twenty-First Century India* (New Delhi: Oxford University Press, 2010).

[33] "MoD Can't Locate Five Key Reports on Military Reforms," *Times of India*, October 14, 2011; also see Anit Mukherjee, "Republic of Opinions," *Times of India*, January 18, 2012.

[34] Vishal Thapar, "1962 War Records Destroyed to Cover up Lapses," *Sunday Guardian*, March 22, 2014.

Overview of the Book

Chapter 1 describes the conceptual approach adopted in this book. It begins by discussing the contrasting views of Samuel Huntington and Eliot Cohen on the preferred role and "balance" of civil–military relations. Next, it examines patterns of democratic civil–military relations to argue that they are shaped largely by three factors—the struggle over military autonomy, the issue of civilian expertise, and institutional design, specifically the manner in which the MoD interacts with the services. The next section discusses the concept of military effectiveness as adopted in this book. Drawing inspiration from previous works, I delineate five variables associated with effective militaries: weapons procurement, jointness, professional military education (PME), officer promotion policies, and defense planning (these variables are discussed in separate chapters).

Chapter 2 examines the historical evolution of civil–military relations in India. In doing so it analyzes civil–military relations under five wartime prime ministers—Jawaharlal Nehru, Lal Bahadur Shastri, Indira Gandhi, Rajiv Gandhi, and Atal Bihari Vajpayee. This approach captures patterns and variation in civil–military relations over time as each of them had his or her own unique ways of dealing with the military. Relying on recently available archival material, it shows the crucial role played by Nehru in ensuring the newly created MoD was accorded the requisite authority. Moreover, it argues, as others have done, that the overarching narrative emerging from the 1962 war with China was that civilian meddling led to the defeat of the Indian Army.[35] This gave rise to the idea of separate civilian and military domains, which created institutional silos between the two.

The next five chapters examine the effect of civil–military relations on the five variables associated with military effectiveness. While doing so, they focus on the interaction between the MoD and the three services. In addition, where applicable, I draw from the experiences of other democratic countries to highlight differences. Chapter 3 examines the effect of civil–military relations on the weapons procurement process. It begins by highlighting the difficulty and the necessity of an "an iterative dialogue" between all stakeholders—the military, the defense industry, and officials in the defense and finance ministries.[36] However, such a dialogue is difficult in India due to strong civil–military silos. Thereafter, it analyzes major trends in India's weapons procurement process. The problems are not just on the civilian side as there are weaknesses in the military's

---

[35] Srinath Raghavan, "Civil–Military Relations in India: The China Crisis and After," *Journal of Strategic Studies* 32, no. 1 (2009): 172–74.

[36] Nick Witney, "Procurement and War," in *The Oxford Handbook of War*, ed. Julian Lindley-French and Yves Boyer, 534 (Oxford: Oxford University Press, 2012).

approach too. Civil–military relations and the pattern of interaction between them, integral to the absent dialogue argument, accentuate these difficulties. As a result, India is heavily dependent upon the import of arms to equip its military.

Chapter 4 examines jointness—defined as the ability of the three services (army, air force, and navy) to operate together—in the Indian military. It is informed by the widely held assumption that jointness enhances military effectiveness. I claim that there are two different approaches to jointness: integration and coordination. The former requires unity of command, control, and effort with a joint staff under a single commander; and the latter is characterized by a single-service approach. The Indian military follows the coordination model, and this chapter discusses jointness in all of India's wars, to show how this is problematic. The absent dialogue perfectly describes civil–military interaction on this issue. The chapter concludes by explaining why civilians have not intervened more forcefully.

Chapter 5 examines PME in India. Its primary argument is that effective PME requires informed civilian intervention—both of educators and of policymakers. This type of intervention has not happened in India, and PME remains almost exclusively in the military's domain. Civil–military interaction on PME largely validates the concept of the absent dialogue.

Chapter 6 analyzes officer promotion and selection policies in India. It begins with a discussion of the role of civilians in this process in other democracies. Next, it analyzes some major controversies pertaining to promotion policies in India, to highlight the nature of civil–military relations. Thereafter, it makes two broad arguments. First, officer promotion and selection policies are an almost exclusive military affair, and civilians have little to do with the processes. As in other established democracies, senior officer promotions need political approval; but, exceptions apart, there is little evidence that civilians have actively shaped these policies. Second, a lack of civilian guidance exacerbates parochial divisions within the military. There is a need, therefore, for an ongoing dialogue on promotion and selection policies. Such a measure, however, also needs to create safeguards to prevent politicization of the military.

Chapter 7 analyzes defense planning, which is the process of creating future force structures and capabilities. It begins with a conceptual overview of the role of civilians in defense planning. Next, it describes the history of defense planning in India, focusing on the interaction between the three services and the defense and finance ministries. Relying on recently available documents, this chapter reveals the complexities and the problems in this process. This is largely because of a lack of expertise and an institutional design creating strong civil–military silos. As a means to overcome this, there have been periodic attempts at reforming defense-planning structures. However, despite some progress, there needs to be a continuous civil–military dialogue on aspects and assumptions underlying the defense-planning process.

Chapter 8 discusses contemporary civil–military relations in India, engaging with, and occasionally refuting, a number of narratives. It begins with an overview of four main controversies—the dispute about withdrawal of troops from the Siachen glacier; the contrasting views over the AFSPA; the tenure of General V. K. Singh (chief of army staff from 2010 to 2012), and issues arising from pay commission reports and the question of equivalence between civilians and the military. This discussion highlights that there is considerable mistrust between civilians and the military. Next, the chapter analyzes the debates surrounding defense reforms and briefly discusses civil–military relations under Prime Minister Narendra Modi. It also explains why, without addressing the problems of institutional design, military autonomy, and a lack of civilian expertise, civil–military relations in India will continue to be problematic.

The concluding chapter revisits some of the themes mentioned in this book. It begins by examining the relevance of the absent dialogue argument. Next, it poses the question of what, if anything, India's experience of civil–military relations informs us about the actual practice of democratic civil–military relations. Thereafter, the chapter identifies topics for further research, both pertaining to the Indian military and in the comparative realm. Finally, it examines the possibility and sources of change.

Note on spelling and word usage

This book follows US convention in spelling, except for quoted material and proper nouns ("Ministry of Defence" and not "Ministry of Defense"). It also uses older names for cities, Calcutta not Kolkata. Please also note that the use of the term "bureaucrat," throughout this book, is in a neutral sense and is not meant to be pejorative.

1

Forging the Sword

Civil–Military Relations and Military Effectiveness

How do democracies maintain firm civilian control while maximizing the effectiveness of their military? Civil–military relations can be conceptualized as a continuous engagement, sometimes conflictual and at other times not, between politicians, civilian bureaucrats, and senior military commanders over policy matters. This interaction is unique to every democracy—shaped by its history, administrative structures, perceived threat environment, customs and norms, and potentially many other factors including the political power of the military. In turn, civil–military relations shape the effectiveness of the military. This is amply clear in non-democracies as there is a wealth of evidence that coup-proofing policies which ensure a tight control over the military have hurt operational and battlefield performance.[1] However, even democracies suffer from "civil–military dysfunction" which impedes military effectiveness.[2] There are various reasons for this—perhaps because civilians attach more value to control over the military rather than to its effectiveness or because their leaders are more focused on domestic politics, among other issues. The fall of France in May 1940 against the German blitzkrieg is perhaps the most infamous example of the rapid collapse of a democratic army, in part due to decades of mishandled civil–military relations.[3] Moreover, there is no academic consensus on the

---

[1] For an excellent new study, see Caitlin Talmadge, *The Dictator's Army: Battlefield Effectiveness in Authoritarian Regimes* (Ithaca, NY: Cornell University Press, 2015); and James T. Quinlivan, "Coup-Proofing: Its Practice and Consequences in the Middle East," *International Security* 24, no. 2 (1999): 131–165.

[2] Vipin Narang and Caitlin Talmadge, "Civil–Military Pathologies and Defeat in War: Tests Using New Data," *Journal of Conflict Resolution* 62, no. 7 (2018): 8; for a study linking patterns of democratic civil–military relations with military effectiveness, see Robert Egnell, *Complex Peace Operations and Civil–Military Relations: Winning the Peace* (Abingdon, UK: Routledge, 2009).

[3] Jasen J. Castillo, *Endurance and War: The National Sources of Military Cohesion* (Ithaca, NY: Cornell University Press, 2014), 96–100, 126; also see Philip C. F. Bankwitz, *Maxime Weygand and Civil–Military Relations in Modern France* (Cambridge, MA: Harvard University Press, 1967).

"proper" role of civilians in military affairs or the "preferred" level of autonomy for the military. One such dysfunction (or pathology, if you will), which I term an "absent dialogue," best characterizes India's civil–military relations. My primary argument is that the conditions emanating from the absent dialogue have been detrimental to its military effectiveness. While this book focuses on India, parts of this argument resonate with problems in other democracies.

This chapter proceeds as follows. I begin by discussing the contrasting views of Samuel Huntington and Eliot Cohen on the preferred role of civilians and the "balance" of civil–military relations. Next, I examine patterns of democratic civil–military relations and argue that they are shaped largely by three factors—the contest over military autonomy, the issue of civilian expertise, and institutional design, specifically the manner in which the Ministry of Defence (MoD) interacts with the services. An interplay of these factors can, under certain conditions, result in creating the absent dialogue. The next section discusses the concept of military effectiveness in the context of this book. Drawing inspiration from earlier works, I examine five variables associated with effective militaries. These variables, as analyzed subsequently in separate chapters, are weapons procurement, jointness—defined as the ability of the army, navy, and air force to operate together—professional military education, officer promotion policies, and defense planning. This chapter then focuses squarely on India and discusses the study of its military. Thereafter, it asks, counterintuitively, whether there is a need to question the effectiveness of the Indian military. The penultimate section explains India's pattern of civil–military relations and the core of the absent dialogue argument. I conclude by revisiting the analytical framework adopted in the rest of the book.

Contrasting Views: Huntington's Objective Control versus Cohen's Unequal Dialogue

In his book *The Soldier and the State* (1957) political scientist Samuel Huntington proposed a theory of civil–military relations and argued that there are two types of civilian control—objective and subjective control. The objective control model envisages a clear division of responsibility between civilians and the military and requires "the recognition (from civilian authorities) of autonomous military professionalism."[4] Civilians therefore have to acknowledge that the military has an expertise that they should not interfere with. The politician

---

[4] Samuel Huntington, *The Soldier and the State: The Theory and Politics of Civil–Military Relations* (Cambridge, MA: Harvard University Press, 1957), 83.

sets the goal, and the soldier is free to determine how to achieve it. Such an approach, he believed, would maximize military effectiveness while obtaining civilian control.[5] The opposite of objective control, according to Huntington, is "subjective control," which aims at maximizing civilian power by "civilianizing the military, making them the mirror of the state."[6] Crucially, subjective control denies "the existence of an independent sphere of purely military imperatives" and "presupposes military participation in politics."[7] Huntington made clear his preference for objective control.

Huntington's theory has been widely criticized by generations of scholars; however, like Banquo's ghost, his "arguments continue to cast a dark and debilitating shadow."[8] It is beyond the scope of this book to revisit the theoretical debate surrounding his ideas.[9] Notably though, despite criticisms over the years, Huntington's objective control model is the preferred option for military officers as it offers them what they crave most—autonomy. As discussed later, the level of autonomy that civilians should accord the military is deeply contested. To his credit, Huntington had anticipated this problem, arguing that in modern states, where civilian control was not in any danger, the problem was "not armed revolt but the relation of the [military] expert to the politician."[10]

Security studies scholar Eliot Cohen criticized the assumptions underlying the objective control model, describing it as the "normal theory of civil–military relations." Instead, while analyzing four successful wartime commanders, he

[5] Huntington did not explicitly use the term "effectiveness" (perhaps because the concept of military effectiveness was not developed at that time); however, most academics assume that one of the aims of objective control was to maximize military effectiveness. See Suzanne C. Nielsen, "Civil–Military Relations Theory and Military Effectiveness," *Public Administration and Management* 10, no. 2 (2005): 4–5; and Risa Brooks, "An Autocracy at War: Explaining Egypt's Military Effectiveness, 1967 and 1973," *Security Studies* 15, no. 3 (2006): 429.

[6] Samuel P. Huntington, "Civilian Control and the Constitution," *American Political Science Review* 50, no. 3 (1956): 678.

[7] Samuel P. Huntington, "Civilian Control of the Military: A Theoretical Statement," in *Political Behaviour: A Reader in Theory and Method*, ed. Heinz Eulau, Samuel J. Eldersveld, and Morris Janowitz, 380–81 (Glencoe, IL: Free Press, 1956).

[8] Jim Golby, "Improving Advice and Earning Autonomy: Building Trust in the Strategic Dialogue," The Strategy Bridge, October 3, 2017, https://thestrategybridge.org/the-bridge/2017/10/3/improving-advice-and-earning-autonomy-building-trust-in-the-strategic-dialogue

[9] For a critical read on Huntington, see the following: Morris Janowitz, *The Professional Soldier* (Glencoe, IL: Free Press, 1960); Samuel E. Finer, *The Man on Horseback: The Role of the Military in Politics* (1962; repr., New Brunswick, NJ: Transaction Publishers, 2002); José A. Olmeda, "Escape from Huntington's Labyrinth: Civil–Military Relations and Comparative Politics," in *The Routledge Handbook of Civil–Military Relations*, ed. Thomas C. Bruneau and Florina Cristiana Matei, 61–76 (New York: Routledge, 2013); and Peter Feaver, *Armed Servants: Agency, Oversight and Civil–Military Relations* (Cambridge, MA: Harvard University Press, 2003), 20–38.

[10] Huntington, *The Soldier and the State*, 20.

argued that it is necessary for political leaders to actively probe ("querying, prodding, suggesting, arbitrating,") the military's plans and assumptions. Cohen made plain his preference for what he called the "unequal dialogue"—as a more suitable form of interaction between civilians and the military. It is a "dialogue, in that both sides expressed their views bluntly, indeed, sometimes offensively, and not once but repeatedly—and unequal, in that the final authority of the civilian leader was unambiguous and unquestioned."[11] It is pertinent to note, however, that Cohen's analysis overlooked certain key factors. First, his case studies focused only on successful political leaders, and he did not address instances of political intervention leading to military disasters. Second, all his cases were of wars of long duration, which allowed political leaders to learn from their mistakes. Such a luxury is rarely available to leaders who have to deal with short, swift wars. Third, by focusing only on wartime leaders, Cohen missed out on the importance of peacetime decisions. Wars are probably unparalleled in their demand on the time, energy, and focus of politicians. However, peacetime decisions are also crucial to the conduct of war—the massive French investment in the Maginot Line prior to the Second World War being a case in point. Notwithstanding these limitations, the thrust of his argument—that political leaders should closely monitor the military's plans and activities—is irrefutable.

Cohen's book saw some controversy as its publication in the summer of 2002 coincided with America's wars, first in Afghanistan and then in Iraq. President George W. Bush claimed to have it on his reading list, which was interpreted as a signal that civilians wished to reassert control over the military.[12] Defense Secretary Donald Rumsfeld's handling of the Iraq War and his seeming disregard for professional military opinion led to some resentment toward the comport of Cohen's thesis.[13] This triggered an academic debate, with the political scientist Richard Betts (among many others) issuing a corrective and calling for an "equal dialogue, unequal authority," arguing that civilians have conveniently focused on the "unequal" aspect but have ignored the essence of a "dialogue."[14]

---

[11] Eliot A. Cohen, *Supreme Command: Soldiers, Statesmen, and Leadership in Wartime* (New York: Free Press, 2002), 209.

[12] Dana Milbank, "Bush's Summer Reading List Hints at Iraq," *Washington Post*, August 20, 2002, https://www.washingtonpost.com/archive/politics/2002/08/20/bushs-summer-reading-list-hints-at-iraq/599b77a7-d11d-4dd1-8eef-4f416b6849b3/?utm_term=.4884a006ae99

[13] See, for instance, Christopher P. Gibson, *Securing the State: Reforming the National Security Decisionmaking Process* (Burlington, VT: Ashgate, 2008), 93–99. Cohen addressed some of these issues in an afterword written for subsequent editions of the book, see Cohen, *Supreme Command*, 225–40.

[14] Richard K. Betts, "Are Civil–Military Relations Still a Problem?" in *American Civil–Military Relations: The Soldier and the State in a New Era*, ed. Suzanne C. Nielsen and Don M. Snider, 35 (Baltimore: Johns Hopkins University Press, 2009). Also see Hew Strachan, "Making Strategy: Civil–Military Relations after Iraq," *Survival* 48, no. 3 (2006): 59–82. It is pertinent to point out that, as

Apart from Huntington and Cohen, other political scientists have conceived of different theories of civil–military relations, which have their own strengths and weaknesses. Assessing the validity of different theories of civil–military relations is beyond the scope of this book. It is crucial to note, however, that at institutions working closely with practitioners of civil–military relations, usually eschew elaborate theories. For instance, at three prominent research centers— the Center for Civil Military Relations in the Naval Postgraduate School in Monterey, California; the Geneva Centre for the Democratic Control of Armed Forces in Switzerland; and Cranfield University in the United Kingdom—those working on civil–military relations have mostly eschewed theory-building and - testing. The literature on security sector reforms, which emerged at the end of the Cold War, consciously refrained from using any theoretical approaches. Instead, there have been growing calls for a "new conceptualization of civil–military relations" that moves beyond theorizing and focuses on areas like effectiveness and efficiency.[15]

Patterns of Civil–Military Relations

Civil–military relations vary across democracies, shaped by factors like history, strategic culture, threat environment, and political and bureaucratic institutions, among others. It is an interactive process involving institutions and individuals and can vary over time. It would be pertinent to note here that individual procivilities often play a significant role in shaping civil–military relations. The broad pattern of civil–military relations in any country is also determined by institutional, bureaucratic, and procedural rules. As discussed below, they are also extremely important in shaping civil-military relations by influencing factors pertaining tomilitary autonomy, civilian expertise, and institutional design (more specifically how the MoD interacts with the services). To be sure, these

others have done, civil–military relations in the United States are unique ("sui generis") and therefore a "poor base for generalization"; see Lindsay Cohn, Damon Coletta, and Peter Feaver, "Civil–Military Relations," in *The Oxford Handbook of International Security*, ed. Aexandra Gheciu and William C. Wohlforth, 711 (Oxford: Oxford University Press, 2018). Unfortunately, despite this, the US case has figured "prominently in the theoretical development of the field"; see Peter D. Feaver, "Civil–Military Relations," *Annual Review of Political Science* 2 (1999): 213.

[15] Thomas C. Bruneau and Florina Cristiana Matei, "Towards a New Conceptualization of Democratization and Civil–Military Relations," *Democratization* 15, no. 5 (2008): 909–29. For similar appeals, also see Andrew Cottey, Timothy Edmunds, and Anthony Forster, "The Second Generation Problematic: Rethinking Democracy and Civil–Military Relations," *Armed Forces & Society* 29, no. 1 (2002): 31–56; and Robert Egnell, "Civil–Military Coordination for Operational Effectiveness: Towards a Measured Approach," *Small Wars & Insurgencies* 24, no. 2 (2013): 242–43.

factors influence each other, and there is some degree of overlap—for instance, the military can have considerable autonomy if there is a lack of civilian expertise. Despite this, examining civil–military relations in the light of these three factors, I argue, is analytically useful.

Military Autonomy

The "appropriate" level of military autonomy is a deeply contested and controversial topic. In a democratic state, where civilian control is not in danger, this is the primary cause of friction in civil–military relations. There are two different views on this. According to some, civilians should give overall strategic directions and leave their implementation to the military. Huntington's "objective control" is an ideal model for those who subscribe to this view. Unsurprisingly, the military and those who view civilian micromanagement as problematic prefer this position. On the other hand, there are others who believe that civilians should both make the key decisions and be involved in the implementation, even, if required, by overruling the military. Those who hold this view justify it by citing Eliot Cohen's concept of "unequal dialogue"—with its expectation of a constant dialogue informed by the principle of civilian supremacy. Peter Feaver describes the fault line between these two opposing views well:

> scholars agree that military professionals possess (or ought to possess) expert knowledge that civilian leaders must tap if they are to make wise decisions, especially about strategy and operations in wartime. Everyone recommends some sort of give and take between the military and the civilians, at least at the intellectual and advisory levels. What distinguishes different theorists from one another is where they position themselves along this *mushy middle ground* of who should be giving more and taking less.[16]

These two views are both right and wrong. Civilian interference without taking into consideration the concerns of the military and its opposite—granting too much autonomy to the military—have both often led to disaster. Considering this patchy record, there is a lack of clarity, and no academic consensus, on the desired role of civilians in various defense-related activities, like

---

[16] Peter D. Feaver, "The Right to Be Right: Civil–Military Relations and the Iraq Surge Decision," *International Security* 35, no. 4 (2011): 93, emphasis added. He terms these two camps the "professional supremacists" and the "civilian supremacists"; see discussion on pp. 89–90 and 93–97.

the procurement of weapon systems, in military education and in the formulation of operational plans.

Apart from the United States and some countries in western Europe, in most other democracies the military enjoys significant autonomy over issues pertaining to strategy, operations, force structures, education, and training. However, military autonomy has not necessarily served these other democracies well, in terms of effectiveness, control, and efficiency, as some military "processes" require civilian guidance and intervention. As pointed out by the military scholar Suzanne Nielsen, Huntington's claim that militaries left to themselves will develop expertise is problematic as "it underestimates the impact of service culture and service parochialism. Left to their own devices, the services may focus on the capabilities they would like to have rather than the capabilities the country needs."[17] Indeed, in India's case, as I show in later chapters, a high degree of military autonomy leads to problems in jointness, in defense planning, and in other fields.

Civilian Expertise

Another factor that plays a significant role in civil–military relations is that of civilian expertise. As there is no universally accepted definition, I am defining "expertise" as *the knowledge pertaining to the administration, deployment, force structures, and use of the military.* Such knowledge allows for a well-informed dialogue as, in its absence, it is difficult for civilians to understand and confidently engage with the military or to challenge its autonomy. There are three ways to gain such expertise—by serving in the military, by its academic study, or by working in state agencies that engage with the military, for instance, the defense ministry, military academies, and the defense research and industry.

The growth of civilian expertise is a relatively recent phenomenon and is largely a product of administrative structures and the hiring procedures of a state. Some countries, like the United States, have flexible hiring practices, well-developed strategic studies programs, and a system of nurturing expertise—whether in think tanks, in academia, or in government. But that is a rarity as in most other democracies civilian expertise is more an exception than a fact.[18] There are numerous reasons for this—lack of career opportunities,

---

[17] Suzanne Nielsen, "American Civil–Military Relations Today: The Continuing Relevance of Samuel P. Huntington's 'The Soldier and the State,'" *International Affairs* 88, no. 2 (2012): 372.

[18] Civilian expertise has been problematic and difficult to obtain even among some European countries, despite a long tradition of democratic civilian control; see Ursula C. Schröder, "Security Expertise in the European Union: The Challenges of Comprehensiveness and Accountability," *European Security* 15, no. 4 (2006): 471–90.

underdeveloped academic programs, lack of declassification procedures, and administrative practices—however, the fact remains that civilian expertise on defense matters is difficult to obtain. One also cannot underestimate the role of several other factors in the growth of civilian expertise in the United States and the United Kingdom: the realization after the First World War that "total war" required greater civilian involvement, a trend reinforced by the involvement of scientists in the war effort during the Second World War. In addition, in the United States, the totality of nuclear war led to the rise of operations research as nuclear weapons changed the character of war and the meaning of strategy. These developments pushed civilians to invest in encouraging expertise outside the narrow confines of the military.[19] However, expertise has been difficult to nurture in countries other than the United States even as scholars are increasingly drawing attention to its criticality to civil–military relations.[20]

The paucity of civilian expertise is particularly acute in India with underdeveloped academic departments, lack of declassification procedures, and administrative processes which favor generalists over specialists. That scholars cannot access primary military documents is particularly debilitating to the growth of strategic studies and military history. Worryingly, the government is, at times, unable to locate crucial documents.[21] As we shall see in subsequent chapters, for a variety of reasons, this lack of expertise creates considerable problems in civilian control and in the larger context of civil–military relations.

Institutional Design

The ministry of defense is the institution that connects political leaders to the military and, in effect, exercises civilian control. By "institutional design" we refer to the manner in which the ministry is enmeshed in or connected to the services.

[19] I thank Pascal Vennesson for pointing this out to me; also see Ole Waever, "The History and Social Structure of Security Studies as a Pratico-Academic Field," in *Security Expertise: Practice, Power, Responsibility*, ed. Trine Villumsen Berling and Christian Bueger, 76–84 (New York: Routledge, 2015).

[20] Thomas Bruneau, "Development of an Approach Through Debate," in *The Routledge Handbook of Civil–Military Relations*, ed. Thomas C. Bruneau and Florina Cristiana Matei, 22–25 (New York: Routledge, 2013); and Douglas Bland, "Managing the 'Expert Problem' in Civil–Military Relations," *European Security* 8, no. 3 (1999): 25–43. There has been a fascinating debate between Latin Americanists about civilian expertise; for an overview, see Gregory Weeks "Civilian Expertise and Civilian–Military Relations in Latin America," *Latin American Policy* 3, no. 2 (2012): 164–73; Harold Trinkunas, *Crafting Civilian Control of the Military in Venezuela: A Comparative Perspective* (Chapel Hill: University of North Carolina Press, 2005); and David S. Pion-Berlin, "Political Management of the Military in Latin America," *Military Review* (January–February 2005): 19–31.

[21] "MoD Can't Locate Five Key Reports on Military Reforms," *Times of India*, October 14, 2011, http://timesofindia.indiatimes.com/articleshow/10347823.cms?utm_source=contentofinterest&utm_medium=text&utm_campaign=cppst

Broadly speaking, depending on national policies, a ministry of defense can be of three types—military-dominant, civilian-dominant, or integrated. Military-dominant ministries are staffed mostly by military officers, and in such cases, civilian control can be problematic. For instance, in countries like Indonesia and Pakistan, military officers—both serving and retired—occupy prominent posts in the defense ministry, upending the notion of civilian control. Tellingly, in countries transitioning from military or authoritarian rule, for instance, South Korea, Taiwan, and eastern Europe, there has been a push toward "civilianizing" the defense ministries.[22] In the case of civilian-dominant ministries, like in India, there is very little military representation. This may suggest complete civilian control over defense policy, but under certain conditions the military may retain considerable autonomy. Moreover, such an arrangement tends to make for adversarial civil–military relations. Integrated ministries, on the other hand, have a mixed representation of civilians and military officers, working within different departments. Generally, integrated ministries are preferable to the other two as they help mitigate, to a certain degree, the information asymmetry inherent in civil–military relations and, all else being equal, tend to create more collegial relations between civilians and the military.

As an institution, ministries of defence are also of relatively recent origin, coming into prominence only after the Second World War. For instance, the United States established the Department of Defense in 1947, whereas a year later, in France, the Ministry of National Defense grouped together the previously separate Ministries of War, the Navy, and Air. To its credit, India was among the first postcolonial countries to form a ministry of defense, under a cabinet minister, in 1947. By contrast, it was only in 1964 that the United Kingdom established its MoD. Similarly, in the rest of the democratic world, ministries of defense came into being much later.[23] However, while in countries like the United Kingdom, the MoD has changed considerably over time, in India the MoD has not changed its basic structure. To be sure, while there has been significant expansion, it remains civilian-dominant and is not integrated with the services.

---

[22] See the following: Todor Tagarev, "Civilians in Defense Ministries," *Connections* 7, no. 2 (2008): 110–17; Valeri Ratchev, *Civilianisation of the Defence Ministry: A Functional Approach to a Modern Defence Institution* (Geneva: Geneva Centre for the Democratic Control of Armed Forces, 2011); Ki-Joo Kim, "The Soldier and the State in South Korea: Crafting Democratic Civilian Control of the Military," *Journal of International and Area Studies* 21, no. 2 (2014): 119–31; and Aurel Croissant and David Kuehn, "Patterns of Civilian Control of the Military in East Asia's New Democracies," *Journal of East Asian Studies* 9, no. 2 (2009): 187–217.

[23] Thomas C. Bruneau and Richard B. Goetze Jr., "Ministries of Defense and Democratic Control," in *Who Guards the Guardians and How: Democratic Civil–Military Relations*, ed. Thomas Bruneau and Scott Tollefson, 71–77 (Austin: University of Texas Press, 2006).

A closer examination of these three factors—extent of military autonomy, civilian expertise, and institutional design of the defense ministry—reveals the pattern of civil–military relations in a democracy. Various combinations of these factors are possible; however, as described later in this chapter, the one I call the absent dialogue consists of the following: considerable military autonomy, lack of civilian expertise, and a civilian-dominated defense ministry.

Military Effectiveness

Military effectiveness is difficult to assess and therefore has been a problematic concept to study.[24] There are many ways to measure effectiveness, with war outcomes being the most obvious. However, this, as the literature on military effectiveness points out, is not the most efficacious method. This is because wars often do not actually have a clear winner. More importantly, war outcomes can be a misleading indicator as countries can lose wars despite possessing a more effective military. For instance, in terms of war outcomes, the Finnish–Soviet Winter War in 1939–1940 will be considered a Soviet victory, although by no means were the Soviets militarily more effective than the Finns.[25] Another approach is to examine and contrast combat casualties to measure effectiveness. This too can be misleading as some armies may refuse to fight and instead flee the battlefield and suffer fewer combat casualties as a result. More importantly, the records of combat deaths in developing countries are opaque and unreliable. This applies to India, Pakistan, and China—countries most relevant to this book. Given these, many academics have eschewed a formal definition of military effectiveness while still producing influential scholarship.[26]

This book relies on the definition of military effectiveness as proposed by historians Allan Millett, Williamson Murray, and Kenneth Watman. They disaggregated the components of military effectiveness and defined it as the "the process by which armed forces convert resources into fighting power. A fully effective military is one that derives maximum combat power from the resources

[24] For some of the challenges associated with defining and studying military effectiveness, see Risa A. Brooks, "Introduction," in *Creating Military Power: Sources of Military Effectiveness*, ed. Risa A. Brooks and Elizabeth A. Stanley, 1–26 (Stanford, CA: Stanford University Press, 2007); for a useful summary of the literature on military effectiveness, see Pasi Tuunainen, *Finnish Military Effectiveness in the Winter War, 1939–1940* (London: Palgrave Macmillan, 2016), 7–28.

[25] Tuunainen, *Finnish Military Effectiveness in the Winter War.*

[26] Kenneth M. Pollack, *Arabs at War: Military Effectiveness, 1948–1991* (Lincoln: University of Nebraska Press, 2002); and Dan Reiter and Allan C. Stam III, *Democracies at War* (Princeton, NJ: Princeton University Press, 2002).

physically and politically available."[27] More recently, building on this insight, Risa Brooks defined military effectiveness as "the capacity to create military power from a state's basic resources in wealth, technology, population size and human capital."[28] This approach factors in variation in economic, demographic, and technological development and allows for examination of processes which *create* military power. In democracies, the primary institutional processes creating military power lie at the intersection of the defense ministry and the services. It is at this level that big-picture decisions—on strategy, budget, force structures, manpower planning, etc.—are deliberated and acted upon and civil–military relations come into play.

Risa Brooks lists four attributes of military effectiveness: quality, integration, skill, and responsiveness. From this framework, I derive the five dependent variables generally associated with military effectiveness: weapons procurement, interservices integration (or "jointness," as it is commonly called), professional military education, officer promotions policy, and defense planning. In doing so, I have divided "skill" into two separate variables—officer education and promotion policies—as these are two different processes relating to human resource development. Table 1.1 presents the attributes of military effectiveness and their definition and the corresponding variables that I have derived from it.

Several considerations inform this approach to analyzing military effectiveness. First, as the academic literature generally agrees, "military power is a function of both quantity and quality."[29] The advantage of the five dependent variables as listed in the table is that they capture both quantitative (weapons procurement and defense planning) and qualitative (officer education, promotion policies, and jointness) aspects of military power. This is better than the bean-counting method, which stacks up hardware without considering software.

Second, these five dependent variables are commonly understood to be associated with military effectiveness. Hence, effective militaries get the weapons they need to win; are able to implement their defense plans based on political direction; are able to educate and promote their best officers; and have services—army, navy, and air force—that fight battles jointly. However, I do not specifically show or, in political science terms, "prove" that problems in these variables undermine the effectiveness of the military. That would require not only a different research focus but, in the case of India, also access to battlefield data and primary documents, which are not available. Given these constraints,

---

[27] Allan R. Millet, Williamson Murray, and Kenneth H. Watman, "The Effectiveness of Military Organizations," *International Security* 11, no. 1 (1986): 37.

[28] Brooks and Stanley, *Creating Military Power*, 9.

[29] Michael Beckley, "Economic Development and Military Effectiveness," *Journal of Strategic Studies* 33, no. 1 (2010): 44.

Table 1.1 **Attributes of Military Effectiveness**

Attributes of Military Effectiveness	Defined As[a]	Dependent Variables
Quality	"The ability to obtain highly capable weapons and equipment"	1. Weapons and equipment
Integration	"The degree to which different military activities are internally consistent and mutually reinforcing"	2. Jointness
Skill (human resources)	"The ability [of military personnel] to achieve particular tasks"	3. Professional military education 4. Officer promotions
Responsiveness	"The ability to tailor military activity to a state's own capabilities, its adversaries' capabilities, and external constraints"	5. Defense planning

[a]Brooks, "Introduction," 9–15.

I disaggregate military effectiveness into its individual components: weapons procurement, jointness, officer education and promotion policies, and defense planning. These "inputs" are critical to military effectiveness, and studying them has been proposed by many scholars. For instance, Robert Egnell argues that, "instead of analyzing effectiveness in terms of outcomes, a more fruitful approach is to study the processes by which armed forces convert resources into fighting power."[30] All else being equal, militaries which conduct these processes well would likely be more effective than those that do not.

Third, civil–military relations—the central focus of this book—significantly influence these five dependent variables. Almost all of the major decisions pertaining to these variables are made by officials, both civilian and military, usually by a process of close interaction between the defense ministry and the services. Indeed, as other scholars have noted, civil–military relations are a "promising explanation" for

[30] Robert Egnell, *Complex Peace Operations and Civil–Military Relations: Winning the Peace* (London: Routledge, 2009), 12.

military effectiveness.[31] To be sure, there are several other competing factors that influence military effectiveness—culture, leadership, nationalism, group cohesion, technology, social structures, threat environment, to name a few. In practice, however, it is impossible to isolate "the single factor which contributes the most to military effectiveness."[32] In India's case, as discussed in the next section, civil–military relations have been controversial and a subject of much contemporary debate.

The Study of India's Civil–Military Relations

Civil–military relations in India have fetched intermittent attention from scholars. Some of the focus has been on explaining the absence of military intervention in Indian politics.[33] Successful civilian control over the military in India is in stark contrast with the fate of two other nations that were formerly a part of British India—Pakistan and Bangladesh. Therefore, there have been a number of comparative studies on civil–military relations among these countries.[34]

Scholars who have studied the Indian military almost unanimously agree that its civil–military relations are unique among postcolonial states. According to Stephen Cohen, referred to as the "doyen" of security studies in South Asia, "the most remarkable fact about the decision-making process is that the military plays almost no role in it . . . in no other middle or great power is the military's

[31] Alexander B. Downes, "How Smart and Tough Are Democracies? Reassessing Theories of Democratic Victory in War," *International Security* 33, no. 4 (2009): 51. Also see Stephen Biddle and Stephen Long, "Democracy and Military Effectiveness—A Deeper Look," *Journal of Conflict Resolution* 48, no. 4 (2004): 525–46; and Stephen Biddle and Robert Zirkle, "Technology, Civil–Military Relations, and Warfare in the Developing World," *Journal of Strategic Studies* 19, no. 2 (1996): 171–212.

[32] Filipo Andreatta, "Conclusion: The Complexity of Military Effectiveness," in *The Sword's Other Edge: Trade-offs in the Pursuit of Military Effectiveness*, ed. Dan Reiter, 254 (Cambridge: Cambridge University Press, 2017), italics in the original.

[33] Steven I. Wilkinson, *Army and Nation: The Military and Indian Democracy since Independence* (Cambridge, MA: Harvard University Press, 2015); Apurba Kundu, *Militarism in India: The Army and Civil Society in Consensus* (New York: St Martin's Press, 1998).

[34] Maya Tudor, *The Promise of Power: The Origins of Democracy in India and Autocracy in Pakistan* (Cambridge: Cambridge University Press, 2013); Veena Kukreja, *Civil–Military Relations in South Asia: Pakistan, Bangladesh and India* (New Delhi: Sage Publications, 1991); Kotera Bhimaya, *Civil–Military Relations: A Comparative Study of India and Pakistan* (Santa Monica, CA: Rand, 1997); Philip Oldenburg, *India, Pakistan and Democracy: Solving the Puzzle of Divergent Paths* (London: Routledge, 2010); and Paul Staniland, "Explaining Civil–Military Relations in Complex Political Environments: India and Pakistan in Comparative Perspective," *Security Studies* 17, no. 2 (2008): 322–62.

advice so detached from political and strategic decisions."[35] Ashley Tellis echoes this sentiment when he notes that "India has one of the most rigid and ironclad systems in the world for ensuring absolute civilian control over the military."[36] These analyses, however, largely overlook the problems accruing from military autonomy and do not systemically analyze variables associated with military effectiveness.

Among the few academic books examining Indian military effectiveness is Stephen Rosen's magisterial study.[37] Rosen is correct that armies mirroring fault lines within their society will face problems with generating military power. But he also admits of problems in civil–military relations and argues that the Indian military "has been separated from society in a number of ways . . . [and] is viewed with suspicion by the civilian leadership."[38] Civil–military relations therefore offer an important explanation for India's military effectiveness.

More recent scholarship has also discussed issues pertaining to civil–military relations. Srinath Raghavan has written an excellent account of the Nehru years with numerous insights into civil–military relations during that period.[39] He provides a much-needed corrective to the conventional wisdom that exclusively blamed politicians for the defeat of the Indian Army in 1962. Instead, Raghavan shows how senior military officers made operational errors, tendered incorrect advice, and were equally culpable. However, in his eagerness to make this point Raghavan perhaps overcompensates. For instance, his telling of the 1962 war overlooks Defence Minister Krishna Menon's toxic impact on civil–military relations. Minor quibbles aside, Raghavan correctly argues two points pertinent to civil–military relations: there was a "need for greater civilian involvement in operational matters"[40] and the outcome of this war had a major impact on

---

[35] Stephen P. Cohen, *India: Emerging Power* (Washington, DC: Brookings Institution Press, 2002), 76. For his other publications on this topic, see *The Indian Army: Its Contribution to the Development of a Nation* (Berkeley: University of California Press, 1971), 173–74; and "The Military and Indian Democracy," in *India's Democracy: An Analysis of Changing State–Society Relations*, ed. Atul Kohli, 99–143 (Princeton, NJ: Princeton University Press, 1988).

[36] Ashley Tellis, *India's Emerging Nuclear Posture: Between Recessed Deterrent and Ready Arsenal* (Santa Monica, CA: Rand, 2001), 283, italics in the original, also see 283–92 and 662–71. For similar assessments, see George Perkovich, *India's Nuclear Bomb: The Impact on Global Proliferation* (Berkeley: University of California Press, 1999), 450.

[37] Stephen Peter Rosen, *Societies and Military Power: India and Its Armies* (Ithaca, NY: Cornell University Press, 1996).

[38] Rosen, *Societies and Military Power*, 208; the separation of the Indian military from society and polity and resultant problems in civil–military relations is a constant theme, see 198–99, 216, 226, 230–31, 239–41, 253, and 262.

[39] See Srinath Raghavan, *War and Peace in Modern India: A Strategic History of the Nehru Years* (New Delhi: Permanent Black, 2010).

[40] Raghavan, *War and Peace in Modern India*, 316.

the future narrative of civil–military relations.[41] Both aspects are central to the story of Indian civil–military relations and are discussed in later chapters. There have also been some insightful autobiographies; however, they only provide perspectives of a single official during his time in office.[42]

Curiously, Huntington's notion of objective control dominates the academic study and popular discussions of civil–military relations in India. Academics concur that India's civil–military relations most closely resembles the objective control model. Stephen Cohen and Sunil Dasgupta, for example, argue that "India maintains a Huntingtonian form of 'objective' civilian control."[43] While examining society–military relations, Stephen Rosen argued that "the historical examination of India does clearly suggest that the model of the relationship between an army and its host society [is] the model set forth in Huntington's *The Soldier and the State*."[44] Other studies on civil–military relations also refer to Huntington's approach.[45] More importantly, public discussions on civil–military relations in India are greatly influenced by Huntington, without much acknowledgment of its downsides. Hailing Huntington's "widely acclaimed theory" of objective control, Ajai Shukla, a well-respected defense correspondent, noted that it is "a model of civil–military relations that is implemented almost universally."[46] It is referred to most often in commentaries by military officers and

---

[41] For more on this, see Srinath Raghavan, "Civil–Military Relations in India: The China Crisis and After," *Journal of Strategic Studies* 32, no. 1 (2009): 172–74.

[42] For instance, see the following: Yogendra Narain, *Born to Serve: Power Games in Bureaucracy* (New Delhi: Manas Publications, 2017), 105–80; Shankar Roychowdhury, *Officially at Peace* (New Delhi: Viking Publishers, 2002); Arun Prakash, *From the Crow's Nest* (New Delhi: Lancer Publications, 2007); V. P. Malik, *India's Military Conflicts and Diplomacy: An Inside View of Decision Making* (New Delhi: Harper Collins Publishers, 2013); and B. G. Deshmukh, *From Poona to the Prime Minister's Office: A Cabinet Secretary Looks Back* (New Delhi: Harper Collins India, 2004). For a good overview of major controversies in India's civil–military relations, see R. Chandrashekar, *Rooks and Knights: Civil–Military Relations in India* (New Delhi: Pentagon Press, 2017).

[43] Cohen and Dasgupta, *Arming Without Aiming*, 163.

[44] Rosen, *Societies and Military Power*, 265; for other references, see Anshu N. Chatterjee, "Shifting Lines of Governance in Insurgencies," in *The Routledge Handbook of Civil–Military Relations*, Thomas C. Bruneau and Florina Cristiana Matei, 168 (New York: Routledge, 2013); Rebecca Schiff, "Concordance Theory: A Response to Recent Criticism," *Armed Forces and Society* 23, no. 2 (1996): 281; Dipankar Bannerjee, "India: Military Professionalism of a First World Army," in *Military Professionalism in Asia: Conceptual and Empirical Perspectives*, ed. Muthiah Alagappa, 19 (Honolulu, HI: East-West Center, 2001); and Anit Mukherjee, "Civil–Military Relations and Military Effectiveness in India," in *India's Military Modernization: Challenges and Prospects*, ed. Rajesh Basrur, Ajaya Das, and Manjeet Pardesi, 96–229 (New Delhi: Oxford University Press, 2013).

[45] Ray, *The Soldier and the State in India*, 11–14; Wilkinson, *Army and Nation*, 4; and S. Kalyanraman, "The Theory and Practice of Civil–Military Relations," in *India's Defence Preparedness*, ed. Shrikant Paranjpe, 112–29 (New Delhi: Pentagon Press, 2016).

[46] Ajai Shukla, "Muzzling the Military," *Business Standard*, January 12, 2012; also see Ajai Shukla, "The Coup that Wasn't . . . the Threat Within?" *Business Standard*, April 7, 2012.

was mentioned in an essay that won the gold medal in a competition among all officers conducted by the renowned United Services Institute of India.[47] Encapsulating the prevailing sentiment, according to Lieutenant General D. S. Hooda, "in India, objective control has been followed and has stood the military in good stead. There is no real need for change."[48] As I argue, the model of "objective control" as understood and implemented in India has not stood the military in good stead as it has compromised on its effectiveness, and there is an urgent need for change. As argued in this book, military autonomy does not automatically translate into effectiveness, and instead informed civilian intervention is key to overcoming service parochialism and better integrating military plans with political objectives.

In sum, despite many references to India's unique civil–military relations, there is no book that systematically analyzes how civilians exercise control and its influences on variables associated with military effectiveness. Analyzing the interaction between the MoD and the services better illuminates this issue. This is a first cut at telling that story.

Why Question Indian Military Effectiveness?

If militaries are there to serve political objectives, then arguably the Indian military has acquitted itself well. Barring the 1962 China war and to some extent the Indian Peace Keeping Force (IPKF) expedition in 1987 to Sri Lanka, the Indian military has succeeded on most counts. During the 1965 war with Pakistan it was able to prevent both Operations Gibraltar and Grand Slam, aimed at capturing Kashmir, from succeeding; and when ceasefire was declared, India was in a comparatively better negotiating position. During the 1971 Bangladesh and the 1999 Kargil wars India was able to achieve all of its political objectives and attained significant diplomatic victories. Even during the ill-fated IPKF expedition in Sri Lanka, the military successfully facilitated the stated objective of the conduct of elections for Sri Lanka's North Eastern Provincial Council in November 1988. Moreover, the Indian Army has been extensively engaged in countering numerous internal insurgencies and has never been defeated in any

---

[47] Pradeep K. Thakur, "Managing Civil–Military Relations: How to Bridge the Gap," *USI Journal* 146, no. 606 (October–December 2016); also see Dhiraj Kukreja, "Higher Defence Management Through Effective Civil–Military Relations," *Indian Defence Review* 27, no. 4 (2012), http://www.indiandefencereview.com/news/higher-defence-management-through-effective-civil-military-relations/

[48] D. S. Hooda, "Civil–Military Relations: Let's Not Weaken the Corporate Character of Our Forces," News18, January 9, 2018, http://www.news18.com/news/india/opinion-civil-military-relations-lets-not-weaken-the-corporate-character-of-our-forces-1563541.html

of them, nor has it ceded territory to insurgent groups. On the contrary, it has assisted in incorporating "states" within the Indian union—Junagarh, Kashmir, Hyderabad, Goa, and Sikkim. The Indian military has also been involved in numerous United Nations operations, both peacekeeping and peace enforcement, and earned recognition as a professional force. Why then question the effectiveness of the Indian military?

A closer study of all of India's wars, except the 1962 China war, reveals that the Indian military was considerably superior to the enemy in terms of both men and material. Despite that advantage, the Indian military faced problems in exercising force to achieve the stated political objectives. For instance, in the 1965 India–Pakistan war and the IPKF operations in Sri Lanka, there were major problems with interservices integration.[49] Even in the victorious 1971 Bangladesh war, the Indian army required considerable time to prepare for the campaign in the east and permanently lost territory in Chhamb in the west. A fine-grained analysis of India's wars therefore reveals a mixed verdict on India's military effectiveness.

In addition, while Indian nationalists might claim outright victories, historians are divided about the outcome of some of these wars. For instance, it is difficult to convincingly ascertain winners and losers of the 1947–1948 Kashmir war, the 1965 Indo- Pakistan war, the IPKF operations in Sri Lanka, and even the 1999 Kargil war. In each of these, both sides have claimed victory. The point is that narratives of victory tell us very little about military effectiveness. Indeed, historians are still debating the war objectives, combat deaths, and outcomes of these wars. In sum, a closer read of India's military historiography reveals significant problems in civil–military relations, equipment availability, higher command of war, and jointness.

As Millett, Murray, and Watman pointed out, "victory is not a characteristic of an organization but rather a result of organizational activity. Judgments of effectiveness should thus retain some sense of proportional cost and organizational process."[50] Therefore, one must move beyond overly simplistic measures of victory and defeat and closely examine the processes and the resources used to create military power. This will reveal that India has historically faced various problems in almost all aspects (pertaining to equipment, organizational

---

[49] S. K. Chakravorty, *History of the Indo-Pak War, 1965* (History Division, Ministry of Defense, 1992), 272 and 329–30, P. C. Lal, *My Years with the IAF* (New Delhi: Lancer, 1986), 162; and Depinder Singh, *IPKF in Sri Lanka* (Delhi: Trishul publications, 1991), 164. This aspect is explored in detail in Chapter 4.

[50] Allan Millett, Williamson Murray, and Kenneth Watman, "The Effectiveness of Military Organizations," in *Military Effectiveness*, vol. 1, ed. Allan Millett and Williamson Murray, 3 (Boston: Allen and Unwin, 1987).

structures, and coordination) of creating military power. This is a constant refrain among India's strategic community.[51] Reports generated by the Parliament's
Standing Committee on Defence frequently refer to the lack of "defence preparedness"—a corollary to military effectiveness.[52] In 2012, a leak of a top-secret
letter from the chief of army staff to the prime minister mentioned problems in
the "preparedness of the army" and "hollowness in the system" stemming from
procedural rules and a "lack of urgency at all levels."[53] Popular media often refers
to a deteriorating security scenario, lack of preparedness, and the urgent need
for reform.[54] Even in the country's internal insurgencies the Indian military has
suffered due to a lack of bulletproof jackets, inadequate base security measures,
and its civil–military relations.[55] In sum, despite no egregious military debacles
(apart from the 1962 war), there is a critical need to improve India's military
effectiveness. As Peter Feaver warns, "an inadequate military institution may be
worse than none at all . . . it could lull leaders into a false confidence, leading
them to rash behavior and then failing in the ultimate military contest."[56] This
is especially pertinent for India as it faces challenges from two hostile, nuclear
weapons–armed neighbors (China and Pakistan) with disputed and, in some
sectors, violent boundaries.

[51] Arun Prakash, "Civil–Military Dissonance: The Bane of India's National Security," *Maritime Affairs: Journal of the National Maritime Foundation of India* 10, no. 1 (2014): 1–19; Shekhar Dutt, "The Conundrum of Indian Defense and Civil–Military Relationship," in *Core Concerns in Indian Defence and the Imperatives for Reforms*, ed. Vinod Misra, 9–18 (New Delhi: Pentagon Press, 2015); and Bharat Karnad, *Why India Is not a Great Power (Yet)* (New Delhi: Oxford University Press, 2015), 303–409.

[52] For a recent report, see Standing Committee on Defence, *Forty Second Report: Demand for Grants (2018–19)* (New Delhi: Lok Sabha Secretariat, March 2018).

[53] Saikat Datta, "DNA Exclusive: General VK Singh Tells PM Some Hard Truths," *Daily News and Analysis (DNA)*, March 28, 2012.

[54] Manoj Joshi, *Scraping the Bottom of the Barrel: Budgets, Organisation and Leadership in the Indian Defence System*, ORF Special Report no. 74 (New Delhi: Observer Research Foundation, August 2018); "Know your own Stregnth," *The Economist*, 406, no. 8829, March 30, 2013, https://www.economist.com/briefing/2013/03/30/know-your-own-strength and K. S. Venkatachalam, "Is India's Military Actually Ready for War with China?" *The Diplomat*, August 10, 2017, https://thediplomat.com/2017/08/is-indias-military-actually-ready-for-war-with-china/

[55] "Defence Ministry, Services Squabble over Cost of Strengthening Military Bases," Rediff News, March 13, 2017, http://www.rediff.com/news/report/defence-ministry-services-squabble-over-cost-of-strengthening-military-bases/20170513.htm; for weaknesses in India's approach to counterinsurgency due to its civil–military relations, see Anit Mukherjee, "India's Experience with Insurgency and Counterinsurgency," in *Handbook of Asian Security Studies*, ed. Sumit Ganguly, Andrew Scobell, and Joseph Liow, 140–59 (London: Routledge, 2009).

[56] Peter Feaver, "Civil–Military Relations," *Annual Review of Political Science* 2 (June 1999): 214.

India's Pattern of Civil–Military Relations

Even with firm civilian control, civil–military relations in India have been problematic. According to Admiral Arun Prakash, former chief of naval staff, "a primary fault-line in the existing system is civil–military dissonance."[57] The absent dialogue, as I characterize it, best captures the pattern of India's civil–military relations and emerges from an interplay of three factors: civilian expertise, institutional design, and military autonomy.

There is a lack of civilian expertise on military issues at both the political and bureaucratic levels. Therefore, defense policymaking, with all its intricacies and complexities, rarely get the attention it deserves. Few politicians, less than 1% of the members of Parliament (MPs) in the 16th Lok Sabha (2014–2019), have served in the military.[58] They are therefore unable to have an informed debate or question the actions of the executive.[59]

Given their lack of expertise, politicians, ironically, tend to rely on the bureaucracy for advice on defense affairs. However, bureaucrats also themselves do not have the requisite knowledge. The lack of specialization among bureaucrats can be traced back to the colonial era, with its emphasis on the generalist cadre. In fact, the functioning of most public institutions in India is still constrained by such practices.[60] Acknowledging problems arising from this, the government has given longer tenures than usual to civilian bureaucrats posted in the MoD—but this policy has been followed only erratically. In the absence of in-depth knowledge and hindered by information asymmetries inherent in civil–military relations, most bureaucrats tend to focus only on the process of decision-making but without due consideration of the objective. Moreover, they are unable to challenge the military on its logic and find it difficult to arbitrate between competing sectional interests. According to Shakti Sinha, a former civil

---

[57] Arun Prakash, "Civil–Military Dissonance: A Chink in India's Armour," Third K. Subrahmanyam Memorial Lecture, India International Centre, New Delhi, January 20, 2014, https://www.globalindiafoundation.org/Admiral%20Arun%20Prakash%20Speech[1].pdf

[58] In contrast, in the United States, military veterans constitute 19% of the Congress, and the corresponding figure is 8% among British parliamentarians; see Amit Ahuja and Rajkamal Singh, "Not Even 1% of Indian MPs Have Served in the Military. And That's Concerning," *The Print*, August 2, 2018, https://theprint.in/opinion/not-even-1-of-indian-mps-have-served-in-the-military-and-thats-concerning/91832/

[59] Vipin Narang and Paul Staniland, "Democratic Accountability and Foreign Security Policy: Theory and Evidence from India," *Security Studies* 27, no. 3 (2018): 427.

[60] For the importance of expertise among civil servants, see K. Subrahmanyam and Arthur Monteiro, *Shedding Shibboleths: India's Evolving Strategic Outlook* (New Delhi: Wordsmiths, 2005), 346–55. Also see S. N. Das, *Building a World-Class Civil Service for Twenty-First Century India* (New Delhi: Oxford University Press, 2010).

servant who served in the prime minister's office, because it lacks expertise, the MoD "is essentially seen blocking decision-making instead of questioning the Services and collaborating with them to achieve national security targets. It has also failed to develop appropriate policies that would lead to improved military effectiveness."[61]

At the same time, it needs to be noted that there are structural reasons underlying the lack of civilian expertise in India. Flawed information-dissemination policies, mainly in relation to declassification, make it extremely difficult to gain expertise on defense affairs. Such knowledge should be imparted at the university level, but since scholars are unable to access primary sources, the existing departments of strategic and defense studies have little to offer.[62] Moreover, there are limited career opportunities for defense specialists and therefore very few incentives for civilians to gain expertise in military affairs. Information-dissemination policies therefore influence the ability to nurture expertise and thereby the quality of civilian control, an aspect mostly ignored by current scholarship.

The second factor in the absent dialogue framework is the institutional design of the MoD. Given that it is a civilian-dominant ministry, there are strong bureaucratic controls; and this, at times, leads to the exclusion of the military from policymaking. At the time of independence and in later years, some Indian political leaders feared a military coup.[63] According to a narrative popular within the military, civilian bureaucrats used this as a pretext to strengthen their powers. All matters that had financial implications—a strong measure of control—had to be cleared by civilian bureaucrats. The rules of business were thus amended to ensure that the services function as "attached offices" of the MoD and had to have all their proposals cleared by it. Over time, this has led to a situation of "intrusive bureaucratic monitoring."[64] Currently, there is a widespread belief within

---

[61] Shakti Sinha, "Inter-ministerial and Inter-departmental Coordination," in *Defence Reforms: A National Imperative*, ed. Gurmeet Kanwal and Neha Kohli, 134 (New Delhi: Pentagon Press, 2018).

[62] For a good analysis of this issue, see P. K. Gautam, "The Need for Renaissance of Military History and Modern War Studies in India" (IDSA occasional paper 21, Institute for Defence Studies and Analyses, New Delhi, 2011); also see Swaran Singh, "The State of Security Studies in India: Limitations and Potential," *Millennial Asia* 6, no. 2 (2015): 191–204; and Amitabh Mattoo and Rory Medcalf, "Think Tank and Universities," in *The Oxford Handbook of Indian Foreign Policy*, ed. David M. Malone, C. Raja Mohan, and Srinath Raghavan, 271–84 (New Delhi: Oxford University Press, 2015).

[63] Kundu, *Militarism in India*, 109–18, 163; and Harsh Pant, "India's Nuclear Doctrine and Command Structure: Implications for Civil–Military Relations in India," *Armed Forces and Society* 33, no. 2 (2007): 242–43.

[64] Kalyanraman, "Theory and Practice of Civil–Military Relations," 125; for a good analysis of the concept of attached officers, see R. Venkataraman, "Integration of MoD and Defense Planning," *Air Power* 5, no. 2 (2010): 25–51.

the military that they are not under "political control but are under bureaucratic control."[65]

Ordinarily, this level of bureaucratic control would not have been a problem or exceptional; for instance, a powerful Department of Defense administers the US military. However, unlike the United States, in India the MoD is comprised almost exclusively of civilians who lack expertise. Moreover, as the ministry is not integrated with the services, it leads to a situation where the military is often excluded from policymaking.[66] While the armed forces are consulted before decisions are made on the use of force, in crucial interagency deliberations the services are not adequately represented. A study of the almost nonexistent role of the Defence Ministers Committee (DMC), originally created soon after independence and involving service chiefs in decision-making, serves as a barometer of civil–military interaction.[67] According to General V. P. Malik, the chief of army staff during the 1999 Kargil war, the military felt "isolated from policy planning and the decision-making processes, leading to increasing suspicion and friction between the civilian bureaucrats in the Ministry and the service headquarters."[68] To be sure, especially after the 2001 defense reforms process, there has been a greater effort at ensuring involvement of the military in matters pertaining to national security. However, recent scholarship shows that, despite these efforts, the military continues to feel excluded from policymaking.[69] Tellingly, as discussed

[65] The narrative of bureaucratic instead of political control has largely been internalized within the Indian military. For some typical perspectives, see Arun Prakash, "Keynote Address," in *Proceedings of USI Seminar on Higher Defense Organization* (New Delhi: United Service Institution of India, 2007), 10; Kapil Kak, "Direction of Higher Defense II," *Strategic Analysis* 22, no. 4 (1998): 504; and Vinod Anand, *Delhi Papers 16: Joint Vision for the Indian Armed Forces* (New Delhi: Institute for Defence Studies and Analyses, 2001), 86.

[66] See the following: Vinod Anand, "Management of Defense: Towards an Integrated and Joint Vision," *Strategic Analysis* 24, no. 11 (2001): 1973–87; Raj Shukla, *Civil Military Relations in India*, Manekshaw Papers 36 (New Delhi: Centre for Land Warfare Studies, 2012), 28–34; and Gurmeet Kanwal, "Military's Voice Is Missing in National Security Decision Making Process," *Hindustan Times*, April 9, 2015, https://www.hindustantimes.com/ht-view/military-s-voice-is-missing-in-national-security-decision-making-process/story-mAYi7nJpF1FhasvsDQroyL.html

[67] The DMC atrophied in the years following independence and was only resurrected after the 1962 India–China war. Even then it existed in the form of the unstructured "morning meetings" and has performed erratically dependent upon the operating style of the defense minister; see S. K. Sinha, "Higher Defence Organisation in India," USI National Security Lecture 10 (New Delhi: United Service Institution of India, 1991), 26–28.

[68] V. P. Malik, *India's Military Conflicts and Diplomacy: An Inside View of Decision Making* (New Delhi: Harper Collins Publishers, 2013), 258.

[69] George Perkovich and Toby Dalton, *Not War, Not Peace? Motivating Pakistan to Prevent Cross-Border Terrorism* (New Delhi: Oxford University Press, 2016), 49–53; Rory Medcalf, "Imagining an Indian National Security Strategy: The Sum of Its Parts," *Australian Journal of International Affairs* 71, no. 5 (2017): 522–27; and Manoj Joshi, "Higher Defence Management: Evolution and Reform,"

in the penultimate chapter of this book, the contemporary debate surrounding defense reforms acknowledges the continued existence of this problem.[70]

A civilian-dominant MoD tends to perpetuate a sense of "us versus them" between civilians and the military.[71] As is fairly well known, there is considerable resentment within the military on what they perceive as civilian-led "intrusive bureaucratic monitoring."[72] This resentment arises from the fact that military personnel have to constantly approach civilians, whom they perceive as uninformed, for clearing their files. However, on the other hand, some argue that military officers themselves lack the expertise to handle the policy processes especially on issues which extend beyond their area of competence, that is, military operations.[73]

The third factor characterizing civil–military relations is the autonomy that the military has over its own affairs. While the concept of bureaucratic control alongside military autonomy appears paradoxical, the entire process plays out as a complicated game of negotiations, bargaining, and generally accepted norms of behavior and practice. As a matter of practice political leaders and bureaucrats rarely interfere in "purely" military affairs or activities considered within its domain. For instance, there is very little civilian participation in issues pertaining to doctrine, training, force structures, integration, and military education. As a result, the military is allowed to do most of what it wants in what it considers to be its own sphere of activities—training and education, threat assessments, force structures, doctrine, welfare activities, etc.[74] It is not even clear whether the services share their operational plans with the MoD or fully explain them to the political leaders.[75] To be sure, there are exceptions to all three factors: lack of

in *Military Strategy for India in the 21st Century*, ed. A. K. Singh and B. S. Nagal, 249–74 (New Delhi: Knowledge World, 2019).

[70] For instance, in 2011 the government constituted a committee, called the Naresh Chandra Committee, to revisit the defense reforms process; and its report had an extensive discussion on this issue; see *Report of the Task Force on National Security* (New Delhi: National Security Council Secretariat, 2012), 20–25.

[71] Srinath Raghavan, "Manohar Parrikar's Must-Do List Is Long," *NDTV News*, December 11, 2014; and Narain, *Born to Serve*, 134–38.

[72] Kalyanraman, "Theory and Practice of Civil–Military Relations," 125.

[73] Prakash Menon, "Military Education in India: Missing the Forest for the Trees," *Journal of Defence Studies* 9, no. 4 (2015): 49–69; and Rumel Dahiya, "Faulty Manpower Policies in Indian Armed Forces: Time for Action," *IDSA Issue Brief* (New Delhi: Institute for Defence Studies and Analyses, June 2011), 1.

[74] This notion of military autonomy challenges most conventional accounts of Indian civil–military relations. For instance, Stephen Cohen once described India as suffering from an "almost crushing dominance" by civilians; see Cohen, "Civilian Control of the Military in India," 47.

[75] According to a former service chief, who did not want to be identified, the Indian model does not encourage civilians to deliberate upon operational plans; interview, New Delhi, April 21, 2011.

expertise, institutional design leading to bureaucratic control, and considerable military autonomy. For instance, K. Subrahmanyam, P. R. Chari, and Shekhar Dutt were MoD officials who acquired a fair degree of expertise. However, all of them supported the idea that civilian bureaucrats needed to acquire defense expertise.[76] In addition, politicians like Arun Singh, minister of state for defense from 1985 to 1987, and Jaswant Singh, defense minister in 2001, took a keen interest in military affairs. Not by coincidence, as described in Chapter 2, both played a leading role in the defense reforms process. Similarly, on certain issues, the military is a powerful actor vitiating against the notion of an institutional design which leads to strong bureaucratic control. There are also instances where civilians, especially political leaders, have interfered in what is considered the domain of the military—usually to promote favored officers. There is thus more evidence of negative, or politically motivated, interference rather than any efforts to enhance overall military capability.

The absent dialogue is the pattern of civil–military relations that emerges from a combination of these three factors For example, there is little evidence of civilians engaging in a well-informed, result-oriented dialogue with military leaders on issues like jointness and professional military education. Instead, civilians seem content with maintaining their authority and control, whereas the military, on the one hand, "wants greater say in policy matters, but on the other it wants to keep the civilians out of its domain."[77] The problem is that in peacetime there is almost no genuine, meaningful dialogue between the military and the civilian authorities on aspects pertaining to force structures, operations, doctrines, and future technology in war.[78] Civilians falsely assume that there is a trade-off between control and military effectiveness and privilege the former over the latter. But the academic literature on this is clear, "the majority

---

Also see General V. N. Sharma, "India's Defense Forces: Building the Sinews of a Nation," *USI Journal* 64, no. 518 (1994): 458–59.

[76] Interviews with K. Subrahmanyam, New Delhi, October 1, 2010, and Shekhar Dutt, New Delhi, September 22, 2015; also see P. R. Chari, "Civil–Military Relations in India," *Armed Forces and Society* 3, no. 1 (1977): 15.

[77] Srinath Raghavan, "Defence Policy Has to Be a Joint Effort Between Civilians and the Military," *Hindustan Times,* May 11, 2017, https://www.hindustantimes.com/columns/defence-policy-has-to-be-a-joint-effort-between-civilians-and-the-military/story-55KtLiHsr63M1buTG7li3N.html

[78] For instance, see the following: B. D. Jayal, "Civil–Military Relations in India: An Unending Saga of a Deepening Crisis and Time for a New Beginning," *CASS Journal* 1, no. 1 (2014): 63–77; Christopher Clary, "Personalities, Organizations, and Doctrine in the Indian Military," *India Review* 17, no. 1 (2017) 100–21; Ali Ahmed, "Doctrine in Civil–Military Relations," *Indian Defence Review,* May 16, 2015, http://www.indiandefencereview.com/spotlights/doctrine-in-civil-military-relations/, Barret F. Bradstreet, "Rearming India: Responses to Military Innovation in India since 1947" (PhD diss., Princeton University, 2016); and Vivek Chadha, *Even If It Ain't Broke Yet, Do Fix It: Enhancing Effectiveness Through Military Change* (New Delhi: Pentagon Press, 2016), 158–59.

of researchers who have addressed the relationship between control and effectiveness confirm ... the positive effect of active involvement and strict civilian control in defense and military issues on military effectiveness."[79]

Conclusion

In most democracies, when faced with a crisis the stakeholders—politicians, bureaucrats, and military officials—quickly close ranks and focus on resolving the situation. However, after the crisis blows over, the patterns of behavior revert to what they were before. Such an approach is suboptimal primarily because, as students of military organizations know too well, building both capability and proficiency in military operations takes years, if not decades. It is usually too late to attend to capability development and address operational shortcomings during a crisis, thus the defiant refrain from the military that it will "fight with whatever we have."[80] However, such refrains, perhaps aimed at lifting morale and indicating resolve, do little to address institutional weaknesses.

The main argument in this book is that among the consequences of India's pattern of civilian control—the absent dialogue—is its pernicious influence on variables generally associated with military effectiveness. Civil–military relations in India are broadly shaped by three factors—lack of civilian expertise, strong bureaucratic control, and considerable military autonomy. In turn, I examine how this shapes the five components of military effectiveness—weapons procurement, jointness, professional military education, officer promotion policies, and defense planning. The next chapter describes the historical evolution of civil–military relations, focusing on wartime leaders

---

[79] Aurel Croissant and David Kuehn, "Introduction," in *Reforming Civil–Military Relations in New Democracies: Democratic Control and Military Effectiveness in Comparative Perspectives*, ed. Aurel Croissant and David Kuehn, 9 (Heidelberg, Germany: Springer, 2017).

[80] At the onset of the Kargil war in 1999, General V. P. Malik, then chief of army staff, famously made this statement; see V. P. Malik, "The Tehelka Impact: Defence Preparedness, Procurement Procedures and Corruption," *Rediff.com*, April 9, 2001, http://www.rediff.com/news/2001/apr/09malik.htm

2

Convenient Narratives

Historical Evolution of Civil–Military Relations

Relations between politicians and soldiers are unique to every country—shaped by its history, political structures, and norms, among many other factors. This is also path-dependent, as norms and forms of behavior emerge over time. To understand these norms, and the paths which lead us to the present, one has to analyze the issue historically. Accordingly, this chapter examines the evolution of civil–military relations in India. While doing so it highlights the different precedents and norms that have led to its "unique civil–military relationship."[1] The uniqueness is primarily a function of three factors: lack of civilian expertise, an institutional design which favors civilian bureaucratic control, and significant military autonomy over its internal processes.

Independence and the partition of India and Pakistan were strange in many respects. Horrific massacres and the largest transfer of population in history accompanied an "otherwise" peaceful transfer of power from the British. The creation of two independent states with new borders, constitutions, currencies, and legal and administrative structures presented formidable challenges. Both countries also had to forge a national identity encompassing diverse religious, ethnic, caste, and linguistic differences. Moreover, they had to divide their armies, which within months after independence went to war over Kashmir. Civil–military relations in both countries were shaped by these circumstances and by the personalities and precedents that were put in place in these first few decades. One of India's main successes was the establishment of firm civilian control, an issue that most other developing countries could not, and some still do not, take for granted. The strength of India's democracy and the maturity and wisdom of its political leaders were critical to this effort. Equally important was

---

[1] K. Subrahmanyam, "Commentary: Evolution of Defense Planning in India," in *Defense Planning in Less-Industrialized States: The Middle East and South Asia*, ed. Stephanie Neuman, 266 (Lexington, MA: Lexington Books, 1984).

the professionalism of the military that internalized the need to remain apolitical. The absence of a coup, however, does not mean that all was well with civil–military relations. Instead, this chapter explains how there has been a continuous contest over policy between politicians and bureaucrats on one side and the military on the other. In this, at times silent at times not, struggle for power all three stakeholders have come to a mutually acceptable solution—a strict separation between the civilian and military domains.

In order to understand the evolving nature of civil–military relations, it is crucial to focus on the interaction between politicians, military officers, and civilian bureaucrats. This interaction becomes more urgent during wartime, with constant meetings and relatively clear outcomes regarding their efficacy. This chapter therefore focuses on civil–military relations under five wartime prime ministers—Jawaharlal Nehru, Lal Bahadur Shastri, Indira Gandhi, Rajiv Gandhi, and Atal Bihari Vajpayee. Together they were at the helm of affairs for almost five decades after independence and significantly shaped civil–military relations. For analytical purposes, their roles are examined through the prism of "supreme commanders," that is, as leaders of the armed forces during war.[2] Next, the chapter focuses on an essential element shaping civil–military relations— the interaction between civilian bureaucrats and military officers. It concludes by highlighting the emergence of the absent dialogue pattern that best describes India's civil–military relations. As with writing history, this chapter relies on access to archival papers; and hence, there is greater discussion of events that go further back in time.

The Nehru Era, 1947–1964: Setting the Stage

Due to the nature of the Indian political system marked by continuing dynasties, Nehru's legacy is still a political issue, and a matter of controversy. It is difficult to engage in an honest debate as writers are often judged on the basis of their perceived political ideology. That notwithstanding, most historians agree that India was fortunate to have Nehru as its first prime minister. His wisdom in adopting a consensual style of leadership and emphasis on a parliamentary democracy instead of authoritarian rule, an easy temptation for most leaders in the developing world, helped embed democratic norms in Indian polity. His views

---

[2] As per custom, the president of India is the supreme commander of the armed forces; however, in this context, "supreme commander" refers to the highest political leader directing the military. As the leader of the cabinet, in India's case, this responsibility rests with the prime minister. For the concept of supreme commander, see Eliot Cohen, *Supreme Command: Soldiers, Statesmen, and Leadership in Wartime* (New York: Free Press, 2002).

on secularism, liberalism, toleration, foreign policy, and rule of law created an idea of India that exists, with imperfections to be sure, to this day.

On civil–military relations, Nehru's greatest accomplishment was the establishment of firm civilian control, but he also oversaw many controversies. This section begins by describing the post-independence relations between politicians and soldiers. It then discusses the unique role of Louis Mountbatten, the last British viceroy and the first Indian governor general, in shaping India's defense policy during this period. Next, it examines major controversies including the tenure of Krishna Menon as defense minister, the resignation of Chief of Army Staff General K. S. Thimayya, and Nehru's overall relations with his generals leading up to the 1962 China war. It then gives an overall assessment of Nehru as a supreme commander.

Dhotiwallahs and Brass Hats: A Clash of Cultures

Upon independence, officers in the Indian military had to deal with the unfamiliar experience of working with their newly appointed political masters and a civilian Ministry of Defence (MoD)—tasks for which they were ill prepared and untrained. The British, as a matter of policy, denied Indian military officers the opportunity to serve in important posts; and, in any case, most officers were junior in service.[3] In addition to the lack of familiarity, Indian military officers had to overcome the awkwardness of dealing with politicians who had made many sacrifices in the freedom struggle while they served, and benefited from, the empire.[4] Hence, there was awkwardness, unfamiliarity, and a lack of experience all around. The outbreak of the first Kashmir war in 1947 and the need to face that crisis helped to overcome some mutual apprehensions, but relations between politicians and military officers were far from comfortable. Indicative of the distrust, shortly after independence, General Rajendra Sinhji, who later became the second Indian chief of army staff, allegedly advised his junior to be careful in dealing with the newly ensconced politicians: "our present leaders are Indians. They do not behave like the British. Their techniques are different. They behave more like the princes. You have to be more of a courtier."[5]

---

[3] V. Longer, *Red Coats to Olive Green: A History of the Indian Army, 1600–1974* (New Delhi: Allied Publishers, 1974), 272–90.

[4] For the gap between political and military leaders during this period, see Kaushik Roy, *The Armed Forces of Independent India, 1947–2006* (New Delhi: Manohar Publishers, 2010), 68–92.

[5] As confided to then brigadier and later chief of army staff J. N. Chaudhuri in December 1947, see Oral History Transcripts, General J. N. Chaudhuri no. 426, Nehru Memorial Museum & Library (hereafter NMML), New Delhi, 17.

At a fundamental level, it represented a clash of cultures between the politicians and military officers. There was also a sociological divide as some Indian officers were considered "more British than the British."[6] Fortunately for India's democracy, the political class successfully asserted itself, although there is little evidence to suggest that the military harbored praetorian tendencies. Nehru played a key role in this process. In a symbolic move, he shifted into the then residence of the commander in chief of the British Indian Army at Teen Murti House. More importantly, he supported his political and bureaucratic leaders in their attempt to assert control. But his leadership style, questionable choice of advisers, and almost obsessive focus on civilian control created unintended and disastrous consequences.

H. M. Patel, the defense secretary from 1947 to 1953, best reflected a commonly held view when he dismissively argued, "actually no one in parliament knows anything about defence policy."[7] Patel's arrogance was probably born out of his long experience in the ministry, but it was also true that, at the turn of independence, few politicians knew much about defense. Baldev Singh, a prominent Sikh leader, was the first defense minister and held the post for nearly five years. He played an important role in supporting and building up the civilian staff in the MoD.

After independence, there was some confusion regarding the working relation between civilians and the military. Previously, the British officer who was the chief of the Indian Army sat in the viceroy's council and thereby deliberated upon defense policy. This arrangement was more attuned for imperial control and had to be replaced by one appropriate for a parliamentary democracy— the cabinet system. Accordingly, a civilian defense minister sat in on cabinet meetings, and their decisions were to be implemented by the MoD and the armed forces. The defense minister, aided by the ministry, was thereby procedurally tasked to control the military. Nehru and Baldev Singh played an important role in this process, assisted by two able civil servants—H. M. Patel and H. C. Sarin.[8] This gave rise to an impression that Baldev Singh was "more or less

[6] Stories about General Cariappa's anglicized manner were legion; see Harbaksh Singh, *In the Line of Duty: A Soldier Remembers* (New Delhi: Lancer Publications, 2000), 384–86. Within the army there was also a divide between the Kings Commissioned Officers and the Indian Commissioned Officers.

[7] "Interview with H. M. Patel, March 9, 1964," Stephen Cohen Papers, Brookings Institution. For similar sentiments and harsh assessments of all defense ministers except Krishna Menon from one of the most well-connected "political generals" of that era, see "Interview with Lt. Gen. B. M. Kaul, December 28, 1964," Stephen Cohen Papers, 4–5.

[8] For a good description of post-independence changes in civil–military relations, see Lloyd Rudolph and Susanne Rudolph, "Generals and Politicians in India," *Pacific Affairs* 37, no. 1 (1964): 9–10.

run by his Personal Secretary and staff."[9] Despite his efforts, as discussed later in this chapter, there were considerable tensions between the bureaucrats and the military.

From 1952 onward there began a widely acknowledged drift in the MoD. Gopalaswami Ayyangar replaced Baldev Singh as the defense minister, but his tenure was only for nine months. From 1953 to 1955, Nehru kept the defense minister's portfolio; however as he was juggling numerous responsibilities, he appointed Mahavir Tyagi to the unique position of minister of defense organization (a post he held from 1953 to 1957). The military resented Tyagi, who was a soldier before he joined the independence movement; and his allegedly eccentric ways earned him the unfortunate moniker of "unguided missile."[10] Matters did not improve when Kailash Nath Katju was the defense minister from 1955 to 1957.[11] Appointing such non-performers to this post reflected either Nehru's lack of priority or his intention to keep the MoD firmly under his control. He exercised this control in one of the more consequential episodes during this time—the controversy over the designation of the service chiefs.

A "Very Obvious Manoeuvre": Change in Designation of Service Chiefs

At the time of independence, the service chiefs had two designations, the "chief of army/navy/air staff" and the "commander in chief, army/navy/air." In practice, they had dual responsibilities—in New Delhi they were the chiefs of staff, and when visiting forces in the field they became the commanders in chief and, therefore, were considered both staff and operational commanders. In 1953, as a result of a long-running feud, Defence Secretary H. M. Patel was "very anxious to clip the wings of the Army C-in-C [General K. M. Cariappa]."[12] Accordingly, the MoD suddenly produced a paper proposing to drop the "commander-in-chief" title. It claimed that this had the approval of the three chiefs, and the paper would have been considered approved if no comments were received within

[9] S. S. Khera, *India's Defence Problem* (New Delhi: Orient Longman, 1968), 66.

[10] Personal letter from Admiral Mark Pizey to Mountbatten dated December 31, 1954, in MB 1/J-341/2, Mountbatten Papers, Hartley Library, University of Southampton (hereafter referred to as Mountbatten Papers). Years later Lt. Gen. B. M. Kaul was more unforgiving, calling him a "a monkey, a lunatic, a little shrimp"; see "Interview with Lt. Gen. B. M. Kaul, December 28, 1964," Stephen Cohen Papers, Brookings Institution, 4.

[11] For more about the drift in the Defence Ministry during this time, see Khera, *India's Defence*, 67–69.

[12] Personal and confidential letter from Admiral Mark Pizey, then Indian chief of naval staff to Admiral Mountbatten, dated February 1, 1955, in MB1/I 225 folder 2, Mountbatten Papers. The rest of this account relies on an exchange of letters which are a part of this collection.

forty-eight hours. Noticeably this paper was circulated the day General Cariappa left on tour. Admiral Pizey argued that the assertion that the three chiefs had been consulted was a "complete fabrication" and that this entire move was a "very obvious manoeuvre."[13] The service chiefs then had to personally appeal to the prime minister and with "utmost difficulty" were told that a "decision would be taken in due course in consultation with the Defence Minister."

Two years later, in January 1955, the service chiefs were informed that the changes in designation would be effective from the tenure of General S. M. Shrinagesh who was replacing General Rajendra Sinhji as the chief of the army. This decision, according to Defence Secretary M. K. Vellodi, was taken during a cabinet meeting presided over by Nehru. Immediately afterward, Nehru left for a visit to the United Kingdom. This led Admiral Pizey, with the concurrence of the other two chiefs, to request Mountbatten to talk to Nehru and convince him to reverse his decision. Mountbatten tried to do so; however, Nehru was adamant and countered that the "commander-in-chief" title in India had a particular historical connotation that was associated with colonial rule and ill-suited for a parliamentary democracy. According to Mountbatten, Nehru "felt it was essential that the position of heads of the Services as being subordinate to the Government should be made clear, as was the case in other countries."[14] But Mountbatten surmised that Nehru was either ill-advised or ill-informed. While urging Pizey to take a conciliatory stance, he wrote, "the thing to stress is that the title "Commander-in-Chief" is used in all other countries far more freely. We used to have no less than nine Commanders-in-Chief in the British navy alone! I do not think he has full[y] realised this."[15] When so advised by Mountbatten, and after a personal discussion with Nehru, the service chiefs accepted this decision.[16] However, to sell what they considered to be a militarily unpopular decision, they requested Nehru to personally announce the change in designation.[17] Nehru accepted this request and announced the change of designation in Parliament. Crucially, while doing so, he promised that gradually the system

[13] Personal and confidential letter from Admiral Mark Pizey to Admiral Mountbatten dated February 1, 1955, in MB1/I 225 folder 2, page 2, Mountbatten Papers.

[14] Personal and strictly confidential letter from Mountbatten to Admiral Pizey titled "Title of Commander-in-Chief," undated in MB1/I225 Mountbatten Papers. Mountbatten instructed Pizey to destroy the letter after reading it.

[15] Personal and strictly confidential letter from Mountbatten to Admiral Pizey titled "Title of Commander-in-Chief," undated in MB1/I225, Mountbatten Papers.

[16] Secret and personal letter from Admiral Pizey to Admiral Mountbatten dated February 22, 1955, in MB1/I225, Mountbatten Papers.

[17] Personal and confidential letter from Admiral Pizey to Admiral Rhoderick McGrigor, first sea lord and chief of naval staff, dated March 18, 1955, in MB1/I225, Mountbatten Papers.

would consist of service councils and boards, like in the United Kingdom.[18] This was never done.[19]

This episode created a lasting impact on the institutional structure of the Indian military and revealed significant trends in civil–military relations. In terms of legacy, the change in designation without changing the job description (or creating service councils) created the strange chiefs of staff system in India wherein service chiefs functionally continue to wear two hats.[20] The episode also provides an insight into the struggle between the civilians and the military and the role and thinking of Nehru on this subject. H. M. Patel's clumsy attempt in 1953 to strip the chiefs of the "commander-in-chief" title was successfully stalled; however, in 1955, Nehru used his authority and overruled all objections—including the advice of Mountbatten. Another possible explanation for this change in designation was offered by Admiral Pizey:

> We think that certain high-ups in the Party feel that the Commanders-in-Chief have got, or are getting, too much popularity, and, perhaps, power. . . . We believe that in certain quarters there is a feeling of danger if the Services' Chiefs get too much in the public eye as they may follow the same "practice" as certain Service Chiefs in other countries have done! I think this is a dreadful thought, but, nevertheless, I believe it is at the back of their minds—though certainly not the P.M.'s.[21]

Admiral Pizey was careful in excluding the prime minister from harboring such a "dreadful thought," perhaps being mindful of Mountbatten's obvious affection for him; but Nehru was deeply concerned about upholding the principle of civilian control. Nehru felt that the commander-in-chief may lead to a mistaken notion, "particularly in the army . . . of being above the government."[22] Time and again, including during the controversy over General Thimayya's

---

[18] This idea came from Mountbatten, and he told both Nehru and Admiral Pizey that the best possible outcome was to move toward the council system; see personal and strictly confidential letter from Mountbatten to Admiral Pizey titled "Title of Commander-in-Chief," undated in MB1/I225, page 2, Mountbatten Papers.

[19] The opposition to the idea of service councils came from the chiefs; see G. M. Hiranandani, *Transition to Guardianship: The Indian Navy, 1991–2000* (New Delhi: Lancer Publishers, 2009) 280.

[20] Anit Mukherjee, "Facing Future Challenges: Defence Reforms in India," *RUSI Journal* 156, no. 5 (2011): 33; also see K. Subrahmanyam, "India's Strategic Challenges," *Indian Express*, February 4, 2012.

[21] Personal and confidential letter from Admiral Mark Pizey to Admiral Mountbatten dated February 1, 1955, in MB1/I 225 folder 2, page 3, Mountbatten Papers.

[22] Personal and strictly confidential letter from Mountbatten to Admiral Pizey titled "Title of Commander-in-Chief," undated in MB1/I225, page 1, Mountbatten Papers.

resignation, Nehru would cite the necessity to uphold civilian supremacy. His thinking was undoubtedly influenced by concerns arising from coups in other developing countries.

Admiral Pizey's other assumption that some political figures were resentful of the military's popularity held more than a kernel of truth to it. Senior military officials at that time, more so than ever before or since, were national celebrities; and their visits and statements were covered prominently in the local and national press. They were frequently invited to speak at Rotary Clubs and social functions, and the public adulation they attracted must have created some uneasiness in the political class.[23] This uneasiness would have increased manifold when in later years two very popular officers fell out with Nehru—General Thimayya and Lieutenant General S. P. P. Thorat, both of whom enjoyed widespread support and attracted sympathetic press coverage.[24]

A final insight from this episode was the lack of communication and dialogue between Nehru and his service chiefs both in 1953 and in 1955. In both instances the proposals were sprung upon the military as a fait accompli, and ironically Nehru discussed matters with the service chiefs only after Mountbatten's intervention. Admiral Pizey's last letter on this subject to Mountbatten conveyed the news that they had decided to accept the change in designation but added significantly, "if it had not been for the fact that the decision was taken by the Cabinet before he left for the U.K., he would have seriously considered postponing the change after the talk he had with you."[25] Clearly, Nehru had no discussions either with his service chiefs or with Mountbatten before the proposal was cleared by the cabinet. It is entirely plausible, though not proven, that Nehru was influenced by H. M. Patel's failed attempt to change the designations in 1953. Nehru, perhaps relying on feedback from civilian bureaucrats, may then have imagined this measure as crucial in upholding the principle of civilian control. It is not surprising then that Nehru kept his service chiefs in the dark. Once the cabinet made the decision, Nehru felt he could not back down, despite Mountbatten's lobbying. If anything, this episode was indicative of an absent dialogue between politicians and the military as the service chiefs in India needed Mountbatten as a secret go-between

[23] For the unease among the political class stemming from the popularity of General K. M. Cariappa, see Ramachandra Guha, *India after Gandhi: The History of the World's Largest Democracy* (New Delhi: Picador Macmillan, 2007), 748–49.

[24] For numerous press clippings that attest to the popularity and controversies concerning these officers, see Subject Files 5, 10, 13, 16, 17, 18, and 20, Thimayya papers, and Subject Files 4, 5, 7, and 19, Thorat papers, NMML.

[25] Personal letter from Admiral Pizey to Admiral Mountbatten dated March 18, 1955, in MB1/I225, Mountbatten Papers.

to communicate their perspectives to the prime minister. It was also indicative of Mountbatten's continued role in shaping India's defense policy in this period.

Mountbatten of India

Mountbatten's unique relationship with Nehru had the mark of a true friendship—it is still unclear who used whom. Both benefited from it and used the friendship to further their national interests. Besides their association during partition and shared history over the "Kashmir problem," Mountbatten also had an abiding interest in higher defense management in India and, later in his career, in the United Kingdom. This was understandable as he along with Lord Ismay, upon Nehru's invitation, were the architects of India's higher defense structure.[26] His influence on defense policies was mainly, but not exclusively, on three issues—weapons procurement, arbitrating differences between the civilians and the military, and an attempt, ultimately unsuccessful, to create a more rational higher defense organization by, among other measures, appointing a chief of defense staff.

A difficult question facing Indian defense managers during this period was the allocation of scarce resources, especially foreign exchange, among the three services. They had to not only build up the air force and the navy, both of which had inherited very few assets upon independence, but also keep the army prepared to deal with emerging threats. In an analysis of defense spending during this era, Raju Thomas expressed a commonly held view: "until the year after the 1965 Indo–Pakistan war, the navy was faced with a government policy of benign neglect."[27] On the contrary, the Indian Navy gained considerable resources during this period, emerging as possibly the strongest navy in the developing world, far ahead of expected rivals China and Pakistan. The official navy history admitted that the navy's share of the budget rose from "4% in 1950–51 [and] it more than doubled to 9% in 1956–57 and reached 12% in 1959–60."[28] In making decisions regarding interservices allocation of resources and general weapons procurement, Mountbatten played an important role both because Britain was the largest supplier of military equipment and because he was consulted often

[26] For more about this structure, see S. K. Sinha, "Higher Defence Organisation in India," in *USI National Security Lecture, 1990*, 17–24 (New Delhi: New Statesman Press, 1980).

[27] Raju G. C. Thomas, "The Armed Services and the Indian Defense Budget," *Asian Survey* 20, no. 3 (1980), 288–89.

[28] Satyindra Singh, *Blueprint to Bluewater: The Indian Navy, 1951–65* (New Delhi: Lancer International, 1992), 305.

and widely.[29] However, Mountbatten's advice did not serve India well due to a fundamental, if understandable, conflict of interest—as a naval officer, he was partial toward building up the Indian Navy. Worse, this was under the assumption that the Indian Navy would help the Commonwealth in a possible world war against communism. India's non-aligned policy might have precluded a military pact, but it appears that Mountbatten was able to convince both British and Indian officials to quanttitatively build up the Indian Navy.[30] This suited the British Navy as it could dispose of some of its aging ships. Building up the Indian Navy was a laudable objective; however, it was done without a sense of proportion to the most likely threats—the Pakistani and Chinese Navies. For instance, Mountbatten played a crucial role in convincing India to buy the aircraft carrier HMS *Hercules* in January 1957 and in his justification wrote that

> the possession of a carrier would put your navy into a different category and raise it to the technical level of great Navies, i.e. British, American, Canadian, Australian and French. Yours would be the only carrier to be possessed by any African or Asian nation and so would consequently dominate all other navies against whom she might have to operate. . . . From the prestige point of view you would have a magnificent ship which would make a great impression in ports that your ship may visit and which would overshadow in every way other Asian navies.[31]

In short, Mountbatten's justification was primarily "prestige" and a desire to catapult the Indian Navy to be among the "great navies" without any mention of role and threat environment. Apart from communicating with the Indian policymakers, Mountbatten also secretly lobbied British officers still serving in the Indian Navy.[32] Finally, he took advantage of the special relationship he shared

---

[29] This is covered in greater detail in Chapter 3. During 1947–1962, Britain was the source for around 70% of India's defense imports, which was adjusted against the sterling debt accumulated during the Second World War.

[30] Mountbatten continuously lobbied for enhancing the capability of the Indian Navy, both in London and in Delhi; see Secret File, "Minutes of Meeting with the First Sea Lord," Naval HQ, New Delhi, dated March 16, 1956, in MB1/I-508 folder 1(1 of 2) and letters exchanged between Mountbatten and Admiral R. D. Katari, 1959–1960, in MB1/J236 India 1959–65, Mountbatten Papers. Also see Jaswant Singh, *Defending India* (New Delhi: Macmillan India, 1999), 114–24.

[31] Secret letter from Mountbatten to Defence Secretary M. K. Vellodi dated December 21, 1956, MB1/I-225 First Sea Lord (1 of 3 folders), 1955–1959, Mountbatten Papers.

[32] Secret and "strictly personal" letter from Mountbatten to Vice Admiral S. H. Carlill, chief of naval staff, Indian Navy, dated December 21, 1956, in MB1/I-225 First Sea Lord (1 of 3 folders), 1955–1959, Mountbatten Papers.

with Nehru and lobbied him too.[33] To be sure, his efforts to sell British equipment were not just restricted to naval hardware but extended to the other two services.[34] But perhaps because of his service loyalty and connections within the Indian and British Navies, he was more successful in facilitating the sale of assets to build up the Indian Navy.

It would be misleading, however, to overstate Mountbatten's influence in interservices prioritization as Nehru was inclined beforehand to building up the navy and air force, over the army. For instance, as early as 1953, after a deliberation on interservices allocation of resources by the Defence Committee of the Cabinet, chaired by Nehru, Chief of Army Staff General Rajendra Sinhji attested to the outcome of the meeting by congratulating his naval counterpart, Admiral Mark Pizey, for "the greatest naval victory after Trafalgar!"[35]

In a prescient note written in 1949, General Roy Bucher foresaw many of the difficulties in interservices allocations and warned against neglecting the requirements of the army: "a serious blunder will be made, if during the next few years the Royal Indian Air Force and the Royal Indian Navy are so unduly expanded as to cause a serious shortcoming in money for reasonable arming and re-equipment of the army."[36] Perhaps Bucher's foreboding arose from his close association with Mountbatten and a premonition that his influence on Indian policymakers may lead to a material neglect of the Indian Army. Or maybe Bucher anticipated Nehru's thoughts on this matter and the subsequent trends in resource allocation. But, in any case, his warning proved to be in vain.

Besides weapons acquisition, Mountbatten also got involved in another aspect of Indian defense policy—arbitrating disputes between civilians and military officials. In the course of his correspondence, usually but not exclusively with British officers serving in India, Mountbatten was apprised of the strange civil–military relations emerging at that time.[37] Based on these inputs, Mountbatten frequently counseled Indian political leaders to fix problems in the MoD. In January 1958, he wrote to the incoming defense minister, Krishna Menon:

[33] Secret letter dated January 7, 1956, to First Lord, et al. in MB1/I-225 First Sea Lord (1 of 3 folders), 1955–1959, Mountbatten Papers.

[34] For his successful efforts in lobbying Nehru to buy the Hunters in addition to the French Mystere, thanks, in part, to an excellent brief prepared by the British Ministry of Defence, see personal letter from Mountbatten to Walter Monckton, Minister of Defence, dated July 11, 1956, in MB1/225 file 3, Mountbatten Papers.

[35] Singh, *Blueprint to Bluewater*, 50.

[36] Secret report titled "Report by General Roy Bucher, Officer on Special duty, Ministry of Defence, New Delhi, dated 17 March 1949," in 7901-87 (13 to 49), Bucher Papers, National Army Museum, London.

[37] Personal letter from Admiral Mark Pizey to Mountbatten dated December 31, 1954, in MB1/J341/2, Mountbatten Papers.

You may remember that in the course of various gossips about your new job I referred to the top heavy set up which I felt that your Ministry of Defence suffered from. So far as I know your Ministry of Defence is full of civil servants with practically no representation from Service Officers at all, whereas the three Service Headquarters appear to have a lot of officers with very little help from the professional civil servants. I discussed this aspect of the case with Carlill [then chief of naval staff] . . . and was interested to know that he shared my views.[38]

This letter apparently had an effect, at least for a while, for within a short time, in a private letter to Mountbatten, Admiral Carlill suggested that Krishna Menon was interested in reorganizing the MoD and that this had the concurrence of all of the service chiefs.[39] However, it is unclear what happened to this effort; and despite Mountbatten's counsel, he was unable to prevent the subsequent breakdown in civil–military relations.

Finally, any analysis of Mountbatten's role would be remiss without discussing an issue that he was passionate about even until a few months before his death— the creation of the chief of defence staff post in India.[40] A discussion of this issue requires a little historical background. In 1947–1948, when Mountbatten along with General Ismay created India's higher defense organization, they had discussed the need for a permanent chairman of the chiefs of staff committee.[41] However, Mountbatten thought that the creation of this post should be deferred by around twelve years as "the Indian Army was one generation ahead of the other two in producing experienced senior officers since the Indian Air Force and Navy were started so much later." Mountbatten felt that the other two services would require this much time to produce capable officers and it was "clearly essential this job should not be permanently held by any one service."

Precisely twelve years later, in 1960, Mountbatten wrote to Nehru requesting him to create a permanent chairman of the chiefs of staff committee, or the

[38] Personal and private letter from Mountbatten to Krishna Menon dated January 10, 1958, MB1/I-225 First Sea Lord (1 of 3 folders), 1955–1959, Mountbatten Papers. The letter later advises Krishna Menon to have an honest chat with Admiral Carlill.

[39] Private letter from Stephen Carlill dated January 17, 1958, MB1/I-225 First Sea Lord (1 of 3 folders), 1955–1959, Mountbatten Papers.

[40] See letter written by Mountbatten to Lt. Gen. M. L. Chibber on September 27, 1977, reproduced in V. P. Malik and Anit Mukherjee, "Jawaharlal Nehru and the Chief of Defence Staff," *IDSA Issue Brief* (New Delhi: Institute for Defence Studies and Analyses, July 2011).

[41] The following account relies on a note titled "Creation of the Chief of the Defence Staff for India," prepared by Mountbatten for Defence Minister Y. B. Chavan on May 7, 1965, that he shared in a strictly personal and private letter with General J. N. Chaudhuri, MB1/J235/56, Mountbatten Papers.

chief of defence staff (CDS) as Mountbatten understood it to be.[42] In this letter, Mountbatten recounted a conversation with Defence Minister Krishna Menon on this topic. Krishna Menon was opposed to it as it was "politically difficult." Moreover, he was even more opposed when he heard that Mountbatten thought Thimayya would make an ideal choice as the first CDS. While Mountbatten "fundamentally disagreed" with Menon's assessment of Thimayya, he understood that he could not be appointed if "Krishna won't have him." "However," Mountbatten wrote, "I am not writing to recommend any one person for the job, but merely to urge you to create the job." Nehru, however, was not convinced; and nothing came of this effort. Mountbatten was to assume later that it was primarily on account of opposition from Krishna Menon.[43]

After 1962, upon the departure of Krishna Menon, Mountbatten renewed his efforts to appoint a CDS. In a forceful letter, he countered all of Nehru's previous objections and uncharacteristically pleaded, "I beg you to consider Thimayya for the appointment."[44] Nehru responded to this by saying that Thimayya, along with Rajendra Sinhji and Thorat, had been made members of the Military Affairs Committee of the Defence Council and "to some extent, what you suggest has been done, though not in a formal way. We are giving thought to your proposal; however you will appreciate that there are all manner of considerations to be borne in mind."[45]

Mountbatten was not overly attached to the idea that only Thimayya should be the CDS and was willing to settle with someone else, as long as the post was appointed. Accordingly, in the summer of 1963 he once again approached the Indian government. A secret assessment written by then British military adviser Brigadier I. M. Christie describes the fate of that effort:

> In May 1963, the C.D.S. [Mountbatten] advised the Minister of Defence [Y. B. Chavan] to consider the question of adopting the CDS concept and organisation. General Chaudhuri is known to be much in favour, and it was strongly rumoured at one time that he himself would become the first Chairman. However, virtually no progress has been made

[42] Mountbatten wrote this letter in December 1960 more than a year after he was appointed as the CDS in Britain; see personal and private letter to Nehru dated December 9, 1960, in MB1/J302, Mountbatten Papers,.

[43] Letter from Mountbatten to Lt. Gen. M. L. Chibber dated September 27, 1977, which was first published by *Indian Defence Review* 16, no. 2 (2001): 130–32. http://www.indiandefencereview.com/spotlights/mountbatten-on-cds/

[44] Personal and confidential letter from Mountbatten to Nehru dated December 31, 1962, in MB1/J302, Mountbatten Papers.

[45] Personal and confidential letter no. 290-PMH/63 from Nehru to Mountbatten dated February 9, 1963, in MB1/J302, Mountbatten Papers.

in this respect, and from information received from various sources, it now looks as if the Government would oppose such a move for the reason that they would not accept a Service Chief in any position which might afford him the opportunity of effecting a coup d'état.[46]

In the course of his conversations with Mountbatten on the subject of the CDS, Nehru at different times offered different explanations of why this could not be done. While earlier it was opposition from Krishna Menon, later "all manner of considerations" prevented him from doing so. It can be reasonably assumed that Nehru was never convinced about the need to appoint a CDS. To be sure, there might have been other sources of opposition. The air force and the navy chiefs, for instance, might have feared an army-dominated CDS. Curiously, the defense secretary at that time, P. V. R. Rao, would cite this as the primary reason for his opposition.[47] However, this might have been a convenient excuse as it was never proposed that the CDS always had to be from the army.[48] Instead, civilians in the MoD might have opposed this post as they feared that they would be dominated by a CDS and that this would upset the delicate civil–military balance and control that they had achieved post-independence.[49] Their fears would then feed into Nehru's own fear of a loss of civilian control. It appears then that Nehru was willing to trade whatever gains might accrue in military effectiveness against any perceived loss of civilian control. As Brigadier Christie rightly guessed, the specter of a "man on horseback" haunted Nehru and, one can argue, the Congress Party both at that time and since.[50]

After Nehru's death, Mountbatten doggedly made another effort and this time suggested to Defence Minister Chavan that General J. N. Chaudhuri, then

---

[46] Secret report titled "A Valedictory Report on the Indian Army by Brigadier IM Christie, Military Adviser to the British High Commissioner in India, New Delhi, March 12, 1965," 8–9, in DO 164/84, Kew Archives, London.

[47] P. V. R Rao, *Defence Without Drift* (Bombay: Popular Prakashan, 1970), 318–19.

[48] Mountbatten's original decision in 1948 to not appoint a permanent chairman was to give time to the other services to grow. After 1960, Mountbatten argued that this post could be held by one of the three service chiefs, whoever was "well suited to be an *impartial* Chairman" (emphasis added); see personal and private letter to Nehru dated December 9, 1960, in MB1/J302, Mountbatten Papers.

[49] Many would argue that the defense secretary had become the "de facto CDS" and was unwilling to give up or share his power; see Vinod Anand, "Management of Defence: Towards An Integrated and Joint Vision," *Strategic Analysis* 24, no. 11 (2001): 1975. For more on sources of opposition to the CDS, see S. K. Sinha, "The Chief of Defence Staff," *Journal of Defence Studies* 1, no. 1 (2007).

[50] The Congress internalized these early fears about military rule, and hence it was not surprising that one of the strongest sources of political opposition to the appointment of the CDS in 2001 came from the Congress; see Anit Mukherjee, "Failing to Deliver: The Post Crises Defence Reforms in India, 1998–2010" (IDSA occasional paper 18, Institute for Defence Studies and Analyses, New Delhi, March 2011), 29–30.

army chief, was ideally placed to assume this post. This was meant to support the latter's own efforts, mostly in private, to appoint himself as the CDS.[51] But these efforts also did not make any headway. With every change of prime minister, Mountbatten was willing to take his chances. Even when attending Shastri's funeral in Delhi in 1966 he promised to discuss this matter with the incoming prime minister, Indira Gandhi.[52] A decade later, in 1977, he would still not lose hope and offered to do so when Morarji Desai came to power. His efforts mirrored those of successive army chiefs including Manekshaw, T. N. Raina, K. V. Krishna Rao, V. P. Malik, N. C. Vij and Bikram Singh, who would all lobby for creating this post. To date, however, this remains a controversial topic.

Mountbatten's overall contribution in shaping India's defense policies has been immense. With the benefit of hindsight, while it might be tempting to criticize some of his advice, it is crucial to note that he was doing this while serving in the British admiralty far from the subcontinent. More importantly, he was not completely in the loop about India's changing foreign and defense policies. Hence, there was a constant tension between the Commonwealth and Britain being a founding member of NATO and India's desire for non-alignment. His ultimately futile efforts in lobbying for a CDS in India and suggestions for more mature civil–military relations should thus be viewed sympathetically because after 1957 Mountbatten's influence on India's defense policies began to wane as the man described by Nehru as a "brilliant mind" took ownership of the MoD.[53]

A Dark Shadow: Krishna Menon in the MoD

After winning parliamentary elections in 1957, Nehru appointed his good friend Krishna Menon as the defense minister. When shortly thereafter General Thimayya, hailed by Mountbatten as "one of the finest Generals in any Army in the world,"[54] was appointed the chief of army staff, there were expectations that the previously moribund MoD would galvanize into action. Indicative of Nehru's faith in Thimayya, in appointing him the chief, the government

---

[51] D.O. no. 70012/10/COAS letter from General J. N. Chaudhuri to Vice Admiral R. V. Brockman dated February 10, 1964, in MB1/J599: Tour Far East 1964, India (1 of 2), Mountbatten Papers.

[52] "Note of conversation between Lord Mountbatten and Gen Chaudhuri in Rashtrapati Bhavan on 12 Jan 1966: Admiral Brockman was present," in MB1/K 146, Mountbatten Papers.

[53] For a description of the relationship between Nehru and Krishna Menon, see Steven Hoffman, *India and the China Crisis* (Berkeley: University of California Press, 1990), 44–46.

[54] Personal and confidential letter from Mountbatten to Nehru dated December 31, 1962, in MB1/J302, Mountbatten Papers. Earlier, in 1960, Mountbatten had recommended Thimayya for the CDS post and had then called him "the most outstanding General that I have ever come across in any country"; see personal and private letter to Nehru dated December 9, 1960, in MB1/J302, Mountbatten Papers.

overlooked "two very successful and well regarded" generals.[55] However, within a few years Krishna Menon was to play a central role in a near total breakdown in civil–military relations, culminating in the resignation of General Thimayya. Ironically, by a strange turn of events, he emerged even more politically powerful from that episode and could only be removed after the finality of the Indian Army's defeat in the 1962 China war.

The controversy over General Thimayya's resignation, which he later withdrew, has attracted much speculation both at that time and since. Even when the story leaked to the press, the prime minister was quick to downplay the incident and argued that it was due to "temperamental differences" over "trivial subjects." According to some, differences between the defence minister and the army chief were primarily over officer promotions as the former wanted to interfere in the process. Another account of the differences blames it on Menon not heeding Thimayya's warnings about the threat from China.[56] In an otherwise excellent piece of scholarship, Srinath Raghavan dismisses these explanations and instead argues that the differences were primarily over policy. He argues that Thimayya was keen to arrange for the prime minister to meet President Ayub Khan of Pakistan in connection with talks on a joint defense arrangement. As Krishna Menon did not like this idea, there was fallout between them, leading to the resignation of the general. "The Thimayya affair, then," Raghavan writes, "was not so much about civilian interference in professional matters as about military intrusion into the realm of policy."[57] However, a closer reading of the document cited by Raghavan does not support this thesis. Instead, what emerges is a complete loss of confidence and trust between the army chief on one side and the prime minister and defense minister on the other. While for all public appearances their differences were patched up, the working relations between them were poisoned, leading to an unprecedented series of allegations against Thimayya. In short, there was an almost total breakdown in civil–military relations.

Raghavan's argument that Thimayya's attempted intrusion into the realm of policy was the precipitating cause of *l'affaire* resignation has never been made before—by observers at that time or scholars since. This is because he makes this claim based on a secret document written by the British high commissioner.

[55] Steven I. Wilkinson, *Army and Nation: The Military and Indian Democracy since Independence* (Cambridge, MA: Harvard University Press, 2015), 110. Both generals were Sikh officers, and, according to Wilkinson, this could have been a potentially coup-proofing strategy.

[56] C. B. Khandhuri, *Thimayya: An Amazing Life* (New Delhi: Knowledge World Publishers, 2006), 251–52. The author claims that he was given privileged access to some of the papers kept in Army headquarters, which informed his research.

[57] Srinath Raghavan, *War and Peace in Modern India: A Strategic History of the Nehru Years* (New Delhi: Permanent Black, 2010), 269.

This document and the claims made therein are both problematic. To begin with, the report qualifies its findings with the following disclaimer: "the full story of his [Krishna Menon's] relations with General Thimayya is still not known, but a good deal can now be recounted and *conjectured*." Crucially, the report admits "what follows is based on evidence of debates in Parliament, information derived from army contacts by my Military Adviser and Mr. Krishna Menon's own account of the events which he recently gave to me."[58] Simply put, the first and perhaps only time that we hear of this account of the underlying cause of the resignation was a conjecture based on Krishna Menon's self-exculpatory account of events as recounted two years later. Hence, without fresh evidence, Raghavan's thesis should be discounted.

Instead, a closer reading of General Thimayya's resignation letter suggests something more than just temperamental differences between him and the defense minister:

> A few days ago I mentioned to you how impossible it was for me and the other two Chiefs of Staff to carry out our responsibilities under the present Defence Minister and that we sought your advice. Since then you have conveyed our feelings to the Minister of Defence and he *quite rightly* feels that my talking to you directly is an act of disloyalty to him. Under these circumstances you will understand how impossible it is for me to carry out my duties as Chief of the Army Staff under Mr Krishna Menon.[59]

Besides what was widely known at that time—that Krishna Menon and Thimayya could not stand each other—the letter suggests that Thimayya felt betrayed that Nehru conveyed sentiments expressed in a private conversation to Krishna Menon. Thimayya therefore does not begrudge Krishna Menon for "quite rightly" considering it as "an act of disloyalty." This suggests a loss of confidence between the prime minister and his army chief and a breakdown in their personal relations.[60] Matters did not improve when Nehru, while speaking in Parliament, forcefully defended the defense minister and, metaphorically,

---

[58] Secret note titled "Krishna Menon and the Generals," dated May 5, 1961, in DO 196/209, Kew Archives (TNA), page 2.

[59] Confidential letter from General Thimayya to Prime Minister Nehru, August 31, 1959, in correspondence with Nehru, emphasis added, Thimayya papers, NMML.

[60] There was a lot of speculation about the underlying causes of the resignation; for an account suggesting a loss of confidence between the prime minister and the army chief, see "Crucial Link in Thimayya's Resignation Theory," *Tribune*, September 8, 1959 in Sub File 16 (c), page 24, Thimayya Papers, NMML. This article appears to have been informed either by General Thimayya or by sources close to him.

threw Thimayya under the bus. Strongly countering opposition charges that substantial policy differences including the promotion of senior officers were the underlying cause of the resignation, Nehru instead argued that Thimayya had just discussed "trivial subjects" of no consequence. In an anguished type-written note, Thimayya responded to Nehru's dismissal of the "trivial subjects discussed" and mentioned three discussion points, "of the many."[61] However, in public, Thimayya held his peace and did not speak then or later about the underlying reasons for the resignation and its subsequent withdrawal.

This controversy was tumultuous for civil–military relations at the time; however, in the longer run it set the correct precedent. If Thimayya had resigned and had gone public with his differences with the defense minister, then in all likelihood the prime minister would have been unable to save Krishna Menon. This would most certainly have empowered the military, which could have wielded the resignation threat in any future policy disagreements with civilians. This could have created an unhealthy precedent and led to a more politically powerful military. In any event, Thimayya chose to suffer through personal humiliation; and, whether intended or not, his conduct was right for civil–military relations, the principle of civilian control, and India's democracy. Some argue, however, that Thimayya's "weakness" leading to a withdrawn resignation contributed to the debacle of 1962 as this was the last opportunity to stop Krishna Menon.[62] Indeed, after this episode, Krishna Menon's power in the MoD increased as Thimayya lost some of his sheen and influence.[63] Thimayya's clash with both Krishna Menon and Nehru, however, would not end with this episode and instead would culminate in a more serious, if less public, fashion.

On April 11, 1961, Krishna Menon's biggest opponent in parliament, J. B. Kriplani, popularly known as Acharya Kriplani, severely criticized the defense minister in what would be described as "perhaps the greatest speech that has been made on the floor of that house since independence."[64] The defense minister was criticized for politicizing the army's promotion policy, encouraging the formation of cliques in the army and thereby demoralizing it, and for pursuing

---

[61] See unsigned and undated typed note in Thimayya Papers, NMML. While there is no date on this note, presumably it written around the time of this controversy. The three points mentioned by him were the war psychosis against Pakistan, the apathetic attitude regarding Chinese moves, and the defense minister's opposition to a meeting between the prime minister and President Ayub Khan of Pakistan.

[62] Khanduri, *Thimayya*, 265.

[63] For a perspective on Thimayya's loss of prestige after the resignation controversy, see S. K. Sinha, *A Soldier Recalls* (New Delhi: Lancer International, 1992), 156.

[64] Quoted in Guha, *India after Gandhi*, 326. Acharya Kriplani was a fierce critic of Krishna Menon and in October of 1961 fought, and lost, a highly publicized Lok Sabha election that he contested against him.

ill-conceived defense policies that ignored the threat posed by China. In light of later events, Kriplani's charges were tragically prescient; however, it was half-informed and, at times, factually inaccurate. As a result, it was easily repudiated by the defense minister, who once again emerged politically stronger from this episode. However, within days an unprecedented letter was written alleging collusion between the chief of army staff and Acharya Kriplani. This episode reveals much about civil–military relations and the prevailing atmosphere at that time.

On April 23, 1961, the chief of army staff designate Lieutenant General P. N. Thapar wrote two personal and top secret letters, which were delivered by officer couriers.[65] They were addressed to General Thimayya, who was the army chief on "leave pending retirement," and to the soon-to-retire Eastern Army commander, Lieutenant General S. P. P. Thorat. Titled "allegations," the letters claimed that they were written on the directions of the prime minister and had his concurrence. The prime minister, the letters said, wanted "to request your comments on the following allegations."[66] The allegations against Thimayya were of a serious nature—he was accused of colluding with Acharaya Kriplani, making injudicious statements against the political leadership, not repaying financial loans, and meeting with arms dealers. One allegation dated back to 1954 when he was in Korea! Thimayya was told not to leave the country until the matter was cleared. The allegations against Thorat were less damaging but included making statements against the defense minister. Most certainly both letters were informed by inputs from the Intelligence Bureau. Thimayya and Thorat wrote back repudiating all the charges.[67] According to one account, Nehru sought the advice of other cabinet ministers and, in order to avoid a controversy, decided to drop the matter.[68]

These letters were unprecedented on several levels. First, it was against military ethos for a junior officer to write such letters.[69] It makes sense then that either General Thapar was told to write them or he did so readily—both explanations

---

[65] These letters are referred to in Khanduri, *Thimayya*, 313–14. According to the author, a letter was also sent to Lt. Gen. S. D. Verma.

[66] Personal and top secret letters DO no. PNT/1 from Lt. Gen. P. N. Thapar in correspondence with Thapar, Thimayya papers; and personal and top secret letters DO no. PNT/1 from Lt. Gen. Thapar dated April 23, 1961, in Subject File 6, Thorat papers (both letters dated April 23, 1961), NMML.

[67] General Thimayya's response is referred to in Khanduri, *Thimayya*, 313. For Thorat's reply, see personal and confidential letter no. 750113/AC dated April 24, 1961, in Subject File 6, Thorat papers, NMML.

[68] Khanduri, *Thimayya*, 314.

[69] Logically, the defense minister or even the prime minister should have written the letters instead of "directing" his new, incoming chief of army staff to write such difficult letters to his seniors, who were popular within the military.

being problematic. If he was told to write them and he readily accepted, then it indicates character traits that Thapar was later criticized for—that he failed to "stand up" to the civilians, was made the army chief because of his "perceived pliability,"[70] and that he easily went along with ill-conceived civilian directions. The British high commissioner was partial to this line of thinking, writing the following in an assessment during the war which ironically ended up praising Thimayya:

> an awful lot of chickens are coming home to roost—the wishful outlook of the Government, the failure of the services, particularly the Army, really to stand up to this policy and either make a row about it or do things quietly without telling the minister—a tactic which Thimayya used sometimes to employ.[71]

If, on the other hand, General Thapar wrote the letters readily, an unlikely prospect, then it indicates the divisions within senior ranks of the Indian Army. Lieutenant General B. M. Kaul, a politically savvy, immensely ambitious, and therefore controversial army officer, was central to this and exploited his proximity to both Nehru and Krishna Menon.[72] Brigadier D. K. Palit, who was then in army headquarters, while hinting at this episode, blamed it on Kaul ("earned him nothing but calumny for a bungled intrigue") and argued that he "did not know if Menon had a hand in this shabby attempt . . . but I doubt it."[73] It is entirely possible that this was an attempt by Kaul, in collusion with Thapar, to get back at his perceived enemies. However, that they could use the prime minister's name in making such serious allegations suggests that either they were confident in their ability to obtain political cover or, and this is more likely, they had Nehru's permission beforehand. In addition, as the letters appear to be informed by intelligence agencies, in all likelihood the contents of the letters were known to Krishna Menon, Nehru, and B. N. Mullick, the director of the Intelligence Bureau.

Regardless of the brains behind this episode, the letters shed light on the intrigue, suspicions, and divisions among senior officers under Krishna Menon.[74]

---

[70] Wilkinson, *Army and the Nation*, 22.

[71] See confidential note from P. H. Gore-Booth to Sir Saville Garner, CRO, dated October 26, 1962, 2–3 in PREM/11, 3838, TNA, Kew Archives.

[72] For a description of the influence wielded by Kaul during this time, see Sinha, *A Soldier Recalls*, 157–64; for more on the divided officer cadre, see K. V. Krishna Rao, *In the Service of the Nation: Reminiscences* (New Delhi: Penguin India Books, 2001), 36.

[73] D. K. Palit, *War in the High Himalayas: The Indian Army in Crisis, 1962* (New Delhi: Lancer International 1991), 74.

[74] These divisions continued even after the departure of Thimayya and Thorat as Kaul had problems with Manekshaw and many other officers; see Palit, *War in the High Himalayas*, 70–78.

Indicative of his lack of judgment, Krishna Menon was distrustful of the only officer who emerged relatively unscathed from the 1962 debacle—Lieutenant General Daulet Singh, the Western Army commander. While reposing faith in other officers, Menon expressed doubts about the capability of Daulet Singh, calling him a "paper tiger."[75] Shortly thereafter Krishna Menon would be proved disastrously wrong—on all his judgments regarding individual competency, military strategy, and assumptions regarding the international system.

After the appointment of General Thapar as chief of army staff in May 1961, Krishna Menon's hold on the MoD and on the army increased. Capturing the prevailing mood in Delhi months before the 1962 war, the British high commissioner would write evocatively,

> The "dark shadow" is a real thing. Increasingly people beyond the immediate area of the Ministry of Defence do things, or refrain from doing them, lest what they have done or not done should get back to Krishna Menon, and his displeasure be visited on them. Therefore to a degree which seemed most unlikely a year ago, his influence now pervades public life, his slant on policy penetrates public speech, and opposite views tend to be muted because of either a general or specific fear.[76]

Nehru and His Generals

Nehru's relationship with the military is still a matter of debate. To many in the military he is singularly responsible for downplaying their contribution to nation-building and thereby denying them a role in polity and the eventual humiliating defeat in 1962. Nehru is therefore frequently vilified by members of India's strategic community.[77] More nuanced scholarship on the 1962 war has pushed back against this notion and focused on other factors, including

Also see K. C. Praval, *Indian Army after Independence* (New Delhi: Lancer International, 1990), 206–9; and S. D. Verma, *To Serve with Honor: My Memoirs* (Pune: New Thacker's Fine Art Press, 1988), 108–27.

[75] Secret note titled "Krishna Menon and the Generals," dated May 5, 1961, in DO 196/209, Kew Archives (TNA), 5. Ironically, the officers that Menon reposed faith in—Thapar, L. P. Sen, and Kaul—have been largely blamed for the debacle in 1962.

[76] Secret note on "Indian Political Situation" written by Ambassador P. M. Gore-Booth dated February 3, 1962, in PREM 11/4865, Kew Archives.

[77] For some typical perspectives, see Eric Vas, "Truly, an Extraordinary Fellow," *Rediff.com*, May 18, 2014 http://www.rediff.com/news/special/special-truly-an-extraordinary-fellow/20140518. htm; R. V. Parasnis, "You Can Scrap the Army," *Rediff.com*, December 5, 2002, http://www.rediff. com/news/2002/dec/18chin.htm

shortcomings within the military.[78] However, even the most ardent of Nehru's supporters would admit that he had problems engaging and getting along with his military commanders.

Nehru appointed Cariappa as the first Indian chief of army staff, but he was not his first choice. According to some accounts, he had approached Nathu Singh and then Rajendra Sinhji, both of whom demurred because they were junior to Cariappa.[79] Nehru's subsequent relations with Cariappa and his successor, Rajendra Sinhji, were known to range from tense and conflict-laden to indifferent and characterized by mutual incomprehension.[80] The next chief, Shrinagesh, had better relations with both political leaders and civilian bureaucrats. Perhaps due to this, he was the first chief to be appointed as a governor, first of Assam and then later of Andhra Pradesh. This set in an unwritten belief—a sentiment that if the chiefs conducted themselves "appropriately" vis-à-vis civilian authorities, then they stood a chance of being rewarded after retirement. In later years this became an important tool, wielded by civilians to incentivize and control the behavior of senior military officers.

With the next chief, Thimayya, Nehru initially had good relations before they fell out over the role of Krishna Menon and B. M. Kaul. Nehru's unequivocal support for both Krishna Menon and Kaul, referred to as a "political general"[81] by his critics, further undermined Thimayya. Kaul was later appointed quartermaster general and posted in Delhi—Thimayya was reluctant to post him but was prevailed upon by Krishna Menon.[82] After Thimayya's retirement, Kaul was appointed chief of general staff and became the most prominent military adviser—by virtue of his proximity to Nehru and Krishna Menon. Kaul's career, however, came to an end when he failed in a spectacular fashion as a corps commander

---

[78] Raghavan, *War and Peace in Modern India*, 270–308; and Praveen Swami, "Lessons from the Gate of Hell," *The Hindu*, March 21, 2014. For a good overview of the "blame" literature surrounding the 1962 war, see Jabin T. Jacob, "Remembering 1962 in India, 50 Years on," in *The Sino-Indian War of 1962: New Perspectives*, ed. Amit R. Das Gupta and Lorenz M. Luthi (London: Routledge, 2017), 238–40.

[79] V. K. Singh, *Leadership in the Indian Army: Biographies of Twelve Soldiers* (New Delhi: Sage Publications, 2005), 38 and 289; and C. B. Khanduri, *Field Marshal KM Cariappa: His Life and Times* (New Delhi: Lancer Publishers, 1995), 210–13.

[80] Khanduri, *Field Marshal KM Cariappa*, 207–81. There are few accounts of Nehru's relations with General Rajendra Sinhji, but it appears as if they kept to themselves.

[81] For criticism of Kaul's relationship with politicians, see "Interview with Lt. Gen S. P. P. Thorat, undated" and "Interview with Lt. Gen. L. P. Sen," Stephen Cohen Papers. Kaul, on the other hand, was to boast that his proximity to politicians represented "a unique record"; see "Interview with Lt. Gen. BM Kaul, December 23, 1964," Stephen Cohen Papers, 2.

[82] The partnership between Nehru, Menon, and Kaul was strongly criticized after the war; see Palit, *War in the High Himalayas*, 70–78; and Lorne Kavic, *India's Quest for Security, 1947–1965* (Berkeley: University of California Press, 1967), 163–66.

during the 1962 war. In a secret assessment written after a visit to the forward area immediately after the war, General Richard Hull, the British chief of general staff, put the blame entirely on Kaul and argued, "at the crucial time I consider that the Corps Commander failed to exercise proper command."[83]

Nehru also had an additional consideration, that of dealing with officers who retired at a comparatively young age—Nathu Singh at 51, Cariappa at 53, Thorat and Thimayya at 55, and Rajendra Sinhji at 56. In part, this was the result of a policy, introduced shortly after independence, of fixed tenures (initially four years but later reduced to three years) for chiefs of army staff and army commanders. Nehru insisted upon this policy as he was apprehensive in case senior army officers "got too secure and developed political ambitions."[84] "The decision was unfortunate," according to one analyst, "as it removed the top leadership of the Indian Army at an age when they had several years of useful life still left, and the Nation could have benefitted from their experience. The rule did not apply to the civil bureaucracy, or to the Navy or the Air Force."[85] Nehru therefore could have, but largely chose not to, utilize their experience in some sort of an administrative position. But with the exception of Shrinagesh (who was appointed governor of Assam from 1959 to 1962), he instead sent some of them on assignments outside the country. It appears therefore that Nehru was careful to ensure that civilian power was unrivaled and discouraged a potentially militaristic "cult of personality." His critics could claim though that Nehru thought like a crafty politician—ensuring that a popular military personality did not have a public role. Despite his efforts, some of them, like Cariappa and Nathu Singh, dabbled in politics and participated in elections—which they both lost.[86] The point remains though that, of all his officials, Nehru had the hardest time understanding and earning the trust and confidence of his generals.

However, the wheel would turn full circle after the 1962 debacle as Nehru re-engaged with the generals that he had metaphorically exiled. After the war, in order to have a more professional approach to formulating defense policies, the government created the Military Affairs Council.[87] This council would meet frequently and, among others, consisted of Thimayya, Thorat, and Rajendra Sinhji. The team that Nehru had previously chosen and certainly favored—Krishna Menon, Thapar, and Kaul—was no longer around. Nehru, an intelligent and

[83] Secret UK eyes only letter no. CIGS/PF/515 dated December 3, 1962, 2 in PREM 11/3876, Kew Archives, London.

[84] Wilkinson, *Army and the Nation*, 105.

[85] Singh, *Leadership in the Indian Army*, 143.

[86] For a description of the post-retirement activities of Nathu Singh, see Singh, *Leadership in the Indian Army*, 81–82; and on Cariappa, see Khanduri, *Field Marshal KM Cariappa*, 322–38.

[87] For more about this committee, see Subject File 21 (c), Thimya Papers, NMML.

thoughtful man, could not have been unaware of the irony of listening to his former generals, some that he had treated badly, when he all but ignored and slighted them earlier.

The definitive account of Nehru's relations with his generals remains to be written as there are still competing interpretations of this period. However, almost all agree that leading up to the 1962 war civil–military relations were possibly at their worst.[88] There was an absence of a free and frank dialogue and a *"structured gap in communication* between the government and the military."[89] Instead, favoritism, palace intrigues, and conspiracies were rife, with the "after Nehru, who?" query dominating conversations. Krishna Menon, disparagingly referred to as an "evil genius,"[90] played a central role in these intrigues; and he seemed to have an unnatural hold on Nehru. Again, according to the British high commissioner,

> Mr. Nehru himself could stop all this with a word or gesture. He knows, it appears, as much as anyone, about Krishna Menon's congenital dishonesty and power-hunger. He even has some realisation of the irrational side of Krishna Menon's behavior. . . . But he will not stop it. Thus in an involved way he is becoming an accomplice to a conspiracy against himself, against his own position and reputation, and against so much that he has done in the past.[91]

Nehru as a Supreme Commander

Nehru clearly failed as a wartime commander, and the 1962 war has forever tarnished his legacy. Four qualities in particular served him badly in his role as a supreme commander—his style of functioning, lack of attention to detail, distraction with global events, and choice of advisers.

As a political leader Nehru was open to a democratic style of functioning, making it a point to communicate even with his rivals. However, in his administrative duties Nehru was not particularly fond of the organized, committee style

---

[88] Wilkinson, *Army and the Nation*, 28.

[89] Palit, *War in the High Himalayas*, 2, emphasis added; for more on problematic civil–military relations during this period, see Yaacov Vertzberger, "Bureaucratic-Organizational Politics and Information Processing in a Developing State," *International Studies Quarterly* 28, no. 1 (1984): 77–81.

[90] Sunil Khilnani, "Nehru's Evil Genius," *Outlook India*, March 19, 2007. For a good account of the influences on Krishna Menon and his intellectual legacy, see Ian Hall, "'Mephistopheles in a Saville Row Suit': V. K. Krishna Menon and the West," in *Radicals and Reactionaries in Twentieth Century International Thought*, ed. Ian Hall (New York: Palgrave Macmillan, 2015), 191–216.

[91] Secret note on "Indian Political Situation" written by Ambassador P. M. Gore-Booth dated February 3, 1962, in PREM 11/4865, Kew Archives.

of functioning. Instead, he favored quick decisions often made in informal, small group settings without adequate staff work. As a result, important issues were considered ad hoc; and many committees, including the Defence Committee of the Cabinet, became moribund or served a perfunctory function and were generally ineffective.[92] This prevented contrarian perspectives from being aired and encouraged a lazy "groupthink" that took its cues from the prime minister.[93] One of the most consequential assumptions that emerged from this groupthink was the idea that China would not attack India. In a sense, Nehru undid the basis and logic of the committee system that Mountbatten and Ismay had so carefully established.

A related quality of Nehru that ill-served him was a lack of attention to detail— an important trait in successful wartime commanders. Nehru assumed that if orders were passed, they would be quickly and efficiently implemented, which was not always the case. For instance, one of the major causes of the Indian Army's defeat in both the northern and eastern sectors was the lack of road communication networks that would have enabled rapid transport of troops and logistical supplies. According to some reports, the Himmatsinghji Committee in 1952, created to recommend measures to strengthen defenses along the China border, had recommended that such roads be rapidly constructed. Funds were allocated from time to time, but progress on this was tardy as different bureaucracies did not understand the urgency. To his credit, Krishna Menon recognized this as a priority and was instrumental in establishing the Border Roads Organization in 1959. Despite this effort, road-building did not improve substantially, and inadequate logistical infrastructure contributed to the defeat. Similarly, Nehru did not pay attention to many other factors including operational deployment and planning, logistics, operational readiness, and coordination and instead left all of these matters to the respective bureaucracies to sort out. Mountbatten picked up on this quality of Nehru, and after what was probably his last meeting, advised him, perhaps unwisely in light of Nehru's aversion to the man, to emulate Churchill: "During the war Winston used to write at the end of a decision 'report position in () days' (It was usually 14). By this means he was able to see not only that decisions were being faithfully carried out but that they were being carried out expeditiously."[94]

Instead, Nehru displayed an organizational naiveté wherein he assumed that once orders were passed they would be readily and quickly implemented.

[92] Rao, Defence Without Drift, 309.

[93] For a good analysis of the decision-making system during this time, see Hoffman, India and the China Crisis, 237–70; also see Vertzberger, "Bureaucratic-Organizational Politics," 84–90.

[94] Letter from Mountbatten to Nehru January 30, 1964, MB1/J599: Tour Far East 1964, India (1 of 2), Mountbatten Papers.

A combination of these two qualities—eschewing a formal, committee-based work culture and lack of attention to detail—contributed in large part to his failure as a supreme commander. One diplomatic assessment on the eve of the 1962 war criticizes Nehru for his lack of urgency and overall administrative skills while describing the "unGovernment" and "strange absence of concentrated authority" in New Delhi.[95] P. M. S. Blackett, who observed Nehru closely, mirrored this assessment when he said, "he was not a good administrator. Rather he was a superb leader, an outstanding leader. But he did not know how to get things done very well."[96]

In the years leading up to the 1962 war, Nehru was like a colossus on the global stage—consulted by both the super blocs and the wider international community on a variety of issues. India's position—on issues arising from decolonization, deliberations within the United Nations, and regional issues in Indo-China, Lesotho, Congo, Eastern Europe, the Korean Peninsula, and elsewhere—was widely sought by diplomats on all sides. Nehru, along with Krishna Menon, was dealing with all of these issues and thinking about the wider problems of the atomic age and the continued threat of a global war. These engagements frequently took them outside the country—and Nehru's time and attention were at a premium. With the benefit of hindsight, Nehru spent too much time and energy on global affairs and neglected matters closer to home. By contrast, China's premier, Chairman Mao, hardly ever stepped out of the country and delegated this function to others, like Zhou Enlai. Tellingly, after this war, China's diplomatic prestige increased, whereas Nehru, and India's global role, diminished significantly.

Finally, and perhaps most consequentially, Nehru suffered from a fatal flaw in any leader—he chose his advisers badly. Krishna Menon, Thapar, and Kaul were clearly the most important advisers who let him down, but the director of the Intelligence Bureau, B. N. Mullick, also came in for some criticism. From a civil–military perspective, Nehru wanted to "rein in the military intelligence services"[97]—perhaps to consolidate civilian control. This had an unintended consequence as the military was unprepared, lacked relevant intelligence inputs, and was completely dependent upon Mullick's assessments. Seemingly in agreement with this line of thinking, according to Vice Admiral Ronald Brockman—who accompanied Mountbatten on his visit to India after

---

[95] Confidential note from P. H. Gore-Booth to Sir Saville Garner, CRO, dated October 26, 1962, 1–2 in PREM/11, 3838, TNA, Kew Archives.

[96] Oral History Transcripts, PMS Blackett, no. 284, NMML, 10; for more on Blackett's criticism about Nehru, see Robert S. Anderson, "Patrick Blackett in India: Military Consultant and Scientific Intervenor, 1947–72, Part I," *Notes and Records of the Royal Society* 53, no. 2 (1999): 256–57.

[97] Wilkinson, *Army and the Nation*, 106.

the war—Mullick, backed by civilian ministers, had "achieved too much power vis-à-vis the Services."[98]

One must, however, resist the temptation to put the entire blame on Nehru, more so because of a number of extenuating circumstances. First, Nehru was handling too many portfolios and was intimately involved with a vast range of issues— economic planning, developmental aid, atomic energy, industrial research, and foreign and defense policies, to name a few. The demands on his time had led to a state, according to one assessment, of "permanent fatigue."[99] As a result, his attention to detail and micromanagement of issues were made more difficult. Second, by the time of the China crisis Nehru was almost 73 years old and suffering from uncertain health. Age and a punishing schedule had taken their toll, creating a complete contrast from Nehru's wartime command during the 1948 Kashmir war. Many who dealt with Nehru before the war noticed his distracted state and surmised that others were running India.[100] These reports reached Mountbatten, who feared that Nehru was "ill and losing his grip at a time when India needs his help and guidance more than ever."[101] Finally, the debacle of 1962 was a result of strategic, diplomatic, intelligence, military, operational, and tactical failures at, more or less, all levels. Nehru could not have foreseen that the Indian Army would collapse as disastrously as it did in the eastern theater or that his chosen team would let him down so much.

Shaping the Narrative: Nehru's Legacy on Civil–Military Relations

In a forthright account of the operational, tactical, and leadership failures in the 1962 war, Shiv Kunal Verma captures the prevailing narrative within India's strategic community, which believes that Nehru's "biggest failing" was the "virtual destruction of his own military thanks to his deep rooted insecurities . . . Nehru played an active part in weakening the confidence and capability of his military."[102] Historians, however, generally agree that he deserves a large part of the credit for

---

[98] Letter from Sir Ronald Brackman to Roy Bucher dated March 6, 1969, in 7901/87-9, Bucher papers, National Army Museum, London.

[99] Secret note on "Indian Political Situation" written by Ambassador P. M. Gore-Booth dated February 3, 1962, in PREM 11/4865, Kew Archives.

[100] For a description of Anglo-American concerns over Nehru's health during this period, see P. M. McGarr, "After Nehru, What? Britain, the United States and the Other Transfer of Power in India," *International History Review* 33, no. 1 (2011): 116–20.

[101] Letter from Mountbatten to Vijayalakshmi Pandit dated June 20, 1962, in MB1/J325, Mountbatten Papers.

[102] Shiv Kunal Verma, *1962: The War that Wasn't* (New Delhi: Aleph Books, 2016), 394.

laying the "foundations of firm civilian control of the military."[103] Nehru's major accomplishment, civilian control, thus contrasted with his biggest failure, defeat in war. Did one come at the cost of the other? Did Nehru's obsession with civilian control blind him to a fault and contribute to the defeat in 1962?

Nehru was clearly concerned about the principle of civilian control and paid extra attention to upholding it, even at the cost of offending senior military commanders. Cognizant of the popularity of the military, he consciously took steps to bring it under democratic control. His emphasis on upholding civilian supremacy was crucial to the emergence of the MoD and its gradual role in exercising civilian control. Later, however, Nehru's obsession with upholding civilian control, however conceived, prejudiced his interactions with the military. The reluctance to appoint a CDS and a general neglect of the army suggest that Nehru laid more priority on civilian control than on military effectiveness. Some of these strategies, described elsewhere as "coup-proofing" mechanisms, created tensions with the military.[104] Later, his support of Krishna Menon and B. M. Kaul resulted in a falling out with sections of the military. Did Nehru's liberal ideas blind him to the use of force in interstate relations? Did he suffer from an intellectual dissonance in his dealings with the military? These are topics worthy of a separate book and require further research, but maybe, just maybe, Nehru did not get the military mind.[105]

Nehru's extended premiership was crucial to establishing the norm of civilian control in India. But the humiliating defeat in 1962 shaped civil–military relations to a considerable degree, even to this day. There were two major narratives that emerged from this war. First, there was a strong belief that civilian meddling in operational details led to the defeat. Historians may challenge such a simplistic account, but within the military there is a strong notion that the Nehru–Krishna Menon combination was largely responsible.[106] As a result, military officials have strongly resisted any perceived civilian interference in operational matters, and "a convention was established whereby the civilian leadership restricted itself to giving overall directives, leaving operational matters to the military."[107] As

[103] Sushant Singh, "The Man Who Saw the Future," *Indian Express*, November 13, 2016; also see Srinath Raghavan, "Soldiers, Statesmen and India's Security Policy," *India Review* 11, no. 2 (2012): 120.

[104] Wilkinson, *Army and the Nation*, 101–107.

[105] According to some accounts, Nehru was unhappy with the annexation of Tawang in 1951 and the use of force against Goa in 1961. For the classic work on liberal ideals and the use of force, see Michael Howard, *War and the Liberal Conscience* (New Brunswick, NJ: Rutgers University Press, 1989).

[106] For a well-considered account of events leading to this war, see Raghavan, *War and Peace in Modern India*, 270–308.

[107] Srinath Raghavan, "Civil–Military Relations in India: The China Crisis and After," *Journal of Strategic Studies* 32, no. 1 (2009): 167.

described in Chapter 1, such an arrangement resembled Huntington's "objective control" model, which envisaged strict separation between the civilian and military domains under the (flawed) assumption that politicians have only to set the broad directives and leave their implementation entirely to the soldiers.

Another narrative that emerged from this war focused on the role of B. M. Kaul, described as a "political general" who not only divided the military but also failed at the operational level. The military perceived civilian interference in favoring Kaul as an egregious instance of politicization that contributed to defeat in battle. As a result, as discussed in greater detail in Chapter 6, hereinafter senior officer promotions would favor seniority over merit and would resist civilian interference and favoritism. In turn, officers were discouraged from interacting with politicians under an unwritten norm, which argued that as professional soldiers were apolitical, they had to maintain a distance. Instead, civilian bureaucrats emerged as a preferred intermediary between them. However, within a few years, the military would resent this partnership and complain that instead of political control they were under bureaucratic control.

The Shastri Era, 1964–1966: Hold Steady and Reassure Policy

The death of Nehru was one of the most momentous events in the life of the young republic. For years, there were speculations, mainly from the Western press, about the fate of India's democracy after Nehru—and many predicted that the military would take over. Belying these predictions, shortly after Nehru's death, the Congress Party elected Lal Bahadur Shastri, who was sworn in as the next prime minister. However, after around five months, in an unusual move, Lieutenant General S. H. F. J. (Sam) Manekshaw moved from the command of the Western Army to that of the Eastern Army in Calcutta. Therein lay a tale.

Upon the death of Nehru, some units from the Western Army Command moved to Delhi amid confusion over orders and intent.[108] Some asserted, without much evidence, that this was an unauthorized move which momentarily threatened civilian control. Others argued that this was on the orders of General J. N. Chaudhuri, the chief of army staff, to control the massive crowds expected at Nehru's funeral. Still another account has it that President Sarvepalli Radhakrishnan as the supreme commander had given these orders to the army

[108] This account relies on Shubhi Sood, *Leadership: Field Marshal Sam Manekshaw* (Noida, India: SDS Publishers, 2006), 41–43; Singh, *In the Line of Duty*, 323; and R. D. Pradhan, *Debacle to Revival: Y. B. Chavan as Defense Minister, 1962–65* (New Delhi: Orient Longman, 1998), 204–6.

chief directly. As a fallout from this episode, Manekshaw, who was commanding the Western Army, which is located close to Delhi, was shifted farther away to Calcutta. While seemingly a minor misunderstanding, this episode revealed civilian apprehensions over the possibilities of a coup. Apart from this hushed-up non-incident, still shrouded in mystery, Prime Minister Shastri had good relations with the military. A large part of the credit for this goes to Defence Minister Y. B. Chavan, who held the post from 1962 to 1966. Their ability to get along with the military served them well when war was forced upon them by India's traditional foe, Pakistan.

1965: The Reluctant Warriors

In August 1965, around 9,000 Pakistani army troops infiltrated deep into Indian Kashmir in an attempt to foment a mass uprising. Their plans began to fall apart when the Kashmiris rejected their calls to revolt and the Indian Army began rounding up the infiltrators, putting military pressure on their staging bases across the Line of Control. The Pakistani response was the audaciously named "Operation Grand Slam," which envisaged a quick armored thrust to cut off Indian troops operating in Kashmir. For a while, this held the promise of a spectacular victory; however, Pakistani indecision and, later, an Indian counterattack in the Lahore sector ended that dream. The 1965 war ultimately proved to be disastrous for Pakistan and allowed the Indian military to retain some of its self-confidence, which was badly shaken after the China war.

From the perspective of civil–military relations, the 1965 war was praised within the Indian military as a model. According to Lieutenant General S. L. Menezes, "the relationship between the Prime Minister and the Army Chief was sound right through 1965. . . . Any decisions taken by the political leadership were left to the military leadership to carry out unfettered."[109] A closer reading of the war, however, leads to another conclusion—this was a flawed model of civil–military relations as there were major problems with the operational conduct and in the higher direction of war. However, such an admission would have been inconvenient, so all stakeholders quickly claimed victory. A misreading of this war therefore helped perpetuate the idea that civilians should not interfere in the military's domain.

The conduct of the 1965 war was problematic across three areas: in the operational domain, in matters pertaining to jointness, and in the absence of strategy. In the operational domain, the performance of the chief of army staff, General

---

[109] S. L. Menezes, *Fidelity and Honour: The Indian Army from the Seventeenth to the Twenty-First Century* (New Delhi: Viking Publishers, 1993), 494.

Chaudhuri, was much criticized. Faced with aggressive Pakistani attacks, he allegedly gave an order for large-scale withdrawal across the Beas River. That such an order could be given without referring to political leaders indicates that the military had considerable operational autonomy. Fortunately, his field commander did not act upon this order.[110] In another instance, toward the end of the war, General Chaudhuri was asked by the prime minister whether prolonging the war would serve India's interests. Without checking with his staff, he incorrectly argued that ammunition stocks were running low and tank losses were high. Based on this advice, India accepted the ceasefire. Some call this episode the "crowning blunder of the war."[111]

Another problem was the absence of jointness, especially the lack of army–air force cooperation.[112] As discussed in greater detail in Chapter 4, the services enjoyed considerable autonomy and were content to plan and execute single-service operations. There were a number of blue-on-blue attacks, or "friendly fire" incidents, and a lack of interoperability. Civilians stayed away from arbitrating interservice disputes and did not force the services to work together.

The final, and perhaps most significant, problem was the absence of strategy. Simply put, civilians and the military never really came together to have a substantial discussion around war aims, goals, and overall strategy. Arzan Tarapore, who has conducted the single best operational study of the 1965, 1971, and Indian Peace Keeping Forces (IPKF) operations, writes that "the civil leadership's primary failing . . . was their lack of articulating how military action would further the nation's political goals."[113] The absence of a clear-cut political and military strategy has given rise to a contested historiography.

According to some, the military was reluctant to engage in a full-scale war. Analysts point to the "inaction" and the inherent reluctance on the part of the air force and the navy.[114] The charge of being reluctant warriors was also leveled against the army. According to then defense secretary P. V. R. Rao, "the Government pressed the Army to attack. The Chief of the Army Staff wanted all the three services to participate. In my opinion, he was never serious about this but was trying this gambit to support his inaction."[115] For some, politicians

---

[110] Singh, In the Line of Duty, 351–52; also see R. D. Pradhan, 1965 War: The Inside Story (New Delhi: Atlantic Publishers, 2007), 62–63. For a critical appraisal of General Chaudhuri, see Palit, War in the High Himalayas, 424–28.

[111] Pradhan, 1965 War, 112.

[112] Srinath Raghavan, "Civil–Military Relations in India," 170.

[113] Arzan Tarapore, "Strategies of Stalemate: Explaining Indian Military Effectiveness, 1965–90" (PhD diss., Kings College, London, 2017), 59. I thank the author for sharing this with me.

[114] S. Hiranandani, Transition to Triumph: History of the Indian Navy:1965–1975 (New Delhi: Lancer Publishers, 2000), 51–55; and S. Krishnaswamy, "Out of the Blue," Indian Express, August 3, 2006. This aspect is discussed in greater detail in Chapter 4.

[115] Hiranandani, Transition to Triumph, 53.

should have more actively intervened and probed the military on its plans and assumptions—and this would have obtained a better outcome for India. "The politicians' refusal to delve deeply into military matters or to ask searching questions," Srinath Raghavan writes, "resulted in the war ending in stalemate."[116]

The criticism of the military, however, overlooks one of the biggest contradictions of this war—politicians did not want a full-scale war.[117] Therefore, the "stalemate" which India obtained was perhaps precisely the desired political outcome. This explains their reluctance to enlarge the theater of operations into East Pakistan or authorize the navy to undertake offensive operations. The three service chiefs, therefore, could have been taking their cues from their political masters and were understandably diffident about undertaking a more expansive and prolonged war.

Resolving these differing interpretations of political directives and military goals will require greater access to the archives; however, Raghavan's larger point is correct—civilians did not probe military operations, and strategy fell through the cracks. According to India's official history of this war, "neither strategic planning nor strategic struggle was made, and no strategic decision was reached. . . . The Field Commanders were not very clear about their goals . . . although at the later stage of the war General Chaudhuri spelt out that it was a war of attrition."[118] If it really was a war of attrition, then General Chaudhuri should have more closely tracked the state of logistics. That he did not do so and thereby misled the prime minister suggests that there was no overall strategy and that General Chaudhuri's claim of an "attrition strategy" was just an afterthought.[119] In short, there was little substantive discussion between civilians and the military.

The politicians most closely associated with the higher direction of the 1965 war were Prime Minister Shastri and Defence Minister Chavan. Both were aware of the narratives emerging from the 1962 war and were careful not to give an appearance of micromanaging or meddling in the affairs of the military. As a result, the Emergency Committee of the Cabinet—the highest decision-making body—"never discussed operational matters but only political issues."[120] At the same time, it would be wrong to say that the politicians were completely uninvolved in operational matters as they were regularly briefed—even if with the

---

[116] Raghavan, "Civil–Military Relations in India," 172.

[117] Hiranandani, *Transition to Triumph*, 40.

[118] B. C. Chakravorty, *History of the Indo–Pakistan War, 1965* (New Delhi: Ministry of Defence 1992) 334.

[119] Nitin A. Gokhale, *1965 Turning the Tide: How India Won the War* (New Delhi: Bloomsbury, 2015), 210.

[120] P. V. R. Rao, *India's Defense Policy and Organizations since Independence* (New Delhi: United Services Institute, 1977), 15, 19, 21; also see Pradhan, *1965 War*, 120.

sketchiest of details.[121] It was a strange form of civilian control then as it appears that the politicians merely approved plans made by the chiefs and provided political sanction for their decisions.

Civilian bureaucrats had a limited role to play in this war. Like politicians, they were careful not to meddle in operational matters and confined their role to intergovernmental issues and matters concerning civilian population or diplomacy. However, they also had a ringside view and carefully observed mistakes that were committed in this campaign. Reflecting an organizational learning, during the next war, in 1971, civilian bureaucrats acted upon many of these mistakes.

Separate Domains: Shastri, Wartime Command, and Civil–Military Relations

The war in 1965 was forced upon India and was waged under the shadow of the 1962 debacle—which weighed heavily on all concerned. The war proved to be a disaster for Pakistan in the long run and provided a much-needed boost to the Indian military.[122] India's political leaders were reluctant to wage an all-out war but were decisive when required. Once again, and not for the last time, their resolve surprised Pakistani calculations. A study of this war highlights two major issues pertaining to civil–military relations.

First, politicians did not have the expertise to sift good military advice from bad, and they were getting both. For instance, General Chaudhuri and Lieutenant General Harbaksh Singh had differences over operations, including withdrawing to the Beas; but the political class did not arbitrate their differences. In another instance, General Chaudhuri's misrepresentation with regard to war stocks led to a hasty—and, some argue, ill-advised—acceptance of a ceasefire.

Second, politicians ceded operational space to the military, which thereby had almost complete autonomy in planning and executing their operations. A misreading of this war and the general euphoria after it—when conveniently everyone claimed "victory"—cemented the narrative of separate civil and military domains. Therefore, the war helped perpetuate the belief that politicians are expected to set the broad directions and the military retains full operational freedom.

After the 1965 war, Defence Secretary P. V. R. Rao criticized this pattern of civil–military relations. He

---

[121] A close reading of Defence Minister Chavan's wartime diary indicates he was only cursorily briefed on operations; see Tarapore, "Strategies of Stalemate," 59–60.

[122] Farooq Bajwa, *From Kutch to Tashkent: The Indo–Pakistan War of 1965* (London: Hurst and Company, 2013), 367–91.

vigorously attacked the notions that civilian and military can or should be separated and that there is a sphere of activity in which civilians may not trespass. Not true, he argues, for two important reasons: the civilian minister may have to intervene in operational matters to 'ensure that there is effective coordination,' and civilians cannot legally or politically delegate responsibility—even for operations—to the military.[123]

Rao's logic was impeccable but inconvenient, and unfortunately, the resounding victory in 1971 drowned out his argument.

The Indira Gandhi Era, 1967–1977 and 1980–1984: The Best and Worst of Times

After Prime Minister Shastri suddenly passed away during the Tashkent peace talks in January 1966, the Congress "Syndicate"—a term used to describe its power brokers—settled upon Indira Gandhi as the ideal replacement. They expected her to be a diffident and pliable leader—a *goongi gudiya* ("dumb doll"). And, at first, she played the role. Even before she was sworn into office, there were tensions with the acting prime minister, Gulzari Lal Nanda, who allegedly called for detachments from the paramilitary Border Security Force to be sent to New Delhi. Indira Gandhi feared that this was an "attempted coup" engineered by Nanda. However, Nanda would later justify it as his pre-emptive move to prevent a military coup.[124] This episode was indicative of the constant expectation and speculation on behalf of both Western and Indian analysts after the 1962 war until the late 1970s of the "inevitable" military coup in India. Fortunately for India's democracy, the military stuck to its apolitical stance and refused to be drawn into partisan political battles.

From the perspective of civil–military relations, Indira Gandhi's weak political standing gave rise, once again, to fears about a military takeover. In March 1966, a few months after she assumed office, in a remarkable conversation, Defence Minister Chavan bluntly discussed the possibility of a military coup with his chief of army staff, General Chaudhuri. The general later recounted this discussion to the British high commissioner. According to the note prepared by the British diplomat, General Chaudhuri had apparently reassured Chavan that a coup was inconceivable. This conversation, both with Chavan and with the

---

[123] Cited in Stephen Cohen, "India's China War and After: A Review Article," *Journal of Asian Studies* 30, no. 4 (1971): 856. For Rao's view on this subject, see his *Defence Without Drift*, 327–28.

[124] Pupul Jayakar, *Indira Gandhi: An Intimate Biography* (Pantheon Books: New York, 1988), 128.

British high commissioner, was remarkable—first for its candor and second for its impropriety by repeating a private conversation with the defense minister to a foreign diplomat. The general further confided to the diplomat that,

> COAS [chief of army staff] had considered the possibility that, in situations of political and administrative chaos, the President of India might, independently of the Union government or even against its wishes, order the army to take over from the civil authority. . . . He believed that presidential authority would be adequate cover and that the operation could probably be carried out successfully.[125]

General Chaudhuri therefore believed that a coup was a possibility if ordered by the supreme commander of the armed forces, viz. the president of India. This indicated the tense relations between President Radhakrishnan and successive prime ministers including Nehru, Shastri, and Indira Gandhi.[126] The army was caught in the middle of these political intrigues. Indira Gandhi then, like her father, also suffered from a fear, whether justifiable or not, of a military coup. However, this fear dissipated over time as she gradually gained confidence and learned how to engage with the military. The contrast would be complete when, much later, she manipulated rules to favor selected military officers.

One of the first challenges that Indira Gandhi faced when she became the prime minister was assembling a team that she could trust in her battle for control against the Congress syndicate. After some setbacks, including criticism for rupee devaluation and soaring prices, she picked P. N. Haksar, a protégé of Krishna Menon, to serve as the secretary to the prime minister in early 1967.[127] Haksar went on to play an important role in her administration and shaped many of her policies.[128] One of his early ideas was that of a "committed bureaucracy," an expectation that bureaucrats should be loyal to the political party, its ideology, and the elected leader. In a letter to Indira Gandhi selling her this idea, he wrote, "Lord Curzon once said that, 'epochs arise in the history of every country when

---

[125] "Note on Conversation" by John Freeman, the British high commissioner to India dated April 5, 1966, reproduced in *The British Papers: Secret and Confidential India–Pakistan–Bangladesh Documents, 1958–1969* (Karachi, India: Oxford University Press, 2002), 480–81.

[126] This issue is explored further in A. G. Noorani, "Our Secrets in British Archives," *Frontline* 20, no. 4 (2003).

[127] Ashok Mitra, "India's Daughter," *India Today*, December 26, 2011.

[128] For a description of the prominent role played by the prime minister's office after 1968, see Oral History Transcripts, Govind Narain, II, no. 631, 420–25, NMML; also see Ashok Mitra, "The P N Haksar Story," Rediff on the Net, December 12, 1998, https://www.rediff.com/news/1998/dec/12mitra.htm. Jairam Ramesh, *Intertwined Lives: P.N. Haksar and Indira Gandhi* (New Delhi: Simon & Schuster, 2018).

the administrative machinery requires to be taken to pieces and overhauled and readjusted to the altered necessities or the growing demands of the hour.' "[129] At the time of its implementation this policy did not extend to the armed forces—as Indira Gandhi was keenly aware that her father was criticized for politicizing promotion policies.[130] However, much later, the logic of this argument—personal loyalty to the prime minister—crept into the selection of senior officers in the armed forces. As discussed in Chapter 6, there were a number of controversies around this issue. To be fair, Haksar was no longer the principal secretary when most of these controversies occurred, and his biggest contribution was to assist her in leading the Indian military to its greatest victory—one that significantly exorcised the trauma of 1962.

India's Finest Hour: 1971 Bangladesh War

The 1971 war between India and Pakistan led to the emergence of a new country, Bangladesh, and dealt a significant blow to the "two-nation theory" as the Bengali Muslims broke away from those residing in West Pakistan. India played a significant role, undertaking a humanitarian intervention when the term was not in fashion and stopping the genocide unleashed by the Pakistani Army on the people of East Pakistan.[131] To be sure, India had a stake in the conflict as it was host to around 10 million refugees fleeing the conflict. After a sharp and intense three-week war, the Pakistani forces in the east unconditionally surrendered. The 1971 war is therefore hailed as the military's finest hour. In terms of civil–military relations, the "conventional wisdom concerning 1971 is almost a caricature of the 'objective control' model of civil–military relations. In this telling, largely based on accounts from the military leadership, the military provided stern and prudent advice to the political leadership, which enabled India to

---

[129] Letter from Haksar to Indira Gandhi, March 4, 1966, correspondence with Indira Gandhi, PN Haksar Papers, Installment I and II, NMML; for another view on Haksar's attitude toward politicians and bureaucrats, see Thomas Abraham, "Need for New Concepts of Administration," in *PN Haksar: Our Times and the Man*, ed. Bidyut Sarkar, 42–47 (New Delhi: Allied Publishers, 1989).

[130] The idea of extending the "committed bureaucracy" argument to the armed forces was debated within the military; see Stephen Cohen, "The Military and Indian Democracy," in *India's Democracy: An Analysis of Changing State–Society Relations*, ed. Atul Kohli, 128–31 (Princeton University Press, 1988).

[131] For more on the birth of Bangladesh, see Srinath Raghavan, *1971: A Global History of the Creation of Bangladesh* (New Delhi: Permanent Black, 2013); Gary J. Bass, *The Blood Telegram: Nixon, Kissinger, and a Forgotten Genocide* (New York: Vintage, 2013); and Richard Sisson and Leo Rose, *War and Secession: Pakistan, India, and the Creation of Bangladesh* (Los Angeles: University of California Press, 1990).

properly triumph when the war did come."[132] Indeed, the dominant narrative within the Indian military regarding this war was that civilians "gave them a free hand to deal with the military situation as it developed. Unambiguous political goal setting for the armed forces . . . and excellent tri-Service coordination were the hallmarks of the military campaign."[133] A closer reading of the war, however, does not support this view. Instead, indicative of some organizational learning from the 1965 war, civilians played a much more active role—although they preferred to do so behind the scenes. This ensured greater coordination between the services and marked a departure from the previous model of civil–military relations. At the same time, this effort did not go far enough, and there were continuing problems in the operational domain.

Prime Minister Indira Gandhi and Defence Minister Jagjivan Ram were the politicians most closely involved in working with the military. They met regularly with their service chiefs and built up a healthy rapport that enabled a frank exchange of views. Continuing the narrative that emerged from the 1962 and 1965 wars, both of them were careful not to overtly "meddle" in operational matters. But, indicative of greater civilian oversight, they along with key civilian bureaucrats encouraged the services to regularly present, discuss, and share their war plans and sometimes sat in on these discussions. D. P. Dhar, as the chairman of the policy planning committee in the Ministry of External Affairs, played a very important role as the point person responsible for coordinating the diplomatic and military responses.[134] His task was made easier by the special relationship he developed with General Manekshaw—they had worked together during the first Kashmir war in 1947–1948. In this task, he was ably supported by Defence Secretary K. B. Lall, who played an important role in coordinating interservices operations including ensuring joint briefings, some of which he personally attended.[135] As a result of all this, the military was on board with the overall strategy. In short, unlike what is popularly believed, civilians played a much more prominent role in preparing the military for this war.

Despite these efforts, civilians were hampered by a lack of expertise and were careful to not "interfere" in the operational domain. As a result, there were problems in the conduct of the war. For instance, there is a controversy over the operational goal of the campaign in the eastern theater. According to the

[132] Tarapore, "Strategies of Stalemate," 98–99; also see Raghavan, "Soldiers, Statesmen, and India's Security Policy," 123.

[133] Kapil Kak, "India's Grand Strategy for the 1971 War," *CLAWS Journal* (Summer 2012): 97.

[134] For more on Dhar's role, see Raghavan, *1971: A Global History*, 216–26.

[135] For an account of civil–military relations during this period, see Oral History Transcript, K. B. Lall, Part II, no. 780, 437–49. In addition, other bureaucrats like Secretary to the Prime Minister P.N. Haksar, later replaced by P. N. Dhar; Home Secretary Govind Narain; and Foreign Secretary T. N. Kaul also played a constructive role.

chief of staff of the Eastern Army Command, Lieutenant General J. F. R. Jacob, army headquarters did not have the capture of Dhaka as its war aim and instead envisaged capture of a portion of East Pakistani territory so as to install a Bangladeshi government.[136] Accordingly, Eastern Command issued its operational plans in August 1971. However, whether by accident or design, the outline of the plan got leaked, and the Pakistani army in the east redeployed accordingly.[137] Ironically this left Dhaka undefended and helped the Indian Army in its eventual victory. While the army deserves compliments for its operational flexibility, the unconditional surrender was not ordained as it could have ended differently.[138] That there were no operational directives to capture Dhaka until the very end has been admitted by the official history of the war, which states that, "it was only on December 11 that the Prime Minister issued a written directive to the Chiefs of Staff for the total liberation of Bangladesh."[139] As noted by Tarapore, the war was conducted not as much by directives from Delhi but at the operational level of command, viz. Eastern Command.[140]

An unfortunate consequence stemming from a lack of civilian probing into operational details was a little discussed episode of the war on the western front—the loss of Chhamb. Due to a lack of operational clarity and confusion over tactical plans, India lost territory in the Chhamb salient.[141] The Shimla agreement ratified this loss, and India ended up accepting twenty thousand refugees.[142] Finally, as discussed in Chapter 4, despite some improvement from the previous war, jointness remained problematic.

Another popular, though mistaken, narrative that emerged from this war was about General Manekshaw "standing up" to the civilians to postpone the planned invasion of East Pakistan. According to this telling, politicians were keen to send the army in and liberate East Pakistan in April 1971, but Manekshaw opposed it

---

[136] J. F. R. Jacob, *Surrender at Dhaka: Birth of a Nation* (New Delhi: Manohar Publishers, 1997), 158–59; also see S. N. Prasad, *Official History of the 1971 War* (New Delhi: History Division, Ministry of Defence, 1992), 789–92.

[137] Prasad, *Official History of the 1971 War*, 786.

[138] For the manner in which General Niazi, the commander of the Pakistani forces in East Pakistan, was virtually "blackmailed" to surrender, see Jacob, *Surrender at Dhaka*, 138–44; this is not to suggest that Bangladesh would not have gained independence as the circumstances against West Pakistani forces were formidable. However, the unconditional surrender was not necessarily assured.

[139] Prasad, *Official History of the 1971 War*, 788. The war ended six days later.

[140] Tarapore, "Strategies of Stalemate," 76; also see Raghavan, *1971: A Global History*, 236–40.

[141] Sukhwant Singh, *Defence of the Western Border*, vol. 2 (New Delhi: Vikas Publishing House, 1981), 60–77.

[142] As a result of the Shimla agreement, India gained some territory in the Kargil area but accepted the loss of Chhamb; see Singh, *Defence of the Western Border*, 401–23.

forcefully and even offered to resign.[143] This is "perhaps the most tenacious of all myths about the 1971 crisis,"[144] which has wide acceptance within the military. Manekshaw's "embellished" account is constantly retold as an example of how senior officers should stand up against "misguided" civilian orders to protect the notion of rightful military autonomy.

After the victory, Indira Gandhi's popularity and political stature were unchallenged. Perhaps secure in her victory and her political power, she explored the possibility of appointing a CDS—the post that Mountbatten had long envisaged. General Manekshaw staked a claim to be the first CDS. However, there was vehement opposition from Air Chief Marshal P. C. Lal.[145] His opposition was convenient as civilians, both politicians and bureaucrats, were, in the end, reluctant to change the command and control structures that were in place. As Steven Wilkinson argues, they did not want to politically empower the military out of a fear that it might compromise civilian control.[146] Their focus, then as in now, is more on control than effectiveness.

The overwhelming nature of the military's victory in the 1971 war helped perpetuate certain myths in India's civil–military relations. First, an overly simplistic reading of the war cemented the narrative that envisaged a strict separation between the civil and military domains. Instead, civilians played an active role in facilitating jointness and in helping the military plan for its operations. D. P. Dhar played an important role in bridging the gap between civilians and the military, but his ad hoc position was never formalized. Second, there was a belief that India's higher defense management worked perfectly, so there was no need to change. Victory, as is usually the case, was a terrible teacher; and problems in joint operations and in higher defense management were glossed over.

Democracy's Darkest Hour: The Emergency Years, 1975–1977

In June 1975, faced with an adverse judgment from the Allahabad High Court and large-scale political protests, Prime Minister Indira Gandhi declared a

---

[143] Interview with General Manekshaw in *Quarterdeck*, reproduced in Hiranandani, *Transition to Triumph*, 114–15; also see Prasad, *Official History of the 1971 War*, 107–17.

[144] Raghavan, *1971: A Global History*, 67; also see Chandrashekhar Dasgupta, "The Decision to Intervene: First Steps in India's Grand Strategy in the 1971 War," *Strategic Analysis* 40, no. 4 (2016): 321.

[145] Top secret letter from P. N. Haksar to Indira Gandhi, December 24, 1972, Subject File no. 56, P. N. Haksar Papers (I and II Installment), NMML; also see P. C. Lal, *My Years with the Air Force* (New Delhi: Lancer International, 1986), 326–28.

[146] Wilkinson, *Army and the Nation*, 138–41.

state of emergency. Over the next two years, the government arrested political leaders, suspended civil liberties, and imposed press censorship, among other authoritarian measures. In the events leading up to the Emergency there were renewed fears in some quarters about a potential loss of civilian control. These were accentuated by statements from some politicians, like J. P. Narayan, openly calling upon the armed forces to disobey "illegal orders."[147] However, there was never any serious danger of a coup, and the armed forces remained strictly apolitical, refusing to take sides with any political figure or party. Moreover, the civilian MoD "provided a stable bureaucratic buffer that insulated the military from politics and politics from the military."[148] The military's desire to stay aloof was made easier by the presidential sanction for the imposition of the Emergency and by not having to implement repressive policies. Instead, this was left to the paramilitary and state police forces, which since the 1960s had significantly grown in number—from twenty thousand in 1960 to around two hundred thousand by 1980.[149] This arrangement was indicative of the unspoken arrangement between the civilians and the military, wherein the latter expected to maintain its "apolitical" nature and focus on its own domain.

A few months after the declaration of the emergency, Bansi Lal, a close associate of Sanjay Gandhi, Indira Gandhi's younger son, was appointed as the defense minister. A confidential assessment by the British defense attaché captured the tensions between the minister and the service chiefs:

There has been a running battle between the Chiefs and the Minister. It was reported that the new Minister tried to restrict the Chiefs right of access to the Prime Minister. . . . M. M. Sen [secretary of defense production] was on the brink of leaving his job. I believed this to be precipitated by undue interference in the management of Defence Production by Mr. Bansi Lal's special personal assistant Mr. S. K. Mishra (who came from Haryana with the Minister). The Chiefs were also upset by the uncouth behaviour of the Minister and his attempt to interfere in their command of their individual services.[150]

[147] This episode is described in Stephen Cohen, "Civilian Control of the Military in India," in *Civilian Control of the Military*, ed. Claude E. Welch Jr., 59–61 (Albany: State University of New York Press, 1976).

[148] Aqil Shah, "The Dog That Did Not Bark: The Army and the Emergency in India," *Commonwealth and Comparative Politics* 55, no. 4 (2017): 3, https://doi.org/10.1080/14662043.2017.1354856.

[149] Wilkinson, *Army and the Nation*, 143. The increase in number was primarily to relieve the army from its internal security mission; however, it also played a potentially useful role in "hedging" against the army power and in coup-proofing, see pages 143–46.

[150] Confidential U.K. Eyes Only "Brief for HE Mr. JA Thompson by Major General TA Richardson," dated January 18, 1977, A-4 in DEFE 11/ 845, Kew Archives, London.

The service chiefs were seemingly upset that the defense minister wanted to "interfere" in their command—therefore upsetting the traditional arrangement of separate civil and military domains. To prevent further controversy, Prime Minister Indira Gandhi had to step in and "take them all to task and tell them to stop squabbling."[151] Bansi Lal's tenure was controversial, however; probably due to media restrictions during the Emergency, these episodes did not fetch public attention. A final episode of the emergency, unsubstantiated and therefore not widely discussed, was about Sanjay Gandhi's alleged attempt to use the army to sustain Congress rule even after it lost the elections held in 1977. According to one version of events, General T. N. Raina, the chief of army staff, refused to entertain this suggestion and thereby upheld the army's apolitical nature.[152]

A Contested Legacy: Indira Gandhi as a Supreme Commander

Indira Gandhi's reign continues to evoke strong responses as she has her share of admirers and critics. With respect to civil–military relations, like on many other issues, she left a mixed legacy. On the positive side, she passed the ultimate test as a supreme commander—leading the country to victory in the 1971 war.[153] Unlike what is popularly believed, she did this, in part, by making her civilian advisers work closely with the military. This period, therefore, indicated a variance in the pattern of civil–military relations. To a significant extent, this was because of Indira Gandhi's personal leadership capabilities and reflected years of observation and experience.

Indira Gandhi had the advantage of being constantly by Nehru's side during his premiership. She took advantage of this and observed him closely, learning from his mistakes—especially his mishandling of the military leading up to the debacle in 1962. Even during the 1965 war, when she was the information and broadcasting minister, she made it a point to stay in the Kashmir Valley during the war and visited troops in the Haji Pir Pass, which had been captured by India.[154] Clearly, she internalized many lessons that emerged from the 1962 and 1965 wars and acquired leadership traits that her father lacked. Hence, she understood the importance of teamwork and invested in building

[151] Confidential U.K. Eyes Only.

[152] For more on this episode, see Eric A. Vas, *Fools and Infantrymen: One View of History (1923–1993)* (Meerut, India: Kartikeya Publishers, 1995), 238; and Wilkinson, *Army and the Nation*, 147–48.

[153] For an assessment of Indira Gandhi's leadership by the then home secretary, see Oral History Transcripts, Govind Narain, Vol. II, 631, 543–45, NMML.

[154] Jayakar, *Indira Gandhi*, 125.

personal relations with both civilians and the military. While she was careful not to give the appearance of meddling with operational details, at the same time she worked with D. P. Dhar, who was a useful messenger and troubleshooter. She also respected professional military opinion and encouraged a free and frank dialogue. Remarkably, even after the victory, she did not rest on her laurels; and one note in particular indicates how deeply she cared about defense preparedness. Barely six months after the Bangladesh victory she expressed concern over reports about Pakistani rearmament and wrote to the defense minister, "hope our defence forces are on alert and that everything possible is being done to re-equip them satisfactorily and adequately to meet any threat or eventuality."[155]

However, Indira Gandhi also had her negative qualities. One of the biggest was her focus on personal ties and disregard for institutions. Despite her personal leadership capabilities, clearly evident during the Bangladesh crisis, Indira Gandhi was not one for institution-building. As a result, the Defence Minister's Committee never came into prominence; and other initiatives, like creation of the Apex Committee for defense planning (which is discussed in Chapter 7) or appointing D. P. Dhar to integrate civilian and military functions before the 1971 war, could not be sustained. In addition, her singular focus on personal loyalty led to controversies over the promotion of senior military officers—as discussed in Chapter 6—creating turbulence within the military. This was part of a pattern—she had similarly undermined the presidency, the Congress Party, the judiciary, and the civil services by repeatedly making appointments based on personal loyalty.[156]

The underlying compact of civil–military relations was set during Indira Gandhi's extended premiership. This compact consisted of two main features, foreshadowing the idea of the absent dialogue—bureaucratic control and military autonomy. It was under Indira Gandhi that civilian bureaucrats played an increasingly important role in framing defense policies and, at times, excluded the military from this process. Writing about policymaking during this time, Stephen Cohen noted that the military was "bureaucratically and politically contained by the powerful Ministry of Defense. The ministry must approve all service-originated proposals. . . . The civilian officials of the defense ministry regard themselves as the pivot on which the defense policy process revolves."[157]

---

[155] Top secret note to defense minister dated May 13, 1972, in Sub File 294, III Installment 1, PN Haksar papers, NMML. This triggered a useful assessment of plans within army headquarters and led to a number of reports and correspondence including with General Manekshaw on the state of defense preparedness.

[156] Ramachandra Guha, *India after Gandhi: The History of the World's Largest Democracy* (London: Macmillan, 2007), 473–75, 499–500, 517–19.

[157] Stephen Cohen, "Military and Indian Democracy," 116–17.

The military expressed its unhappiness over this from time to time—most famously in a widely read, landmark study titled "Higher Defence Organisation in India"—but it also benefited from this arrangement which gave it considerable autonomy.[158] As a result, the idea that there was a strict separation between the civilian and military domains took hold. In later years, a deliberate misreading of the 1962, 1965, and 1971 wars led to a narrative that the military should stand up to resist civilian intervention in professional matters. As Raghavan points out, the belief that the military *should* have almost complete autonomy in its "own" domain turned into a type of "morality pageant"[159]—and became widely accepted within the community.

The Rajiv Gandhi Era, 1984–1989: Trying to Change, Quickly

Indira Gandhi's assassination in October 1984 thrust her elder son, Rajiv Gandhi, into the prime minister's chair. Riding on a wave of sympathy, he won the biggest landslide in Indian electoral history. His premiership was marked by a number of crises and controversies involving the armed forces, which illuminates different aspects pertaining to civil–military relations. Like before, this analysis examines the role of politicians, military officers, and bureaucrats during this period.

Rajiv Gandhi was India's youngest prime minister and keen to lead the country "into the twenty-first century"—a euphemism for getting things done quickly. Distrustful of traditional politicians, he inducted some of his close friends and associates into the government. One of them was Arun Singh, who, after a short stint in the prime minister's office, was appointed minister of state for defense in September 1985.[160]

The Short-Lived Renaissance: Arun Singh and Defense Policies in the 1980s

Arun Singh was an accidental politician—coming into power by virtue of his friendship with Rajiv Gandhi. Intellectually, and from a very young age, he was interested in the military and read up extensively on it.[161] In a way, therefore, he

---

[158] S. K. Sinha, "Higher Defense Organization in India" (USI Paper 7, USI Publications, New Delhi, 1980).

[159] Raghavan, "Soldiers, Statesmen and India's Security Policy," 121.

[160] Harihar Swarup, "Arun Singh—A Master in Defence Planning," *The Tribune*, July 11, 1999.

[161] Interview with Arun Singh, New Delhi, April 22, 2008.

was comfortable working with the military and got along well with them. Here was a rare instance of a politician who, arguably, possessed some expertise and was willing to partner with the military. And, fortuitously, the service chiefs at that time—General K. Sundarji, Admiral R. H. Tahiliani, and Air Chief Marshal Denis La Fontaine—enjoyed a moment of rare unity, getting along well with each other. As a result, the partnership between Arun Singh and the military led to a number of creative, and unprecedented, initiatives, touching upon various aspects of defense policy. For instance, and as discussed in greater detail in subsequent chapters, they created the Defence Planning Staff and the Committee for the Review of Training of Officers for the Services and resolved many contentious interservices issues, one of which resulted in the creation of Army Aviation. These efforts were made possible by a significant increase in budgetary allocations for the military and increased investment in missile development programs. In short, this was an era of change and reform, and there was a sense that it marked a clear departure from past practices.

The bonhomie between Arun Singh and the military chiefs was unlike the typical pattern of civil–military relations, and their direct interaction undercut the civilian bureaucracy, which, for the first time, felt that "it was out of the loop."[162] The cabinet secretary at that time, B. G. Deshmukh, described it in as many words: "unfortunately, Arun Singh, mainly on account of his inexperience in government, was completely bowled over by the Service Chiefs . . . and, therefore, the Service Chiefs during this period came to overshadow the bureaucratic civil structure of the Ministry."[163] There was a concern, therefore, that the military had become powerful and was driving policy. These fears were accentuated with the 1986–1987 Brasstacks crisis between India and Pakistan. This was triggered by the largest peacetime training exercise undertaken by all three services of the Indian military. Pakistan felt threatened and, perceiving it as a pretext for an all-out war, mobilized its army—leading to a tense face-off along the border. The Brasstacks crisis revealed serious shortcomings in Indian decision-making, and some argued that Prime Minister Rajiv Gandhi was not fully briefed by Arun Singh or the military. In the midst of this crisis, the prime minister shifted V. P. Singh from the Finance Ministry and appointed him defense minister.[164] Later, with the looming storm over the Bofors deal (a Swedish artillery gun which got embroiled in a corruption scandal), there was a falling out between Rajiv Gandhi

---

[162] Interview with P. R. Chari, who was in the Ministry of Defence at that time, New Delhi, February 27, 2012.

[163] B. G. Deshmukh, "A Systemic Failure," *Frontline*, 16, no. 2 (January 16-29, 1999).

[164] Rajiv Gandhi was apparently unhappy with V. P. Singh's handling of the Finance Ministry and may have used the Brasstacks crisis as a convenient excuse to move him; see Prabhash Joshi, "The Uncommon Catalyst," *Tehelka* 5, no. 50 (December 20, 2008).

and Arun Singh. In July 1987, for unexplained reasons, Arun Singh suddenly resigned. A few months later, V. P Singh was replaced by K. C. Pant, with the latter intent on regaining the civil–military "balance." One of his first decisions was to bring civilian bureaucrats back as the "pivot" of the ministry—and thereby return to the traditional pattern of strong bureaucratic control. One columnist argued that with this move, "there is now firm assertion of political control over the formulation of policy on such matters without letting the defense establishment influence such decisions on purely tactical considerations."[165] The experiment of a direct partnership between the politician and the military was over.

The General in His Labyrinth: Sundarji's Military Adventures

From 1987 to 1990, the Indian military was deployed in Sri Lanka as part of the IPKF, a costly political and military misadventure. They were sent there for peacekeeping under the India–Sri Lanka Accord but ended up in a peace enforcement mission and fought the Liberation Tigers of Tamil Eelam (LTTE), which wanted to establish a separate homeland. As with any failure, one in which the Indian Army lost about twelve hundred soldiers, there was much finger-pointing. The dominant view within the military was that they were let down by the political and diplomatic leadership and handed a nearly impossible mission.[166] Moreover, the military felt that different government agencies were working at cross purposes and that it had to fight "with one arm tied behind its back on account of the inherent political restrictions."[167]

Rajiv Gandhi was a hands-on leader and was quick with his decisions, often impatient with ceremony or what he perceived to be laborious bureaucratic processes. Most analysts, therefore, with the benefit of hindsight, criticize his "great haste" in the signing of the India–Sri Lanka Accord in July 1987, which committed the Indian Army to Sri Lanka.[168] At the political level, Rajiv Gandhi depended upon advice from relatively junior ministers like Natwar Singh and

[165] G. K. Reddy cited in P. R. Chari, Pervaiz Iqbal, and Stephen Cohen, *Four Crises and a Peace Process: American Engagement in South Asia* (New Delhi: Harpercollins, 2008), 60.

[166] Harkirat Singh, *Intervention in Sri Lanka: The IPKF Experience Retold* (New Delhi: Manohar, 2009); Depinder Singh, *Indian Peacekeeping Force in Sri Lanka, 1987–1989* (Dehra Dun, India: Natraj, 2001).

[167] V. P. Malik, *India's Military Conflicts and Diplomacy: An Inside View of Decision Making* (New Delhi: Harper Collins, 2013), 3.

[168] Ashok Mehta, "25 Years on, IPKF Awaits a Fitting Tribute Back Home," *Times of India*, July 29, 2012, https://timesofindia.indiatimes.com/home/sunday-times/all-that-matters/25-years-on-IPKF-awaits-a-fitting-tribute-back-home/articleshow/15243476.cms.

P. Chidambaram and ignored the views of experienced politicians like Narasimha Rao, who had suggested "not to rush into an agreement."[169] Moreover, around the time of the signing of the accord there was considerable change in personnel in the MoD (V. P. Singh was appointed as the defense minister in January but quickly replaced by K. C. Pant in April, and Arun Singh resigned in July). The political leadership therefore was in considerable turmoil.

In April 1987, to handle the Sri Lanka crisis, a "core group" was established, which functioned directly under Prime Minister Rajiv Gandhi. It consisted of representatives from the three services, the foreign ministry, intelligence agencies, and the prime minister's office and was responsible for overall coordination.[170] The formation of the core group itself was indicative of the weaknesses in the national security architecture, and, according to one analyst, the "main issue that confronted the decision-making at that point of time was the absence of proper structure to study issues concerning national security."[171] However, continuing with the traditional pattern of civil–military relations, politicians did not interfere in the operational conduct of the Sri Lankan campaign. This resulted in continuing problems in jointness—the ability of the three services to operate together, as discussed in greater detail in Chapter 4. Moreover, political interference in operational matters would have been difficult because it would have been resisted by the chief of army staff—who was a larger-than-life figure.

General K. Sundarji has been called India's "most brilliant, ambitious and controversial chief of army staff."[172] Even before the Brasstacks crisis, in 1986, General Sundarji was also at the heart of a border standoff with China, in what was called "Operation Falcon." This operation, which included the airlifting of troops, was Sundarji's forceful response to an alleged Chinese attempt to change the status quo along the border with India. Caught unaware, the Chinese upped the ante and threated India, leading Prime Minister Rajiv Gandhi to convene a meeting in the operations room of the army headquarters. According to one account, after Sundarji explained the situation and the steps he had taken to counter China's actions, he offered to step aside in case civilians wanted other

---

[169] S. Kalyanraman, "Major Lessons from Operation Pawan for Future Stability Operations," *Journal of Defense Studies* 6, no. 3 (2012): 35.

[170] Bharat Kumar, *Operation Pawan: Role of Airpower with IPKF* (New Delhi: Manohar Publishers, 2015), 38; there is some confusion about the precise composition of the Core Group, see 52n52.

[171] N. Manoharan, "National Security Decision Making Structures in India: Lessons from the IPKF involvement in Sri Lanka," *Journal of Defence Studies* 3, no. 4 (2009): 58.

[172] Kuldip Singh, "Obituary: General Krishnaswami Sundarji," *Independent*, February 10, 1999, https://www.independent.co.uk/arts-entertainment/obituary-general-krishnaswami-sundarji-1069842.html

advice. But under the impression that "civilian interference in operational matters was what had led to the disaster of 1962,"[173] civilians did not dare over-rule the general. Eventually, the situation was defused after some intense diplomatic negotiations.

Sundarji had called the civilian bluff and he would brook no interference on operational matters, entirely in keeping with the agreed model of civil–military relations. In addition, his "domineering personality kept the civil servants at bay."[174] B. G. Deshmukh, the cabinet secretary, would complain about Sundarji's obvious annoyance—more than once—at civilian "probing" of his claims.[175] In addition, Sundarji was known to be a man in a hurry, and his off-the-cuff assessments more than once got the Indian Army into trouble. For instance, as the Western Army commander during Operation Blue Star, the code name for the army's operations in the Golden Temple in Amritsar in June 1984, he allegedly promised that the operation would be over in a day (it took three days and the use of armor). Similarly, he grossly underestimated the fighting capability of the LTTE and reportedly claimed that the "Indian armed forces would be able to neutralize them militarily within two weeks."[176] The Indian Army could never completely neutralize the LTTE.

Eventually, perhaps because he was unable to deliver on his promises, Sundarji lost the confidence of the prime minister. According to Lieutenant General Depinder Singh, who commanded forces in Sri Lanka and worked closely with the general, "the lack of rapport between the COAS and the Prime Minister—undesirable in normal times, [is] completely fatal in an emergency. I am not aware of why such a situation developed . . . what I do know is that when I queried the COAS as to why our point of view was not being projected, his revealing reply was, 'Woh Sunta Nahi Hai' (he does not listen)."[177] It was a sad ending for Sundarji, who had come into office with so much promise and, at least for some time, had enjoyed complete access to the prime minister. General Sundarji's overall legacy is still highly contested, but the numerous military

---

[173] Manoj Joshi, "Operation Falcon: When Gen Sundarji Took the Chinese by Surprise," *The Quint*, March 14, 2018, https://www.thequint.com/voices/opinion/operation-falcon-sundarji-took-china-by-surprise

[174] Shekhar Gupta, "General Krishnaswamy Sundarji, Soldier of the Mind Who Rewrote India's Military Doctrine," *The Print*, February 8, 2018, https://theprint.in/opinion/general-krishnaswamy-sundarji-soldier-mind-rewrote-indias-military-doctrine/34227/.

[175] B. G. Deshmukh, *From Poona to the Prime Minister's Office: A Cabinet Secretary Looks Back* (New Delhi: Harper Collins, 2004), 163–66.

[176] On this episode, see J. N. Dixit, *Assignment Colombo* (Delhi: Konark Publishers, 1998), 156; also see Singh, *Intervention in Sri Lanka*, 78.

[177] Cited in A. G. Noorani, "Shocking Disclosures," *Frontline* 24, no. 18 (2007).

setbacks under his tenure ended the period of a direct partnership between the politicians and the military in India.[178]

The role of civilian bureaucrats during this time was somewhat controversial. The defense secretary was S. K. Bhatnagar, who held the post for a little under four years—which was a rarity. He became deeply embroiled in the Bofors controversy, and as a result, some felt that he could not exercise his authority vis-à-vis the military.[179] His successor was T. N. Seshan, who had the opposite problem: he was "assertive and aggressive," and the "relationship between the service chiefs and Seshan became increasingly difficult."[180] Fortunately, he served for only ten months, replaced by Naresh Chandra, who had a more balanced temperament and brought a degree of calm efficiency to the MoD.

In addition, two foreign service officers, J. N. Dixit and Ronen Sen, played an important role in shaping defense policies during this period. Dixit especially, due to his controversial tenure in Colombo, was resented by many in the military for his allegedly domineering ways.[181] Ronen Sen played a less public but an important role in the prime minister's office.[182]

A Missed Opportunity: Rajiv Gandhi as a Supreme Commander

Unlike his mother, Rajiv Gandhi was not known to pay careful attention to detail and was prone to taking whimsical decisions without adequate deliberation.[183] He also lacked the experience that his mother gained by being constantly at Nehru's side, before becoming the prime minister. Rajiv Gandhi's premiership was eventful from the perspective of civil–military relations. In the early days, when he kept the defense minister's portfolio, he partnered with Arun Singh; and they were accused of bypassing the civilian bureaucracy and directly interacting with the service chiefs. This was the form of political control that

---

[178] For more on General Sundarji's legacy, see Inderjit Badhwar and Dilip Bobb, "General Sundarji Leaves Behind a Legacy Most Fiercely Disputed in the History of the Army," *India Today*, May 15, 1988, https://www.indiatoday.in/magazine/cover-story/story/19880515-general-sundarji-leaves-behind-a-legacy-most-fiercely-disputed-in-the-history-of-the-army-797243-1988-05-15; Satish Nambiar, "His Many Frontlines," *Outlook India*, February 22, 1999, https://www.outlookindia.com/magazine/story/his-many-frontlines/207021; and Manoj Joshi, "General Krishnaswami Sundarji Passes Away," *India Today*, February 22, 1999.

[179] Vinay Kumar, "Serious Flaw in Bhatnagar's Conduct," *The Hindu*, November 20, 2002.

[180] Deshmukh, *From Poona to the Prime Minister's Office*, 164.

[181] For a particularly scathing, even if motivated, critique, see Singh, *Intervention in Sri Lanka*.

[182] P.R. Chari, "The IPKF Experience in Sri Lanka" (ACDIS occasional paper, University of Illinois at Urbana-Champaign, February 1994), 14–15.

[183] For an assessment of his style of leadership, see Chari, *IPKF Experience in Sri Lanka*, 8, 14–15.

the military had long been advocating for. And, indeed, many contentious issues were resolved, helped in part by Arun Singh's knowledge and interest in the military. His tenure was, therefore, the closest exception to the generalization about a lack of expertise in the political class. However, there was a gradual falling out between Rajiv Gandhi on one side and Arun Singh and General Sundarji on the other—accentuated by the Brasstacks crisis, the Bofors corruption allegations, and the debacle in Sri Lanka. These controversies also served to discredit the direct political control model. In later years, the bureaucracy would cite these setbacks as indicative of the costs that would be incurred if they are bypassed and if the military gets to drive policy.

There was a silver lining, however, that emerged from the Sri Lanka episode. In 1989, after V. P. Singh became the prime minister, he appointed Arun Singh to lead a reform committee. Ostensibly set up to reduce defense expenditure, this committee (called the Committee on Defence Expenditure) assumed a wider remit and allegedly recommended changes in higher defense organization—including in the MoD and the services. But since these reforms were inconvenient for both civilian bureaucrats and the military, the report was quietly buried.[184] Arun Singh's efforts and the Sri Lanka debacle were the trigger for a vibrant intellectual debate within India's strategic community, which was hankering for major national security reforms. The weakness in India's higher defense management—and by definition its civil–military relations—was self-evident, but it would require a crisis to gather the momentum to bring about changes. And, perhaps fortunately, such a crisis occurred about a decade later in the form of the Kargil war.

Atal Bihari Vajpayee, 1998–2004: The Reluctant Reformer

Atal Bihari Vajpayee was the first non-Congress prime minister to complete a full term in office. Widely acknowledged as a great orator and a keen intellect, his Bhartiya Janata Party–led coalition government was credited with a number of foreign and defense policy transformations. His premiership literally began with a bang as in May 1998, within two months of coming to power, India conducted five underground nuclear tests. Interestingly, the service chiefs were not informed until the very last moment.[185] Despite that, it was expected that relations between the military and India's first right-of-center government would be

---

[184] Mukherjee, "Failing to Deliver," 9–10.
[185] Interview with General V. P. Malik, then chief of army staff, New Delhi, June 30, 2009.

strong. However, these expectations were soon belied due to tensions between civilians and the military culminating in an unprecedented event—the sacking of the chief of naval staff, Admiral Vishnu Bhagwat. As described in greater detail in Chapter 6, the admiral became embroiled in a clash of will with the government over personnel issues, leading to his dismissal. To deflect criticism arising from this controversy, Defence Minister George Fernandes publicly announced plans to establish a group for "restructuring of the services and integration of the services and the ministry of defence."[186] Ostensibly then, it was intended that "a wholly new structure" would be recommended that would serve the twin purposes of allowing a greater say for the military in the decision-making process while decreasing civilian bureaucratic interference. However, despite making this announcement, no such group was set up. Instead, as in many other democracies, change was forced upon the MoD and the overall national security apparatus by an unanticipated war.

The Kargil War: Challenging Traditional Notions of Civil–Military Relations

The 1999 Kargil war was triggered by an incursion of Pakistani troops across the Line of Control that divides the two countries in Kashmir. India's initial response to this was slow and confused as they lacked knowledge about the identity of the infiltrators. However, by the end of May 1999, with growing awareness of the situation, the political leadership told the military to escalate its operations, both on land and in air. While doing so, it only gave an overriding directive— that the Line of Control would not be crossed by either land or air forces. This was a very specific operational directive which violated the traditional pattern of India's civil–military relations—where civilians were not supposed to intervene in operational matters. What explains this anomaly?

The Kargil war occurred a little over a year after the nuclear tests conducted by both countries, and India was under considerable diplomatic pressure for seemingly breaking an international moratorium against nuclear testing. The outbreak of the war added to fears in the international community about the India–Pakistan rivalry and focused attention on the Kashmir dispute. They were concerns therefore about a potential nuclear war on the subcontinent. These concerns played an important role in shaping Indian decision-making.[187] India's political leadership was anxious not to legitimize two narratives: that India

---

[186] "Fernandes Sets Up Panel to Restructure Defence Ministry," Rediff on the Net, January 8, 1999, http://www.rediff.com/news/1999/jan/08def.htm

[187] Interview with civilian official who worked in the prime minister's office during the Kargil war, June 30, 2009, New Delhi.

behaved irresponsibly and that India–Pakistan relations, more specifically the Kashmir issue, required the attention of the international community. As a result, India's political class decisively intervened in what ordinarily should have been considered the military's domain—the operational conduct of the war. Indian leaders calculated, correctly as it turned out, that they would gain significant diplomatic advantage from such a measured and responsible approach.

The directive not to cross the Line of Control created problems for the Indian military, and there was a strong perception that as a result it was taking in more losses.[188] Initially, the service chiefs accepted these restraints; but as the war dragged on, they faced mounting criticism from within their organization and were under pressure, including from the National Security Advisory Board, to challenge this operational directive.[189] However, after Indian troops won the Battle of Tololing on June 13, 1999, the tide of the war turned and the pressure to revisit the do-not-cross the Line of Control decision reduced. This episode is crucial in examining civil–military relations as it was one of the few instances where politicians disregarded professional military advice and placed restrictions on their operations. More importantly, it demonstrated for the first time that politicians could interfere in what could have been construed as a "purely military" activity if they were firm and explained their reasons clearly to the military leadership. This reflected a maturity and confidence in civil–military relations that contrasted from earlier years. Crucially, it also reflected a dilemma of overt nuclearization in the sub-continent. After the nuclear tests of 1998, civilians were forced to pay greater attention to military plans.

The Kargil crisis forced politicians, civilians, and the military to work together under pressure; and much of the bitterness that was created due to previous controversies, like the dismissal of Admiral Bhagwat in December 1998, was set aside. General V. P. Malik, the chief of army staff, observed that "the three chiefs were closely enmeshed in the political–military decision-making process [which was] open and direct . . . and after discussions, the concerned executive authorities, including the three chiefs, received directions from the prime minister and the national security adviser, Brajesh Mishra."[190] Later, there were accounts praising this teamwork, wherein civilians made the strategic decisions and the military had tactical autonomy.[191]

That civilians and the military worked together while facing a crisis is not unusual or surprising, but after it was over, it was business as usual. The military

---

[188] Narayan Menon, "The Ghosts of Kargil," *Indian Defence Review* 25, no. 3 (2010): 123.

[189] Chari, Cheema, and Cohen, *Four Crises and a Peace Process*, 131.

[190] V. P. Malik, *Kargil: From Surprise to Victory* (New Delhi: HarperCollins, 2007), 132.

[191] Ashok Krishna, "Lessons, Precepts, and Perspectives," in *Kargil: The Tables Turned*, ed. Ashok Krishna and P. R. Chari, 166 (New Delhi: Manohar, 2001).

was to complain again about its neglect, and in later years General Malik would emerge as one of the leading critics of the system of higher defense management and the tenor of civil–military relations.[192] However, the war also triggered a public outcry, and this led to the most significant reforms in India's national security apparatus.

Change, at Last: The Post-Kargil Defense Reforms

As a result of the Kargil war, the Vajpayee government established what has become popularly known as the Kargil Review Committee, headed by K. Subrahmanyam, considered the doyen of strategic studies in India. This committee submitted its report, which was tabled in Parliament on February 23, 2000. The report reaffirmed a commonly held view: India's national security and system of higher defense management required major overhaul. "An objective assessment of the last 52 years will show," the report argued, "that the country is lucky to have scraped through various national security threats without too much damage, except in 1962. The country can no longer afford such ad hoc functioning."[193] Presciently, it also cautioned that it would not be easy to change as the "political, bureaucratic, military and intelligence establishments appear to have developed a vested interest in the status quo."[194]

One of the main recommendations of the Kargil Review Committee was the need to conduct a thorough review of the national security system. Accordingly, in April 2000, the government set up the Group of Ministers (GoM). This body was created to deliberate upon reports submitted by four task forces examining aspects pertaining to intelligence, internal security, border management, and defense. The one most relevant for civil–military relations was the Task Force on Defence, which was headed by Arun Singh, the former politician turned recluse turned military reformer—back for seemingly his last innings.

This task force recommended major changes including appointing a CDS to head a joint staff, among many others.[195] While implementing many of its recommendations, the government demurred from creating the post of CDS.

---

[192] V. P. Malik, "Higher Defence Management and Defence Reforms: Towards Better Management Techniques," in *Call for Change: Higher Defence Management in India*, IDSA Monograph 6 (New Delhi: Institute for Defence Studies and Analyses, July 2012), 37–51; V. P. Malik, "Decoding the Civil–Military Relations," *ORF Analysis*, May 18, 2009.

[193] Kargil Review Committee, *From Surprise to Reckoning: The Kargil Review Committee Report* (New Delhi: Sage Publications, 2000), 259.

[194] Kargil Review Committee, 252.

[195] For more on the recommendations, see Group of Ministers, *Reforming the National Security System: Report of the Group of Ministers on National Security* (New Delhi: Government of India, 2001), 97–117.

This was because of opposition from different quarters—the Indian Air Force, civilian bureaucrats, and even the Congress Party.[196] Not appointing a CDS, according to Admiral Arun Prakash, member of the Arun Singh Task Force and later chairman of the chiefs of staffs' committee, "ripped the heart out of the GoM recommendations."[197] Indeed, the services maintained their individual autonomy, and jointness continued to be problematic.

The Arun Singh Task Force, however, largely left unchanged the interaction between the defense ministry and military headquarters. Indicative of a difference of opinion within the task force, this meant that the civilian bureaucracy continued to function as before.[198] To be sure, there were some improvements. For instance, a joint staff, called the Integrated Defence Staff was established in 2001 and has gradually come into prominence, greater financial powers were allocated to the military and the joint Andaman and Nicobar Command has been established. But there have also been arguments about how even these reforms have been subverted in practice by different bureaucracies, both civilian and military.[199]

As a result, since around 2009 there have been persistent calls to revisit the defense reforms process; and, indeed, the government appointed two committees (the Naresh Chandra Committee in 2012 and the Shekatkar Committee in 2015), with an explicit mandate to do so. But despite submission of the reports of these committees, there has been no substantial change. Why did the government fail to act more decisively, for instance, by appointing a CDS, post-Kargil and since?

There are two main explanations for this. First, India's political class is uncomfortable with the idea of altering the strict form of civilian control that was shaped during the Nehru era. They believe that the current structure of civil–military is *efficient enough* to deal with the current threats. Therefore, and this cuts across political parties, they are unwilling to appoint a CDS. Second, the status quo is, as the Kargil Review Committee correctly pointed out, suitable for all of the existing stakeholders. Simply put, the services do not want jointness

---

[196] For more on this, see Mukherjee, "Failing to Deliver," 17–49.

[197] Arun Prakash, "India's Higher Defence Organisation: Implications for National Security and Jointness," *Journal of Defence Studies* 1, no. 1 (2007): 24.

[198] Mukherjee, "Failing to Deliver," 20–22.

[199] Gurmeet Kanwal, "Defence Reforms: CDS and Theatre Commands Are an Operational Necessity," *Synergy* (July 2016): 19, https://cenjows.gov.in/upload_images/pdf/Layout%20 Inside_Synergy.pdf; Ajai Shukla, "Why India's Defence Planning Is a No-Brainer," Rediff News, May 13, 2014, http://www.rediff.com/news/report/defence-news-why-indias-defence-planning-is-a-no-brainer/20140513.htm; and Anit Mukherjee, "The Unsinkable Aircraft Carrier: The Andaman and Nicobar Command," in *India's Naval Strategy and Asian Security*, ed. Anit Mukherjee and C. Raja Mohan, 86–105 (London and New York: Routledge, 2015).

or to have a CDS with a mandate to enforce it. Similarly, civilian bureaucrats are reluctant to tinker with the procedural rules governing civil–military relations. The political class, which is ultimately responsible, is also reluctant to enforce radical change without gaining consensus from all of the constituencies.

Shortly after the Vajpayee government implemented some of these changes, it was faced with another military crisis—the 2001–2002 border mobilization crisis, also known as Operation Parakram. This was triggered by an attack on December 13, 2001, by Pakistani terrorists on the Indian Parliament. In response, the government ordered a large-scale military mobilization, which accentuated war fears on the subcontinent. Eventually, the crisis was resolved after eight months, but it also revealed a major disconnect in civil–military relations. It was not, and is still not, entirely clear what was the overall political objective and if this was clearly communicated and understood by the military.[200] Moreover, it was evident that the political leadership did not understand the military options and that the military, in turn, did not plan and prepare for a short, swift conflict with Pakistan.[201] This revealed the need for a continuous dialogue between civilians and the military over political aims, military doctrines, plans, and operations. However, the Vajpayee government was seemingly intellectually exhausted with constant military crises, and no effort was made to analyze the lessons emerging from this operation.

Another Missed Opportunity: Vajpayee's Legacy

Prime Minister Vajpayee assembled a team that showed greater enthusiasm than its predecessors on issues pertaining to national security. His principal secretary and national security adviser, Brijesh Mishra, played a hands-on role while dealing with different crises. L. K. Advani and Jaswant Singh were other senior members of the cabinet that advised the prime minister. The defence minister, George Fernandes, had a mixed legacy. Like the infamous Krishna Menon, his initial actions, including sending civilian bureaucrats to visit forward posts on the Siachen glacier, endeared him to the military. However, he was later embroiled in numerous controversies and forced to temporarily step down after corruption charges were brought against him following an investigative report by *Tehelka* magazine. This proved to be a blessing in disguise as Jaswant Singh,

[200] Verghese Koithara, "Nuclear Weapons in India's Defence Policy: Achieving Conventional-Nuclear Synergy," in *Handbook of Indian Defence Policy: Themes, Structures and Doctrines*, ed. Harsh Pant, 388–91 (New Delhi: Routledge India); also see "Operation Parakram after Parliament Attack Lacked Clear Objectives: Ex-Navy Chief Sushil Kumar," *Times of India*, November 6, 2011.

[201] Praveen Swami, "Gen. Padmanabhan Mulls over Lessons of Operation Parakram," *The Hindu*, February 6, 2004, http://www.thehindu.com/2004/02/06/stories/2004020604461200.htm

who served in the army for a short while, assumed temporary charge of the MoD. He used this opportunity to bring Arun Singh into the MoD to implement the post-Kargil defense reforms. Together they were able to make some changes but could not overcome opposition, especially to the proposal of creating a CDS. After Fernandes was cleared of corruption charges, he was reinstated to the cabinet; and this effectively ended the defense reforms process.

The Kargil war, forced upon India, led to the most significant reforms in the Indian military. This was, therefore, an opportunity to address structural weaknesses in civil–military relations. Perhaps Vajpayee thought it best to adopt an incremental approach to change; but, with the benefit of hindsight, it is clear that he did not go far enough. It would not be overly harsh therefore to consider this a setback for Vajpayee's overall legacy.

Perhaps however one should be kinder on Vajpayee as that type of transformational reforms has not even been pushed by his successors. As one analyst pessimistically argued, "the only consistency in reforming India's moribund and bureaucracy-ridden security architecture remains ensuring that no comprehensive reform occurs.... The reorganization of India's higher defense management, started after the Kargil War, continues to languish despite the lapse of nearly 16 years."[202] An important part of any such reorganization, will have to address one of the main points of friction in its civil–military relations—the relationship between the soldier and the bureaucrat.

An Uncomfortable Relationship: Bureaucrats and the Military

A refrain, constantly repeated within the Indian military, is that they are "not under political control but under bureaucratic control."[203] Such sentiments represent one of the most enduring sources of tension in its civil–military relations: the equation between bureaucrats and the military. The origins of this

---

[202] Saikat Datta, "Intelligence, Strategic Assessment, and Decision Process Deficits: The Absence of Indian Learning from Crisis to Crisis," in *Investigating Crises: South Asia's Lessons, Evolving Dynamics, and Trajectories*, ed. Sameer Lalwani and Hannah Haegeland, 112–13 (Washington, DC: Stimson Center, 2018).

[203] For some typical perspectives, see Arun Prakash, "Keynote Address," in *Proceedings of USI Seminar on Higher Defense Organization* (New Delhi: United Service Institution of India, 2007), 10; Kapil Kak, "Direction of Higher Defense II," *Strategic Analysis* 22, no. 4 (1998): 504; and Vinod Anand, *Delhi Papers 16: Joint Vision for the Indian Armed Forces* (New Delhi: Institute for Defence Studies and Analysis, 2001), 86.

issue go back to the early years after independence.[204] India's political leaders consolidated control over the military by increasing the prominence of the defense minister. The military was comfortable with accepting a political leader as its head, but its attitude toward civilian bureaucrats in the ministry was another matter.

As mentioned earlier in this chapter, there was considerable animosity between the first Indian chief of army staff, General Cariappa, and H. M. Patel, defense secretary from 1947 to 1953. It was more than a clash of personalities, however, and was indicative of the initial teething troubles in formalizing working relations between the civilians and the military. The military chiefs resented Patel's manner of functioning—especially his insistence that they approach the defense minister through his office. In a letter to Mountbatten, H. M. Patel defended his actions and, in turn, criticized the Warrant of Precedence (a document which formally delineates the order of hierarchy within the government):

> I see that you have come to hear of the differences between the service chiefs and myself. It is quite true that there do exist differences . . . for some reason the Service Chiefs seem to have come to the conclusion that they can only deal direct with the Defence Minister. This was manifested, for instance, in their decision not even to send to me the Agenda of the Chiefs of Staff Meetings! This was, of course, quite impractical and so far as I can see scarcely conducive to the most efficient discharge of work. However these and other barriers which were attempted to be build up, partly under the unreasonable influence that that horrible document, the Warrant of Precedence, seems to exercise on some minds are getting removed through sheer necessity, as I always imagined they would. The Defence Ministry is an integral part of the Defence Organisation, and any attempt to ignore it is merely to ignore the essential constitution and other organizational necessities.[205]

The crux of the problem was twofold. First was the principle of seniority. The chiefs resented the defense secretary and other junior officials in the MoD questioning the decisions made by the services. They felt that as seniors, under the terms of the Warrant of Precedence, military officers should interact directly with the defense minister. Within a few years, using the argument of democratic and civilian consolidation, the Warrant of Precedence was successively

---

[204] Stephen Cohen goes back even earlier and traces these tensions to the Curzon–Kitchener dispute; see Cohen, "Civilian Control of the Military in India," 45–46.

[205] Letter from H. M. Patel, defence secretary of India, to General Roy Bucher dated February 26, 1950, 7901-87-32, Bucher Papers, National Army Museum, London.

revised.[206] Initially, political leaders were designated above the service chiefs; however, later it gave prominence to leaders of other institutions like the judiciary and the election commission, among others.[207] This represented the inevitable lowering of status from an imperial to a democratic army; however, it added to the indignation in some circles within the military.[208] The issue of alleged downgrading of status, seniority and equivalence between military officers and civilian bureaucrats remains a sore point to date.

The second problem pertained to the rules of business. After independence, there was a lack of clarity about the precise functions and relations of the MoD and services. In 1952, H. M. Patel prepared a report that designated the services as "attached offices" to the secretariat.[209] The chiefs had serious disagreements with this report and requested a discussion. But their request was denied, and the report was quietly implemented. Indicative of a lack of dialogue, "no correspondence or interaction took place between the Chiefs and the political authority on this vital issue."[210] This report formalized an arrangement wherein the services had to clear all of their files from the ministry and empowered the latter. A common complaint then arose—that the bureaucrat had emerged as the interlocutor between the politician and the military. Stephen Cohen argues that "the administrative and organizational changes introduced after independence indicate a fairly effective alliance between the civil service and the politicians, an alliance created for the purpose of reducing the role of the military in the decision-making process."[211]

Institutionalizing the bureaucracy's role in the MoD was necessary to consolidate civilian control in India—praetorian states and fragile democracies are almost always characterized by the absence of such civilian bureaucracies (this argument is admittedly tautological: weak civilian control is a result of weak civilian bureaucracy and vice versa). In all democracies, relations between civilian bureaucrats and the military have been delicate, and require careful handling

[206] Lloyd Rudolph and Susanne Rudolph, "Generals and Politicians in India," *Pacific Affairs* 37, no. 1 (1964): 9–10.

[207] Currently, the chiefs are placed twelfth in the table of precedence, see president's secretariat letter no. 33-Pres/79 dated July 26, 1979, http://mha.gov.in/sites/default/files/table_of_precedence.pdf.

[208] The complaint about lowered warrant of precedence is commonplace in Indian military literature and is often touted as an example of the military's loss of prestige; see S. K. Sinha, "Soldiers Lost in the Babu Maze," *Asian Age*, September 15, 2010.

[209] In 2011 responding to Right to Information request, the Ministry of Defence claimed that it could not locate this report; see "MoD Can't Locate Five Key Reports on Military Reforms," *Times of India*, October 14, 2011.

[210] Hiranandani, *Transition to Guardianship*, 280, also see 278–81.

[211] Stephen P. Cohen, *The Indian Army: Its Contribution to the Development of a Nation* (Berkeley: University of California Press, 1971), 171.

from all sides. In India's case however, over the years, the lack of trust and respect between the military and civilian bureaucrats is a "real problem."[212]

Conclusion

This chapter examined the historical trajectory of India's civil–military relations, focusing on five wartime commanders. As we have seen, there was a variance in the pattern of civil–military relations under them.

Nehru failed the wartime test, due to the defeat in the 1962 war, however he deserves credit for imbibing the principle of civilian control. At the same time, the rules of business that were controversially enacted set in motion policies that later created discord between civilians and the military. Shastri had a mixed record during the 1965 war—he was successful in denying Pakistan its war aims but there were major operational shortcomings. Among the narratives that emerged from this war is that the military should have near complete autonomy in the operational realm—an assumption that still largely holds true. Out of all these leaders, Indira Gandhi stands out as the best—not just for the scale of the victory during the 1971 Bangladesh war but also for her handling of the military before, during, and even after the war. She relied on the advice of competent officials and earned the trust of her military commanders by, at times, probing them on their plans and state of preparedness. However, ironically, under her premiership the civilian bureaucracy gained prominence in the decision-making process through a system of strong financial controls.

Rajiv Gandhi's premiership was unusual as he got Arun Singh—a politician with some knowledge about the military, as his de facto defense minister. This led to some wide-ranging defense reforms, as Arun Singh partnered directly with the military. However, this arrangement was resented by the civilian bureaucracy; and after Arun Singh's departure, status quo was restored. Vajpayee had to deal with the 1999 Kargil war; and, contrary to not interfering in the military's operational realm, he placed clear operational limits on the army and air force. Vajpayee also undertook the most significant defense reforms process since independence but was unwilling to alter civilian control by, for instance, appointing a CDS.

India's military defeat in 1962 was blamed entirely on civilian incompetence and interference in military affairs, so a narrative emerged that the military should have complete autonomy in the operational domain. A selective reading

---

[212] Srinath Raghavan, "Military–Bureaucracy Brinksmanship," *Economic and Political Weekly* 51, no. 39 (September 24, 2016).

of the 1965 and 1971 wars reinforced this narrative despite significant problems in higher defense management. Over time, these narratives have evolved into "norms and rules" of behavior that typically shape the conduct of politicians, bureaucrats, and soldiers. This pattern of civil–military relations, which is best described as an absent dialogue, can be imagined as having three broad characteristics: lack of civilian expertise, institutional design with strong bureaucratic control and high degree of military autonomy in its domain. The next five chapters examine civil–military relations and the manner in which they influence five variables generally associated with military effectiveness—weapons procurement, jointness, professional military education, officer promotion policies, and defense planning.

3

The False Promise of Self-Reliance

The Weapons Procurement Process

Equipping a military with appropriate weapons is a complex but critical task, with potentially high costs of failure. It is a function of a number of factors including economic considerations, changes in the international situation, military capabilities and doctrine of potential adversaries, technological change, and defense production capability. According to Thomas McNaugher, weapons acquisition is "both a technical and a political process—technical, in that it involves the development and production of sophisticated weapons, and political, because it uses public money to supply part of a public good called national security."[1] Weapons procurement therefore is thus one of the core functions of civil–military relations, requiring constant interaction between civilians and the military, usually through a multitude of agencies. This process is unique to all countries.

This chapter examines civil–military relations and the weapons procurement process in India. Weapons procurement or acquisition (the two terms are used interchangeably in this chapter and in the literature) "refers to the research, development, production and procurement of a weapon."[2] The main argument is that the pattern of interaction between civilians and the military combined with the processes within their organizations contributes to long delays, misplaced priorities, wasteful expenditure, and, at an extreme, "less-than-optimal weapon performance."[3] This pattern, the absent dialogue argument, includes the lack of

---

[1] Thomas L. McNaugher, "Weapons Procurement: The Futility of Reform," *International Security* 12, no. 2 (1987): 65.

[2] Theo Farrell, *Weapons Without a Cause: The Politics of Weapons Acquisitions in the United States* (London: Palgrave Macmillan, 1997), 1.

[3] Richard A. Bitzinger, "Comparing Defense Industry Reforms in China and India," *Asian Politics & Policy* 7, no. 4 (2015): 535.

civilian expertise, strong bureaucratic controls which exclude the military from policymaking, and considerable military autonomy.

The first section of this chapter begins with a conceptual and comparative discussion of the role of civil–military relations in weapons procurement in different countries. In doing so, it highlights the importance of a constant and "iterative" dialogue between civilians and the military. Next, it identifies two desirable features in the procurement process—institutional design and the need for expertise in both civilian and military bureaucracies. Thereafter, it analyzes major trends in India's weapons procurement process by dividing them into different periods since 1947. This highlights the inability of state-owned domestic industry to meet the demands of the military. The next section analyzes problems accruing from the current structure of civil–military relations. The penultimate section examines the relevance of the absent dialogue argument and concludes by summarizing the major arguments presented in this chapter.

It is important, however, to begin with a distinction between acquisitions and procurement—a point missed by most. Acquisition focuses on generating capabilities and involves a series of activities including design, development, testing, user feedback, and production. Procurement, on the other hand, is the procedure to buy usually off-the-shelf weapons. In India, there is a major confusion—agencies speak at cross purposes—as state-owned entities tout "acquisitions" but the military, disillusioned with repeated failures, prefers procurement. As discussed later, the Kelkar Committee, set up in 2004, emphasized the importance of differentiating these terms.[4] However, most official documents in India have used the terms interchangeably; and to avoid confusion, this chapter does the same.

Role of Civil–Military Relations in Weapons Procurement: A Comparative Overview

The crux of the civil–military issue on weapons procurement comes down to a relatively straightforward question: how much autonomy should the military have in choosing its weapons? This issue lacks consensus, and weapons procurement in different countries is shaped by a variety of factors including political structures, production capabilities, bureaucratic procedures, export policy, and the institutional power of the military. Unsurprisingly, militaries would prefer

---

[4] Ministry of Defence, *Towards Strengthening Self Reliance in Defense Preparedness*, April 2005 (hereafter referred to as the *Kelkar Committee Report*), 84. Also see Mrinal Suman, "Defence Production and Acquisitions: Enhancing Capability Through Integrated Approach," *CLAWS Journal* (Summer 2013): 133.

to have maximum autonomy in this regard. However, civilians, keeping in mind larger economic, societal, diplomatic, and strategic interests, vet proposals from the military. The role of the defense industry also adds an element of complexity, and, almost inevitably, these factors give rise to tensions between civilians and the military. The manner in which these tensions are resolved is indicative of the institutional power of these bureaucracies. Examining the experience of different countries highlights the complexity of these factors.

With the largest, most expensive military in the world, the United States has an elaborate weapons procurement process and a complex relationship between the civilians and the military. In general, the various branches of the military are important players and have been "able to promote their institutional interests in weapons acquisition because they have more influence over the process than any other actors."[5] Over the years, however, civilians have consolidated their powers in the acquisitions process and have been assertive, depending on the personality of the defense secretary, in arbitrating differences among the services (sometimes within the services) and with the defense industry.[6] The Office of the Secretary of Defense, which consists of both civilian and military officials, is chiefly responsible for oversight, policy formulation and implementation. This office generally has a high level of expertise, which is crucial to its ability to integrate military procurement plans with overall strategic goals and to arbitrate differences between the military and the defense industry. Significantly, weapons production is entirely in the hands of the private sector.

A comparative study of weapons procurement in France and Britain illuminates the crucial role of expertise, weapons exports, and institutional design. In 1961, France established the Ministerial Delegation for Armament by merging service-specific armament directorates. Renamed the Directorate General of Armaments (DGA) in 1977, this organization is solely responsible for all weapons acquisition functions, including program management, research and development, testing, production, and export. It comprises engineering and technocratic officials, some of whom hold military rank, and functions directly under the defense minister. This arrangement gives it significant bureaucratic power, which it has used to support the defense industry, including by seeking out export markets, turning it into a front-line and profitable weapons producer. However, the French defense industry, primarily due to its tutelage under the DGA, has been accused of not being responsive to the demands of its military.

---

[5] Farrell, *Weapons Without a Cause*, 72.

[6] For an account of varying levels of civilian involvement by bureaucrats in the weapons-acquisition process, see Quentin Hodgson, *Deciding to Buy: Civil–Military Relations and Major Weapons Programs*, The Letort Papers (Carlisle, PA: US Army War College, 2010); and Farrell, *Weapons Without a Cause*, 140–49.

This is especially applicable to the French Air Force, which lost many bureau-cratic battles to the DGA, leading one analyst to argue that the French "may count themselves fortunate that the Air Force's fears about their preparedness for a full-scale war were never put to the test."[7]

In Britain, on the other hand, the military has been a more dominant actor vis-à-vis its defense industry. Compared to the French, the British obtained weapons "well suited for their designated missions."[8] However, this came at a cost as it hurt the British defense industry. Crucially, unlike the Americans or the French, civilian bureaucrats or technocrats have not played a significant role in shaping weapons procurement. As Marc De Vore notes, "non-technically trained civil servants run British procurement institutions, which has created a disparity of technical expertise that has hindered the ability of British procure-ment officials to contest the technological demands of the armed services or the claims of industry."[9]

Examining a non-democracy like China might seem counterintuitive; how-ever, the similarities between India and China make for a suitable comparison. China faced many of the same, if not worse, predicaments as India in its defense industry in the 1990s. Unlike India, which was, over time, able to access tech-nology from most advanced weapons-producing countries, China faced an arms embargo after the Tiananmen Square massacre in 1989. Moreover, the Chinese defense industry was deeply involved in producing goods for the civilian market and worse, from a professional point of view, the Chinese People's Liberation Army (PLA) had significant commercial interests. Like the Indian Department of Defence Production, in China defense research, development, and production were under the control of a civilian ministry called the Commission for Science, Technology, and Industry for National Defense (COSTIND). Uncannily mirroring India's experience, "the interests between COSTIND and the PLA diverged to such an extent that their relationship had essentially broken down by the late 1990s. The military lacked the effective means to compel the defense economy to follow its instructions."[10] However, in 1998 a decision was made to dissolve the military–business complex and for commercial divestiture by the PLA. More importantly, the PLA emerged "as the dominant actor in guiding defense S&T research and production activities since the late 1990s [which] has been an important factor in raising the performance of the defense economy."[11]

---

[7] Marc De Vore, "Armed Forces, States and Threats: Civil–Military Institutions and Military Power in Modern Democracies" (PhD diss., Massachusetts Institute of Technology, 2009), 398.

[8] De Vore, "Armed Forces, States and Threats," 471.

[9] De Vore, "Armed Forces, States and Threats," 419.

[10] Tai Ming Cheung, "The Chinese Defense Economy's Long March from Imitation to Innovation," *Journal of Strategic Studies* 34, no. 3 (2011): 350.

[11] Cheung, "Chinese Defense Economy's Long March," 350.

Within the few years the Chinese defense industry exhibited an ability for innovation. This remarkable turnaround was primarily due to "far reaching organizational changes to curb the authority and influence of the conservative defense industrial administrative apparatus embodied in the Commission for Science, Technology and Industry for National Defense (COSTIND), a revamping of loss-making defense conglomerates, and a *more influential and direct role* for the PLA in the management of the defense research, development, and acquisition process."[12] In short, changing the pattern of civil–military relations and bringing the PLA within the decision-making process was one of the key policy measures that improved the efficiency, quality, and responsiveness of China's defense industry.

Brazil, like India, also professes the idea of self-reliance in its defense industry. Unlike India, Brazil's civil–military relations have been tumultuous as its military has usurped power and civilian control is a relatively recent phenomenon. It was only in 1999 that it created a ministry of defense, and since then civilians have gradually asserted control.[13] However, the military retains considerable influence with research institutes and the defense industry. Unlike India, a majority of its industry is in the private sector, and a successful implementation of offset clauses facilitates technology absorption. Brazil has been relatively successful in both self-reliance and defense industrialization. Laxman Behera concludes that India has much to imbibe from Brazil's experience, including "a strong policy framework, user participation in defense projects, a strong offset policy and greater trust with the private sector."[14] Once again, like in China, user participation appears to be an important explanatory factor.

Where does this discussion of weapons procurement in different countries lead? First, there is no normative answer to how much autonomy the military should have in choosing its weapons. Countries have adopted different approaches to undertake this task. Second, institutional structures and their bureaucratic powers are extremely crucial to outcomes. As we have seen, empowering the military over the defense industry and favoring industry over the military lead to different outcomes. This point especially calls attention to the patterns of civil–military relations and the manner in which they shape weapons acquisition.

[12] Tai Ming Cheung, "Explaining China's Improving Defense Industrial and Innovation Capabilities," in *Defense Acquisition*, ed. Laxman Behera and Vinay Kaushal, 251 (New Delhi: Institute for Defence Studies and Analysis 2013). Emphasis added.

[13] Lytton Guimares, "Civil–Military Relations and Brazil's Defense Policy: Challenges and Prospects," *Boletim do NEASIA* no. 76, June 7, 2010, 7–13.

[14] Laxman Behera, "LAAD Exhibition: Showcase of Brazilian Self-Reliance," IDSA Comment, April 25, 2013, https://idsa.in/idsacomments/LAADExhibitionShowcaseofBrazilianSelfRelia nce_lkbehera_250413.

The Necessary Dialogue: Civil–Military Relations and Weapons Procurement

Weapons procurement is an inherently difficult enterprise, often marked by failure.[15] Even without a normatively correct answer regarding the type of civil–military relations most conducive to weapons procurement, one can discern certain desired features. First, and perhaps most importantly, there is a need for expertise within different bureaucracies involved in this process. The two agencies most involved are officials in the defense ministry and in the military. It is desirable to have a mix of expertise within these bureaucracies—technical, financial expertise related to project management and on military-focused operational matters. Expertise would enable the civilian bureaucracy in the Ministry of Defense (MoD) to understand and, if necessary, challenge and arbitrate the claims from the military and the defense industry. Some technological expertise among those in the military involved in this process would also be helpful as they can understand the complexity and challenges associated with producing weapon systems. Expertise, by definition, is hard to acquire; and to overcome this, bureaucracies usually cross-post officers—military officers in civilian bureaucracies and civilian officers in military offices. In addition, they may create special provisions for allowing their officials to have extended tenures without harming their careers. Without such measures, weapons acquisition, an inherently challenging activity, is bound to be even more difficult.

Second, the institutional design should create conditions for an "iterative dialogue" among different agencies involved in this process.[16] Institutional design, in this case, refers to the structure of decision-making between three main bureaucratic actors—the military, the defense industry, and civilian officials in the defense ministry. To be sure, on major issues, it is ultimately a political decision; however, these bureaucracies, by virtue of possessing privileged information and access, can significantly shape the outcome. As De Vore points out, "by empowering certain groups rather than others, the institutional structure of procurement decision-making ultimately shapes values and calculations embodied in a weapons acquisition program."[17] For instance, if the defense industry is not responsive to the military, its primary customers, then this will shape its organizational performance and incentives and it may develop sectional interests. However, if the military emerges as the most powerful actor, then, without

---

[15] For a good overview of the difficulties in procurement across countries, see Nick Witney, "Procurement and War," in *The Oxford Handbook of War*, ed. Julian Lindley-French and Yves Boyer, 531–42 (Oxford: Oxford University Press, 2012).

[16] Witney, "Procurement and War," 534.

[17] De Vore, "Armed Forces, States and Threats," 418.

civilian guidance, it may procure weapons ill-suited to the strategic goals of the country. Alternatively, like in the case of Britain, it may not closely collaborate with domestic industry—leading to its decline and growing foreign dependency.

The "iterative dialogue" involving all stakeholders (the military, the defense industry, and officials in the defense and finance ministries) will inevitably be contentious, involving trade-offs between efficiency, economy, effectiveness, and commercial potential.[18] "Civilians and military officers should vigorously debate military requirements," writes former Pentagon official Quentin Hodgson, as "the differences in perspectives are essential to democracy and contribute to better results in the end."[19]

India's Weapons Procurement

As argued in the previous section, expertise and institutional design are conducive to the "iterative" dialogue, which is necessary to balance various agencies involved in weapons procurement. Such dialogue however is not possible under India's current pattern of civil–military relations. This pattern, the absent dialogue argument, consists of three main factors: lack of civilian expertise, an institutional design characterized by strong bureaucratic control, and military autonomy.

A lack of expertise applies to both the civilian and the military officials. Civilian officials dealing with acquisitions in the ministry serve on a rotational basis and lack expertise on weapon systems, the defense industry, the military, and project management. The military also deputes its officers on a rotational basis and lacks expertise pertaining to technical and engineering knowledge and project management. To be sure, there is a slight variance between the services as the navy is better at nurturing design expertise than the other two services. However, largely, a lack of expertise makes it difficult to conceive of a well-informed dialogue between different stakeholders.

The institutional design of various bureaucracies is also not conducive for a healthy, even if contentious, dialogue. India's state-owned defense research and industry functions directly under the defense minister and has not been responsive to its consumers, the armed forces. In assessing competing claims from the defense industry and the military, the defense minister perforce has to rely on

[18] For a good analysis of different trade-offs, see Anessa L. Kimball, "What Canada Could Learn from U.S. Defence Procurement: Issues, Best Practices and Recommendations," *SPP Research Papers*, 8, no. 17 (2015): 6.

[19] Hodgson, *Deciding to Buy*, 87.

the advice of the generalist bureaucracy. Moreover, there is diffused accountability and a lack of oversight, leading to delays and a lack of ownership.

In addition, the military enjoys considerable autonomy in its internal processes to acquire capabilities which, at times, can be problematic. A combination of all these factors leads to an adversarial relations between all stakeholders.

The next section describes the history of the weapons acquisitions programs in India highlighting its efforts to build defense industry while ensuring military preparedness.

History of the Weapons Acquisition Process, 1947–2018

The following analyzes major trends in India's weapons acquisition process under five broad phases: 1947–1962, 1963–1991, 1992–2004, 2005–2014, and 2015–2018. This division, admittedly artificial, coincides with significant milestones in the procurement process. The first period, 1947–1962, is an obvious one since the China war shocked the system and subsequently led to a major armament program. The second period, 1963–1991, examines the growth of India's defense industry and is bookended by the end of the Cold War and by India's most significant economic crisis. The third period, 1992–2004, examines the power of different bureaucratic lobbies and defense reforms after the 1999 Kargil war. Next, I analyze weapons acquisitions from 2005 to 2014. During this time, following the logic of economic liberalization, there was a realization in some quarters that the private sector should participate in defense production, an idea opposed by entrenched bureaucracies. All the same, a number of reform committees were created and measures were taken to enhance the technical expertise within the MoD. Finally, in the period 2014–2018, we examine the reforms introduced by Prime Minister Narendra Modi and the success of the "Make in India" campaign, which was meant to attract foreign companies to invest in India. There have been significant procedural reforms, but there has been no structural change. As a result, there are continuing weaknesses in India's defense industry.

1947–1962: A Structure Takes Shape

India's security policy from 1947 until the 1962 India–China war has, somewhat unfairly, been characterized as the "age of idealism"[20] or one shaped by Nehru's

---

[20] Timothy Hoyt, *Military Industry and Regional Defense Policy: India, Iraq and Israel* (London: Routledge, 2006), 28–33.

"idealistic romanticism."[21] Analyzing defense spending during this period reveals, however, that it was more an era of misplaced priorities in terms of interservices prioritization, threat assessments, and an ill-timed emphasis on defense production. In 1947, defense expenditure as a percentage of total government expenditure was approximately 46%.[22] Perceiving this to be an imperial legacy, Mahatma Gandhi and some of his followers wanted to drastically curtail defense expenditure and favored the idea of a demilitarized nation, like postwar Japan. Jawaharlal Nehru, however, like he did with many of Gandhi's visions, put on hold such radical ideas.[23] Instead, along with his home minister, Vallabhbhai Patel, Nehru understood the utility of the armed forces in protecting and consolidating the still-fragile union. This became a mainstream view when the military proved its utility in suppressing the communist insurrection in Telangana and in securing Junagarh, Kashmir, Hyderabad, and, much later, Goa.[24] A study of the defense acquisitions during this period reveals the following trends.

First, the salience of the "guns versus butter" argument meant that most political leaders viewed defense expenditure as wasteful and unproductive. In light of human development indices of that time, the main priority was to provide the basic requirements to millions of impoverished citizens. Defense spending was given a lower priority as it was perceived to be at the cost of development and was seen to be a set of "alternate choices in a zero-sum equation."[25] This notion was helped by a perception that there was no immediate threat to India's security.[26] The parliamentary debates of the time do not indicate any political party advocating for an increase in military spending.[27] This feeling was prevalent even among bureaucrats in the MoD as former defense secretary H. M. Patel

[21] Jaswant Singh, *Defending India* (New Delhi: Macmillan India, 1999), 34.

[22] See Appendix III in Lorne Kavic, *India's Quest for Security: Defence Policies, 1947–1965* (Berkeley: University of California Press, 1967), 226.

[23] For an exposition of Nehru's views on this idea, see his note to Shriman Narayan, "Need for Non-violent Defense Techniques," May 4, 1957, in *Selected Works of Jawaharlal Nehru*, 2nd Series, ed. Mushirul Hasan, 430–36 (New Delhi: Oxford University Press, 2008).

[24] Srinath Raghavan, *War and Peace in Modern India: A Strategic History of the Nehru Years* (New Delhi: Permanent Black, 2010).

[25] Jasjit Singh, *India's Defence Spending: Assessing Future Needs* (New Delhi: Knowledge World, 2000), 3. For more on the defense versus development debate, see Raju Thomas, *The Defence of India: A Budgetary Perspective of Strategy and Policy* (New Delhi: Macmillan, 1978), 125–35.

[26] This assessment gradually changed as Pakistan acquired sophisticated arms and equipment from the United States; see Stephen Cohen, "US Weapons and South Asia: A Policy Analysis," *Pacific Affairs* 49, no. 1 (1976): 52.

[27] While some parties, most prominently the Swatantra and the Praja Socialist Party, argued for a hawkish posture vis-à-vis China and Pakistan, they did not favor an increase in the defense expenditure; see Thomas, *Defence of India*, 48–53.

admitted, "we [in the MoD] fought against increasing the defence budget."[28] Due to these factors "the defence budget, though it increased in absolute terms, fell from over 30% of the central budget in 1950–51 to 15% in 1961–62."[29] This sentiment was strengthened by a belief that military security was "a function of rapid and effective development."[30] In later years, K. Subrahmanyam, wrote a number of articles arguing against the consequences of assuming such a simplistic trade-off between defense and development.[31] However, soon after the 1971 Bangladesh war the "guns versus butter" argument staged a comeback, at least in academic circles, which echoes till today.[32] Crucially, due to the defeat in the 1962 China war, few politicians publicly made this argument.

Second, weapons and equipment were procured primarily to deal with the threat from Pakistan, and little attention was paid to the possibility of a border war with China. By joining anticommunist pacts, Pakistan obtained significant US military aid including advanced combat aircraft, modern tanks, and other front-line stores.[33] This alarmed Indian policymakers, and in response they spent precious foreign exchange reserves to match the Pakistani buildup. [34] However, the types of weapons procured indicated that interservices prioritization, crucial to ensuring that the military's strategy is conjoined with foreign policy, was not given much thought. Therefore, resources were allocated more toward building up the air force and the navy than the army. In 1947 the Indian Air Force (IAF) had around seven squadrons and "by end-1962, the actual strength of the IAF

---

[28] H. M. Patel, "Basic Factors in Indian Defense," in *Defence of India* (New Delhi: Press Institute of India, Vikas Publications, 1969), 61.

[29] P. V. R. Rao, *Defence Without Drift* (Bombay: Popular Prakashan, 1970), 5; also see Kavic, *India's Quest for Security*, 221.

[30] Lloyd Rudolph and Suzanne Rudolph, "Generals and Politicians in India," *Pacific Affairs* 37, no. 1 (1964): 10.

[31] K. Subrahmanyam, "Five Years of Indian Defence Effort in Perspective," *International Studies Quarterly* 13, no. 2 (1969): 174–81; "Indian Defence Expenditure in Global Perspective," *Economic and Political Weekly* 8, no. 26 (June 30, 1973): 1155–58; and *Defense and Development* (Calcutta: Minerva, 1973).

[32] This argument is periodically resurrected in academic debates in India; see Ved Gandhi, "India's Self-Inflicted Defence Burden," *Economic and Political Weekly* 9, no. 35 (August 31, 1974): 1485–94; P. Terhal, "Guns or Grain: Macro-Economic Costs of Indian Defence, 1960–70," *Economic and Political Weekly* 16, no. 49 (December 5, 1981): 1995–2004; Jean Dreze, "Militarism, Development and Democracy," *Economic and Political Weekly* 35, no. 14 (April 1–7, 2000): 1171–83; and Pavan Nair, "An Evaluation of India's Defense Expenditure," *Economic and Political Weekly* 44, no. 51 (December 19–25, 2009) 40–46.

[33] Sultana Afroz, "The Cold War and United States Military Aid to Pakistan 1947–1960: A Reassessment," *South Asia: Journal of South Asian Studies* 17, no. 1 (2007): 57–72.

[34] Thomas, *Defence of India*, 37–39; and Chris Smith, *India's Ad Hoc Arsenal: Direction or Drift in Defense Policy* (New York: Oxford University Press, 1994), 56–59.

was a total of 36 squadrons,"[35] which represented "an astounding institutional victory for the IAF throughout the 1950s."[36] Similarly, the navy's share of the defense budget, which was 2% at the time of independence, increased to almost 10% by 1962 despite "the absence of a major regional naval adversary."[37]

During the same period, army modernization plans were largely sidelined.[38] The Indian Army, which had seven divisions in 1950, had added only two more by 1962—including an armored division meant for the western front.[39] Army acquisition consisted mainly of tanks, towed guns, and other weapons systems which could be used primarily in the plains. Nehru himself admitted that "requests from the Army authorities when referred to the Defense Committee of the Cabinet were 'possibly' agreed to by the Committee to the extent of one-tenth of what was asked."[40] Building up the air force and the navy was understandable as they had limited capital assets; however, this was done with little thought to the possibility of a border conflict with China. As a result, in the years preceding the 1962 war, the military was not prepared—doctrinally, in terms of weapons and equipment, and logistically (especially road networks and transport fleet) to implement the type of "forward policy" envisaged by its political leaders.[41]

Third, Krishna Menon, defense minister from 1957 to 1962, played a crucial role in shaping the overall weapons procurement process during this period. To his credit, Krishna Menon took a keen interest and is hailed for laying the foundation for India's defense industry.[42] He oversaw a growth in defense production and was instrumental in creating the Department of Research and Development (later renamed the Defense Research and Development

---

[35] Jasjit Singh, *Defence from the Skies: Indian Air Force Through 75 Years* (New Delhi: Knowledge World Publishers 2007), 67. These thirty-six squadrons included auxiliary and transport squadrons. According to one account, Nehru approved the expansion plans of the air force after the war scare with Pakistan in 1951; see P. C. Lal, *My Years with the Air Force* (New Delhi: Lancer International, 1986), 72.

[36] Smith, *India's Ad Hoc Arsenal*, 58.

[37] Hoyt, *Military Industry and Regional Defense Policy*, 30, 203n85.

[38] Kavic, *India's Quest for Security*, 89n13, n14; Singh, *India's Defence Spending*, 63; and Smith, *India's Ad Hoc Arsenal*, 55.

[39] Only one division was raised in the three years preceding the 1962 China war; see Kavic, *India's Quest for Security*, 89, 242.

[40] Cited in Kavic, *India's Quest for Security*, 89.

[41] For more on this policy, see Rajesh Rajagopalan, "Re-examining the 'Forward Policy,'" in *Security Beyond Survival: Essays for K. Subrahmanyam*, ed. P. R. Kumaraswamy, 103–26 (New Delhi: Sage Publications, 2004). For the complacency within the government regarding the China threat, see Kavic, *India's Quest for Security*, 89.

[42] For Krishna Menon's role in the development of defense production, see Lal, *My Years with the Air Force*, 84; also see Kavic, *India's Quest for Security*, 126–40.

Organisation [DRDO]). The emphasis on indigenous defense production led to the establishment of a number of factories. However, this was achieved with some unintended consequences. Due to its considerable time lag, the emphasis on indigenization and import substitution created weakness within the military at an operationally critical time. Moreover, his style of functioning—a combination of outright rejection and an inability to make decisions—delayed or prevented the acquisition of weapons systems including the standard infantry weapon, twenty-five-pound field artillery, mountain howitzers, mortars, and helicopters.[43] As a result, immediate requirements for military modernization could not be met in time for the 1962 war.[44] According to some assessments, differences in equipment were a crucial factor in the outcome of tactical battles.[45] This was even highlighted in the official history of the 1962 conflict, which argued that, "for establishing indigenous weapons manufacture, money had to be found by cutting arms imports. The armed forces would be short of equipment and stores for several years till the new arms factories started producing.... A period of transition was inevitable, during which the fighting machine would not be fully efficient and would be vulnerable. Therein seems to lie the *basic cause* of the debacle of 1962."[46]

Fourth, during this period there were tensions between civilians and the military over ownership of defense research and production facilities. This contest—never satisfactorily resolved—laid the foundation for subsequent problems between the military, the scientific community, and the defense industry. In 1948, ordnance factories (OFs) were transferred from the control of the army, where they functioned under the master general of ordnance, to the MoD. The army was unhappy as a "major limb" of about "60,000 factory personnel" was taken away.[47] After this, there was a routine "battle royal" between the army and the OFs as the latter "failed to meet targets of production."[48] It did

---

[43] For more on problems with replacing the standard issue infantry rifle, see S. L. Menezes, *Fidelity and Honour: The Indian Army* (New Delhi: Oxford University Press, 2001), 472–74; for problems in procuring other weapons, see Kavic, *India's Quest for Security*, 91–92 and Lal, *My Years with the Air Force*, 108–9.

[44] The problem arising from Krishna Menon's misplaced emphasis was acknowledged by the then chief of general staff; see "Interview with Lt Gen BM Kaul, December 25, 1964," Stephen Cohen Papers, 3.

[45] For more on the superiority of Chinese small-arms, mortar, and communication equipment, see Kavic, *India's Quest for Security*, 184. For a contrary view, see Pranab Dhal Samanta, "Poor Military Leadership, not Equipment, Led to 1962 Debacle: Report under Wraps," *Indian Express*, October 14, 2012.

[46] S. N. Prasad, P. B. Sinha, and A. A. Athale, *History of the Conflict with China 1962* (New Delhi: History Division, Ministry of Defence, 1992), xxiii, emphasis added.

[47] B. D. Kapur, *Building a Defence Technology Base* (New Delhi: Lancer International, 1990), 6.

[48] Kapur, *Building a Defence Technology Base*, 6.

not help that Krishna Menon encouraged a policy of using the defense industry for producing civilian goods. This was justified on the grounds of fully utilizing excess or idle industrial capacity "during slack periods of demand."[49] After the 1962 war, this move was criticized as many complained that coffee percolators and consumer items were being produced while the needs of the military were being ignored.[50] However, after a few years, this criticism abated; and later, in the 1980s and 1990s, civilian production in the state-owned defense industry picked up in a big way.[51] Eventually, this diversified the goods produced in these industries and made them less dependent on, and responsive to, the needs of the military.

Another point of civil–military contention emerged with the creation of the DRDO in 1958. The military was strongly opposed to establishing a research entity separated from production, but its objections were overruled by Krishna Menon.[52] This created the cadre of the defense scientists divorced from the production of weapons and equipment. Over time defense research became an additional bureaucracy, which at times made extravagant claims and justified budgets under the buzzwords "self-sufficiency" and "self-reliance." As a result of all these measures, the institutional design of the different bureaucracies made both the scientific community and the state-owned defense industry not as responsive to the demands of the user community, the armed forces.

Finally, the government implemented policies that discouraged private sector participation. In a move that was to have far-reaching consequences, the industry policy resolution of 1948 (revised in 1956) designated the defense industry as a public sector as it was felt that private industry due to its profit motive would be unable to provide for adequate defense capability.[53] Control over the entire defense industry was exercised under the Industries Act of 1951, which made licensing compulsory and encouraged the growth of defense production in the public sector. This essentially crippled the growth of the private defense industry and created a monopoly for the public sector. Predictably, in the absence of any competition, this arrangement over time led to major inefficiencies.[54]

---

[49] Deba Mohanty, "Changing Times?" (BICC Paper 36, Bonn International Center for Conversion, Bonn, Germany, 2004), 32.

[50] Pratap Narain, *Indian Arms Bazaar* (New Delhi: Shipra Publications, 1994), 67–68.

[51] Mohanty, "Changing Times?" 32–34.

[52] Kapur, *Building a Defence Technology Base*, 30–36.

[53] Amit Gupta, "The Indian Arms Industry: A Lumbering Giant?" *Asian Survey* 30, no. 9 (1990): 847.

[54] For problems arising from monopoly, see Anuradha Prasad, "Indian Ordnance Factories: An Agenda for Change," 283; and Ravinder Pal Singh, "Capacity Building for Defense Technology Acquisition and Oversight," 393–98; both in Laxman Behera and Vinay Kaushal, eds., *Defense Acquisitions*.

How should this period be assessed from the perspective of weapons procurement and civil–military relations? There was a general lack of experience and expertise among almost all stakeholders—politicians, civilian bureaucrats, and military officers. Krishna Menon played an important role in creating and establishing defense scientific research and the domestic defense industry. However, the institutional design of the bureaucracies made both of them not as responsive to the military—a trend which became more prominent over time. Gradually, civilians—whether in the MoD, the DRDO, or the defense industry—played an increasingly important role, and the military became marginalized.

1963–1991: Licensed Production and the Self-Reliance Mantra

There are five major trends that can be observed while analyzing weapons acquisition from 1963 to 1991. First, after the 1962 debacle, India's immediate focus was on increasing its defense budget and the size of its armed forces, both of which it was able to do reasonably successfully. To illustrate, in the decade before 1962 the defense budget averaged at around 2% of the national product, but in the decade after it nearly doubled to 3.6%.[55] This era has therefore been rightly called the "armament phase" of Indian security policy and was shaped largely by the five-year defense plan sanctioned in 1964.[56] In simple numerical terms, the size of the army increased from 500,000 to 830,000 between 1962 and 1973, and the combined size of the air force and navy increased from 45,000 to 130,000.[57]

Second, changes in the international situation, especially the Sino–Soviet split, the Pakistani-arranged US–China rapprochement, and the resultant Indo–Soviet strategic embrace, influenced India's procurement policies. The main result of these shifting "alliances" was an increasing reliance on weapons supplied by the Soviet Union. The Soviets not only agreed to licensed production but also offered easy credit terms and rupee payment—an important consideration for a country short on foreign exchange. Later, in an effort to diversify sources of supply, India turned to European countries, primarily the United Kingdom, France, and West Germany.[58] This partial shift coincided with the Janata

[55] Raju Thomas, "The Armed Services and the Indian Defense Budget," *Asian Survey* 20, no. 3 (1980): 281–82.

[56] Ministry of Defence, *Annual Report 1964–65* (New Delhi: Government of India Press, 1965), 1–2; for details of this rearmament, see Smith, *India's Ad Hoc Arsenal*, 80–82.

[57] Thomas, *Defence of India*, 152; also see Amit Gupta, "Determining India's Force Structure and Military Doctrine: I Want My MiG," *Asian Survey* 35, no. 5 (1995): 444–48.

[58] Inder Malhotra, "Planning for Defence: Changed Strategic Environment," *Times of India*, January 25, 1979.

government coming to power in 1977, which, critical of an overly pro-Soviet stance, announced a policy of "genuine non-alignment."[59] When Indira Gandhi returned to power in 1980, the old arrangement of buying heavily, though not exclusively, from the Soviet Union resumed. In sum, during this period changes in the international situation and, to an extent, domestic politics influenced India's weapons procurement.

Third, an emphasis on domestic and licensed production helped meet most of the targets of the armament plan, but despite rhetoric favoring self-reliance and self-sufficiency, indigenous weapons development programs failed to deliver. The idea of domestic defense production, initially championed by Krishna Menon, gained prominence in India for three main reasons—to guard against reliance on any one foreign supplier, to encourage technological and industrial development, and to conserve foreign exchange.[60] Accordingly, within the MoD, the Department of Defence Production was set up in 1962, followed by the Department of Defence Supply in 1965. This armament program was successful in equipping the army with relatively low-technology infantry weapons, artillery guns, ammunition, vehicles, instruments, and other defense stores.

Most of the relatively high-technology items, however, were produced under licensed production agreements signed with numerous foreign governments and firms. Accordingly, factories were established all over the country for licensed production of Vijayanta and T-72 Ajeya tanks; Gnat, MiG, and Jaguar fighters for the air force; Aloutte-III helicopters; trucks; etc.[61] These contracts were signed under the assumption that there would be technology transfer, but licensed production primarily meant assembling knocked down and semi–knocked down kits with little, if any, technological assimilation. In part, this was because of the exclusion of the private sector as, without any competition, public sector units did not feel the need to innovate or assimilate technology. According to Jaideep Prabhu, "Indian policy was always that it would try to buy equipment along with the full transfer of technology, barring which it would negotiate to manufacture in-country on license . . . [but] the structure of the economy prevented the private sector from receiving the benefits from foreign know-how and government research organizations were unable to learn from

[59] Raju Thomas, "Indian Defense Policy: Continuity and Change under the Janata Government," *Pacific Affairs* 53, no. 2 (1980): 234–38.

[60] Ministry of Defence, *Annual Report 1964–65*, 50–51. For more on reasons favoring indigenous weapons production in India, see David Kinsella and Jugdep S. Chima, "Symbols of Statehood: Military Industrialization and Public Discourse in India," *Review of International Studies* 27, no. 3 (2001): 355–58.

[61] For a good overview of defense production during this period, see Thomas, *Defence of India*, 158–66 for army programs, 184–97 for air force programs, and 210–17 for naval programs.

their imports."[62] Indigenous weapons development programs were, therefore, unable to meet their objectives; and, according to one study, "by the late 1970s, the Indian arms industry was in doldrums as its indigenous projects had not come to fruition."[63]

The fourth trend in defense procurement during this period was the emergence of bureaucratic actors and pressures from multiple interest groups representing the defense scientific and industrial lobby. This consisted of three main organizations—the DRDO, defense public sector units (DPSUs), and OFs. The DRDO was created mainly as a research enterprise to help equip the military and provide scientific solutions to the problems faced by them. DPSUs are responsible for the majority of high-tech defense production, including aircraft, ships, missiles, and submarines. Some of them were created when the government took control of privately owned defense production companies. OFs, however, are engaged in assembling items like tanks (T-72 and T-90) and producing low-technology defense items including ammunition, small arms, and other stores.

After 1962, there was an exponential growth in all three. At the time of its formation in 1958, the DRDO consisted of ten institutions/laboratories, but by 1969 it had "expanded into thirty three R&D laboratories and two training institutions."[64] Similarly, five of the nine existing DPSUs and eighteen of the current forty-one OFs were either acquired or established after 1962.[65] According to a former defense secretary, all of these constituted "the *single largest* industrial organization in the country but outwardly this fact was not known because of the defense angle."[66] These organizations not only employed a large workforce but also created bureaucratic pressures in favor of domestic production.

These three institutions were run by the Departments of Defense Production and Defense Supply. Both were manned at senior levels by generalist bureaucrats on a rotational basis, who did not necessarily have expertise. As a result, they had limited capacity to develop the defense industrial base. Moreover, part of

[62] Jaideep A. Prabhu, "Indian Scientists in Defence and Foreign Policy," in *The Oxford Handbook of Indian Foreign Policy*, ed. David M. Malone, C. Raja Mohan, and Srinath Raghavan, 318 (London: Oxford University Press, 2015).

[63] Gupta, "Determining India's Force Structure and Military Doctrine," 449; also see Smith, *India's Ad Hoc Arsenal*, 147.

[64] Ramadas P. Shenoy, *Defence Research and Development Organisation: 1958–1982* (New Delhi: Desidoc, 2006), 66.

[65] There were only three DPSUs before 1962: Bharat Electronics Limited, Mazagon Docks Limited, and Garden Reach Shipbuilders.

[66] Oral History Transcripts, Govind Narain, no. 631 (vol. 2), 399, emphasis added, Nehru Memorial Museum and Library (NMML), New Delhi. Mr. Narain was also a former secretary of defense production.

their job was to keep these numerous public sector companies running—and the workforce employed. Due to this institutional design, the defense industry was more responsive to the ministry than to the military. In turn, as the ministry lacked expertise, on both technical and military subjects (there were no service officers in the ministry), it was unable to judge between good and bad advice—whether from the industry or the military.

Finally, it was during this period that allegations of corruption surfaced, linking political parties with high-value weapons sales from foreign companies.[67] The first murmur about this surfaced due to the conduct of L. N. Mishra, who was the minister of state for defense production under Indira Gandhi. Described as a "fund raiser for the Congress party," he was "not quite objective and rational" in his negotiations and had to be counseled by his bureaucrats.[68] But the first major arms deal which attracted allegations of widespread political corruption was the acquisition of the deep penetration strike aircraft the Jaguar in 1979.[69] Although difficult to prove, over time a trend began whereby political parties filled their coffers by brokering, and claiming to influence, defense sales. According to former chief of army staff, General K. Sundarji, "generally many governments have been getting a percentage of many of these large deals. . . . It's been going on for some time. The fact is that irrespective of which weapon is chosen, if the intention is to cream a certain amount off the top for party purposes or whatever, it could be creamed off whichever weapon is chosen."[70] This trend led to the Bofors arms scandal in 1987, with allegations that commissions were paid, including to top political leaders, while purchasing an artillery gun from Sweden. This story dominated media headlines for a few years and contributed to the electoral defeat of the Congress Party in 1989. Despite that, there were, and continue to be, periodic allegations of corruption in defense sales.

Two main consequences emerged from the allegations of corruption. First, there was marked reluctance on the part of officials to make decisions on weapons procurement, leading to considerable delays.[71] As allegations of corruption in defense sales became a political weapon—opportunistically used by all parties—there was a slowdown in decision-making. Unfortunately, the armed forces have had to bear the brunt of this slowdown, leading to a "devaluation of

[67] The "jeep scandal" had rocked the political scene in 1948; however, those allegations, dropped in 1955, were made only against an individual (Krishna Menon) and not a political party.

[68] Oral History Transcripts, Govind Narain, 418–20.

[69] Interview with two former Ministry of Defence officials who were still serving at that time, New Delhi, 2008; see Smith, *India's Ad Hoc Arsenal*, 101; Thomas, "Indian Defense Policy," 241–42.

[70] Ramindra Singh, "Interview with General K. Sundarji," *India Today*, September 15, 1989, 29.

[71] For a good analysis of the influence of corruption allegations on arms procurement, see Rahul Bedi, "India's Bizarre Arms Procurement Policy," *Economic and Political Weekly* 35, no. 42 (October 14–20, 2000): 3716–19.

India's military deterrent."[72] Second, as a result of the Bofors scandal, the MoD promulgated the first defense procurement procedure in 1992.[73] As discussed later, this, perhaps inadvertently, strengthened the bureaucratic power of the DRDO.

In sum, the emphasis on self-sufficiency, self-reliance, and the resultant institutional design of weapons acquisition marginalized the military.[74] The inability of the domestic defense industry to meet the requirement of the armed forces adversely shaped military effectiveness. In an analysis of indigenous weapons programs, Raju Thomas concludes that the "goal of self-sufficiency had generally been at the cost of *efficiency* both in terms of delivery time with the accompanying risk of obsolescence, and in terms of the quality of the weapon demanded by the services."[75] The military would express its frustration with cost and time overruns, substandard equipment, and unfulfilled and extravagant claims; but civilians would brush aside their protests under the mantra of self-reliance and self-sufficiency. The growth of India's defense industry were entirely in keeping with its state-led approach to industrialization wherein the public sector gained the "commanding heights" of the economy. However, as with the rest of the economy, this soon changed; and a gradual paradigm shift was hastened by the 1991 economic crisis and, later, the 1999 Kargil war.

1992–2004: A (Gradual) Paradigm Shift

The 1991 balance of payments crisis in India came as a shock and led to a gradual economic liberalization. The military had to bear the brunt of the crisis as the defense budget was drastically curtailed. There were three notable trends in weapons acquisitions during this period.

First was the emergence of the DRDO as a major bureaucratic player. The 1992 Defense Procurement Procedure formalized the role of the DRDO in the acquisitions process, by giving it the first option of refusal. Hereafter, the DRDO could deliberate upon the military's requirements and, regardless of its capability, could claim the wherewithal to meet it. The downside of this arrangement became evident with the case of the weapons-locating radar. The military had expressed an interest in acquiring these radars by importing them, but

[72] Ajai Shukla, "The Cost of Antony's Halo," *Business Standard*, February 23, 2010.

[73] Standing Committee on Defense, *Sixth Report: Procurement Policy and Procedure* (New Delhi: Lok Sabha Secretariat, 2005), 10.

[74] For a good analysis of self-sufficiency and self-reliance, see Manjeet S. Pardesi and Ron Matthews, "India's Tortuous Road to Defence—Industrial Self Reliance," *Defence & Security Analysis* 23, no. 4 (2007): 419–38.

[75] Thomas, "Indian Defense Policy," 240 (emphasis added).

the DRDO opposed this and claimed that it had the capability to make them. However, the DRDO was unable to do so when the 1999 Kargil war broke out. The chief of army staff during that war, General V. P. Malik, would later argue that "if the DRDO had not come in the way we would have got them [weapons-locating radars] before the Kargil war and that would have definitely reduced our casualties."[76]

The DRDO also benefited from its ability to directly lobby political authorities, bypassing the armed forces. To be sure, this trend had started earlier as during the 1980s the DRDO expanded its defense labs by over 33% and "R&D funding for advanced weapons increased by 800%."[77] This was on account of the Integrated Guided Missile Development Program, which was launched in July 1983 to produce a variety of missiles. The military would later complain about the glacial pace of DRDO projects and argued that it wanted "a more intense involvement in the Acquisition process, as this would help in cutting short delays."[78] Despite such appeals, the DRDO maintained its institutional autonomy. In addition, its involvement in the nuclear weapons and missile delivery program gave it the ability to directly interact with political leaders and protect their institutional interests. This was facilitated by a bureaucratic norm wherein the chairman of the DRDO was also co-appointed as the scientific adviser to the defense minister. All of these measures led to a situation whereby the DRDO was presiding "over an overly distorted system, with serious implications for the armed forces' growing requirement for high-quality conventional weapons."[79]

The DRDO also proved to be an astute bureaucratic actor, and in 1992, recognizing the political urgency to save precious foreign exchange, it formulated a plan to increase the "self-reliance index"—a measure of percentage share of domestic procurement to total procurement—from 30% to 70%. The self-reliance index is difficult to calculate, but, according to one well-considered study, in 2011 it "stood at 38.5%."[80] According to its critics, and the DRDO has many, this plan was another instance of the organization overpromising and then not delivering.[81] Ironically, within a decade and a half, the government would be

[76] "Kargil Toll Could Have Been Lower but for DRDO, Says Former Army Chief Malik," *Hindustan Times*, September 7, 2009, https://www.hindustantimes.com/india/kargil-toll-could-have-been-lower-but-for-drdo-says-former-army-chief-malik/story-INQ9SH5MYck3sbTRmsAGZI.html.

[77] Hoyt, *Military Industry and Regional Defense Policy*, 42, also see 27.

[78] *Kelkar Committee Report*, 34, also see 42.

[79] Bibhu Prasad Routray, "Armed Forces versus Technologists in India's Military Modernisation," *Defence Studies* 13, no. 1 (2013): 33.

[80] Laxman Kumar Behera, *Indian Defence Industry: Issues of Self-Reliance*, IDSA Monograph Series (New Delhi: Institute for Defence Studies and Analyses, July 21, 2013), 51; also see Standing Committee on Defence, *Fourteenth Report: Defence Research and Development Organization* (New Delhi: Lok Sabha Secretariat, March 2007), 4–5.

[81] Manoj Joshi, "Way off Target," *India Today*, November 24, 1997.

taking steps to dismantle its bureaucratic empire, focus on core technologies, and make it more responsive to its users—the services.[82]

Second, during this time steps were taken to encourage private sector participation in the defense industry. Using the logic of economic liberalization, the private sector, represented by the Confederation of Indian Industries, lobbied the government; and six task forces were set up "to assess and consider the involvement of the private sector in defense production."[83] As a result of these efforts, in May 2001 the government allowed, subject to licensing, private sector participation up to 100% in the defense sector and foreign direct investment (FDI) up to 26%. These measures were an acknowledgment of the growing success of the private sector in the Indian economy and of the need of foreign capital to help it grow further. Both of these were revolutionary ideas, and in challenging the monopoly of state-owned enterprises, they were viewed with some trepidation. As described later, once the Congress Party came back to power in 2004, there was a marked reluctance to encourage private sector participation in the defense industry. And, belying expectations of policymakers, FDI in defense was simply not forthcoming—between 2000 and 2016, it attracted only US$5 million, representing 0.002% of total FDI inflow in the country.[84]

Third, procurement structures underwent a sea change after the 1999 Kargil war. As described in Chapter 2, there were comprehensive defense reforms based on the reports of the Kargil Review Committee and the Arun Singh Task Force. The latter noted that defense acquisitions, "suffers from a lack of integrated planning; weaknesses in linkages between Plan and Budget; cumbersome administrative, technical and financial evaluation procedures; and an absence of dedicated professionally equipped procurement structure within the MOD."[85] In addition, it made what amounted to a devastating indictment: "existing structure for procurement has led to sub-optimal utilisation of funds, long delays in acquisition and has not been conducive to the modernisation of the Services."[86] The report clearly identified problems arising from both institutional design and lack of expertise within the MoD.

---

[82] In 2009, recommendations along these lines were made by a committee established to streamline the functioning of the DRDO; see Manu Pubby, "DRDO Revamp: Antony Appoints High-Level Panel," *Indian Express*, June 12, 2009.

[83] Arindam Bhattacharya and Navneet Vasishth, *Creating a Vibrant Defence Manufacturing Sector* (Boston: Boston Consulting Group, March 2012), 21.

[84] Laxman Kumar Behera, "Making FDI Count in Defence," IDSA Comment, June 22, 2016, https://idsa.in/idsacomments/making_fdi_count_in_defence_lkbehera_220616.

[85] Group of Ministers, *Reforming the National Security System: Report of the Group of Ministers on National Security* (New Delhi: Government of India, 2001), 98.

[86] Group of Ministers, *Reforming the National Security System*, 105.

As a result of its recommendations, a number of new organizations were established to streamline defense procurement.[87] Among other changes, a separate acquisitions wing was established within the MoD, headed by a director general. From the perspective of civil–military relations, the most important step was the creation of three offices in the Acquisitions Wing, called technical managers (of land, air, and naval systems). These offices, comprising senior military officers from each of the services, were meant to advise the ministry on the technical aspects of the acquisitions process. This was the ministry's way of addressing its lack of expertise and was a positive development as, for the first time, service officers were working side by side with civilian bureaucrats. This was precisely the sort of change that many in the military were arguing for.

In addition, other steps were taken based on the recommendations of the reform committees. Limited financial powers were delegated to the military, speeding up the acquisition process. Starting in 2002, the Defense Procurement Procedure for capital and revenue items was released, and in subsequent years it was frequently revised and amended. Reacting to criticism, there has been an unprecedented level of user interface and dialogue between the DRDO/ DPSUs and the services. One former MoD official, closely involved with the 2001 changes, argued that there has been a sea change in the functioning of the ministry with "the blurring of lines between civilian and the military, making it a more collegial system than it had ever been in the past."[88]

This period, therefore, marked the beginning of a twofold paradigm shift. First was the idea of private sector participation in the defense industrial base. Second was an acceptance that civilians needed some expert advice in the acquisitions process. However, as argued in the next section, the entry of the private sector was opposed by the Congress Party, which led a coalition government from 2004 to 2014, and the issue of expertise did not go far enough.

2005–2014: Smoke and Mirrors

In 2004, defying the prediction of pollsters, the Congress Party came back to power as part of a coalition government. Five years later, it was re-elected to office and remained in power until 2014. A. K. Antony was the defense minister for almost eight out of those ten years and, as an important member of the party, had an enormous influence in shaping defense policies. As we shall see, his

---

[87] Standing Committee on Defense, *Sixth Report*, 12–13.

[88] Interview with Dhirendra Singh, who served as a joint secretary and additional secretary, Department of Defense Production in the Ministry of Defense, August 26, 2010, New Delhi.

legacy was largely uncontested—most analysts considered it a disaster. From the perspective of weapons acquisitions, this period had three major trends.

First, the Congress government discouraged entry of the private sector or FDI in India's defense industry. In 2004, its predecessor, the Bharatiya Janata Party coalition government had set up a committee to review the defense procurement procedure to integrate users, the MoD, and domestic industry. The report of this committee, which is more widely known as the Kelkar Committee, focused mainly on developing the private sector defense industry. However, Antony, who took over as the defense minister in 2006, was not politically inclined toward private sector participation.In addition, the government resisted widespread calls for increasing the FDI limit above 26%.

Simply put, the government did not want the private defense industry to challenge state-owned public enterprises. Therefore, despite government assurances to the contrary, the stranglehold of the DRDO/DPSU on defense production continued. As in the past, these measures were justified under politically acceptable terms like self-reliance, indigenization, and, instead of import substitution, offsets.[89] Within five years of the Kelkar Committee report, in 2010 India emerged as the world's largest weapons importer. In a scathing assessment, the journalist Sandeep Unnithan would argue that "Antony's socialist leanings, his refusal to reform the defence Public Sector Undertakings (DPSU) and suspicion of the private sector, may be the root cause of the failure of indigenous defence capability to meet India's requirements."[90]

Second, corruption scandals, real and alleged, hobbled the acquisition process. Haunted by the Bofors scandal, the Congress Party feared corruption allegations in arms deals and appointed Antony, who was widely respected for his probity and integrity. But Antony's "obsessive quest for unblemished weapons procurement"[91] delayed many critical acquisition programs. To fend off potential corruption allegations, there was an institutional preference for most big-ticket items to be purchased through government-to-government sales.

Third, during this time a number of reform committees were set up to examine defense procurement, expenditure, and indigenous weapons development. These committees submitted reports with wide-ranging recommendations; however, for the most part, their implementation has been ineffectual—hindered by

[89] See comments made by A. K. Antony, "Keynote Address at National Seminar on Defence Acquisition," October 27, 2009, http://www.idsa.in/node/3408.

[90] Sandeep Unnithan "The Worst Defence Minister Ever," *India Today*, March 7, 2014, https://www.indiatoday.in/magazine/special-report/story/20140317-ak-antony-defence-minister-scams-upa-ii-800422-2014-03-07.

[91] Ajai Shukla, "The Cost of Antony's Halo," *Business Standard*, February 23, 2010.

bureaucratic turf wars and a lack of political will. Table 3.1 describes some of the major acquisition reform committees.

To its credit, under the Congress government, progress was achieved in some sectors especially in building up bureaucratic institutions. For instance, the office of the director general (acquisitions) and, within it, those of the technical managers came into prominence. The latter grew in number, and military officers were brought into the ministry to provide technical input on proposals emanating from the services. In addition, the office of the Integrated Defense Staff (IDS) was increasingly utilized by the MoD "to provide entire secretarial and domain expertise"[92] to vet proposals sent by the services. To an extent, these measures helped address the lack of expertise within the ministry. This was a sea change from how the ministry used to operate earlier and brought about a level of professionalism in the interaction between the military, the ministry, and the defense industry.

Despite these improvements, however, in 2012 a letter written to Prime Minister Manmohan Singh by the chief of army staff, General V. K. Singh, was leaked to the press. This letter presented a "grim picture of the operational capabilities" of the army, with depleting ammunition stocks and obsolete and inadequate weaponry, and indirectly blamed "the long-winded arms procurement process and the recalcitrant bureaucracy."[93] While generating a political firestorm, the letter revealed a larger truth—the military's unhappiness with the civilian bureaucracy. Despite all the committee reports, the MoD under A. K. Antony was widely perceived to be suffering from a "policy-paralysis" which slowed down procurement and resisted the growth of the private sector or FDI.[94] Arguably then, in light of Antony's well-known reluctance to change, setting up all these committees was useful to deflect attention and criticism. Unsurprisingly, members of these committees would later complain about the lack of implementation.[95] The stage was set for a decisive break from the past— and the next government came into power promising just that.

---

[92] Shekhar Sinha, "Role of Integrated Defence Staff in Defence Procurement," *Bharat Shakti*, December 30, 2015, http://bharatshakti.in/role-of-integrated-defence-staff-in-defence-procurement/.

[93] "Army Chief's Letter to PM: General V K Singh Exposes Chinks in Armour," *Times of India*, March 29, 2012, https://timesofindia.indiatimes.com/india/Army-chiefs-letter-to-PM-General-V-K-Singh-exposes-chinks-in-armour/articleshow/12447751.cms.

[94] Jaideep Prabhu, "India's Defence Preparedness Has Hit Rock Bottom under AK Antony," *DNA*, March 31, 2014, http://www.dnaindia.com/analysis/standpoint-india-s-defence-preparedness-has-hit-rock-bottom-under-ak-antony-1973750.

[95] Manoj Joshi, "The Unending Quest to Reform India's National Security System" (RSIS Policy Brief, S. Rajaratnam School of International Studies, Singapore, March 2014). The author was a member of the Naresh Chandra Committee. Also see Vinod Misra, "Overview," in *Core Concerns in Indian Defence and the Imperatives for Reforms*, ed. Vinod Misra, xix (New Delhi: Pentagon Press, Institute for Defence Studies and Analysis, 2015).

Table 3.1 **Acquisition Reform Committees, 2005–2014**

Year/Acquisition Reform Committees	Remarks
2005: The Kelkar Committee suggested measures to allow private companies in defense production.	Most recommendations were not accepted, and there is still limited private sector participation in defense production.
2007: Following the recommendation of the Kelkar Committee, the Prabir Sengupta Committee is set up to recommend suitable private sector defense companies as Raksha Udyog Ratnas (RuRs), or champions of the defense industry, putting them on par with the public sector.	The committee recommended fifteen out of forty companies for RuR status. However, under pressure from trade unions and left-wing political parties, the government did not accept this recommendation.[a]
2007: Sisodia Committee established for "improving defence acquisition structures in the Ministry of Defence."	Report submitted in July 2007, but most of its recommendations were not implemented.
2007: Rama Rao Committee established to conduct an external review of the functioning and performance of the DRDO.	Government claims that it has accepted many of its recommendations, but the military is still unsatisfied with DRDO.[b]
2008: Defense Expenditure Review Committee, also known as the VK Misra Committee, established to recommend measures to streamline defense expenditure.	Many of its far-reaching recommendations were not implemented, and the report was allegedly put "in limbo."[c]
2012: Task Force on National Security to review national security management system (also known as the Naresh Chandra Committee).	The task force suggested major acquisition reforms, and its recommendations have been accepted to a varying degree.
2012: Ravindra Gupta Task Force on Defence Modernisation and Self-Reliance: Report was critical of research and development efforts in public sector defense companies.[d]	It is unclear how this report was acted upon, but research and development in the public sector are still problematic.

[a]Shukla, "MoD Scraps Plans for Raksha Udyog Ratnas."

[b]Press Information Bureau, "MoD Announces Major DRDO Restructuring Plan" May 13, 2010, http://pib.nic.in/newsite/erelcontent.aspx?relid=61808.

[c]Behera, *Indian Defense Industry: Issues of Self-Reliance*, 72.

[d]Josy Joseph, "HAL's Import, Assemble, Supply 'Model,'" *The Hindu*, February 5, 2016, http://www.thehindu.com/news/national/hals-import-assemble-supply-model/article8194894.ece.

2015–2018: Changing Procedures, Unchanged Outcome

In May 2014, Prime Minister Narendra Modi's government came into power with high expectations that it would be strong on national security. The first few years were marked by a flurry of activities including approval of long pending acquisitions. In terms of weapons acquisitions, there have been three major trends.

First, there have been significant procedural reforms. In September 2014, the Modi government announced a flagship scheme to create manufacturing jobs through its "Make in India" campaign. Defense industry was considered an essential part of this campaign, and a number of steps were taken to encourage it. For instance, the government brought clarity in granting industrial licenses, tried to level the field between public and private sectors, increased the automatic FDI limit to 49%, simplified rules for offsets and public–private partnerships, and made it easier to export defense materiel.[96] Acting on one of the recommendations of the Naresh Chandra Committee, the government, for the first time, separated the posts of Chairman of the DRDO and the scientific adviser to the defense minister.[97] This was construed as a signal to the DRDO that it should be more responsive and deliver on its promises. The government also pressured the industry to work with the military in, for instance, developing an artillery gun, leading one officer to enthusiastically claim that "such collaboration never happened in the past."[98] All of these measures were welcomed by analysts, the defense industry, and the user community, the military. However, as described later, within a few years serious doubts emerged regarding its commitment to private industry and allocating funds for military modernization.

Second, a number of committees were set up to examine different aspects of the acquisitions process, especially to promote private sector participation and spur defense production. Accordingly, in 2015, a committee of experts (also called the Dhirendra Singh Committee) was set up to suggest amendments to the Defense Procurement Procedure to facilitate "Make in India" projects. This committee recommended a "strategic partnership" model, and the government

---

[96] For an overview of these changes, see Laxman Kumar Behera, *Indian Defence Industry: An Agenda for Making in India* (New Delhi: Pentagon Press, 2016), 14–17.

[97] National Security Council Secretariat, *Report of the Task Force on National Security* (New Delhi: National Security Council Secretariat, 2012), 29 (hereafter referred to as the *Report of the Naresh Chandra Committee*); also see Ajai Shukla, "In a First, Defence Minister Gets His Own Tech Advisor," *Business Standard*, May 30, 2015, https://www.business-standard.com/article/economy-policy/in-a-first-defence-minister-gets-his-own-tech-advisor-115053000028_1.html.

[98] Pradip R. Sagar, "Shots on Target, finally," *The Week*, May 06, 2018, https://www.theweek.in/theweek/specials/2018/04/27/shots-on-target-finally.html.

set up a task force (called the V. K. Aatre Task Force) to "lay down the criteria for selection of strategic partners for various platforms from the private sector industry."[99] In addition, the government announced its intention to set up two defense industrial corridors, in Tamil Nadu and Uttar Pradesh, to promote domestic production in both the public and private sectors. Not all of the committees, however, worked as per plan. For instance, among the more ambitious efforts was a committee, led by V. K. Rae, for restructuring the Acquisitions Wing of the MoD. Later, suggesting a difference of visions, Rae resigned from this committee; and it is not entirely clear whether there was any actual outcome.[100]

Finally, despite all of these procedural measures, the Modi government's vision for private sector participation, Make in India and FDI, has largely failed to materialize. As noted by *The Economist*, "foreign investment in the defence industry, touted as a centerpiece of the government's Make In India campaign to boost domestic manufacturing, amounted to less than $200,000 from 2014 to 2017, out of some $60bn of FDI in 2017 alone."[101] Most analysts are therefore skeptical of governmental claims regarding Make in India and private sector participation in the defense sector.[102]

Despite much promise, Prime Minister Modi's government has not been able to make much headway. To be charitable, ushering in institutional reforms and building up private sector industry takes time and perhaps conditions have been created for a potential transformation. But institutional design and the lack of expertise remain problematic, as discussed in the next section.

Never-Ending Story: India's Floundering Defense Industry and Its Military

India's state-owned research and defense production capabilities consist of fifty-two DRDO laboratories, nine DPSUs, and forty-one OFs. In

---

[99] Ministry of Defence, *Report on the Task Force of Selection of Partners*, 2016, 8.

[100] Manu Pubby, "Vivek Rae Resigns after Differences over Basic Concept of New Procurement Wing," *Economic Times*, November 3, 2016, https://economictimes.indiatimes.com/news/defence/vivek-rae-resigns-after-differences-over-basic-concept-of-new-procurement-wing/articleshow/55232964.cms.

[101] "India Spends a Fortune on Defence and Gets Poor Value for Money," *The Economist* 426, no. 9085 (March 31, 2018): 56, https://www.economist.com/asia/2018/03/28/india-spends-a-fortune-on-defence-and-gets-poor-value-for-money.

[102] Manu Pubby, "For the Defence Sector, Make in India Ended Before It Began," *The Print*, December 22, 2017, https://theprint.in/opinion/for-the-defence-sector-make-in-india-ended-before-it-began/24280/; Rajat Pandit, "Defence Gets Its Aim Right, but Still Far from Hitting Reforms Target," *Times of India*, May 23, 2017; and Ajai Shukla, "Weaponry Development Subsidy Scrapped: Indian Firms Won't 'Make' Anymore," *Business Standard*, June 6, 2018.

2011, "with a turnover of over \$10.5 billion and a workforce of nearly 180,000 these enterprises constitute one of the largest defence industrial bases in the world."[103] This vast bureaucratic–scientific–industrial complex functions under the MoD. The declared objective of the ministry was to make the country self-sufficient and self-reliant in defense production; however, it has failed to achieve this goal, as India is currently the largest arms importer in the world. While the research division was moderately successful in strategic weapons programs—including nuclear and missile technology, its conventional weapons development capabilities have been mired in controversy.[104]

Analytically, problems in India's weapons procurement process can be put under two broad categories—those arising from institutional design and others from the lack of expertise. This section describes each of these problems and then explains how the pattern of India's civil–military relations plays a role in perpetuating them.

Problems Due to Institutional Design

In this chapter, institutional design refers to the structure of decision-making between three main bureaucratic actors—the military, the defense industry, and civilian officials in the MoD. This captures the formal interaction between these institutions. Two main problems emerge from the current institutional design: it creates an adversarial work culture as the military feels that state-owned enterprises are not responsive to it and there is a lack of oversight and accountability.

Adversarial Work Culture and a Lack of Responsiveness to the Military

Instead of a collaborative approach to weapons systems development and acquisitions, the existing structures of interaction between different agencies create an adversarial work culture. This results in a lack of information sharing, turf wars, and a lack of coordination. Problems arise between the military, on

---

[103] Laxman Kumar Behera, "Defence Innovation in India: The Fault Lines" (IDSA occasional paper 32, Institute for Defence Studies and Analyses, New Delhi, 2014), 28.

[104] For a critique of the DRDO's performance, see the eight-part exposé titled "Delayed Research, Delayed Organisation," in the *Indian Express* by Shiv Aroor and Amitav Ranjan, November 11–19, 2006. For a different view, see the three-part series by Kaushik Kapisthalam, "DRDO: A Stellar Success," Rediff News, January 2005, https://www.rediff.com/news/special/spec2/20050119.htm.

one side, and civilian bureaucrats in the MoD and the scientists, technocrats, and defense industry, on the other.

As described throughout this book, there are considerable tensions between the military and the bureaucrats in the MoD. In the acquisitions process, the services feel that bureaucrats, holding the office of secretary (defense production)—responsible for all DPSUs and the OF Board (OFB), are not as cognizant of the interests and issues raised by the military. They also feel that the acquisition managers in the ministry work against them. The appointment of technical managers (manned by military officers) under the director general (acquisitions) was meant to create a more collegial working atmosphere. Despite some improvement, however, as a former technical manager (land systems) argues, "although the bureaucracy and the Services are required to function as an integrated team to provide the Services with the required equipment, a culture of 'we versus them' has vitiated the working environment."[105]

These problems are magnified when we examine the relationship between the user, the military, and other agencies—the DRDO, DPSU, and OFB. There have been long-standing problems between the military and the DRDO. Generations of military officers have complained about the manner in which the DRDO obtained project approval by making unrealistic claims with respect to capability, delivery schedule, and cost. This problem has also been accepted by former DRDO officials. For instance, V. S. Arunachalam, head of the DRDO in the 1980s, admitted, "in our eagerness to get major projects, we gave unrealistic timeframes and very low budgets."[106] More recently, Vasudev Aatre, who headed the DRDO from 2000 to 2004, argued that the DRDO had a vested interest in making "exaggerated promises."[107]

The military also feels that the DRDO is not responsive to their requirements. Historically, the military has complained that the scientific adviser to the defense minister, who until recently was also the head of the DRDO, did not devote adequate time and attention to their needs. According to a former defense secretary,

> There was a lot of interaction by the world scientists with the Scientific Adviser as a scientist. . . . So, the calls on his time from seminars and meetings and visits abroad were many. They took away a lot of his time.

---

[105] Mrinal Suman, "Defence Production and Acquisitions," 136.

[106] Cited in Hoyt, *Military Industry and Regional Defense Policy*, 64.

[107] Amitav Ranjan, "Advice from Ex-Chief: Accountability Absolute Must," *Indian Express*, November 19, 2006.

Often there was a complaint by the three Chiefs that they did not get enough time with the Scientific Adviser, which they were entitled to. So the forward planning and thinking about future requirements of the Defence Services did not receive as much time from the Scientific Adviser as was intended."[108]

That the DRDO was not responsive to the military was observed by multiple reform committees. For instance, in 2008, the Defence Expenditure Review Committee, which was tasked to review procurement procedures, identified this as a problem and argued that "there is a pressing need for sustained and regular peer reviews for all major ongoing DRDO projects [and] full oversight by Steering Committees headed by User Service's functionaries."[109] In 2012, the Naresh Chandra Committee was even more scathing when it argued that the "DRDO fell short of expectations by often misjudging the complexity of programs. . . . Consequent of criticism, DRDO drifted away from meeting the needs of the military through indigenous route (which was the objective of forming DRDO) to 'futuristic products' that were at the frontier of technology such as Missile Defense and hypersonic craft."[110]

There are similar problems with the DPSUs and OFB. The nine DPSUs have been the mainstay of India's defense industry, and they have been successful in the licensed production of foreign-origin weapons systems. Despite transfer of technology agreements, however, most DPSUs merely assemble these systems; and there has been very little transfer of expertise and technical know-how.[111] Part of the problem was the separation between research and production, a move that was opposed by the military.[112] Like the DRDO, the responsiveness of the DPSUs to the user community, the military, has been

[108] Oral History Transcript, Govind Narain, 425.

[109] *Defense Expenditure Committee Report*, Executive Summary, 4. I thank an unnamed non-official for sharing this report. For similar views also see *Kelkar Committee Report*, 2005, 42.

[110] *Report of the Naresh Chandra Committee*, 29.

[111] Vinay Shankar, "Catalysing the Defence Industry," *Indian Defence Review* 21, no. 4 (October–December 2006): http://www.indiandefencereview.com/news/catalysing-the-defence-industry/0/; for a good account of problems with transfer of technology, state of science and technology, and the defense industrial base, see Ravinder Pal Singh, "An Assessment of Indian Science and Technology and Implications for Military Research and Development," *Economic and Political Weekly* 35, no. 31 (July 29–August 4, 2000): 2762–75.

[112] Kapur, *Building a Defence Technology Base*, 30–32; for problems arising from this, see 52–60.

in question.[113] As a result, the DPSUs have been repeatedly criticized by the military community. Acknowledging this as a problem, the Naresh Chandra Committee argued in favor of inducting "experienced service personnel in the [D]PSUs at an appropriate managerial level to provide the user interface and helping DPSUs become more focused."[114]

The military has also expressed its unhappiness with the functioning of the OFB, and there have been numerous complaints about substandard quality, price, and even safety. A detailed study of the OFB argued that a lot of its "problems could be sorted out with close cooperation between the OFs and the armed forces."[115] The OFB, in its current avatar, is more responsive to the Department of Defence Production than to the military. Once again, the Naresh Chandra Committee recommended staffing this department with service officers to make it more professional and attuned to the requirements of the military.

It would be unfair and misleading, however, to put the onus of the blame for the failure of India's domestic defense industry entirely on the civilians. To a significant degree, the military also bears responsibility in its approach to technology (or its institutional capacity) and its staffing and deputation policies.[116] These factors result in a miscommunication and further vitiate the working relations between civilians and the military.

India's military is not monolithic, and there are significant differences among the services and in their approach to weapons and technology acquisitions. The variance is most apparent in their "institutional capacity," defined as the ability to "design military technological systems."[117] The army and air force did not build up, until very recently, this capability and have struggled to communicate and work with the defense industry. In 2016, in an attempt to address this shortcoming, the army established an Army Design Bureau, however this remains a work in progress.

By contrast, the navy has a much better interface with the defense industry because of the quality, education, and training it imparts to officers deputed to the

[113] Bedi, "India's Bizarre Arms Procurement Policy," 3717; and Ravinder Pal Singh, "India," in *Arms Procurement Decision Making, Volume I: China, India, Israel, Japan, South Korea, and Thailand,* ed. Ravinder Pal Singh (Oxford: Oxford University Press, 1998), 70.

[114] *Report of the Naresh Chandra Committee,* 30.

[115] Laxman Kumar Behera, "India's Ordnance Factories: A Performance Analysis," *Journal of Defense Studies* 6, no. 2 (2012): 70.

[116] For a scathing critique of the Indian military's approach to technology and weapons development, see Bharat Karnad, *Why India Is not a Great Power (Yet)* (New Delhi: Oxford University Press, 2015), 303–409.

[117] Srinath Raghavan, "Military Technological Innovation in India: A Tale of Three Projects," *India Review* 17, no. 1 (2018): 125.

DRDO and DPSUs.[118] Significantly, officers were trained in-house on subjects like warship design, acquiring technical knowledge which facilitated their engagement with the scientific community.[119] It helped that some of the DRDO laboratories were not only located close to major naval bases like Kochi and Vishakhapatnam but also exclusively devoted to serving the navy. The DPSU shipbuilding yards were also responsive as their chief managing directors were almost always former naval officers. All these factors played a role in enhancing the interaction between the scientific, production, and naval communities and making them responsive to each other. However, even then the navy had reason to complain about the go-alone attitude in some DRDO laboratories.[120]

Relations between the DRDO, DPSUs, OFs, and the services are made more problematic because of the staffing and deputation policies adopted by the military. Displaying a lack of organizational emphasis, the services (especially the army) do not post their best officers to these organizations, as a result of which it is considered an unattractive career choice.[121] Many of the officers deputed to these organizations are often superseded within their parent arm and have little professional incentive. As a result, user interface, crucial for development of weapons systems, is problematic. Embarrassingly for the army, the competency of these military officers was called into question by a MoD official while explaining the reasons for underperformance by the DRDO.[122] The army's deputation of officers and its interface with the OFs were also criticized by the Defense Expenditure Review Committee, which argued that it is "important that the army HQ [headquarters] is mandated to depute suitable representatives to participate in these important activities."[123]

In sum, there are problems in the working relations between the DRDO, DPSUs, and OFs, all under the MoD, and the user community, the armed forces. Military officials have mixed views about the domestic defense industrial base, with some doubting its capacity to deliver and others embracing its logic. To deflect the criticism, DRDO officials claim that military officers prefer foreign products and lack institutional capacity or emphasis.[124] The point remains,

---

[118] Standing Committee on Defense, *Fourteenth Report*, 34–35. The navy established its own design cell for warship construction in 1962 and has encouraged engineering and technical education.

[119] Email from Vice Admiral P. S. Das to author, May 13, 2013.

[120] *Kelkar Committee Report*, 44.

[121] Problems arising from the manner in which service officers are deputed to the DRDO had been discussed and corrective measures suggested by the Arun Singh committee in 2001, see Group of Ministers, *Reforming the National Security System*, 111–12.

[122] See comments made in Standing Committee on Defence, *Fourteenth Report*, 42.

[123] *Defense Expenditure Committee Report*, 5.

[124] For a description of problems between the DRDO and the military, see Standing Committee on Defense, *Fourteenth Report*, 33–38.

however, that there is an adversarial working relationship and a lack of responsiveness between the military and defense research and production units. Inevitably, delays, shoddy products, or failures in projects create tension between the services and MoD officials, technocrats, research scientists, and production factories. These are compounded when casualties occur due to faulty products.[125]

Many Heads, No Headmaster: Oversight and Accountability

Another problem that can be blamed on the institutional design of the weapons procurement process is the absence of an independent oversight body and diffused or even absent accountability.[126] Financial accountability is enforced by the Comptroller and Auditor General (CAG), but other forms of accountability pertaining to equipment capability, plan implementation, timelines, cost overruns, and overall ownership are either diffused or lacking. As the ownership of programs, plans, and financial outlays is diffused between the Ministries of Defence and Finance, services, the DRDO, and the Department of Defence Production, there is little systemic accountability. This concept is best explained by Air Commodore Jasjit Singh: "the civil bureaucracy in the Ministry of Defence is too small, is overburdened by routine (and crisis) management, and has too little professional expertise to manage this task. . . . The result is a large amount of Service HQ–Ministry–Service HQ correspondence and debate which is not only time consuming with its built-in delay factors, but also *diffuses accountability*."[127]

Indeed, one of the measures to improve the functioning of the DRDO as suggested by its former head, is the "absolute must for accountability."[128] In 2007, the Sisodia Committee argued that "the dispersed and diffused defense acquisition framework of the MoD, as it exists in India today, leads to

---

[125] A number of T-72 tank barrels burst when conducting firing practice between 1992 and 1997, killing around twenty crew members. Later it was blamed on inadequate tempering of steel barrels by the Indian production agency. Interview with one of the investigators into these incidents, Pune, September 2, 2009. Similarly, a number of ammunition blasts have also been blamed on the quality control and defective manufacturing by OF, see Deepak Sinha, "A Different India but an Unchanged Ministry of Defence," *Times of India*, July 3, 2017, https://blogs.timesofindia.indiatimes.com/para-phrase/our-defence-ministry-remains-firmly-wedded-to-mid-twentieth-mindset/.

[126] Singh, *Arms Procurement Decision-Making*, 83–86.

[127] Singh, *India's Defence Spending*, 75, emphasis added.

[128] Ranjan, "Advice from Ex-Chief."

inordinate delays; shortfall in operational capabilities, which may sometimes remain unnoticed; time and cost overruns; and lack of accountability."[129] However, enforcing accountability is easier said than done. In the first place, none of the agencies involved are inclined to allow scrutiny over their activities, making accountability an alien concept. Crucially, the MoD, which serves as the nodal agency for procurement decisions, does little to enforce accountability, despite having considerable powers to do so. Expressing his helplessness, one defense secretary observed that "though it is an integrated procurement system, the delays are there and I cannot pinpoint exactly who is guilty or who is not guilty."[130]

The problem of diffused or absent accountability continues to exist, even after recent organizational changes, like the creation of the director general (acquisitions) and the IDS. A classified study conducted by the IDS while examining delays in weapons acquisition blamed "multiple and diffused structures with no single-point accountability, multiple decision-making heads, duplication of processes-avoidable redundant layers doing the same thing over and over again, delayed comments, delayed decision, delayed execution, no real-time monitoring, no program/project-based approach, tendency to fault-find rather than to facilitate."[131] In short, due to organizational complexity—there is a resultant lack of accountability.

Lack of Expertise

There are problems which also arise from lack of expertise. In India's case this applies to the civilian bureaucracy in the MoD and to the military.

The Acquisition Managers: (In)Capacity in the MoD

The senior leadership in the MoD handling acquisitions usually are deputed from the Indian Administrative Services. They serve on a rotational basis and

[129] *Report of the Committee on Improving Defense Acquisition Structures in MoD*, July 2007, 57. I thank an unnamed official for sharing this report with me (hereafter referred to as the *Sisodia Committee Report*).

[130] Standing Committee on Defence, *Fifteenth Report: Demand for Grants (2012–2013)* (New Delhi: Lok Sabha Secretariat, April 2012), 27.

[131] Sandeep Unnithan, "Budget Squeeze Threatens Indian Army's Preparedness for Possible Two-Front War," *India Today*, May 3, 2018, https://www.indiatoday.in/magazine/cover-story/story/20180514-defence-budget-squeeze-indian-army-unprepared-for-wars-1226462-2018-05-03.

have little expertise in the complexities of advanced weapons systems. According to Air Marshal M. Matheswaran, who served in the IDS, the "Director General (Acquisitions) has no military background and rarely has had tenures serving in the Defence Ministry. As a result, the officer does not understand the problems, nuances and operational challenges and the overall decision-making structure makes for an adversarial relationship."[132] Put another way, the MoD does not have qualified, professional staff with adequate expertise to focus exclusively on the acquisition process. To be sure, some bureaucrats, especially at the junior levels and those belonging to the Indian Defence Accounts Services, spend more time and gain a measure of expertise; however, this is mainly in financial management, and they rotate frequently between jobs. Expertise, or lack thereof, was a problem acknowledged by the CAG—which in a report argued that the acquisition staff "did not have adequate training or exposure to project management, procurement management or contract management."[133]

This is especially problematic as acquisition managers in the MoD suffer from a lack of manpower while having to deal with organizational complexity. The Sisodia Committee that examined the acquisition process especially singled out an "overburdened staff" and an absence of expertise in the cost and legal cells that led to all-around delays.[134] In terms of organizational complexity, there are "thirteen different agencies each reporting to different functional heads involved in the processing of procurement."[135] In short, the MoD "simply does not have the expertise . . . to analyze and evaluate the Armed Forces' programs."[136] There have been persistent demands for the creation of a separate acquisition cadre and a defense acquisition institute.[137] In 2017, it was reported that the government was considering a proposal to create a separate organization, to be called the Defense Acquisition Organization, with its own professional cadre.[138] However, as of yet, this plan remains on paper.

[132] Email to author, June 19, 2018.

[133] Comptroller and Auditor General (CAG) of India Report, *Union Government (Defence Services) Army and Ordnance Factories no. 4 of 2007 (Performance Audit) for the Year Ended March 2006*, 23.

[134] *Sisodia Committee Report*, 2007, 38–47.

[135] CAG Report, *Union Government (Defence Services)*, 23.

[136] Narendra Singh Sisodia and Amit Cowshish, "Defence Planning, Programming and Budgeting: An Agenda for Reform," in *Core Concerns in Indian Defence and the Imperatives for Reforms*, 103.

[137] Mrinal Suman, "Defense Acquisition Institute: A Viewpoint," *Journal of Defense Studies* 6, no. 2 (2012): 1–12.

[138] Manu Pubby, "MoD Panel for Autonomous Weapons Acquisition Body in Charge of Policy, Acquisition and Exports," *Economic Times*, May 23, 2017, https://economictimes.indiatimes. com/news/defence/mod-panel-for-autonomous-weapons-acquisition-body-in-charge-of-policy-acquisition-and-exports/articleshow/58796326.cms.

The (In)expert Soldier

Most military officers believe that problems in weapons procurement are primarily due to a nexus between the politicians, bureaucrats, and the public sector defense industry. They, military officers further believe, impose sub-standard goods produced by an inefficient public sector defense industry on a helpless military, which then has to suffer the consequences.[139] Like most opinion-driven narratives, this is a half-truth. Instead, one of the bigger problems in the weapons acquisitions process is the generalist culture and a resultant lack of expertise within the military. Simply put, its personnel policies perpetuate a generalist system as opposed to an emphasis on specialization. Quite the contrary, specialization can even harm career prospects as it hinders employability, making it difficult for officers to follow typical career progression pathways. Officers, therefore, usually spend two to three years in any one post before assuming a position often completely unrelated to their previous experience. Hence, by the time they gain experience in one particular job, they are transferred to another. According to a former vice chief, the army "remains rooted to the outdated policies of employing 'generalists' rather than 'specialists' to man the weapon procurement functions at Army headquarters."[140] Ironically then, the military's manpower policies resemble the same generalist system that they criticize in the civilian bureaucracy.

Problems arising from a generalist culture apply to all activities within the military, but in weapons procurement they are particularly consequential in the drafting of General Staff Qualitative Requirements (GSQRs, often called QRs). GSQRs are technical specifications of weapons and equipment, on the basis of which they are evaluated and eventually inducted into service. These are drafted by the services and are considered one of the most important documents as they specify the parameters of the desired weapon systems. However, GSQRs have attracted much criticism on two issues—their manner of drafting and frequent changes made in them.[141]

---

[139] For a particularly strident view, see A. G. Bewoor, "Defence PSU's: The Great Betrayal," *Indian Defence Review* 24, no. 4 (2009): http://www.indiandefencereview.com/spotlights/defence-psus-the-great-betrayl/.

[140] Philip Campose, "Modernizing of the Indian Army: Future Challenges," in *Defence Primer 2017: Today's Capabilities, Tomorrow's Conflicts*, ed. Sushant Singh and Pushan Das, 31 (New Delhi: Observer Research Foundation, 2017).

[141] See Laxman Kumar Behera, "India's Defence Acquisition System: Need for Further Reforms," *The Korean Journal of Defense Analysis* 24, no. 1 (2012): 97–100; and Mrinal Suman, "Weapons Procurement: Qualitative Requirements and Transparency in Evaluation," *Strategic Analysis* 30, no. 4 (2006): 727–28.

Among the complaints made by both domestic and foreign defense companies operating in India are that the services frame GSQRs by choosing "BBC—best of brochure claims" and end up asking for products that do not exist. GSQRs are drafted by generalist officers possessing little specialized knowledge of weapons, and so they rely on brochures and pick and choose features that they would like in their equipment. The GSQRs therefore end up as an amalgamation of characteristics from different systems that no one firm can match. Identifying this as one of the problems in indigenous weapons development, MoD sources noted that "often Air Staff Requirements (ASR)/GSQR's are supersets of various latest technologies available in different foreign products combined together and, therefore, unrealistic for providing a complete or ultimate solution through development."[142]

Another problem with GSQR formulation is the changes and amendments made in them by the services, which set back projects by years.[143] As officers lack specialized training, and have relatively short tenures in comparison to the time taken to develop weapon systems, the GSQRs are often erratically formulated. As a result, in a large number of instances, they have to be reformulated, which understandably "delay[s] the completion of the acquisition process."[144] This has also been a long-running problem, with changes in QRs frustrating research and development projects.[145] As noted by the CAG, "the acquisition process suffered from a major drawback of inaccurate formulation of Qualitative requirements (QRs). In 50% of the procurement cases test checked, specifications were changed after issue of tender/request for proposal."[146]

On their part, the military claims that changes in the GSQRs are often unavoidable as delays in indigenous production combined with technological advancements and changes in the threat environment (acquisition of new weapon capabilities by neighboring countries) render the product obsolescent even before it is inducted. For instance, the GSQR for the main battle tank Arjun, initially drafted in 1974, had to be redrafted in 1985; and even when the prototypes were tested in 1996, they "failed to meet the requirements projected in the GSQR."[147] Similarly, delays in the development of the light combat

---

[142] Standing Committee on Defense, *Fourteenth Report*, 34.

[143] Standing Committee on Defense, *Fourteenth Report*, 34–44.

[144] Standing Committee on Defense, *Sixth Report*, 6.

[145] For instance, radical changes in the air staff requirement for the Advanced Light Helicopter delayed its development considerably, see Smith, *India's Ad Hoc Arsenal*, 164.

[146] CAG Report, *Union Government (Defence Services)*, 1.

[147] Report of the Public Accounts Committee, *Design and Development of Main Battle Tank— Arjun* (New Delhi: Lok Sabha Secretariat, April 2000), 21, also see 14.

aircraft and technological changes led the Indian Air Force to make changes in its weapons definition in 2004, further delaying the project.[148]

The issue of GSQR formulation, and the problems arising from it, has been debated by the various reform committees. In 2005, the Kelkar Committee felt that, at some point in time, this function should be taken away from the exclusive domain of the services and given to a professional body (like the French DGA), composed of both civilian and military personnel.[149] But, by 2015, the Dhirendra Singh Committee had a different view and argued against taking this function away from the military.[150] In effect, GSQR formulation has become a point of contention between the civilians and the military.

India's Civil–Military Relations and the Defense–Industrial Complex

In the weapons procurement process, there are three main stakeholders—the military, civilian bureaucrats in the MoD, and the public sector defense industry consisting of both scientists and weapon producers. Existing institutional structures and norms of interaction indicate a high level of stovepiping within all of these organizations, resulting in the "persistent inability of its domestic military industrial base to meet extant needs on a timely and cost-effective basis."[151] But are the problems due to civil–military relations or just normal organizational pathologies? Some, like Eric Arnett, argue that it is the former. After describing the dysfunctional relationship between the DRDO and the military, he concluded that it was a consequence of "India's eccentric civil–military relations."[152] This view resonates with others and is a commonly held view within the military.[153] How do civil–military relations explain this, and where are the sources of discord?

---

[148] Standing Committee on Defense, *Seventeenth Report: In-Depth Study and Critical Review of Hindustan Aeronautical Limited* (New Delhi: Lok Sabha Secretariat, April 2007), 43.

[149] *Kelkar Committee Report*, 86–87.

[150] Report of the Experts Committee, *Committee of Experts for Amendments to DPP 2013 including formulation of Policy Framework* (July 2015), 8. This report is more commonly known as the *Dhrirendra Singh Committee Report* https://mod.gov.in/sites/default/files/Reportddp.pdf

[151] Sumit Ganguly, "India's National Security," in *Oxford Handbook of Indian Foreign Policy*, 150.

[152] Eric Arnett, "And the Loser Is . . . the Indian Armed Forces," *Economic and Political Weekly*, 33, no. 36/37 (September 5–12, 1998): 2339.

[153] Stephen P. Cohen and Sunil Dasgupta, *Arming Without Aiming: India's Military Modernization* (Washington, DC: Brookings Institution Press, 2010), 30–36; Smith, *India's Ad Hoc Arsenal*; and Routray, "Armed Forces versus Technologists," 37.

As discussed at the beginning of this chapter, a comparative overview of weapons acquisitions in different countries focused on two desirable features— institutional design and expertise. In India's case, both are difficult because of its unique pattern of civil–military relations. This pattern, the absent dialogue argument, consists of three broad features: a lack of civilian expertise, an institutional design characterized by strong bureaucratic controls, and considerable military autonomy.

The lack of expertise is an accepted facet of India's defense procurement structures. Civilians do not only lack military expertise, but also suffer due to a lack of expertise in complex project and financial management, and legal-technical skills. This makes it difficult for them to have effective oversight or even to engage in an informed dialogue with different stakeholders.

It is crucial to note, however, that politicians have periodically intervened in the weapons procurement process. This characteristic contravenes one of the features of the absent dialogue argument. Civilians therefore have stepped in mainly to facilitate the growth and continued patronage of the public sector. Despite widely known problems with efficiency, limited capabilities and delivery failures of the public sector defense industry, politicians have, by and large, chosen to protect and nurture them. In turn, bureaucrats and technocrats in the MoD, DPSUs, the DRDO, and the OFs have touted their employee numbers and used ideological buzzwords like "self-reliance," "self-sufficiency," "import substitution," and "indigenization."[154] This fetches political traction and acceptability. Thus, regardless of the actual track record, politicians find it convenient, both by deflecting pressure from labor unions and for domestic political consumption, to continue their support for defense public sector units.[155] These facilities directly employ around 200,000 workers (besides many more employed by small to medium-sized enterprises and ancillary units that indirectly support them) and possess considerable political power. In the past, politicians discouraged the growth of the private sector in this field and instead protected the monopoly of

---

[154] For the ideology of self-sufficiency and its high costs on equipment quality, see Raju Thomas, "Arms Procurement in India: Military Self-Reliance versus Technological Self-Sufficiency," in *Military Capacity and the Risk of War: China, India, Pakistan, and Iran*, ed. Eric Arnett, 111 (New York: SIPRI and Oxford University Press, 1997); also see David Kinsella and Jugdep S. Chima, "Symbols of Statehood: Military Industrialization and Public Discourse in India," *Review of International Studies* 27, no. 3 (2001), 353.

[155] According to some reports in 2010, opposition from DPSU trade unions stymied plans to allow greater participation by private defense industry in defense production; see Ajai Shukla, "MoD Scraps Plans for Raksha Udyog Ratnas," *Business Standard*, February 11, 2010. Even earlier, indicative of the domestic politics surrounding this issue, the Communist Party of India (Marxist) had expressed opposition; see Convention of Defence Employees, "Scrap Kelkar Committee Report," *People's Democracy* 31, no. 17 (April 29, 2007).

the public sector.[156] However, there appears be a paradigm shift and a willingness to give a role to the private sector in defense manufacturing. The success of this initiative, however, is by no means assured.

Another characteristic of civil–military relations—an institutional design leading to strong bureaucratic controls, accurately describes weapons procurement in India. There are both political and (civilian) bureaucratic pressures to ensure that indigenization programs, though often slow, tardy, or complete failures, continue—even at the cost of operational efficiency. It is the responsibility of the secretary, defense production to ensure that the OFs and DPSUs are provided funds and work-projects. The military has often complained about the lack of responsiveness of defense scientists and industry, however by institutional design they are kept "out of the decisionmaking loop."[157]

The third characteristic of civil–military relations—considerable autonomy to the military—also contributes to problems in weapons procurement. In a manner somewhat similar to that of the civilian bureaucracy, the military is a generalist cadre lacking technical expertise for framing GSQRs and in project, financial and procurement management. Despite occasional complaints the military has not systematically addressed this issue.

A combination of these three characteristics of civil–military relations in India make it difficult to have the "iterative dialogue"—crucial to the acquisitions process. Instead, bureaucracies operate in sectional stove-pipes creating resentments and an "us-versus-them" mentality.

What would it take to address some of these civil–military infirmities? In 2006, the Sisodia Committee was specifically tasked to suggest measures to improve the acquisition structures in the MoD, and it recommended "amalgamation of substantial elements of Departments of Defence Research and Development, Defence Production, and some elements of Integrated Defence Staff, and Service Headquarters and DGQA [Director General Quality Assurance], with DG Acquisition."[158] Among other measures it also suggested cross-posting officers in different bureaucracies and organizational restructuring to make it less of a civil–military divide. However, the report of the Sisodia Committee faced a lot of opposition from, among other sources, the military, which is not at all keen to give up or share its powers with regard to GSQR formulation.

---

[156] For the manner in which the Ministry of Defence protects state-owned enterprises from private industry competition, see Rahul Bedi, "India-Divided Interests," *Jane's Defence Weekly*, May 21, 2003.

[157] Suman, "Defence Production and Acquisitions," 136.

[158] *Sisodia Committee Report*, 2007, 59.

Conclusion

The primary argument in this chapter is that the pattern of civil–military relations contributes to problems in the weapons procurement process. It is important to note, however, that India's pattern of civil–military relations is an important, though not the only, explanatory factor. It will be misleading to assume that achieving a normatively "correct" pattern of civil–military relations will automatically fix all of the problems in the procurement process. Britain, for instance, whose strength is of an integrated MoD, has had problems attributed to "a conspiracy of optimism."[159] In the United States, controversies erupt when domestic political considerations take precedence over the military's wish list.[160] Every country will have its unique set of problems, challenges, and circumstances associated with its weapons procurement. In general, this chapter highlights the need for further research into an undertheorized topic—the role of civil–military relations in weapons procurement.

The unfortunate distinction of being the world's largest arms importer testifies to the failure of the Indian defense industry. India has not achieved its stated goals of self-reliance and self-sufficiency, and the military suffers from repeated delays or nondelivery of weapons systems. A former naval chief captures the prevailing sentiment within the military when he argues that, "delays and shortfalls are in-built into the system and seem to worry only the military that has to live with the consequences in terms of diminished operational capability."[161]

Finally, it is important to note that there has been a gradual change in different bureaucracies involved with weapons procurement in India. The establishment of offices like director general (acquisitions) and technical managers (manned by the military) and of the IDS has improved decision-making and made it more professional. Easing procedural rules for private sector participation and articulating a vision of "Make in India" have sent encouraging signals to industry. Other reforms, like creating the Army Design Bureau in 2016, which has released in the public domain its list of future requirements, are indicative of an unprecedented transparency and willingness to work with academia and the defense industry. Arguably, India is at the cusp of a major transformation in the defense industry. Addressing persistent and recurring civil–military tensions will go a long way toward achieving this transformation.

---

[159] RUSI Acquisition Focus Group, "The Conspiracy of Optimism," *RUSI Defence Systems*, October 2007.

[160] Gordon Adams, *The Role of Defense Budgets in Civil–Military Relations* (Washington, DC: Defense Budget Project, April 1992), 20–22.

[161] V. S. Shekhawat, "Challenges in Defence Planning," *Strategic Analysis* 30, no. 4 (2006): 699.

4

The Coordinators

India's Unique Approach to Jointness

Jointness, defined as the ability of the army, air force, and navy, to plan, train, and operate in a mutually reinforcing manner, has been a matter of debate in all militaries. Some of these debates have been downright vicious, with intense rivalry between the services. While most attribute problems to one of turf battle and control over resources, the services actually differ over their visions of war. Usually, air forces consider counter-air missions, including air defense, to be of primary importance and then tout strategic interdiction and bombing as the preferred way to "win" the war.[1] The army typically wishes to concentrate air assets to deal with the "near enemy"—tactical forces opposing them including the threat from the enemy air force—and prefers the use of air power for close air support. The navy is concerned about fleet protection from a variety of threats including submarines, surface ships, air threats, and missiles. Thus, there is a variance in how different services imagine war and offer different "theories of victory."[2]

Disagreements between the three services are inevitable, whether over roles and missions, budget, or defense plans. These disagreements, some of them crucial to the future of the institution, are, in most cases, only resolved by civilian arbitration. Making decisions relating to integration (another term for jointness[3]) and resolving interservices rivalry thus becomes one of the core functions of civil–military relations. This is especially pertinent for jointness—which

[1] For more on strategic bombing, see Robert A. Pape, *Bombing to Win: Air Power and Coercion in War* (Ithaca, NY: Cornell University Press, 1996).

[2] The term "theory of victory" refers to the fundamental idea of how to wage war, see discussion in Christopher P. Twomey. *The Military Lens: Doctrinal Differences and Deterrence Failure in Sino–American Relations* (Ithaca, NY: Cornell University Press, 2010), 21–22.

[3] The terms "jointness" and "integration" have been used interchangeably by the Indian defense community. To capture the essence of the debate, this chapter follows a similar approach.

requires the subordination of parochial service interests to transition to a more efficient and effective "joint" effort. Jointness therefore requires civilian arbitration, probing, and interference, and is shaped significantly by the form of civil–military relations.

It is widely recognized that jointness tends to enhance military effectiveness. As noted by Millet, Murray, and Watman, an "operationally effective military organization is one that derives maximum benefit from its components and assets by linking them together for mutual support . . . this require[s] complete utilization of combat branches within and between military services. . . . The greater the integration of these disparate elements, the better a military organization will generate combat power from its available resources."[4] Indeed, the advantages of interoperability and of "synergy" between the services leading to increased effectiveness and efficiency have now been widely, if not universally, embraced.

Jointness can be envisioned in two main ways: coordination and integration. The coordination approach allows maximum autonomy to the services and does not require resolution of potentially contentious issues over turf, roles, and, most importantly, command and control. Jointness, instead, is left to the discretion of the service commanders. On the other hand, the integrated model of jointness is one in which there is "unity of effort" wherein the three services operate under a single commander.[5] This approach is informed by the assumption that "unity of command (or control) is one of several elements that make unity of effort possible."[6] Militaries adhering to the integrated model usually appoint a chief of defense staff (CDS) or a chairman of the joint chiefs of staff, have theater commands, and have a joint headquarters at the operational level. Most Western militaries have transitioned from the coordination to the integrated model of jointness. Such is the case even with the Chinese military, which in 2016 undertook reforms to set up joint theater commands.

As discussed elsewhere, civilian intervention is key to jointness.[7] Without civilian intervention we would expect to find the three services settling upon the "coordination model," which maximizes their autonomy. This results in two types of interrelated problems—it perpetuates a single-service approach and

[4] Allan R. Millet, Williamson Murray, and Kenneth H. Watman, "The Effectiveness of Military Organizations," *International Security* 11, no. 1 (1986): 52.

[5] The term "unity of effort" has been defined as a principle which involves "solidarity of purpose, effort, and command. It directs all energies, assets, and activities, physical and mental, towards desired ends"; see John M. Collins, *Grand Strategy: Principles and Practices* (Annapolis, MD: Naval Institute Press, 1973), 28.

[6] James A. Winnefeld and Dana J. Johnson, *Joint Air Operations: Pursuit of Unity in Command and Control, 1942–1991* (Annapolis, MD: Naval Institute Press, 1993), 4.

[7] Anit Mukherjee, "Fighting Separately: Jointness and Civil–Military Relations in India," *Journal of Strategic Studies* 40, no. 1–2 (2017): 6–34.

intensifies turf wars between the services. To be sure, these problems are also present in countries which follow the integration model, but it becomes more acute in countries that do not. This is because the coordination model is inherently divisive as the services battle over roles, budgets, and missions. This is precisely what has happened in India. As its traditional pattern of civil–military relations, best described as that of an absent dialogue, precludes civilian intervention— the Indian military has embraced the coordination approach to jointness. This has adversely shaped its military effectiveness and has been problematic in war. As in other countries, jointness requires civilian arbitration and intervention.

The rest of this chapter proceeds as follows. It begins with a discussion of the British legacy shaping interservices relations after independence. Next, it examines jointness in five major wars—the 1962 China war, the 1965 and 1971 India–Pakistan wars, the military intervention in Sri Lanka in the 1980s, and the 1999 Kargil war. While doing so, it focuses on the higher command of war and the role of civilian policymakers. Next, it examines the dominance of the services and the subsequent single-service approach. Thereafter, it describes developments after the post-Kargil defense reforms to argue that the Indian military has had an "incomplete" transition to jointness. This is primarily because of fitful civilian intervention, which has only served to undermine reformist military officers. The penultimate section examines whether the characteristics of an absent dialogue adequately explain problems in jointness. It concludes by explaining why civilians have not more forcefully intervened on this issue.

Shaped by the Raj: British Legacy on Joint Operations

The three services comprising the Indian military—the army, navy, and air force—existed prior to independence and were shaped both by their rapid expansion and by experiences during the Second World War. The army, the predominant service in numbers and in the share of the defense budget, was relatively confident about its capabilities after its success on the Burma front and, to a limited extent, its participation in the war in Europe. The air force consisted of only seven squadrons and had experience primarily in transport and logistic support operations in the Burma campaign. The navy had even less operational experience as it was tasked predominantly with coastal defense by the British and "possessed but a handful of small ships."[8]

[8] "Outline Plan for the Reorganization and Development of the Royal Indian Navy," cited in Satyindra Singh, *Blueprint to Bluewater: The Indian Navy, 1951–65* (New Delhi: Lancer International 1992), 39.

However, the first India–Pakistan war over Kashmir forced the services to co-operate on tactical issues. The navy had a limited role and was used to transport army troops off the coast of Gujarat to ensure that the princely state of Junagarh acceded to India. The cooperation between the army and the air force during the Kashmir war and during Operation Polo in Hyderabad was of a different magnitude and involved troop transport, air maintenance operations, and tactical air support missions.[9] The air force played a vital role in landing troops in Srinagar, in maintaining the Poonch garrison, in landing and sustaining troops in Ladakh, and in air support missions provided by their Spitfires and Tempest aircrafts. Even then the scale of the effort was relatively minor as only three fighter squadrons, one transport squadron, and one photo reconnaissance flight participated in the operations—roughly half of its existing strength.

Independence, the experience of the Kashmir war, and, most importantly, the colonial experience shaped the attitude and response of the services on the issue of jointness. These influences left four major legacies. First, as Indian officers had limited experience of the higher command of war, including planning, force structures, and operations, they faced a steep learning curve on complex operational issues. Prior to independence, most Indian officers were excluded from manning "sensitive" appointments, partly due to their junior ranks and partly because it was considered a British policy. As a result, they lacked experience in the higher command of war. But after independence, these officers were rapidly promoted to senior ranks, an unavoidable consequence of the speedy exit of British officers. This inexperience in higher defense management characterized the entire defense effort, including on matters pertaining to jointness, for around the first two decades after independence.

Second, even when jointness was discussed, the services' perspective was influenced by British experience and debates. While the navy was too small and had few missions that could realistically envisage major joint operations, the air force and the army had divergent views on the use of air power—mirroring the debates in other countries. Air force philosophy was shaped by the views of its first service chief and a seconded British officer, Air Marshal Thomas Elmhirst.[10] One of his preconditions, while assuming the post of commander-in-chief of the then Royal Indian Air Force (renamed the Indian Air Force [IAF] in 1950) was that it should be "independent" from the army.[11] Modeled on the British setup, this demand stemmed from his short experience as the chief of

[9] For a description of air operations in the Kashmir war, see Bharat Kumar, *An Incredible War: IAF in Kashmir War, 1947–48* (New Delhi: Knowledge World Publishers, 2007).

[10] For an insight into his views on air power, see Thomas Elmhirst, "Lessons of Air Warfare, 1939–45," *Journal of the United Service Institution of India* 68, no. 328 (1947): 477–85.

[11] M. S. Chaturvedi, *History of the Indian Air Force* (New Delhi: Vikas Publishers, 1978), 57.

the Inter-Services Administration—a combined services headquarters or joint command that was created during World War II. Until then, the air force, though established as a separate service in 1932, had operated under the command of the army commander-in-chief.

This desire to be independent, not uncommon in air forces throughout the world, became one of the guiding philosophies of the IAF. Thus, in the operational realm it zealously guarded and later reluctantly parted with functional roles in support of the other two services, like army aviation and naval maritime reconnaissance (these episodes are examined later in this chapter). Its main headquarters was established separate from the other two services and added to the geographical separation that characterizes the location of the command headquarters of all three services.[12] More importantly, the IAF "based much of its thinking on RAF [Royal Air Force] doctrine and practices."[13] Unlike the United States, which had experience of air–ground battle during the Second World War, the RAF philosophy envisaged two primary roles for air power—fighter aircraft for air defense and strategic bombing. The IAF had an institutional preference for the former and was inspired by the folklore around the Battle of Britain, where fighter pilots were seen to have saved the country. This inclination toward fighters in an air defense role became a defining feature of the service culture of the IAF. As a result, it treated cooperation with the army as a secondary task that was best left to transport and helicopter pilots and "there was little joint training even by mid-1950 beyond 'artillery reconnaissance'."[14]

Problems with jointness stemmed not only from the air force's attitude but also from that of the army. The army considered air power essential for transportation and air maintenance tasks but did not fully understand the role that close air support could play in combat operations. Shaped by its own experiences in the Burma theater and, to a limited extent, in the European theater, where allied air forces were dominant, the army did not understand the importance of joint training, planning, and organization. Their planning, training, and doctrine tended to assume that the air force would be useful mainly for sustenance and not so much in actual combat support. The army also thought of itself as the "battle-winning" force, a function of self-glorification; and it was perhaps only

[12] The Indian armed forces have a total of seventeen commands, and with the exception of the joint Strategic Forces Command and the Andaman and Nicobar Command, none of the service commands are in the same location; see Arun Prakash, "Keynote Address," in *Proceedings of USI Seminar on Higher Defense Organization* (New Delhi: United Service Institution of India, 2007), 9.

[13] George Tanham and Marcy Agmon, *The Indian Air Force: Trends and Prospects* (Santa Monica, CA: Rand, 1995), 44.

[14] Jasjit Singh, *The Icon: Marshal of the Air Force Arjan Singh* (New Delhi: Knowledge World Publishers, 2009), 163.

after the experience of the 1965 war that the Indian Army realized the importance of close air support and air superiority.

The third major legacy was that jointness as a concept was confused with
low-level tactical cooperation. In the name of jointness, the services engaged in
minor exercises like aircraft recognition, training for air maintenance operations,
and practice with army artillery observation posts. To facilitate cooperation between the air force and the navy, a combined operations cell was established in
Bombay, later called the Maritime Air Operations cell; but its role was restricted
mainly to coordination.[15] There was a program to facilitate exchange of junior
pilots between the three services. All of these measures enabled low-level tactical cooperation. The only major example of cooperation involved the air force's
transport support to the army to maintain isolated posts in northeast India and
in Ladakh, along the India–China border. This cooperation, crucial as it was, was
restricted to logistics as there was little joint planning and training for combat
operations. According to a former air force officer, "cooperation with the Army
was nonexistent. They made their plans, we made our Counter Air Operation
plans.... Very few IAF officers studied Army ops of war, the Army expected CAS
[close air support] as and when demanded, very much like Arty [Artillery] support, and wanted it to be on call, and under command.... Truly then, in 1962 we
were far from a cohesive Joint operations military machine."[16]

However, some of the ideas in favor of jointness that were introduced
during the last days of the Raj were either continued or resurrected. The Joint
Services Wing, later to be called the National Defence Academy, was established after independence and was one of the first institutions of its kind in the
world where pre-commission training was imparted to cadets of all three services.[17] The combined-services Defence Services Staff College, which in its pre-
independence days was in Quetta, now Pakistan, was established at Wellington
and trained mid-level officers. The National Defence College was established
in New Delhi in 1959, modeled on the British Imperial Defence College, a tri-
services institution to educate senior officers.

Finally, civilians—whether politicians or bureaucrats in the ministry—played
a minimal role in fostering jointness and instead left it to the services. This was
perhaps inevitable as they also lacked expertise and, like the military, faced a

---

[15] Bharat-Rakshak, "IAF in Maritime Operations. Air Vice Marshall (Retd) H. S. Ahluwalia YSM,
VM," June 29, 2006, http://bharat-rakshak.com/cms/srr/64-17.html.

[16] A. G. Bewoor, "Close Air Support in the 1962 War," Bharat-Rakshak, June 12, 2017, http://
www.bharat-rakshak.com/IAF/history/1962war/1019-bewoor.html.

[17] The recommendation for this type of an institution arose out of the deliberations of a committee
that was established by the British in 1945; see V. K. Singh, *Leadership in the Indian Army: Biographies
of 12 Soldiers* (New Delhi: Sage Publications, 2005), 131–33.

steep learning curve. Jointness consequently was a neglected subject within the three services and in the ministry. Ironically, in the late 1950s the British moved toward creating a joint structure and integrating their services. As described in Chapter 2, around this time, Mountbatten urged Prime Minister Jawaharlal Nehru to create a joint staff to be headed by a CDS. However, Nehru opposed it as he was focused more on consolidating civilian control and was apprehensive of appointing a potential "superchief." The services were also reluctant to integrate as they feared a dilution of powers and autonomy. It thereby suited all of the stakeholders to perpetuate the existing arrangement, even at the cost of military effectiveness.

Jointness in War

The following section examines wartime jointness in the Indian military. In doing so it examines five military operations—the 1962 border war with China, the 1965 and 1971 India–Pakistan wars (the latter resulting in the creation of Bangladesh), the 1987–1990 military intervention in Sri Lanka, and the 1999 Kargil war, again with Pakistan.[18] Operations in these wars created many controversies and debates, some of which continue to resonate. As the following analysis shows, the services have preferred the coordination model with its single-service approach, while civilians have largely stayed away from enforcing jointness.

It is important to acknowledge, however, that, as a concept, jointness was not emphasized in most militaries until the 1980s. In the United States, the issue of jointness gained prominence after the ill-fated Iran hostage rescue attempt in 1979 and the invasion of Grenada in 1983. These experiences led to the Goldwater-Nichols Act in 1986, which has been largely responsible for the subsequent revolution in jointness.[19] Criticizing the lack of jointness in the Indian military during the 1962, 1965, and 1971 war is therefore perhaps a little harsh. However, these are assessed to better understand the intellectual debates and evolution of jointness in India.

---

[18] The Indian military also conducted an operation to liberate Goa from Portuguese rule in 1961; but it faced minimal opposition, and jointness was not such an important factor. For a good overview of this operation, see Jagan Pillarisetti, "The Liberation of Goa—An Overview," Bharat-Rakshak, September 22, 2015, https://www.bharat-rakshak.com/IAF/history/1961goa/1012-goa01.html.

[19] For more about the enactment of the Goldwater-Nichols Act, see James R. Locher III and Sam Nunn, *Victory on the Potomac: The Goldwater-Nichols Act Unifies the Pentagon* (College Station: Texas A&M University Press, 2002).

The Great Counterfactual: The 1962 India–China Land War

Jointness did not emerge as a major issue for discussion during the 1962 China war. The navy was completely out of the picture as the war was restricted to land borders. The IAF played a critical role in air transport, sustenance, and casualty evacuation. Its transport and helicopter pilots flew heroic missions to badly maintained airfields, often under adverse weather conditions at high altitudes, and sometimes taking enemy ground fire.[20] However, the air force did not employ offensive air power against Chinese ground forces, and its most direct role in support of the army, besides transportation, was to conduct around twenty-two photo-recce missions with Canberra fighter bombers.[21] According to the official history of this war, "it is felt that during Chinese conflict, had the IAF been used offensively specially in NEFA [North East Frontier Agency] the outcome of the one-sided war might have been different."[22] This has since become one of the major counterfactuals of the war and creates controversy to this day. In 2012, on the fiftieth anniversary of the war, a seemingly off-the-cuff comment from the chief of air staff, Air Chief Marshal N. A. K. Browne, claiming that the use of offensive air power would have changed the outcome of the war, triggered a controversy.[23] While insinuating that it was a political decision and therefore a political blunder, Air Chief Marshal Browne conveniently overlooked, or was perhaps unaware of, the culpability of senior air force leadership.

The reasons behind the non-use of offensive air power are still shrouded in mystery. There are a number of suggested explanations—reluctance of the political leaders to "escalate" the war fearing the Chinese bombardment of Indian cities, incorrect assessment of Chinese air power by the Intelligence Bureau, reluctance on the part of the army that feared losing its transport support, opposition from the IAF itself, and the influence of the US ambassador.[24] Again, according to the official history, "there is no accurate or authentic documentation of the thinking that was behind this decision to desist from use of offensive air

---

[20] For a description of the air transport efforts, see P. B. Sinha and A. A. Athale, "Role of the Indian Air Force," in *History of the Conflict with China, 1962*, 348–55 (New Delhi: History Division, Ministry of Defense, 1992) (hereafter OH 1962).

[21] OH 1962, 348.

[22] OH 1962, 363.

[23] "1962 War Would Have Been Different Had IAF Been on the Offence: ACM," *Indian Express*, October 5, 2012, http://archive.indianexpress.com/news/1962-war-would-have-been-different-had-iaf-been-on-the-offence-acm/1012500/0. Also see Anit Mukherjee, "Where Knowledge Is Free?" *Pragati*, January 11, 2013, http://pragati.nationalinterest.in/2013/01/where-knowledge-is-free/.

[24] For more on this, see OH 1962, 356–65; and R. Sukumaran, "The 1962 India–China War and Kargil 1999: Restrictions on the Use of Air Power," *Strategic Analysis* 27, no. 3 (2003): 332–56.

support."[25] However, some newly available documents suggest that in addition to political reluctance, the IAF itself was unprepared for and unwilling to undertake offensive air operations.

Immediately after the war the British prime minister sent a delegation to evaluate Indian defense requirements. Among the touring officials was Air Vice Marshal P. G. Wykeham, director of the Joint Warfare Staff. His "secret-UK eyes only" report reveals insight into both the lack of air support and the state of the IAF: "the main reason for with-holding close support from hard-pressed army units has been fear of air action escalating into Chinese bombing attacks on Indian cities. Governmental weak nerves on this subject has been further weakened by an intelligence appreciation which over-estimated the enemy air force, and by a lack of self-confidence in the Indian Air Force itself."[26]

The government's uncertainty was matched and perhaps reinforced by the air force's reluctance to engage in a shooting war. The problem in the IAF at that time was probably one of leadership. This aspect was commented on by the visiting British officer:

> I was briefed by the full Air Staff, on two separate occasions and the contrast with the Army was very marked. The Air Staff were full of contradictory excuses, both for the chaotic condition of the Indian Air Force order of battle and for the lack of fighting support for the Army. Air Marshal Engineer, the CAS [Chief of Air Staff], made a very bad impression on me. . . . The leadership at the top is bad, and the CAS is uninspiring and semi-defeatist. The Air Staff has no conception of large-scale force planning, and they seem to receive no help from senior civil servants.[27]

In short, the IAF did not plan or train to fight the Chinese Air Force or for providing offensive air support to the Indian Army. There were no plans or training conducted to operate fighter aircrafts in either NEFA or Ladakh. Admittedly, they were hindered by the directives given by the political leadership as Prime Minister Nehru, mindful of "escalating tensions," ordered them "not to fly recce or fighter sorties within a 24 km belt from the border."[28] This directive, passed on October 20, 1960, was revisited in December 1961 as the army was establishing new posts and "there was an urgent request to waive this condition."[29] However,

[25] OH 1962, 360.

[26] Appendix B in "Secret-UK Eyes Only" letter no. CIGS/PF/515 dated December 3, 1962, in PREM 11/3876, Kew Archives, London.

[27] Appendix B in "Secret-UK Eyes Only" letter no. CIGS/PF/515.

[28] OH 1962, 347.

[29] OH 1962, 347.

Defense Minister Krishna Menon agreed to give clearance to specific flights on a case-by-case basis. It is not yet clear whether the air force pushed for or recommended combat air support throughout this time, although the official history suggests otherwise: "The Defense Minister was probably in favor of full use of the IAF . . . however, it appears that in the light of the weighty professional opinion of Air HQ, the political leadership did not think it wise to use the Air Force in the offensive role."[30] Thus, the political directives and fears of "escalation" were convenient for the air force's own reluctance and lack of training to conduct offensive air operations.

Instead, the main focus of the air force was on air transport and maintenance functions in support of the army. Even with rising tensions on the China border, the air force did not devote time or perhaps did not even have the capability to assess the strengths, capabilities, deployment, and combat potential of the Chinese Air Force.[31] Again, according to the official history, "Air Headquarters does not appear to have conducted any in depth study. In the absence of any professional in-depth and competent technical analysis of the Chinese threat and Indian counters, the spontaneous predominant feeling was that the Chinese enjoyed great superiority in the air, based on sketchy information about their overall strength."[32]

One of the explanations for this is offered by Jasjit Singh when he argues that "the Air Force did not have an institution where employment of air power could be systematically studied."[33] In fact, the School of Land and Air Warfare, which was later called the Joint Air Warfare School and is today known as the College of Air Warfare, was established in 1959 with the mandate to improve the co-ordination between the army and the air force and ought to have played that part. The air force also had experience of close air support during operations in the Congo in 1961–1962.[34] However, this experience was not internalized even though air power played an important role in those operations. In a larger sense, though, Jasjit Singh is right in arguing that the air force did not conduct a professional study into the concept of air power. That type of professional study was only evident under Air Chief Marshal P. C. Lal, who led the air force from 1969 to 1973.

---

[30] OH 1962, 360–61; also see Sukumaran, "The 1962 India–China War and Kargil 1999."

[31] Jasjit Singh, *Defence from the Skies* (New Delhi: Knowledge World Publishers, 2007), 85–87.

[32] OH 1962, 358; also see Singh, *Defence of the Skies*, 82.

[33] Singh, *Defence of the Skies*, 86.

[34] During these operations, in support of the United Nations mission, its Canberra bombers played a decisive role by providing ground support to troops in contact; see Pushpindar Singh Chopra, "Canberras in the Congo," *Bharat Rakshak*, July 20, 2009, http://www.bharat-rakshak.com/IAF/History/52-Congo/1009-Congo01.html.

It would be incorrect, however, to put the entire onus of blame on the leadership of the air force. The Indian Army did not fully understand the utility of air power and focused merely on taking advantage of its airlift capabilities. It does appear as if the army did not fully incorporate air force officers into the decision-making loop and instead treated them as a supporting arm. In sum, higher defense organizations and the interactions between civilians and the military and between the army and the air force were problematic before and during the 1962 war. There was little professional staff work and an "almost total absence of joint planning,"[35] which reflected an amateurish approach to modern warfare.

The Ministry of Defence (MoD), led by the temperamental Krishna Menon, played no role in enabling jointness between the services. Even so, the narrative that emerged from the war blamed civilians for operational meddling, and subsequently, "civilians chose to keep away from operational issues."[36] This unfortunately left jointness entirely at the discretion of the services and cemented a single-service approach to military operations. That arrangement left much to be desired.

The "Supermo" Complex: Jointness in the 1965 India–Pakistan War

The 1965 India–Pakistan war, even by the complicated history of the subcontinent, was one of its strangest wars. A precursor to the war witnessed both armies fighting a localized conflict in the saltwater plains of the Kutch in Gujarat. After a few months of tension, the real war was triggered in August by a Pakistani infiltration deep into Kashmir. Each country charged the other with starting the war, and both claimed victory—as they still do. The war witnessed some of the largest tank and aerial battles since World War II, but civilian casualties were rare. India did not move against the isolated and numerically inferior Pakistani forces in East Pakistan, now Bangladesh—even though they were attacked by Pakistani Air Force (PAF) units based there. There were allegations of an unspoken agreement between the air force commanders not to attack each other's airfields, until the PAF allegedly broke this agreement by carrying out successful raids on Indian airfields. By the time a ceasefire was imposed by the United Nations, the Indian military was in a comparatively better position as attrition, combined with suspension of military aid from the United States, had left the Pakistani military in a precipitous state. Despite this material advantage, however, the Indian

---

[35] Singh, *Defence of the Skies*, 86.

[36] Srinath Raghavan, "Civil–Military Relations in India: The China Crisis and After," *Journal of Strategic Studies* 32, no. 1 (2009): 173.

Army chief, when asked by the political leaders, preferred an immediate cease-fire. Departing from the hostility of the Cold War and to prevent China from playing a significant role, the United States preferred that the Soviet Union host the ceasefire negotiations, which culminated with the Tashkent Agreement in January 1966. In a final twist, the Indian prime minister died of a heart attack within hours of signing the agreement.

With respect to jointness, the 1965 war resulted in many controversies that created much bitterness between the services. During the two phases of the war—limited clashes in the Gulf of Kutch in April–May, followed by the war proper in August–September—interservices operations left much to be desired.[37] There were two major aspects relating to this—inadequate sharing of information, leading to an absence of joint planning, and an organizational inclination toward the single-service approach. On the first aspect, there is an almost complete unanimity of views—there was little, if any, joint planning within the Indian military.[38] Instead, each of the services operated, more or less, independently.

The absence of joint planning has two different explanations. The first, popular within the air force, blames it squarely on senior army leadership, especially the conduct of General J. N. Chaudhuri.[39] While General Chaudhuri was frequently consulted by the senior political leadership, he allegedly did not inform the other services of these discussions. In the run-up to the war, according to most accounts, General Chaudhuri assumed the post of chairman of the Chiefs of Staff Committee (COSC), and it was his responsibility to coordinate the preparation of a joint war plan.[40] That this was not done was attributed to the single-service thinking prevalent at that time as well as General Chaudhuri's alleged "supermo syndrome."[41]

In his defense, General Chaudhuri claimed that he was "in great doubt"[42] as to whether he would receive political permission to launch a full-scale war across

---

[37] Amit Gupta, *Building an Arsenal: The Evolution of Regional Power Force Structures* (Westport, CT: Praeger, 1997), 43.

[38] B. C. Chakravorty, *History of the Indo–Pak War, 1965* (New Delhi: History Division, Ministry of Defence, 1992), 267, 329 (hereafter OH 1965).

[39] P. C. Lal, "Some Problems of Defence," in *USI National Security Lectures* (New Delhi: United Service Institution of India, 1977), 72–73.

[40] There is some dispute over whether Admiral B. S. Soman or General Chaudhuri was the chairman of the COSC during this war. For more on this, see G. M. Hiranandani, *Transition to Triumph: History of the Indian Navy, 1965–75* (New Delhi: Lancer Publications, 2000), 50.

[41] A term used to denote the army's desire for intellectual and perceptual domination; see P. C. Lal, *My Years with the Air Force* (New Delhi: Lancer International, 1986), 163.

[42] J. N. Chaudhuri, "India's Problems of National Security in the Seventies," in *USI National Security Lectures* (New Delhi: United Service Institution of India, 1973), 42.

the International Boundary. As a result, he was unable to give clear instructions to the other two services. There is some strength in this argument. Prime Minister Lal Bahadur Shastri was reluctant to embark on a full-scale war and vacillated over giving operational directives.[43] Therefore a lack of communication and trust between the political and military leadership led to a confused, ill-coordinated response.

The second explanation for a lack of joint plans blames the leadership of the air force and the navy for essentially wishing to "sit out" the war. After the war, Air Chief Marshal Arjan Singh was criticized for his reluctance to employ offensive air power, especially to conduct strike sorties against enemy airfields—either to honor a telephone commitment he made to the previous Pakistani air chief or to prevent an escalation of the conflict.[44] Criticizing the senior leadership, the official history of the war noted that "the IAF, it seems, operated on the basis of ad-hoc decisions, and in the hope that full-scale war would simply not come."[45] Air Chief Marshal Krishnaswamy, then a young fighter pilot, captures the frustration within the air force at that time when he says that he found "[senior] commanders at the desks to be confused and under-confident, lacking imagination and grit."[46]

Similarly, chief of naval staff Admiral B. S. Soman was criticized for not planning offensive operations. To be sure, the government had placed restrictions on the navy's sphere of operations and ordered it not to unilaterally undertake offensive missions.[47] However, it is unclear whether Admiral Soman proposed any offensive missions or was content to sit it out. According to a former naval officer, "naval leaders did not show boldness or initiative during the 1965 war."[48] Admiral Soman refuted these allegations and argued that he tried his best to obtain sanction from the government to undertake offensive actions.[49] While we may never know what exactly transpired, ultimately, the navy had no real role to play in the war. However, on the positive side, the inactivity during this war and the humiliation that was heaped on the navy due to the Pakistani naval

[43] Hiranandani, *Transition to Triumph*, 43.

[44] For a personal note from Air Chief Marshal Arjan Singh admitting this instruction, see Singh, *The Icon*, 197–98, also see 143–47 for a sympathetic view of this episode.

[45] OH 1965, 247.

[46] S. Krishnaswamy, "Out of the Blue," *Indian Express*, August 3, 2006.

[47] For more about this, see Hiranandani, *Transition to Triumph*, 40–55.

[48] OH 1965, 296. Air Chief Marshal Arjan Singh was also of the view that the naval leadership was reluctant to take part in operations; see Hiranandani, *Transition to Triumph*, 50.

[49] Hiranandani, *Transition to Triumph*, 51–53; also see diary entry of then defense minister Chavan in R. D. Pradhan, *1965 War: The Inside Story* (New Delhi: Atlantic Publishers, 2007), 58.

bombardment of Dwarka (on September 07, 1965) spurred them on to be more proactive, which led to spectacular results in the 1971 war.[50]

Another aspect of jointness was that by their operating philosophy, information-sharing practices, and training the services were inherently inclined toward single-service operations. Aviators flying for the navy complained about the attitude and lack of tactical cooperation with the air force.[51] There was "a total absence of a joint Naval–Air Plan for the defense of naval bases."[52] However, the biggest problem was with air force–army cooperation. The official history attributed the infamous "friendly fire" incidents in the Chamb to the "lack of proper wireless network and lack of adequate Army–IAF coordination."[53]

Jasjit Singh argues that the broad strategy of the IAF in the 1965 war was to "be employed essentially in support of the army."[54] The available evidence does not support this claim. Instead, it appears as if each service fought its own war, with little coordination between the two. Just about 18% of the total combat support missions flown by the air force were used for close air support.[55] Even when flying ground support missions, the targeting philosophy was either for general strategic interdiction or to engage "targets of opportunity"[56] and, in most cases, had little impact on the tactical ground battles.[57] This was largely because the existing structures for cooperation were dysfunctional, had little situational awareness, and were not trained or even equipped to execute joint operations.[58] It is not even clear that the IAF had devised a clear operational plan and had carefully thought through the employment of air power.[59] The only operational plan known to exist during this period was one issued by the chief of air staff on September 5, 1965, a day before the Indian Army crossed the International

---

[50] For an account of Admiral Nanda's resolve after the humiliation in 1965, see Hiranandani, *Transition to Triumph*, 118.

[51] Hiranandani, *Transition to Triumph*, 265.

[52] Lal, *My Years with the Air Force*, 164–65.

[53] OH 1965, 328.

[54] Singh, *The Icon*, 171; it is unclear, however, whether this reflects the chief's operations order of September 5, 1965, or is his own deduction.

[55] According to the official history, a total of 696 fighter bomber sorties were launched for close air support out of a total of 3,937 sorties; see OH 1965, 269.

[56] Lal, "Some Problems of Defence," 75.

[57] P. V. S. Jagan Mohan and Samir Chopra, *The India–Pakistan Air War of 1965* (New Delhi: Manohar Publications, 2005), 95, 205, 226–28. An important exception was the IAF raids that blunted and imposed caution on the Pakistani offensive in the Chamb sector.

[58] Mohan and Chopra, *India–Pakistan Air War of 1965*, 308–9; Harbaksh Singh, *War Despatches: Indo–Pak Conflict 1965* (New Delhi: Lancer International, 1991), 170–77; Lal, *My Years with the Air Force*, 164, 175–76; and OH 1965, 268–69.

[59] Tanham and Agmon, *Indian Air Force*, 28, for more on the problems with army–air force cooperation, see 32–33.

Boundary to attack Lahore. In contrast, the PAF had better thought through the employment of air power and had made detailed war plans.[60] It provided more effective tactical air support to its army and imposed caution on the Indian Army. To be sure, the PAF had superior fighters, radar and communication systems, and a clear technological edge. However, possibly due to its cooperation and tutelage under the US Air Force, it also displayed a higher level of professionalism, cogent planning, and better skills at army–air force cooperation.[61] Obliquely admitting as much, the official history attempted to exculpate the performance of the IAF when it argued that "with *low level of professionalism*, lack of proper planning and cooperation with the army, and the aircraft of old vintage, the IAF could not be expected to perform much better."[62]

On its part, the Indian Army also did not display much appreciation for the use of air power. Army planners rarely integrated air power into battle plans and operated under a single-service mentality. Army war games and operations planning were apparently conducted without air force participation, and it is not even clear whether the details of the operational plans were fully shared.[63] Moreover, the functioning of the existing organizations for cooperation, like the Joint Army Air Operation Center, was suspect and problematic.[64] In sum, each of the services operated within its own organizations and there was little sharing of information and overall integration between them.[65]

One must, however, resist the temptation to criticize the service chiefs and other senior commanders too harshly. In the first place, political leaders were hesitant to escalate the conflict, and hence the initiative was with Pakistan. Second, the air force and the army, in particular, were in the middle of major reorganization and expansion in manpower and equipment. Third, the Pakistani military had a technological edge in hardware with superior aircraft, radar, and command and control elements. In fact, it had more tanks in its inventory, including the reputed Patton tanks, than what the Indian Army possessed.[66] Finally, the experience of the defeat in the 1962 war had unnerved senior military commanders, as a result of which they lacked confidence in the capabilities of their commanders and men. Considering all of these factors, senior leaders did the best that they could, and the experience of this war helped prepare them for the next, more consequential one.

[60] OH 1965, 249, 329–30.

[61] For a reference to the influence of American training and concepts on the PAF, see OH 1965, 246–47.

[62] OH 1965, 330 (emphasis added); also see comments made by P. M. Wilson, 273.

[63] Tanham and Agmon, *Indian Air Force*, 25–34.

[64] Singh, *War Despatches*, 170–75.

[65] Lal, "Some Problems of Defence," 72–73.

[66] For a comparison of the opposing forces in the western sector, see Singh, *War Despatches*, 7.

During this war, civilians gave the military considerable leeway and autonomy in planning and operations. Civilian principals directing this conflict, Prime Minister Shastri and Defense Minister Y. B. Chavan, along with advisers like Defence Secretary P. V. R. Rao, did little to encourage or foster jointness within the services. Instead, taking a cue from the main lesson that was internalized after the 1962 war, they stayed away from discussing or questioning operational plans. This pattern of civil–military relations, proved to be "deeply problematic" as the "politicians' reluctance to look closely into military matters resulted in the war ending in stalemate."[67] After the 1962 war, civilians were afraid of the political consequences of engaging, challenging, and, if required, overruling the military. Therefore, hampered by a lack of authority and expertise, civilians did not insist on jointness; and instead, their directives were confined to the broader strategy, leaving the operational conduct of the war to the military. In the absence of joint staff, interservices operations therefore suffered from a lack of coordination, information asymmetries, and even incidents of friendly fire.[68]

Victory, the Terrible Teacher: Jointness and the 1971 Bangladesh War

The 1971 Bangladesh war was the "finest hour" for the Indian armed forces. It not only freed a nation but, while defeating the Pakistani military, captured the largest number of prisoners of war since the Battle of Stalingrad in World War II. This "lightning" campaign erased some of the ignominy of the 1962 defeat and the stalemate of the 1965 war and established India as the dominant power in the subcontinent. In later years, this war was studied as a textbook campaign on political–military interaction, operational freedom for the services, and interservices cooperation. This overly simplistic reading of the war glossed over the crucial role played by civilians in fostering jointness, and is at variance with the idea of complete operational freedom. There were four major aspects to jointness during this war.

First, the three services had adequate preparatory time, which they used wisely to prepare for operations. The Pakistani crackdown in East Pakistan began in March 1971, and war finally broke out in November/December of that year. The Indian military, therefore, had adequate warning and used it by emphasizing joint

---

[67] Srinath Raghavan, "Soldiers, Statesmen, and India's Security Policy," *India Review* 11, no. 2 (2012): 122.

[68] For instance, there was a lack of clarity about the expected duration of the war. Hence, toward the end of the war while the army was fighting high-intensity battles, the air force was sending its pilots for rest and recuperation under the assumption that it would be a long, multiyear war; see Mohan and Chopra, *India–Pakistan Air War of 1965*, 306–7.

planning at all levels. The sense that war was inevitable forced an urgency into the services, and they made extra efforts to engage with each other. Operational plans were made and periodically amended, war games were conducted, formation commanders were briefed, and troops were trained according to their expected tasking.[69] The operational commands of the three services were given specific tasks, and lower formations were suitably reorganized and equipped.[70] Therefore, detailed planning, practice, and organizational changes allowed the three services to operate with a vastly improved degree of jointness.

Second, all three services put into practice the lessons learned from the 1965 war and paid particular attention to joint planning and operations. The attitude of the air force in particular was crucial and this time its performance was a marked improvement. This was because the chief of air staff, Air Chief Marshal P. C. Lal, had been the vice chief during the 1965 war and had an opportunity to learn from that experience.[71] More importantly, the air force made an honest effort to deal with some of its shortcomings. Accordingly, the air force prioritized ground support missions and streamlined the organization and process of army–air force tactical cooperation.[72] As a result, according to the official history, more than 40% of the offensive missions in the western sector were flown in support of the army.[73] And in the eastern sector, "about 60% of the air effort was allocated for close support of the army."[74] The IAF's offensive and force employment strategy turned the tables on the PAF, ironically "doing a 1965" on them.[75] Hence, the PAF concentrated on self-preservation and flew defensive air cover sorties, thereby restricting its ability to interfere with the ground battle. However, this strategy of prioritizing ground support missions came at a high cost to the IAF as its pilots were exposed to enemy anti-aircraft fire. As a measure of its performance, during the 1971 operations a little over 42% of the IAF losses due to enemy action were from anti-aircraft ground fire; and, by

---

[69] For an overview of this, see S. N. Prasad and U. P. Thapliyal, eds., *The India–Pakistan War of 1971: A History* (New Delhi: Natraj Publishers, Ministry of Defence, 2014), 105–8; this is a copy of the official history and hereafter is referred to as OH 1971.

[70] Sukhwant Singh, *Defence of the Western Border: India's Wars since Independence* (New Delhi: Lancer Publishers, 1981), 2:304–9.

[71] For the best description of army–air force cooperation and learning in the interwar years, see Lal, "Some Problems of Defence," 77–85.

[72] Lal, *My Years with the Air Force*, 174–76.

[73] OH 1971, 235.

[74] Lal, *My Years with the Air Force*, 187; according to the official history, the figure is 68%; see OH 1971, 367.

[75] The PAF concept of operations in 1971 had an uncanny resemblance to that of the IAF during the 1965 war; see OH 1971, 238.

contrast, this figure for the 1965 war was around 14%.[76] One consequence of such high casualties was the internalization within the air force that providing close air support in an air defense–rich environment was a waste of air assets.[77] After such a costly experience, the air force turned away from prioritizing and training for close air support and instead concentrated on strategic interdiction missions.

Similarly, the army put into practice the lessons it learned from the 1965 war and emphasized air defense, air cover for its operations, and army–air force tactical cooperation. Formation commanders, in both theaters of operation, were careful to involve air force planners and operators in the run-up to the war, and this working familiarity helped during operations. The navy too made a conscious decision to plan and train for offensive operations, thus avenging the humiliation of 1965, and in doing so worked closely with the other services.[78]

Third, as described in Chapter 2, in a departure from the past, civilian principals played a more active role in facilitating jointness. Just like the military learned from the 1965 war, civilians also internalized the necessity for enhancing interservices coordination. As a result, they made it a point to attend important meetings and facilitate exchange of information among the three services. The political leaders during this conflict, Prime Minister Indira Gandhi and Defense Minister Jagjivan Ram, met regularly with the service chiefs and kept everyone informed about the developing situation. A cohesive political–military strategy was facilitated by bureaucrats like P. N. Haksar, D. P. Dhar, and Defense Secretary K. B. Lall.[79] Despite playing the role of a facilitator, it is not entirely clear if civilians actively intervened and pushed for joint operations.

Finally, while there was considerable improvement, it would be a misreading of the war to suggest that all was well with jointness. The relations between General Manekshaw and Air Chief Marshal P. C. Lal were not cordial, a fact that their operational commanders had to work around.[80] In the western sector, according to Air Chief Marshal Lal, "no detailed plans were drawn up for offensive operations

---

[76] In 1971 the IAF lost fifty-six aircraft due to enemy action, out of which twenty-four were due to anti-aircraft ground fire; see OH 1971, 236. During 1965 operations eight aircraft were destroyed by anti-aircraft ground fire out of a total of fifty-nine lost to enemy action; data compiled from OH 1965, 270–271 and Mohan and Chopra, *India–Pakistan Air War of 1965*, appendix B.

[77] Interview with Air Marshal Vinod Patney, Gurgaon, September 2, 2010.

[78] Hiranandani, *Transition to Triumph*, 118–26.

[79] For a description of civil–military relations during this period, see Oral History Transcripts, K. B. Lal, parts 1 and 2, no. 724, 437–41, Nehru Memorial Library and Museum (NMML), New Delhi, also see Depinder Singh, *Field Marshal Sam Manekshaw: Soldiering with Dignity* (Dehra Dun: Natraj Publishers, 2002), 155.

[80] J. F. R. Jacob, *Surrender at Dhaka: Birth of a Nation* (New Delhi: Manohar Publishers, 2006), 51; and Singh, *Field Marshal Sam Manekshaw*, 135.

to be mounted jointly by the Army and the Air Force."[81] Even the much celebrated naval and air attacks on oil installations in Karachi on December 9, 1971, which were hailed at that time as a perfect example of jointmanship, were later discovered to be fortuitous and not deliberately planned.[82]

While cooperation in the eastern sector was better, there were problems nonetheless with interoperability. For instance, as per plans, naval aircraft operating from the aircraft carrier INS *Vikrant* were expected to provide air support for army operations in the south; but when the war started, "naval authorities said that their pilots had not been trained for the support of forces in the field."[83] In addition, tactical units from different services lacked the capability to directly communicate with each other and instead had to rely on higher formations to ensure coordination. This led to some casualties due to "friendly fire" and an inability to support each other's missions.[84] Acknowledging problems in jointness, the official history went on to argue that there is a "need for joint staff at formation and command levels for proper planning and conduct of operations. . . . On top should be placed the Chief of Defense Staff."[85]

India's resounding victory meant that there was little critical analysis of the war, which stymied further debate and movement toward jointness. To be sure, there was some analysis of the operations and the "lessons learnt about the conduct of joint operations led to the Army/Air HQ Joint Directive for Ground and Air Training, which was issued in 1972."[86] However, this did not significantly change the single-service approach as the MoD and the services falsely believed that the coordination model of jointness had worked well and was appropriate. Success, as is usually the case, was the enemy of change; and there was little incentive to alter the existing structures for interservices cooperation.

Later, a falling out between Air Chief Marshal P. C. Lal and General Manekshaw over the suggested appointment of the latter as the CDS created bitterness between the services. This measure which had been agreed to in principle by the government was scrapped once the chief of air staff protested.[87] The legacy

[81] Lal, *My Years with the Air Force*, 223; the exception was pre-allotment of air assets in support of the 1 Corps offensives in the Shakargarh sector.

[82] S. N. Kohli, *We Dared: Maritime Operations in the 1971 Indo–Pak War* (New Delhi: Lancer International, 1989), 89–93; and Lal, *My Years with the Air Force*, 294–98.

[83] Lal, *My Years with the Air Force*, 210.

[84] Hiranandani, *Transition to Triumph*, 154–57; for another instance of a lack of interoperability, see OH 1971, 385.

[85] OH 1971, 449; also see Lal, *My Years with the Air Force*, 216.

[86] P. M. Mathai, "Building Jointness," in *Air Power and Joint Operations*, ed. Jasjit Singh, 77 (New Delhi: Knowledge World Publishers, 2003).

[87] The chief of naval staff was unhappy with the proposal but kept quiet, while Air Chief Marshal Lal made his opposition clear; see Top Secret letter from P. N. Haksar to Indira Gandhi, December

of this episode vitiated the atmosphere, and soon peacetime disagreements over turf—maritime and army aviation, attack helicopters, etc.—froze any significant move toward jointness.

In Tiger Country: The 1987–1990 Military Intervention in Sri Lanka

The deployment of the Indian Peace Keeping Force (IPKF) in Sri Lanka from 1987 to 1990 was India's first and only expeditionary counterinsurgency operation. This episode came to be known as "India's Vietnam"[88] as, just like in Vietnam, India failed to achieve its political–military goals, suffered high casualties in a guerilla war fought in jungles, and faced domestic political opposition. This was a tri-services operation with the involvement of the air force and the navy, mainly in troop transport, logistical maintenance, and casualty evacuation. In addition, the air force deployed some of its helicopters to provide tactical support to ground troops.[89] The navy was tasked to establish a *cordon militaire* and deployed its ships and aircrafts to prevent movement of militant arms and materials.[90] However, the best indication of the limited combat role of both the air force and the navy was the absence of any battle casualties, while the army suffered more than 1,200 fatalities. On jointness there were two major issues that emerged during this conflict.

First, confusion and rivalry over command and control of the mission between the three services resulted in a lack of ownership, which hampered joint operations. At the apex level, the three service chiefs at that time enjoyed unusually good relations and, even before the operation was launched on July 30, 1987, insisted on establishing the tri-services Overall Forces Headquarters (called HQ OFC). This headquarters was established at Pune and headed by Lieutenant General Depinder Singh with three service component commanders. However, within a fortnight the naval and air force component commanders, in a coordinated move, returned to their respective formations and instead sent their

24, 1972, Subject File no. 56, PN Haksar Papers (I and II Installment), NMML; also see Lal, *My Years with the Air Force*, 326–28.

[88] See special feature "India's Vietnam: The IPKF in Sri Lanka, 10 Years On," Rediff.com, March 2000, https://www.rediff.com/news/2000/mar/23lanka.htm; for a good analysis of this operation, see N. Manoharan, "National Security Decision Making Structure in India: Lessons from the IPKF involvement in Sri Lanka," *Journal of Defence Studies* 3, no. 4 (2009): 49–63.

[89] For a good overview of the air effort in this war, see Bharat Kumar, *Operation Pawan: Role of Airpower with IPKF* (New Delhi: Manohar Publishers, 2015).

[90] For a statistical overview of naval operations during this mission, see G. M. Hiranandani, *Transition to Eminence: The Indian Navy 1976–1990* (New Delhi: Lancer Publishers, 2005), 196.

juniors to act as liaison officers—an arrangement that continued for the duration of the mission.[91] Even though the chiefs of the services wanted a type of theater command with senior component commanders, their formation commanders resisted this idea and instead preferred the older model of liaison officer to "co-ordinate operations." Faced with this opposition from within their own service, the naval and air force chiefs backed down.[92] This resulted in the usual single-service approach to operations wherein the Overall Force Commander of the IPKF did not command the assets of the other two services and instead had to depend upon liaison officers to plan interservices operations.[93] According to Major General Harkirat Singh, whose division was tasked to capture Jaffna and suffered heavily in the process, "the Air Force was commanding its own troops, Army its own troops, Navy its own troops. . . . Everybody went independently, there was no joint command. It was a tri-service operation, Air Force, Navy and Army involved, but there was no joint command. There should have been a single command to take this full force across."[94]

Major General Harkirat Singh partly blamed the disastrous helidrop at Jaffna University, where an entire platoon, save one, got wiped out, on the inability of the air force to deliver on the planned number of helicopters.[95] His was perhaps a motivated account, but without assured support, commanders were averse to planning interservices operations. On this aspect, Lieutenant General A. S. Kalkat, who was subsequently in charge of the IPKF, commented "Air Force and Naval assets were given but they were still taking orders from their headquarters and as they were not dedicated to me this resulted in delays affecting planning and operations."[96]

The second issue pertaining to jointness was the lack of interoperability between the three services. Partly a result of single-service thinking and indicative of organizational priorities, none of the services had planned and prepared for

[91] This account is based on interview with Vice Admiral P. S. Das who was at that time the chief of staff, Eastern Naval Command, New Delhi, July 15, 2010. Later, the navy posted junior liaison officers at different locations in Sri Lanka.

[92] Interview with Vice Admiral P. S. Das, New Delhi, July 15, 2010.

[93] For criticism of interservices operations from the then OFC commander, see Depinder Singh, *IPKF in Sri Lanka* (Delhi: Trishul Publications, 1991), 59–60 and 168–69; also see Kalyanraman, "Major Lessons from Operation Pawan for Future Stability Operations," *Journal of Defense Studies* 6, no. 3 (2012): 43–44.

[94] See interview with Josy Joseph, "Till the LTTE Get Eelam, They Won't Stop," Rediff.com, March 2000, https://www.rediff.com/news/2000/mar/30lanka.htm.

[95] See interview with Josy Joseph, "Nobody Sounded Even a Last Post for Our Dead in Colombo," Rediff.com, March 2000, https://www.rediff.com/news/2000/apr/01lanka.htm; for a very different, and more balanced, view, see Sushant Singh, *Mission Overseas: Daring Operations by the Indian Military* (New Delhi: Juggernaut Books, 2017), 79–148.

[96] Interview with Lieutenant General A. S. Kalkat, New Delhi, October 27, 2009.

joint tactical operations. Unsurprisingly, therefore, the services did not have the technological capability to communicate with each other. On the rare occasion when they carried out joint tactical operations, usually an army radio detachment was physically located with helicopters or naval craft.[97] Among the few instances when naval fire support was requested by the army, it engaged targets two kilometers away from where it was needed.[98] As there were no joint command structures, the services operated within their own silos; and there were even problems with aligning maps. In short, operations in Sri Lanka made it clear that there was no concept of interoperability between the services.

The role of civilians in facilitating jointness was the traditional one—they had little, if anything, to say on operational matters. Instead, the military had considerable autonomy in the planning and conduct of operations. The civilian interface with the military for this operation was provided at two locations— the Indian High Commission in Colombo and the control exercised by a core group that was formed in New Delhi. The former, led by High Commissioner J. N. Dixit, had difficult working with some of the field commanders, most notably with Major General Harkirat Singh.[99] This matter was only resolved when Singh was replaced, apparently on the basis of Dixit's complaint.[100] This episode revealed significant differences between the military and the diplomats amid allegations from the former that it was the "MEA's [Ministry of External Affairs] first war." To coordinate different agencies involved in this operation, an ad hoc core group consisting of officials from the military, intelligence, the cabinet secretary, and other ministries was established in New Delhi.[101] According to Lieutenant General A. S. Kalkat, who took over as General Officer Commanding-in-Chief of the IPKF "the Core group functioned magnificently."[102] However, others were much more critical.[103] On the whole, civilians had little role to play in interservices integration. Instead, the services followed their single-service approach to operations that the coordination model envisaged.

[97] Yashwant Deva, *Sky Is the Limit: Signals in Operation Pawan* (New Delhi: Pentagon Press, 2007), 231–34. For his assessment of interservices communications, see 322–23.

[98] Singh, *IPKF in Sri Lanka*, 169; also see S. C. Sardeshpande, *Assignment: Jaffna* (New Delhi: Lancer Publishers, 1992), 57–59.

[99] Harkirat Singh, *Intervention in Sri Lanka: The IPKF Experience Retold* (New Delhi: Manohar Publishers, 2007), 50–58.

[100] J. N. Dixit, *Assignment Colombo* (Delhi: Konark Publishers, 1998), 211.

[101] For the composition of the Core Group, see Manoharan, "National Security Decision Making Structure in India," 52.

[102] Interview, New Delhi, April 11, 2008.

[103] Singh, *IPKF in Sri Lanka*, 173–74; and Manoharan, "National Security Decision Making Structure in India," 57.

The Air–Land Battle: The 1999 Kargil War

The 1999 Kargil war was triggered by the intrusion of Pakistani troops across the Line of Control in Kashmir. The Indian Navy was on high alert during this conflict and played an important role in signaling resolve, but this was primarily an air–land operation. Indicative of the difference in ordnance usage, the air force dropped around 500 bombs, whereas the artillery alone fired over 250,000 shells, bombs, and rockets. According to some estimates, over 83% of Pakistan's 466 fatalities were caused by combined infantry and artillery fire and 1% were due to air strikes.[104] Despite the difference in scale, however, this was a combined air–land battle which revealed three main problems pertaining to jointness.

First was the acrimonious relationship between the army and the air force at the highest levels in New Delhi. One of the enduring controversies of the war was regarding the promptness of the air force in responding to army requests for close air support. The prevalent view in the army is that the air force dithered over their requests for support. According to an officer who served in the Operations Directorate, "in one of the early COSC meetings held at the Military Operations Room, Air Chief Marshal Tipnis almost gave a shut up call to the VCOAS [vice chief of army staff] who was requesting for air support."[105] Air force officers, on the other hand, argue that the army was not clear or forthcoming about the operational picture and was making unrealistic demands, like using attack helicopters in high-altitude areas.[106] These tensions were partially resolved when chief of army staff General V. P. Malik returned from his foreign visit and lobbied the other chiefs to present a joint plan to their political leaders.[107] However, this episode set the tone, and the war of words between the two services and the bitterness reverberate to this day.[108] The initial tensions and bitterness added to the interservice rivalry and, in turn, encouraged single-service narratives to the conflict. All the same, many participants observed that while relations were stained at senior levels, at the functional level, especially in the lower formation headquarters, they worked well as a team.[109]

---

[104] Author calculations based on data taken from a Pakistani Army website which displayed a list of battle casualties in "Shuhada's Corner" (martyr's corner). This website was later taken down, but the list has been downloaded and hosted at Bharat-Rakshak.com: https://forums.bharat-rakshak.com/viewtopic.php?t=5761.

[105] Mohan Bhandari, "Kargil: An IAF Perspective," *Indian Defence Review* 25, no. 2 (2010): 134. Also see Harwant Singh, "Revisiting Kargil," *Indian Defence Review* 25, no. 2 (2010): 130–33.

[106] Narayan Menon, "The Ghosts of Kargil," *Indian Defence Review* 25, no. 3 (2010): 122–23.

[107] For a description of this, see V. P. Malik, *Kargil: From Surprise to Victory* (New Delhi: HarperCollins, 2007), 119–24.

[108] "Ex-Air Marshal Returns Army Fire," Rediff News, June 8, 2004, https://www.rediff.com/news/2004/jun/08spec1.htm.

[109] Menon, "Ghosts of Kargil," 126.

The second and perhaps more important problem was in the execution of joint operations as they revealed lacunae in the joint planning process, information sharing, and execution. The problems with joint planning started from the top, with the service chiefs in the COSC. The views of the services could not be more different as General V. P. Malik claimed that the COSC is the "worst organization for joint planning,"[110] while a senior air force officer who was present at the meetings called it "a very effective body."[111] This divergence reflected an institutional divide on the proper model for jointness as the air force prefers to continue the "coordination" model and the army argues for the "co-option" one, preferably under its control. Other than problems at the highest level, there were issues at the functional level of planning. The air force made its plans and coordinated operations from liaising with 15 Corps headquarters, based in Srinagar. However, the plans of attack and the actual conduct of operation were done with minimal interference from higher headquarters at 8 Mountain Division headquarters under Major General Mohinder Puri. He had no air force representative to coordinate air force–army activities, despite his lobbying the air chief.[112] As a result, air force operations were almost incidental to the ground attack plans. Tellingly, General Malik was even approached by one of his field commanders to halt the air strikes as they were interfering with his battle plans, but he declined to do so.[113]

A related problem was in the conceptualization of the plan and the sharing of information between the services. Conditioned by a single-service approach, the services maintain separate operations room, and the traditional norms on information sharing result in limited and controlled information sharing. As a result, air force officers argue that the army at different levels—army, command, and corps headquarters—did not fully share their operational plans, future tasking, and contingencies.[114] Instead, the air force was told about the deployment of its own troops to prevent casualties from "friendly fire" and indicated the areas where air power was desired. In short, the planning of operations was not truly integrated.

[110] Interview with General V. P. Malik, Chandimandir, June 1, 2010.

[111] Interview with officer who wishes to remain unnamed, Gurgaon, August 30, 2010.

[112] Interview with Lieutenant General Mohinder Puri, Gurgaon, May 25, 2010. According to him, although the chief of air staff was appreciative of his advice and an air force officer was sent for a few days, he was soon reverted back.

[113] Interview with the General V. P. Malik, Chandimandir, June 1, 2010, and with the field commander who made this request, October 5, 2010. This request was turned down by General Malik as he wanted to maintain interservices unity and continue the diplomatic pressure on Pakistan.

[114] Telephone interview Air Marshal Menon, May 27, 2010; also see his "Kargil—10 Years After," first published in *Indian Defence Review* and reproduced at Bharat-rakshak.com, http://www.bharat-rakshak.com/IAF/History/Kargil/1059-Menon.html.

Writing in 1995 and based on interviews with senior air force officers at that time, George Tanham and Marcy Agmon argued that "support of the Army is a top mission of the Indian Air Force. . . . The current Air Force leadership considers air support to the Army as one of its highest priorities—a position the IAF has not always taken."[115] In 2012, while analyzing the role of airpower in the Kargil war, Benjamin Lambeth supported this notion and argued that "until the early 1990s, it [the IAF] was principally a support entity for the Indian Army."[116] On the contrary, the war in Kargil proved that both sets of authors relied too heavily on the pronouncements of air force officials. Instead, there were serious problems with the air force's training and preparations for close air support. To be sure, the terrain and altitude in Kargil were unique and challenging to both humans and machines, but the capabilities of the air force reflected a lack of organizational emphasis and training for close air support. Hence, lacking ground to air communications and training, troops in contact could not guide aircraft to desired targets.[117] Also, while the air force had experimented with ground-based laser designators since 1983, when faced with difficulties it simply argued that this capability was not required.[118] It can be reasonably argued that had close air support been a priority, the air force would have found ways to overcome this problem.[119] As the air force had not visualized operating in this area, there was no radar coverage; and it was only toward the end of the operations that ground radar was established.[120] There were no forward air controllers in the entire theater as the air force did not feel the need for them. Instead, army aviation helicopters were diverted to be used as airborne forward air controllers, but this ad hoc arrangement, which suffered from a lack of training, proved to be rudimentary and largely unsatisfactory.[121] The localized theater of conflict also

[115] Tanham and Agmon, *Indian Air Force*, 91.

[116] Benjamin Lambeth, *Airpower at 18,000': The Indian Air Force in the Kargil War* (Washington, DC: Carnegie Endowment, 2012), 3.

[117] Y. M. Bammi, *Kargil 1999: The Impregnable Conquered* (New Delhi: Gorkha Publishers, 2002), 401–2.

[118] Interview with Air Marshal Vinod Patney, who argued that "we do not need ground based laser designators," Gurgaon, September 2, 2010. The air force had carried out some tests with these designators but, faced with problems in target acquisition during low-level missions, gave up on such missions.

[119] The literature around military innovation suggests that organizations find solution to problems that they attach high priority to. The fact that the IAF gave up this mission belies its earlier claim that close air support was a priority mission. For more on military innovation, see Adam Grissom, "The Future of Military Innovation Studies," *Journal of Strategic Studies* 29, no. 5 (2006): 905–34.

[120] Menon, "Kargil—10 Years After."

[121] Interview with Air Marshal Vinod Patney, September 2, 2010. Air force jets did not have the capability to communicate directly with army aviation helicopters, and instead information about the accuracy of the air strikes was conveyed to the fighter pilots once they returned to their operations room.

meant that the "Tactical Air Center . . . system did not work."[122] The much celebrated and widely advertised use of laser-guided bombs was also misleading as only two of them were dropped and that too a month after the start of air operations.[123]

Indeed, after the initial reverses suffered on the first two days of operations, the air force shifted to "pre-planned, high-altitude GPS assisted" bombing.[124] While doing so, it was careful not to inflict casualties on its own troops; and this, combined with the challenges of the terrain, meant that it operations were not that germane to the ground campaign. In sum, judging by training, capabilities, and planning, it does not appear as if the air force had prioritized close air support during the preceding years. The prevalent notion within the air force was that the "use of air power in direct support of ground battle is its most inefficient utilization"[125] and that the army only wanted it to be used for "artillery support."[126] The best description of this state of interservices rivalry is provided by Air Marshal R. S. Bedi when he writes, "the Army in its zest to acquire armed helicopters gave a commitment to the Air Force that it would not ask for close air support from the Air Force in the future. Taking the Army's commitment seriously, the Air Force cut short close air support training of its fighter pilots which was subsequently stopped altogether."[127]

It would be incorrect, however, to blame this entirely on the air force as the army was reluctant to share the complete operational picture or to do joint planning for operations.[128] As noted by Air Chief Marshal Tipnis, there was a "total lack of army–air force joint staff work. When the army found itself in difficulties, information/intelligence had not been communicated by Army Headquarters in any systematic manner to Air Headquarters. There had been no call for a joint briefing, leave alone joint planning, both at the service and command headquarters. . . . There had been no joint deliberations at any level."[129]

The third major problem with jointness during the Kargil war was the lack of interoperability between the army and the air force. Most evident while

[122] Telephone interview with Air Marshal Narayan Menon, May 27, 2010.

[123] Lambeth, *Airpower at 18,000'*, 52n111; also see 50n75, which blamed the delay in their use on "ego hassles."

[124] The air force lost two fighter jets and one helicopter on the first two days of the operations. For a description of this GPS-assisted bombing, see Lambeth, *Airpower at 18,000'*, 29.

[125] A. Y. Tipnis, "Operation Safed Sagar," *Force* 4, no. 2 (2006): 11.

[126] Interview with Air Marshal Vinod Patney, Gurgaon, September 2, 2010.

[127] R. S. Bedi, "Kargil: An IAF Perspective," *Indian Defence Review* 25, no. 1 (2010): 152.

[128] Lambeth, *Airpower at 18,000'*, 9–13; and Manmohan Bahadur, "Summer of 1999: View from 5th Floor Air HQ," *Force Magazine*, reproduced at Bharat-Rakshak.com: http://www.bharat-rakshak.com/IAF/History/Kargil/1145-M-Bahadur.html.

[129] Tipnis, "Operation Safed Sagar," 12.

examining communications systems, the three services operated their own systems and did not have the ability to securely communicate with each other. To resolve this, 15 Corps allotted a signals detachment to be co-located with relevant air force units.[130] There were other issues too, for instance, "maps used by army and the air force were completely different and this led to a lot of problems."[131] These problems, however, should not have been too surprising as the concept of interoperability was never emphasized.

Despite these problems, the IAF played a very important part in the Kargil war. While its tactical bombing effectiveness might still be debated, it played a crucial role in strategic signaling and in demoralizing the enemy. The actions of the IAF imposed caution on the PAF and effectively kept it out of the war.[132] Tactically, its air strikes neutralized some enemy maintenance bases such as at Muntho Dhalo. Most importantly, it imposed a feeling of isolation and abandonment in the minds of the infiltrators. They lost their will to fight as they saw the uncontested control of the skies, which not only prevented helicopter support but also ruled out casualty evacuation. Hence, it was not surprising that one of the first demands made by the Pakistani foreign minister when he visited India in June 1999 was to halt these air strikes.[133]

As described in Chapter 2, the role of civilian principals in this conflict was more pronounced, largely because of India's nuclear tests in May 1998. Civilian leaders were careful to project the idea that India was a "responsible" nuclear power and therefore did not want to escalate the conflict. They did this by placing restrictions on the military and disallowing it from crossing the Line of Control dividing India and Pakistan. But apart from this directive, civilians did not insist upon or enforce jointness among the services. Instead, they left the operational conduct of the war entirely to the military.

The lack of civilian expertise and the prevalence of single-service approaches were evident in what could be considered one of the more significant omissions concerning jointness. There was no joint study that examined army–air force operations in this war. Despite the controversy over

---

[130] Telephone interview with Air Officer Commanding (Jammu and Kashmir), Air Marshal Narayan Menon, August 31, 2010. For more on problems of interoperability, see his article "Ghosts of Kargil," 126.

[131] Telephone interview with Air Marshal Narayan Menon, May 27, 2010. The interservices coordination of maps and grid references with satellite imagery was one of the biggest problems faced by planners at all levels in this war.

[132] For the best description of the activities of the PAF, see Kaiser Tufail, "Kargil Conflict and the Pakistan Air Force," *Aeronaut* (blog), January 28, 2009, http://kaiser-aeronaut.blogspot.com/2009/01/kargil-conflict-and-pakistan-air-force.html.

[133] Menon, "Ghosts of Kargil," 126.

the effectiveness of the air campaign and on planning, training, and equipping for joint operations, the services did not initiate a joint study. Instead, the army constituted a study team that wrote a six-volume classified report, while the air force held a number of seminars.[134] The army's study reportedly had a chapter on close air support, but it largely recommended induction of attack helicopters in the army and did not interview air force officials or have access to their files.[135] Neither sought out the views, documents, or experiences of the other. On this matter General V. P. Malik admitted, "no study was conducted/commissioned to examine jointness between IAF and Indian Army because the terms of reference given to the Subrahmanyam Committee were comprehensive. In fact this Committee did comment on this specific aspect in its Report."[136] On the contrary, the Kargil Review Committee was not charged with examining the operational conduct of the war and did not examine jointness.[137] However, as relations between the two services were strained, it is not surprising that they did not share their documents or experiences. Instead, it should have been the responsibility of the MoD to commission such a study. It's probable too that a lack of expertise and procedural norms—such a joint study had never been commissioned before—also prevented the ministry from commissioning such a study. Its inaction could be explained by apprehensions that its findings might have been inconvenient.

An analysis of joint operations in all the wars helps us in identifying six broad trends. First, the "coordination model" of jointness is preferred by all three services as it maximizes their autonomy and allows them to operate independently. Second, the concept of interoperability is almost completely lacking as each of the services acquire capabilities independently. Third, by training, education, and inclination the three services acquire a single-service approach to operations. Fourth, turf battles and peacetime disagreements have contributed to interservices rivalry. Fifth, a result of all the above factors combined with limited information sharing creates major problems in joint planning and operations. And sixth, civilians, both by norm and by a lack of expertise, play a limited to negligible role in fostering jointness. This aspect of the single-service approach is examined in the next section.

[134] The air force seminar was organized by Air Headquarters but excluded officers who played an important part in the war; interview with retired air force officer, September 30, 2010.

[135] This report was prepared under Lieutenant General A. R. K. Reddy, see V. P. Malik, "My Side of the Story," *Asian Age*, June 18, 2002.

[136] Email from General V. P. Malik to author, August 29, 2010.

[137] Interview with K. Subrahmanyam, New Delhi, October 1, 2010.

"I Will Go It Alone": Dominance of the Single-Service Approach

The biggest impediment to jointness is the dominance of the individual services and the prevalence of the single-service approach. The single-service approach can be defined as the characteristic of each service planning, training, and emphasizing its own operational and organizational priorities over any concept of joint operations. This is entirely in keeping with theories of organizational behavior but, as seen from the previous discussion on India's wars, has been problematic in terms of interoperability and the training, planning, and execution of joint operations.

The single-service approach creates problems with interoperability. This is most apparent by the lack of interoperability in terms of telecommunication and data and signal traffic. Due to differing technological equipment and a reluctance to share information on secrecy and telecommunication devices, most units of the three services are unable to tactically communicate with each other. To overcome problems arising from this, local commanders usually embedded radio detachments with elements of the other services. In addition, other aspects pertaining to interoperability, like coordinating maps, have never been emphasized.

At a larger level, problems in jointness stem from an inability on the part of the services to commit to joint operations. The problem starts from the apex level—at the COSC. According to Admiral Arun Prakash, "the COSC system is completely meaningless and a waste of time."[138] This aspect was acknowledged by the Naresh Chandra Committee in 2012, which was tasked to revisit the defense reforms process and which recommended the creation of a permanent chairman of the COSC.[139] According to former chief of army staff General V. P. Malik, the "single-service approach to defense and operational planning at the level of the armed forces chiefs, though outdated, tends to continue in our country due to its peculiar higher defense control organization and due to the fact that there is no chief of defense staff."[140]

Taking their cues from the top and conditioned by the single-service approach, it is not clear if the services and formations below them share detailed operational plans with each other. This complaint is most commonly made by the air force against the other services. According to Air Marshal M. Matheswaran, who

---

[138] Interview, New Delhi, May 16, 2008.

[139] National Security Council Secretariat, *Report of the Task Force on National Security* (New Delhi: National Security Council Secretariat, 2012), 23–25.

[140] Malik, *Kargil: From Surprise to Victory*, 121

served as the senior air planning officer in the Eastern Command, "each of the services do their own planning and do not share it [their operational plans] with each other. This becomes a problem particularly with the Army and the Navy because, given the inescapable necessity of air power's role in all dimensions of military operations, it is imperative for the two surface based services to involve air power from the word go, and hence, the need for joint planning."[141] In the field, the attitude of the army commander is also crucial to creating a congenial working atmosphere as officers from the advanced headquarters of the air commands sometimes complain about being excluded from operational briefings and being treated like "glorified liaison officers."[142]

There has been a call therefore, mainly from air force officers, for a paradigm shift away from single-service planning to joint operations planning. Air Marshal Patney best describes this when arguing that "the term 'planning for joint operations' should be replaced by 'joint planning for operations.' "[143] This is a call for the services to plan their operations jointly from the beginning instead of merely coordinating their operations. The inability to plan jointly can be blamed, in turn, on single-service thinking and on turf wars as the services do not wish to expose their plans to scrutiny from others. Instead, they want to maximize their operational autonomy. According to Admiral Arun Prakash, "at senior levels, especially in the SHQ [service headquarters], there is little evidence of Jointmanship, and information regarding plans, acquisitions and especially new raisings, is carefully kept away from sister services."[144]

Problems in the conduct of joint operations also arise from the single-service approach to doctrine and training. For a long time the services wrote their own doctrines, with limited cross-pollination of ideas. In an assessment of military doctrines, Lieutenant General Vijay Oberoi noticed that "the present concept of 'coordination' continues to be advocated at theater and operational levels. . . . Obviously, common ground between the Air Force and the Army has still not been found and differences persist."[145] Colonel Ali Ahmed supports this view and recommends a "doctrinal adjudication"[146] between different service

---

[141] Email to author, June 25, 2018; the officer was a senior air staff officer, responsible for operational planning in Eastern Air Command in 2011–2012.

[142] Interview with former air commodore who served as head of Advanced Headquarters of the air force in the Southern Army Command Headquarters, New Delhi, May 16, 2010.

[143] Vinod Patney, "Air Power and Joint Operations: Doctrinal and Organizational Challenges," in *Essays on Aerospace Power* (New Delhi: Knowledge World Publishers, 2009), 82–85.

[144] Arun Prakash, "India's Higher Defense Organization: Implications for National Security and Jointness," *Journal of Defence Studies* 1, no. 1 (2007): 28.

[145] Vijay Oberoi, "India's New Military Doctrines: An Analysis," in *India's National Security Review, 2006*, ed. Satish Kumar, 334 (New Delhi: Knowledge World Publishers, 2006).

[146] Ali Ahmed, *India's Doctrine Puzzle: Limiting War in South Asia* (London: Routledge, 2014), 183.

doctrines. However, such adjudication is not forthcoming in the Indian system as the services are dominant and the civilians are both unwilling and unqualified to take on this role.

Similar problems arising from the single-service approach create problems in the training for joint operations. Training, along with maintenance and logistics, is an individual service function. The services therefore train according to their requirements, and officers from the three services train together either during pre-commissioning at the National Defence Academy or much later at the Defence Services Staff College, the College of Defence Management, and the National Defence College. While the experience of the National Defence Academy is good for forming friendships, by the time they get to the other institutions, "mindsets have been developed and joint concepts are more in theory and less in practice, with *single Service concepts* dominating the entire thought cycle of future staff officers and commanders."[147] Joint training in India, therefore, "is episodic and suffers from an absence of joint structures and joint doctrine. Each of the services has a different approach to war fighting and simply assumes that sister-service approaches are complementary."[148]

An Incomplete
Transition: Contemporary Jointness

After the 1999 Kargil war, there were wide-ranging and comprehensive defense reforms.[149] New structures and institutions were created, and there was a greater emphasis on jointness. To get over the problem of inadequate sharing of information, the services currently cross-post officers in the operations directorate. The air force has made an unprecedented effort to reach out to the other two services. The following section describes some of these changes and explains why, despite some improvements, the Indian military's transition to jointness can, at best, be described as incomplete.

The creation of the joint Integrated Defence Staff (IDS) in 2001 to be headed by a CDS was the centerpiece of the reforms process. While an IDS was established, as discussed in Chapter 2, the government demurred from appointing a CDS. This, according to Admiral Arun Prakash, one of the architects of the

---

[147] Arjun Subramaniam, "Jointmanship- Training and Mindset—The Keys to Synergy in the Combined Arms Concept," *Purple Pages* 1, no. 1 (2006): 53, emphasis added.

[148] David Johnson et al., *Preparing and Training for the Full Spectrum of the Military Challenges* (Santa Monica, CA: Rand, 2009), 179.

[149] Anit Mukherjee, *Failing to Deliver: Post-Crises Defense Reforms in India, 1998–2010* (New Delhi: Institute for Defence Studies and Analyses, 2011).

reform process, "ripped the heart out" of their recommendations.[150] Indeed, without a CDS, many have argued that the joint staff is a bureaucratic light-weight that is easily sidelined by the services.[151] To be sure, the IDS has made some incremental progress in ushering in jointness—it has periodically released joint doctrines, has been at the intellectual forefront of propounding jointness, and has been pushing, with some success, for joint training, education, and in-teroperability. But the service chiefs always outrank the head of the joint staff, and, as a result, the IDS is unable to impose its will on the services.

Another transformative idea from the post-Kargil defense reforms was the crea-tion of a joint command on the Andaman and Nicobar Islands. This joint command was imagined as a "template for replication," with the hope that it would usher in other geographically and functionally delineated joint commands.[152] However, this joint command was undermined by the services which did not want it to succeed as it would have resulted in a loss of power and posts.[153] As a result, no more joint commands have been established. On the contrary, in a setback to those arguing for joint commands, the navy may have been given "permanent charge" of this island command.[154] Civilians therefore, by not supporting the rationale behind joint commands, have only undermined military reformers and inadvertently strengthened the single-service approach.[155]

In sum, there are continuing problems with joint training, planning, and operations.[156] Just like before, the army and the air force are deeply divided over the use of air assets during operations, and there is a divergence of views

[150] Prakash, "India's Higher Defense Organization," 24. In the absence of a CDS, a former army chief called the IDS a redundant organization; see S. Padmanabhan, *A General Speaks* (New Delhi: Manas Publications, 2005), 35.

[151] Abhijnan Rej and Shashank Joshi, "India's Joint Doctrine: A Lost Opportunity" (ORF Occasional Paper 139, Observer Research Foundation, New Delhi, January 2018), 4–5.

[152] Mukherjee, "Fighting Separately," 24–26.

[153] Anit Mukherjee, "The Unsinkable Aircraft Carrier: The Andaman and Nicobar Command," in *India's Naval Strategy and Asian Security*, ed. Anit Mukherjee and C. Raja Mohan, 86–105 (London and New York: Routledge, 2015).

[154] Manu Pubby, "Indian Navy to Retain Charge of Andaman Command," *Economic Times*, July 22, 2016, https://economictimes.indiatimes.com/news/defence/indian-navy-to-retain-charge-of-andaman-command/articleshow/53329023.cms.

[155] For the importance of reformist officers in ushering in jointness, see Mukherjee, "Fighting Separately," 13.

[156] For a useful overview, see Vinod Anand, "Evolution of Jointness in Indian Defense Forces: Stuck Between the Services," in *Handbook of Indian Defense Policy: Themes, Structures and Doctrines*, ed. Harsh V. Pant, 173–85 (London: Routledge, 2016); and Shashank Joshi, *Indian Power Projection: Ambition, Arms and Influence*. RUSI Whitehall Paper 85 (London: Routledge, 2015), 96–102.

on the execution of the army's "cold start" doctrine.[157] In addition, there are persistent problems in information sharing as none of the commands of the three services are co-located. Moreover, structures for army–air force operations have peculiarities like Western Air Command having to operate with six army corps, while the rest operate with two or three. The Indian military has therefore undergone an "incomplete transition" to jointness. The services have maintained their autonomy and have successfully resisted reformist ideas. Air Chief Marshal P. C. Lal, among the more perceptive service chiefs, noted that "it takes a war to make our people work together. Peace breaks them up into narrow sectional pieces. We must learn to rise above sectional interests and work for what is best for the country."[158] He perhaps forgot to add that rising above sectional interests takes civilian oversight, which is largely absent in India.

Civil–Military Relations and Jointness in India

Is India's "incomplete" transition to jointness primarily due to its pattern of civil–military relations? As argued elsewhere, civilian intervention is the primary driver for ushering in jointness in other militaries.[159] Logically, therefore, the absence of such civilian intervention is responsible for the Indian military's "incomplete" transition. This section analyzes whether one can attribute this "incomplete" transition to the three characteristics of the "absent dialogue" argument: lack of civilian expertise, an institutional design with strong bureaucratic controls, and considerable military autonomy.

The lack of civilian expertise is a significant factor hindering jointness in India. Civilian bureaucrats in the MoD serve on a rotational basis, and few have knowledge about the operational intricacies and importance of interoperability, training, and planning in facilitating joint operations. Encumbered by their lack of knowledge and a tradition of non-interference, civilians are therefore not in a position to alter the single-service approach or effectively arbitrate when the services battle over turf. Capturing the dilemma faced by the bureaucrat and hinting at the lack of capabilities, former defense secretary V. Shankar noted that, "the ultimate burden of coordination . . . and of settling inter-service rivalries or competing demands largely falls on the Defence Secretary and the Defence

---

[157] Shashank Joshi, "India and the Four Day War," RUSI Commentary, April 7, 2010, https://rusi.org/commentary/india-and-four-day-war.

[158] Lal, *My Years with the Air Force*, 329.

[159] Mukherjee, "Fighting Separately," 13–15.

Minister . . . [but] he (Defence Minister) does not have independent advice at the professional level."[160]

The second characteristic of civil–military relations—institutional design leading to strong bureaucratic control—does not apply in this case. Jointness instead has been left entirely to the military. On the contrary, this is an instance of *weak* civilian control as the services have successfully resisted efforts to usher in jointness. Moreover, the structure of the bureaucracy prevents an integrated approach. As bureaucratic structures within the ministry mirror the single-service approach, they also work in service-specific silos. According to a former official who served in the ministry, "all the divisions in the MOD faithfully replicate those in the Services Headquarters. Hence, they deal with single services and further with the different Directorates in Services Headquarters."[161] As a result of this, there is no bureaucrat in the ministry with a mandate to work on jointness.

The single biggest factor hindering jointness is the autonomy that is given to services, resulting in the single-service approach. The absence of civilian pressure on the military to work together results in their operating in service-specific silos. As each of the services practices and prepares for its own vision of war, there are allegations that they are fighting "independent wars." The operating assumption within the military is that interservices differences should be resolved "in-house" and not projected to the civilians. Moreover, even when tasked to consolidate joint activities and thereby save on costs, they are able to "shirk" from this role. For instance, in 2002, a committee to recommend an outline for a national defense university did not examine consolidating officer training as a separate tri-services committee was doing so.[162] A few years later, in response to the standing committee's report, the MoD claimed that a "tri-Services Committee on Joint Training was constituted under HQ IDS to identify areas at operational and strategic level within the Armed Forces which are common to two or more Services."[163] Conveniently, however, its recommendations left little unchanged and allowed the single services to maintain control over their existing assets.[164] Conveniently, therefore, the services prefer to maintain their organizational and operational autonomy under the coordination model of jointness. Hindered by information asymmetries, lack of expertise, and a tradition of non-interference

[160] Cited in Harsha Kakar, "Enhancing Jointness: Role of Service HQ's and HQ IDS," *Purple Pages* 1, no. 3 (2007): 47; also see A. V. Vaidya, "Blue to Purple," *Purple Pages*, 1, no. 2 (2007): 3–5.

[161] Email from P. R. Chari to author, August 19, 2010.

[162] *Report of the Committee on National Defence University (CONDU)*, vol. 1, 2002, 48–49.

[163] Standing Committee on Defense, *Action Taken Report on the Recommendations/Observations of the Committee Contained in the Thirty-Sixth Report (Fourteenth Lok Sabha) on "Status of Implementation of Unified Command for Armed Forces"* (New Delhi: Lok Sabha Secretariat, December 2009), 14.

[164] Letter from the Ministry of Defence dated May 12, 2009, reproduced in Standing Committee on Defense, *Action Taken Report on the Recommendations/Observations of the Committee*, 14–16.

in operational matters, civilians are unwilling to force the three services to prioritize jointness. The costs are borne by the country in terms of fiscal profligacy and overall military effectiveness.

Conclusion

Admitting weaknesses in jointness, in March 2015, defense minister Manohar Parrikar acknowledged that "integration of the three forces [services] does not exist in the existing structure."[165] These sentiments were echoed by Prime Minister Narendra Modi when, early in his term, he urged his senior military commanders to "promote jointness across every level of our Armed Forces... [and that] Jointness at the top is a need that is long overdue."[166] Despite such statements, however the Modi government has not undertaken any significant higher defense reforms. Why? Why have civilians not forcefully intervened to enforce jointness on the services?

Civilian intervention to enforce jointness in other countries has happened for three main reasons—to increase military effectiveness, to save financial resources, and to emulate other militaries.[167] Civilians in India have not yet emphasized any of these factors to force jointness on an unwilling military. To be sure, the 1999 Kargil war led to a process of defense reforms wherein civilians intervened and made incremental progress in enforcing jointness. Unfortunately, this intervention was not sustained or forceful enough, as a result of which there has only been an "incomplete" transition to jointness. This is attributable to three main factors.

First, the political leadership has misgivings about altering the existing structure of civilian control by appointing a CDS post, among other measures which might enhance jointness. There are fears that unifying the services through forceful intervention will make them institutionally powerful and threaten the balance of power between civilians and the military.

Second, civilians are unwilling to bear the potential costs of overruling professional military advice. The Indian military is opposed to joint structures and attached to its single-service approach, which gives it maximum autonomy.

---

[165] "Must Integrate 3 Services, Says Defence Minister Parrikar," *Hindustan Times*, March 13, 2015.

[166] Press Information Bureau, "PM chairs Combined Commanders Conference on Board INS Vikramaditya at Sea," Prime Minister's Office, December 15, 2015, http://pib.nic.in/newsite/PrintRelease.aspx?relid=133265

[167] Mukherjee, "Fighting Separately," 13–15. In addition, as in the case of China, some argue that military reforms in favor of jointness have been undertaken to consolidate civilian control; see Michael S. Chase and Jeffrey Engstrom, "China's Military Reforms: An Optimistic Take," *JFQ: Joint Forces Quarterly* no. 83 (October 2016): 49–52.

While some reformist officers have been advocating for changes, there is no consensus on it. Faced with this disunity, civilians are unwilling to forcefully intervene, especially as there might be electoral consequences in case of any setbacks. Civilians are also unsure of their technocratic expertise in overruling military advice.

Finally, the existing status quo suits all of the stakeholders. Civilians are comfortable with the current higher defense management structures, without the need for a CDS. They have moreover refrained from enforcing jointness as it is perceived to be in the military's domain. The military is content paying lip service to jointness and enjoys the single-service approach. Without a military crisis which ends badly, there is very little impetus for reforms and for jointness.

In sum, India's unique civil–military relations have had a negative effect on the ability of the army, navy, and air force to operate together. While the ultimate test of the capabilities may only come when faced with a crisis, interviews with serving and retired senior officials suggest that core issues have not been addressed. Many suggest that a far more dramatic and forceful set of reforms is required from the political elite and demand an Indian equivalent of the Goldwater-Nichols Act. Admiral Sureesh Mehta, while serving as the chairman of the COSC, supported such an approach when he argued that, "if true jointness has to be ushered in, with a well-deliberated India-specific model, there is a need to foster much greater understanding of the subject amongst our apex level decision-makers and perhaps even work towards enacting our own version of a 'Goldwater-Nichols' Act."[168] It remains to be seen whether changes, if any, will come because of political pressure responding to institutional demand or will be an incremental process. The least preferred option, of course, will be for reforms to be implemented after the Indian military is found wanting in the field of battle.

---

[168] Admiral Sureesh Mehta, "India's National Security Challenges—An Armed Forces Overview," *Outlook*, August 12, 2009, 7, https://www.outlookindia.com/website/story/indias-national-security-challenges/261738; also see Prakash, "India's Higher Defence Organization," 31.

5

An "In-House" Affair

India's System of Professional Military Education

Professional military education (PME) is the process "through which a military imparts skills and knowledge to its forces, and socializes them to organizational norms and conventions."[1] Military education teaches soldiers how to handle situations, expected and unexpected, that best further the military's objectives. The US Joint Staff defines PME as learning that focuses on "the cognitive domain and fosters breadth of view, diverse perspectives, critical analysis, abstract reasoning, comfort with ambiguity and uncertainty, and innovative thinking, particularly with respect to complex, non-linear problems."[2] It is a powerful tool to shape military perspectives, and authoritarian regimes have used it for indoctrination to ensure regime loyalty.[3] On the other hand, in some countries, it has helped the process of democratization by appropriately shaping the military's views on constitutional loyalty and democratic values.[4]

---

[1] Risa A. Brooks, "Introduction," in *Creating Military Power: Sources of Military Effectiveness*, ed. Risa A. Brooks and Elizabeth A. Stanley, 22 (Stanford, CA: Stanford University Press, 2007).

[2] US Chairman of the Joint Chiefs of Staff. *CJCSI 1800.01D: Officer Professional Military Education Policy (OPMEP)* (Washington, DC: Chairman of the Joint Chiefs of Staff Instruction, 2009), A-1-2.

[3] Caitlin Talmadge, *The Dictator's Army: Battlefield Effectiveness in Authoritarian Regimes* (Ithaca, NY: Cornell University Press, 2015), 172. Also see Thomas Bickford, "Trends in Education and Training, 1925–2007: From Whampoa to Nanjing Polytechnic," in *The "People" in the PLA: Recruitment, Training and Education in China's Military*, ed. Roy Kamphausen, Andrew Scobell, and Travis Tanner, 21 (Carlisle, PA: US Army War College, Strategic Studies Institute, 2008).

[4] Narcis Serra, *The Military Transition: Democratic Reform of the Armed Forces*, trans. Peter Bush, 185–89 (Cambridge: Cambridge University Press, 2010); Todor Tagarev, *The Role of Military Education in Harmonizing Civil–Military Relations (the Bulgarian Case)* (Sofia, Bulgaria: NATO Democratic Institutions Individual Fellowship Project, June 1997); and Thomas C. Bruneau, "Reforms in Professional Military Education: The United States," in *The Routledge Handbook of Civil–Military Relations*, ed. Thomas C. Bruneau and Florina Cristiana Matei, 197 (New York: Routledge, 2013).

PME is also an important determinant of military effectiveness.[5] As it shapes the perception, education, and therefore capability of all soldiers, it plays a significant role in shaping military competency. According to Holder and Murray, "the history of military innovation and effectiveness in the last century suggests a correlation between battlefield performance and how seriously military institutions regarded officer education."[6] While discussing the experience of the US military, Karen Guttieri argues that professional military education has "played a vital role in boosting U.S. military effectiveness by fostering the integration of new technologies in battle, shaping unit cohesion, and enhancing multiservice and multinational warfighting."[7]

Despite being such a powerful tool, PME in most democracies is almost exclusively in the military's domain. As explained later in this chapter, this is primarily because there are few civilians who are qualified to engage with, comment on, and thereby help shape it. In countries where such expertise exists, there have been civilian-led attempts to review military education. These have mainly been either to enhance effectiveness, usually by emphasizing jointness, or to save on financial costs. For instance, in the United States the Ike Skelton report in 1987 led to major changes in military education.[8] This effort was the culmination of a debate triggered by problems in interoperability in military operations in Iran and especially the Grenada invasion in 1983.[9] Similarly, in the United Kingdom the Defence Training Review in 2001 was a civilian-led initiative, with the participation of some military officers, which resulted in considerable changes in PME.[10] We will revisit these cases but, exceptions apart, in most countries civilians rarely intervene in PME.

The main arguments in this chapter are threefold. First, civilian intervention is crucial in designing an effective system for PME. As discussed elsewhere, this

---

[5] Brooks, "Introduction," 22; and Nathan W. Toronto, "Does Military Education Matter?" E-International Relations, May 26, 2015, http://www.e-ir.info/2015/05/26/does-military-education-matter/.

[6] Leonard Holder and Williamson Murray, "Prospects for Military Education," *Joint Forces Quarterly* 18 (Spring 1998): 90.

[7] Karen Guttieri, "Professional Military Education in Democracies," in *Who Guards the Guardians and How: Democratic Civil–Military Relations*, ed. Thomas Bruneau and Scott Tollefson, 255 (Austin: University of Texas Press, 2006).

[8] US House of Representatives, *Report of the Panel on Military Education of the One Hundredth Congress of the Committee on Armed Services House of Representatives [Skelton Report]* (Washington, DC: US Government Printing Office, 1989).

[9] For more on this, see Cynthia Watson, *Military Education: A Reference Handbook* (Westport, CT: Praeger Security International, 2007), 13–19.

[10] Kate Utting, "Beyond Joint-Professional Military Education for the 21st Century: The United Kingdom's Post-Defence Training Review Advanced Command and Staff Course," *Defence Studies* 9, no. 3 (2009): 310–28.

intervention is important not just to enforce jointness but also to emphasize education over training and for creating a role for civilian academics.[11] Second, such intervention has not happened in India, and PME is, almost exclusively, in the military's domain. This has led to considerable duplication within the services and is financially wasteful and not conducive for jointness. Third, India's unique pattern of civil–military relations, the absent dialogue argument, has accentuated weaknesses in its PME. Hindered by a lack of expertise and the norm in civil–military relations, civilians do not actively shape PME, while retaining strong financial controls. This strange pattern of military autonomy with civilian financial control has adversely shaped its PME.

This chapter begins by describing the characteristics of an effective PME. Next, it examines instances of civilian intervention in different countries to shape PME. Thereafter, it describes the history of PME in India, explaining how civilians have mostly stayed away from this process. Next, it explains weaknesses stemming from a lack of civilian participation in military education. The penultimate section analyzes whether the absent dialogue argument accurately captures the dynamics of civil–military relations on this issue. It concludes with a summary of the main findings of this chapter.

What Constitutes Effective PME?

How can we differentiate between an effective and a weak program of PME? The first, and perhaps most important, characteristic is the provision for civilian faculty. It is essential that civilian faculty function as core members for the provision of PME. Only then can military officers potentially get a well-rounded education. It is more likely—but not always necessary—that civilian faculty would be able to challenge prevailing organizational narratives and instill the habits of critical thinking and intellectual curiosity in their students. Without this provision, the faculty would usually consist of military officers, most likely serving on a rotational basis. This is problematic for a number of reasons. Military officers are essential for teaching subjects related to military operations; however, they are rarely in a position to teach nonmilitary subjects. As a result, the curricula, the importance of which is discussed later, would probably lean more toward training than education. In addition, it would be difficult for a serving officer in the faculty to challenge organizational myths and narratives and therefore even harder to instill critical thinking skills in the students. Having the provision for

---

[11] Anit Mukherjee, "Educating the Professional Military: Civil–Military Relations and Professional Military Education in India," *Armed Forces & Society* 44, no. 3 (2018): 476–97.

civilian faculty therefore benefits military education, assuming that they have the freedom, autonomy, and job security that are necessary to teach and publish without fear. In authoritarian countries or those where the military is politically powerful, therefore, one could have civilian faculty; but this need not necessarily enhance military education. While such details matter, overall, civilian faculty tends to enhance PME. The role of civilian faculty in PME perhaps does not have the attention it deserves because in most Western democracies civilians are routinely employed in this position.

The second important characteristic of a strong PME relates to curricula development and focus. Simply put, PME should focus on subjects that instill critical thinking skills. This is one of the most commonly cited goals for PME. According to a white paper released by US chairman of the Joint Chiefs, General Martin Dempsey, in addition to "critical thinking skills" military education should prepare officers to deal with "surprise and uncertainty . . . [and] anticipate and recognize change and lead transitions."[12] Others support such a view.[13] PME, therefore, should strive to broaden the horizons of military officers and inform them about larger political, social, organizational, and economic considerations. According to Randall Wakelam, to achieve its goals military education becomes a "largely intellectual action," which "requires more liberal education than it does training."[14] An effective system of PME therefore focuses on topics other than training and operations. Necessarily, the curricula should also include study of military history, essential to the intellectual development of the officer cadre.[15] However, most militaries are suspicious of what they consider dated historical knowledge and are more interested in applied knowledge attached to the concept of a "usable past."[16] If left to the military, one would expect to see less of an emphasis on military history.

---

[12] Martin Dempsey, "Joint Education" (white paper, Joint Chiefs of Staff, Washington, DC, July 2012), 4, http://www.jcs.mil/Portals/36/Documents/Doctrine/concepts/cjcs_wp_education.pdf?ver=2017-12-28-162044-527

[13] David Barno et al., Building Better Generals (Washington, DC: Center for a New American Security, 2013); and Wilton Park Conference Report, Connected Forces, Educated Minds: Transformation and Professional Military Education (WP1225, 2013), https://www.wiltonpark.org.uk/wp-content/uploads/WP1225-final-report.pdf.

[14] Randall Wakelam, "Education and the General: Educating Military Executives," New Strategist Journal 1, no. 1 (2016): 60.

[15] Michael Evans, "The Role of Military History in the Education of Future Officers," Miscellaneous Papers, Land Warfare Studies Centre, 1998, https://pdfs.semanticscholar.org/82f4/1d317b66d19f5b00c659067847005c4cd558.pdf.

[16] Bradley L. Carter, "No 'Holidays from History': Adult Learning, Professional Military Education, and Teaching History," in Military Culture and Education, ed. Douglas Higbee, 173 (Burlington, VT: Ashgate Publishing, 2010).

Table 5.1 **Characteristics of an Effective PME**

Characteristics	Effective PME	Weak PME
Faculty	Civilian faculty function as core members of PME institutes	No such provision
Curricula development and focus	Apart from operations, education is geared toward broader subjects related to statecraft, diplomacy, and the use of force including international relations, organizational theory, area studies, constitutional law, military history, and security studies.	Primarily focused on training and operations

Table 5.1 summarizes the desired characteristics for an effective PME. In theory, an "enlightened" military can implement all of these measures. It can appoint civilian faculty, embrace a broad-based curricula, and consult closely with professional educators. However, in practice this is highly unlikely as most militaries would be reluctant to give up the control and autonomy that they have over the military education process. This is perfectly understandable from the perspective of bureaucratic politics and organizational theories.

The best way forward then is the idea of a civil–military *partnership*, wherein civilians—policymakers and academicians—work together with the military leadership to enhance PME. As Gregory Kennedy and Keith Nielson argue, "one of the key points brought to light here is the indispensable role of civilian educators in pointing the military in the right direction and being a vital part of any successful process."[17] Such civilian led efforts have happened in other countries, with significant improvements in PME.

Civilian Intervention and PME in Other Countries

PME in most countries is in the exclusive domain of the military. This is primarily due to norm and a lack of expertise. As per customary practice, the military usually controls PME. This should not be surprising in countries where the military is a politically powerful actor. However, this is also the case in countries with strong civilian control. For instance, in the United States, the Skelton panel reform that in 1989 reshaped military education was the "first comprehensive congressional review of PME in the 200-year history of the Congress."[18] Another factor that works against civilian involvement in PME is the lack of expertise. As few civilians possess the experience and the knowledge of military affairs, in most countries the content, structure, and conduct of PME are left to the military. However, in some countries civilians have intervened in PME in order to enhance military effectiveness.[19]

Civilian intervention and partnership of the kind argued for in this chapter is most evident in the United States. The Goldwater-Nichols Act in 1986 and the Ike Skelton Committee in 1989 dramatically transformed the US military, especially with respect to joint education. These civilian-led initiatives, however, faced considerable opposition. The military feared a loss of power and the "individual services fought to maintain their autonomy even though the overall defense system suffered in terms of effectiveness."[20] However, civilians in the legislative branch, in partnership with reformist military officers, serving and retired, and the executive branch forcefully intervened in what was previously considered the military's domain to change military education. By the 1990s, jointness had emerged as the primary intellectual justification for civilian intervention in reshaping military education. One of the architects of Goldwater-Nichols reforms, Arch Barrett, admitted that they viewed "changes in education as the means to change the culture of the organization of the U.S. armed forces."[21] These interventions led to a number of positive changes in military education. The two most important changes were the provisions for civilian faculty and for greater civilian academic input in curricula development. To be sure, there is still some criticism of the American system of military education. However, the scale of the problems appear to be of a different magnitude in comparison to PME in other countries. Significantly, for the main argument made in this chapter, those calling for reform of military education are in favor of greater civilian involvement.[22]

Similarly, in the United Kingdom, civilians in partnership with reformist military officers were at the forefront of efforts to reshape military education. In

[18] Center for Strategic and International Studies, "Professional Military Education: An Asset for Peace and Progress," republished in Paul Bolt, Damon Coletta, and Collins Shackelford, eds., *American Defense Policy*, 8th ed. (Baltimore: Johns Hopkins University Press, 2005), 303.

[19] There are other motivations or drivers for civilian intervention; see Mukherjee, "Educating the Professional Military," 6–7.

[20] Bruneau, "Reforms in Professional Military Education," 198.

[21] Bruneau, "Reforms in Professional Military Education," 199.

[22] Kevin P. Kelley and Joan Johnson-Freese, "Getting to the Goal in Professional Military Education," *Orbis* 58, no. 1 (2014): 125–28.

1997, they overcame opposition from the services and combined their single-service staff colleges into the Joint Services Command and Staff College. Based on the recommendation of the Defence Training Review, undertaken from 1999 to 2001 by a team of civilian and military officers, the Defence Academy was established in 2002. This, along with other measures, created a greater role for civilian academics, as faculty and in shaping policy. For instance, the grant of accreditation for military education within universities (King's College and Cranfield University) forced the military to work with educators like never before. As a result, they cooperate and consult closely together on the issue of curriculum development. According to Kate Utting, the all-around improvement in military education occurred due to a partnership between civilians, including officials in the Ministry of Defence (MoD) and academicians, and the military.[23]

There are also varying levels of civilian intervention in other democracies, like Canada and Australia.[24] However, these countries along with some others in Europe represent an exception rather than a rule. In most democracies, civilians have almost no role to play—either in deciding upon the curricula or as educators. As noted by Bruneau, in "Latin America, Africa, and South East Asia, the militaries themselves control the content of their forces' education."[25] Peter Foot has characterized this as the "in-house" approach to military education. This approach assumes that "its most talented officers" should be taught by "fast track, uniformed individuals" and that "participation in the course is essential for promotion" with "little or no role for a permanent academic staff." In addition, "outsiders, whether government officials or visiting academics . . . [can] participate . . . but the weight of activity is service oriented and inward-looking," and students should conform to the "staff solution—a set of 'answers' drafted by and for the military directing staff."[26] As the following discussion shows, India closely adheres to this "in-house" approach.

History of PME in India

In the early part of the twentieth century, the Raj had established an elaborate system of training of soldiers through the system of regimental centers, but

[23] Utting, "Beyond Joint-Professional Military Education," 311–15.

[24] Geoff Peterson, "Nurturing the Australian Military Mind: A Considered Assessment of Senior Professional Military Education," Shedden Papers, Australian Defense College, March 2012, http://www.defence.gov.au/ADC/Publications/documents/Shedden/2012/SheddenPapers12_120306_Nurturing_Peterson.pdf.

[25] Bruneau, "Reforms in Professional Military Education," 196.

[26] Peter Foot, "European Military Education Today," in *Military Education: Past, Present, and Future*, 199.

officer education was not a priority. The assumption was that officer education would be carried out in Britain. However, reflecting the growing professionalization of the British Indian military and to overcome the logistical problems associated with moving officers over long distances, the Staff College was established at first in Devlali in 1905, which was shifted two years later to Quetta.[27] Prior to independence, some officer training schools were established to cater for the tremendous expansion of the military during World War II.[28] After partition, and on loss of the location at Quetta, the Indian Staff College was established at Wellington to prepare mid-ranking officers for staff appointments. It educated officers from all three services and, along with the National Defence Academy (NDA), formally inaugurated in Khadakwasla in 1955, was among the first interservices institutions of its kind.[29]

British views on professional military education continued to hold sway for the first few decades after independence. The close association between Indian and British officers, the deputation of Indian officers to British schools of instruction, and the retention of British officers for a few years after independence cemented this arrangement. The first commandant of the Staff College was Major General "Joe" Lentaigne, a British Indian Army officer, who served in this position until 1955. During this time, Staff College précis, concepts, and study borrowed heavily from its British counterpart at Camberley. Later, with Indian officers as commandants, they decided to teach concepts more pertinent to Indian conditions. Strangely enough, until 1962, "the Staff College did not remotely study, analyze or examine the possible hostilities with China or Pakistan, lest we upset our policy of 'Panchsheel.'"[30] It is unclear if this was the military's decision or if civilians specifically instructed them not to do so. If it was the latter, then it is among the rare instance of civilians influencing the military education process.

For the most part, civilians had little influence on military training and education. The services proposed courses and the creation of training facilities, which were then usually approved by the MoD. Their main consideration was to examine the proposal for its financial implications and not on its technical or

---

[27] This account of the history of Staff College relies on *The History of the Staff College*, http://www.dssc.gov.in/dssc-history.html.

[28] Vipul Dutta, "Educating Future Generals: An Indian Defence University and Educational Reform," *Economic & Political Weekly* 53, no. 32 (2018): 48–50.

[29] The National Defence Academy was established for pre-commissioning training of cadets for all three services and was the brainchild of Lord Mountbatten; see Trilokinath Raina and G. D. Bakshi, *Forging Warriors: A History of the National Defence Academy* (Pune, India: National Defence Academy, 2008).

[30] "Towards an Indian Identity," in *History of the Staff College*, 17, http://www.dssc.gov.in/history/Towards%20an%20Indian%20Identity.pdf.

logical merit. This was understandable as civilians knew little about the subject and deferred to the military. Accordingly, the School of Land and Air Warfare was established in New Delhi in 1959 on the advice of the services.[31] In the same year, the cabinet approved creation of the National Defence College (NDC) in New Delhi to educate senior military and civilian officers in the higher aspects of strategy and warfare. Concurrently, over time, the services started combat arms and branch-specific courses. For instance, in 1967 two courses were started: a tank technology course at Ahmednagar and the Young Officers course at Mhow.[32] Later, to teach modern management techniques, the military established the Institute of Defence Management in Secunderabad.[33]

It also initiated some courses in response to combat experiences and to address organizational shortcomings. For instance, reflecting the need to prepare troops for counterinsurgency, the army created the Counter-Insurgency and Jungle Warfare (CIJW) School in Mizoram in 1967. Similarly, it introduced a "higher command course" in 1971, ostensibly because of the experience of the 1965 war.[34] In 1974, the Indian Navy commenced with the Command Exam, which was mandatory for all officers who aspired to command ships. Interestingly, in 1972, feeling the need for civilian faculty, the commandant of the Staff College "sought the induction of three civilian professors, one each for International Affairs, Applied Economics and Defence Management."[35] This was an opportunity to induct qualified civilian faculty members however, the Chiefs of Staff Committee—for reasons not entirely clear—did not accept this proposal.

Another issue that involved both civilians and the military was the idea of a defense university. The Chiefs of Staff Committee first made this proposal in 1967, but after much interministerial and interagency discussion, this idea fell by the wayside.[36] The primary motivating factor for this effort was a desire by the military to obtain academic affiliation for post-retirement benefits. After

---

[31] This school has since shifted to Hyderabad and is now called the College of Air Warfare Studies; for more on this, see *College of Air Warfare: Golden Jubilee, 1959–2009* (Hyderabad, India: CAW Publications, 2009).

[32] Ministry of Defence, *Annual Report, 1966–67* (New Delhi: 1967), 15. Over the years such courses were created to teach different subjects and branches pertaining to all three services.

[33] Ministry of Defence, *Annual Report, 1970–71* (New Delhi: 1971), 14. This is now called the College of Defence Management.

[34] Ministry of Defence, *Annual Report, 1970–71*, 13; this also gives details of other new courses.

[35] Sudhir Pillai, "Professional Faculty at DSSC Wellington: A Necessity of Professional Military Education," *Trishul Journal* 17, no. 2 (2015): 51.

[36] This account of the Indian National Defence University relies on the *Report of the Committee on National Defence University (CONDU)*, 1, 2002, 51–62. I thank a member of this committee, who wishes to remain unnamed, for sharing a copy of the report.

lobbying from the military, in 1974, Jawaharlal Nehru University agreed to award a bachelor's degree to cadets from the National Defence Academy and the Army Cadet College but refused to do so for other training institutions, arguing that they had very little in common. In 1980, the Chiefs of Staff Committee constituted a study group under Vice Chief of Army Staff Lieutenant General A. M. Sethna. The study group submitted its report in 1982 and recommended the creation of the Indian National Defence University (INDU). For reasons not entirely clear, there was no action on this.

Instead, only after the urgency of the 1999 Kargil war and based on the reports of the reform committees, there was renewed attention. Accordingly, the government established the Committee on National Defence University (CONDU), led by K. Subrahmanyam, which submitted its report in May 2002. It identified a number of shortcomings in the existing approach to PME.[37] Significantly, while justifying the need for civilian faculty, it proposed that the INDU faculty, when established, "should have a military civilian ratio of 1:1."[38] Eighteen years after its report, however, the government was still struggling with an appropriate intellectual vision for this institution.[39] Worryingly, it appears that the vision for this institution has been left, almost entirely, to the military.[40] Moreover, initial reports about this university suggest that only four tri-services institutions (consisting of the NDC, NDA, Staff College, and College of Defence Management) will be "under the ambit" of the university.[41] Even with the establishment of a defense university, the services therefore will likely retain control over key aspects of military education.

In December 1986, reflecting a general trend for a widespread restructuring and re-examination within the services, a committee was set up to examine officer training "starting from the NDA right up to the NDC."[42] Called the Committee for the Review of Training of Officers for the Services (CORTOS), this interservices committee was curiously not under the Chiefs of Staff Committee. Created on the orders of the minister of state for defense, Arun Singh, it had representatives of all three services.[43] It had two primary aims—to

---

[37] Mukherjee, "Educating the Professional Military," 11–12.

[38] Report of the Committee on National Defence University, 2002, 172.

[39] Devesh Kapur and Anit Mukherjee, "A Fleeting Opportunity," The Hindu, August 10, 2016; and Dutta, "Educating Future Generals."

[40] Implementation for the Defence University has been given to the directorate of the Indian Defence University, manned exclusively by military officers, under the Integrated Defense Staff.

[41] EdCil (India), Detailed Project Report for Establishment of Indian National University (New Delhi: February 2013), 11.

[42] G. M. Hiranandani, Transition to Triumph: History of the Indian Navy, 1965–1975 (New Delhi: Lancer Publishers, 2000), 282.

[43] The following account of the CORTOS relies on an interview with a member of the committee, Vice Admiral (retd.) Barin Ghosh, Gurgaon, June 25, 2011.

increase the technical content of services training and to increase interservices interaction in training.[44] Consisting of eight different reports, this committee made a number of recommendations including the establishment of the Naval War College (subsequently established at Karanja), changes in the Defence Services Staff College (DSSC) and in pre-commissioning training at the NDA, and that the last leg of the respective higher command courses of the three services be conducted together.[45]

The overall implementation of the recommendations of this committee was, according to one of its members, "tardy, ineffectual and overcome by changing events."[46] Crucially, this was an entirely in-house affair handled by the services, and civilians had little role to play in the deliberations of the committee. This created problems in the implementation of the report of this committee, especially when it involved agencies outside the control of the military. Admitting as much, according to the chairman of the committee, Admiral J. G. Nadkarni "the effects of the implementation of our report has been somewhat mixed. In certain areas, which were well within the powers and purview of the Chiefs of Staff, we have already implemented a number of recommendations of this Committee. But where some outside agencies were concerned, the progress has not been very satisfactory."[47]

Around the same time, based on a study team that examined the US Navy's training system, the Indian Navy reorganized its training structures, syllabi, and focus. It designated Southern Command at Cochin as the lead agency for training purposes and revamped its approach to encourage specialization. In 1992, the Indian Navy introduced the concept of Flag Officer Sea Training (FOST) modeled on the experience of the Royal Navy.[48] Meanwhile, inspired by the US experience with Training Command, then army chief General K. Sundarji, by no coincidence a product of the US Army Command and General Staff course at Fort Leavenworth, floated the idea for an army training command. Established in 1991, this organization, as discussed later, was unable to live up to its potential and suffered from a disagreement between civilians and the military. There were changes even in the air force and "in 2006 the training pattern of the IAF [Indian Air Force] underwent a sea change with major restructuring of courses

[44] Hiranandani, Transition to Triumph, 282.

[45] For more about the recommendations of this committee, see Hiranandani, Transition to Triumph, 282–83.

[46] Interview with Vice Admiral Barin Ghosh, Gurgaon, June 25, 2011.

[47] "Interview with Admiral JG Nadkarni: Chairman Chiefs of Staff Committee and Chief of Naval Staff," Indian Defence Review (July 1990): 22.

[48] For more on the Indian Navy's experience with FOST, see Indian Navy, "Flag Officer Sea Training (FOST)," https://www.indiannavy.nic.in/content/flag-officer-sea-training-fost.

for officers."[49] In this manner, the three services incrementally added to their training and education.[50]

In sum, training and education have been largely driven by the respective services, and civilians have had little role to play. The MoD's role is mainly to grant financial approvals, and it does not have the authority or the knowledge to shape the structure and content of PME. Civilians, whether politicians or bureaucrats, were not motivated by considerations of military effectiveness or jointness but focused mostly on financial implications. For the most part they readily agreed to the military's proposals to start courses in India as doing so reduced the number of officers deputed abroad, thereby saving precious foreign exchange.[51] As discussed in the next section, this non-involvement of civilians, both as educators and in shaping policy, accentuates weaknesses in PME.

Weaknesses in India's System of PME

Officers in the Indian military are the best trained out of all government officials and undergo an extensive system of classroom and "on the job" learning with frequent field training and exercises. As the Indian military is operationally active—along the borders with Pakistan and China and against numerous insurgencies—the senior leadership of the military emphasizes operational readiness. According to Lieutenant General B. L. Narasimhan, former commandant of the Army War College, the biggest strength of India's PME is that it is "operationally/job oriented to prepare the person for the next assignment."[52] Perhaps inadvertently though, as discussed later, this reveals the inability to distinguish between training and education. Based on our previously defined metrics (see Table 5.2), India's approach to PME is not effective. There are mainly two reasons for this.

First, the Indian military does not allow civilian faculty to teach at its war colleges. The faculty instead consists of serving military officers—usually outstanding students from the previous courses. Most of these career officers find it difficult to challenge prevailing narratives or organizational myths. Moreover, as the faculty serve on a rotational basis, they are unable to develop deep

---

[49] *College of Air Warfare: Golden Jubilee*, 31.

[50] For the current course design for officer education, see P. K. Mallick, "Professional Military Education—An Indian Experience" (occasional paper, Vivekananda International Foundation, New Delhi, September 2017), 30–32; also see Dharmendra Singh, "Rejuvenating Indian Army Education and Training," *Delhi Business Review* 6, no. 1 (2005): 27–44.

[51] Ministry of Defense, *Annual report, 1966–67*, 14.

[52] Interview, Singapore, September 8, 2016.

competency or expertise on any one subject. The teaching therefore tends to focus on subjects that the military faculty is more comfortable with—generally tactics and operations. According to a former commandant of the NDC, military education in India is "weighted towards the tactical level in all stages of professional development."[53] It is not surprising therefore that Indian war colleges struggle to shape, or even engage with, the intellectual discussions within the military. While assessing the faculty of study, typically embedded in war colleges, Lieutenant General Gautam Banerjee argued that, "given the close-structured environment these have to conform to, there is little of note, besides mundane drills and tactical tweaks here and there ... the output from the plethora of military's in-house 'faculty of studies', 'perspective planning' etc. remain anything beyond modest, mundane and stagnant."[54] To compensate for the lack of civilian faculty, some war colleges have constituted a system of guest lectures delivered by eminent personalities, serving officials, or academics. However, these are skewed more toward military speakers, both serving and retired, than civilians.[55] In short, the lack of civilian faculty seriously undermines PME in India.[56]

Second, the curriculum development for PME is left, almost entirely, to the discretion of the military. To be sure, the war colleges are affiliated for accreditation purposes to different universities.[57] However, these universities do not significantly shape curriculum development; instead, their role is limited to mainly five activities: ensuring contact hours adhere to university guidelines, a three-day capsule explaining research methods, conducting viva, evaluating dissertations written by student officers, and offering advice on dissertation topics. Admittedly, this generalization glosses over the variation among different PME institutes. For instance, the College of Defence Management teaches concepts closer to management studies and therefore, similar to technical schools, has greater inputs from civilian faculty. However, apart from specialized subjects, the curricula are shaped largely by the military. According to Professor Utham Kumar Jamadhagni, the head of the Department of Defence and Strategic Studies at Madras University—which grants degrees to students from the DSSC, the formal interaction between them and the military is "limited to civilians handling a few capsules like Research Methodology & International

---

[53] Prakash Menon, "Military Education in India: Missing the Forest for the Trees," *Journal of Defence Studies* 9, no. 4 (2015): 49.

[54] Gautam Banerjee, "Think Over ..., Think-Tanks!" *Indian Defence Review* (blog), September 2, 2015, http://www.indiandefencereview.com/think-over-think-tanks/.

[55] Mukherjee, "Educating the Professional Military," 14.

[56] Pillai, "Professional Faculty at DSSC Wellington."

[57] For details of the accreditation of war colleges with universities, see Mukherjee, "Educating the Professional Military," 13.

Relations besides lectures by eminent persons, as the DSSC have their own emphasis and *own their curricula*."[58]

As the military retains strong control over the curricula, it emphasizes training over education.[59] The tendency to train and "school" instead of educate has been noted by almost all analysts of PME in India. According to Lieutenant General Rakesh Sharma, military education retains "the classic fervor of military training as against education. The academic rigor and research . . . is noticeably absent, including at the highest institutions of learning."[60] Another analyst, a former colonel, criticized the "tactical orientation of instruction during formal teaching that focuses on rote learning rather than holistic understanding of issues."[61] This is not specific to a branch or service as analysts have criticized the Indian Air Force too for confusing training and education.[62]

Another unfortunate byproduct of leaving curricula development to the military has been the neglect of military history. Considered the bedrock of strategic studies, PME in India does not emphasize the study of military history. It is a subject for the Staff College entrance exam—a competitive process to select students who attend the course—but beyond that, it is not taught as a discipline.[63] Therefore, war colleges do not cultivate or engage with military historians, adding weight to the argument that there is "a distinct absence of a culture of military history in the Indian Armed Forces."[64] After analyzing publications in professional military journals, Stephen Rosen concludes, "the Indian army has not been promoted either by its own wars or by the wars of others to engage in an effort to rethink its basic concepts in the light of military events after WWII."[65] A lack of documented studies results in an inability

---

[58] Email to author, November 21, 2016, emphasis added.

[59] For a good account of the difference between the two, see Joan Johnson-Freese, "The Reform of Military Education: Twenty-Five Years Later," *Orbis* 56, no. 1 (2012): 136–38.

[60] Rakesh Sharma, "Professional Military Education and Producing Thought Leaders for the Army," *Indian Defence Review* (blog), July 17, 2017, http://www.indiandefencereview.com/professional-military-education-and-producing-thought-leaders-for-the-army/.

[61] Vivek Chadha, *Even If It Ain't Broke Yet, Do Fix It: Enhancing Effectiveness Through Military Change* (New Delhi: Pentagon Press, 2016), 76; also see Harsh Pant, "The Soldier, the State and the Society in India: A Precarious Balance," *Maritime Affairs* 10, no. 1 (2014): 29.

[62] Maneesh Misra, "Towards Continuous Military Education in the IAF: A Need for Yesterday," *Air Power Journal* 3, no. 1 (2008): 95–103.

[63] For a good overview of this issue, see P. K. Gautam, "The Need for Renaissance of Military History and Modern War Studies in India" (IDSA occasional paper 21, Institute for Defence Studies and Analyses, New Delhi, November 2011); and Arjun Subramaniam, *India's Wars: A Military History, 1947–71* (Annapolis, MD: Naval Institute Press, 2016), 17–25.

[64] Jaideep Chanda, "A Historiographic Analysis of the Military History of Post-Independent India" (Manekshaw paper 64, Centre for Land Warfare Studies, New Delhi, 2016), 18.

[65] Stephen Peter Rosen, *Societies and Military Power: India and Its Armies* (Ithaca: Cornell University Press, 1996), 234; for a critical appraisal of PME in India, also see 233–237.

to honestly analyze and learn from the past.[66] There is a broader disconnect between the military and academia, a fact admitted by two official reports—the 2001 Group of Ministers and the 2002 CONDU reports.[67]

As military officers—either those posted as commandants or faculty members at the different war colleges—are not professional educators, they usually focus on what they know best—operations and training. Nonmilitary subjects like international relations, strategic studies, political science, area studies, organizational theory, and human resources are either taught by military officers or not emphasized. Lamenting this state of affairs, a former instructor at the Army War College argued, "there is a total absence of high caliber, qualified academic faculty to cover strategic issues relating to broader subjects concerning international and national security."[68]

Civil–Military Relations and PME in India

India's pattern of civil–military relations has left its imprint on PME. This pattern, the absent dialogue argument, consists of three main characteristics: a lack of expertise, an institutional design with strong bureaucratic control, and considerable military autonomy.

The lack of civilian expertise on PME, at both the political and bureaucratic levels, is self-evident. There were only two instances of civilian initiatives to review education and training. The first, in the form of the CORTOS, was under Minister of State for Defence Arun Singh, who had a keen intellectual interest in military affairs. This relatively minor attempt was undone when he prematurely left the political scene in the aftermath of the Bofors scandal. In another instance, after the 1999 Kargil war, the CONDU revisited military education. However, as on 2019, the national defence university is still to be established, and it is uncertain whether it will prove to be transformative.

The second characteristic of civil–military relations—an institutional design leading to strong bureaucratic control—applies to a limited degree to some aspects of military education. The military has almost total freedom in designing its education and training courses; however, if new facilities have

---

[66] For relearning lessons in counterinsurgency, see Gautam, "Need for Renaissance of Military History," 20; also see Anit Mukherjee, "India's Experience with Insurgency and Counterinsurgency," in *Handbook of Asian Security*, ed. Sumit Ganguly, Andrew Scobell, and Joseph Liow, 149 (London: Routledge, 2009).

[67] Group of Ministers on National Security, *Report of the Group of Ministers on National Security* (New Delhi: Government of India, 2001), 99; and *Report of the Committee on National Defence University (CONDU)*, 24–27.

[68] Personal communication from Lieutenant General Amitava Mukherjee to author, June 3, 2011.

to be built, additional posts created, or officers sent abroad for educational purposes, then it has to obtain civilian sanction. This otherwise entirely reasonable procedure causes considerable friction between civilians and the military. There are two contrasting narratives on this. Civilians argue that they serve as a check and balance on military expenditure and in its natural organizational desire to expand. In addition, they argue that the military is always seeking opportunities to travel abroad. Military officers, on the other hand, argue that civilians—without much expertise, constantly (and pointlessly) question their proposals, causing delay and hindering their professional development. The truth is somewhere in between and is context-dependent—differing from case to case.

The third characteristic of civil–military relations—considerable autonomy to the military—is the primary factor responsible for most of the existing problems in PME. The concept of strong bureaucratic control vitiates against the argument about military autonomy; however, in practice, there is little that civilians can do to shape military education. Civilians play a minimal role, either as educators or as policymakers, in the functioning of institutions for PME and instead have left this to the services. According to a former commandant of the NDC, "there is minimal interference or instructions from the Ministry."[69] The military, in turn, has enacted policies preventing civilian faculty in its war college, preferring instead the "in-house" approach to military education. The military partners with some civilian universities; however, it is mainly to obtain accreditation, and there are no full-time civilian instructors involved in officer education.[70] This perpetuates the divide between the Indian military and its society as the former is bereft of civilian perspectives. Curricula development, critical to the education process, has also been left to the military. With both these measures, in general, PME leans more toward training than education.

Another problem due to the autonomy within the military is the lack of historiography. As the military does not declassify its files, the study of military history is unable to develop. But on this issue there is a curious catch-22. Military officials claim that they do not have instructions from the ministry regarding declassification. MoD officials, on the other hand, claim that only the classifying

---

[69] Interview with former commandant of NDC, who wishes to remain anonymous, New Delhi, May 4, 2011.

[70] As a counterexample for the relationship between the military and civilian universities in the United Kingdom, see John Kiszely, "Defence and the Universities in the Twenty-First Century," *RUSI Journal* 149, no. 3 (2004): 34–39.

agency can declassify![71] Due to this confusion, it is unclear whether this problem stems from military autonomy or strong bureaucratic control.

Conclusion

There is a normative element to the expectation of civilian intervention to address weaknesses in military education. The main theoretical justification for civilian "interference" to shape military education comes from Clausewitz's famous dictum that "policy is the guiding intelligence and war only the instrument, not vice versa. No other possibility exists, then, than to subordinate the military point of view to the political."[72] If wars are fought for political purposes, then military officers—at the operational and strategic levels—must be well acquainted with the larger political goal. Militaries therefore have to be aware of, and educated about, larger political, diplomatic, economic, and social goals. Indeed, in Latin America, while making the case for reforms in military education, David Pion-Berlin and Rafael Martínez note that its objective should be

> to mold soldiers to be citizens and public servants and not just warriors. A democracy wants to cultivate a greater awareness and sensitivity among soldiers that they are members of society, not a separate, privileged caste; that their purpose is to fulfill the policy aims of the government, not self-defined goals. For all this to occur, soldier-students need a full slate of courses in humanities and social sciences; they should benefit from the expertise of well-educated civilian professors; and they should get out of the barracks to interact with civilian students at the universities.[73]

In India, civilians have little knowledge *and* no mandate to influence military education and training. Instead, there is considerable autonomy given to the services. On this issue, the interaction between the MoD and the military—to use Verghese Koithara's memorable term—is one of a "depthless interaction."[74]

---

[71] Interviews with senior officials in the Services and a civilian bureaucrat in the Ministry of Defence, all of whom requested anonymity. Also see Anit Mukherjee, "Republic of Opinions," *Times of India*, January 18, 2012.

[72] Carl Von Clausewitz, *On War* (Princeton, NJ: Princeton University Press, 1976), 605.

[73] David Pion-Berlin and Rafael Martínez, *Soldiers, Politicians, and Civilians: Reforming Civil–Military Relations in Democratic Latin America* (New York: Cambridge University Press, 2017), 213.

[74] Verghese Koithara, *Managing India's Nuclear Forces* (Washington, DC: Brookings Institution Press, 2012), 184.

Neither of them are specialists, or well informed, when it comes to education; and therefore, it is difficult to imagine a productive dialogue between the two. India needs a partnership between civilian policymakers, academics, and the military to review its system of PME.[75] Its experience stands in contrast to that of some other established democracies wherein informed civilian intervention, collaborating with reformist officers and academics, has qualitatively improved PME. Whether such a partnership can be forged in India remains to be seen.

[75] This intervention must be well informed and predicated on improving military education and effectiveness; for the danger of ill-informed civilian intervention, see Mukherjee, "Educating the Professional Military," 15–16.

6

Simply the Best?

Officer Promotion and Selection Policies

The idea of heroic commanders leading their armies to victories resonates throughout history, celebrated through memorials and statues across the world. There is romance in this notion and an attachment to the belief that "great men" win great battles. Despite the vast literature eulogizing such military commanders, the study of military effectiveness as a function of promotion policies has not fetched much attention. To be sure, there has been scholarship on the politicization of military promotions and its influence on military effectiveness.[1] However, it has focused mainly on autocratic or ideological regimes and the effects of "coup-proofing" on military effectiveness.[2] There is very little literature on civil–military relations shaping promotion policies in democracies. This is surprising as selecting appropriate senior officers is one of the most important tasks of civilian leaders and one that can potentially cause friction in civil–military relations. Moreover, leadership plays an important role in military effectiveness as officer selection, rotation, and promotion policies "can influence effectiveness by affecting the criteria by which individuals are selected for positions of responsibility in the chain of command."[3] Choosing skilled military

---

[1] Caitlin Talmadge, *The Dictator's Army: Battlefield Effectiveness in Authoritarian Regimes* (Ithaca, NY: Cornell University Press, 2015); Timothy Hoyt, "Social Structure, Ethnicity, and Military Effectiveness: Iraq, 1980–2004," in *Creating Military Power: The Sources of Military Effectiveness*, ed. Risa Brooks and Elizabeth Stanley, 55–79 (Stanford, CA: Stanford University Press, 2007); and Ulrich Pilster and Tobias Bohmelt, "Coup-Proofing and Military Effectiveness in Interstate Wars, 1967–99," *Conflict Management and Peace Science* 28, no. 4 (2011): 331–50.

[2] James T. Quinlivan, "Coup-Proofing: Its Practice and Consequences in the Middle East," *International Security* 24, no. 2 (1999): 131–65; also see various references to the politicization of military promotions in Aurel Croissant, David Kuehn, and Philip Lorenz, *Breaking with the Past? Civil–Military Relations in the Emerging Democracies of East Asia*, Policy Studies 63 (Honolulu, HI: East-West Center, 2012).

[3] Risa Brooks, "Introduction," in *Creating Military Power: Sources of Military Effectiveness*, ed. Risa A. Brooks and Elizabeth A. Stanley, 21 (Stanford, CA: Stanford University Press, 2007).

commanders or firing unsuccessful ones is therefore one of the most crucial tasks for a nation's polity.

Considering its importance, why is there so little discussion of civil–military relations, officer promotion policies, and military effectiveness? Perhaps one reason is the difficulty in establishing a causal link between officer promotion policies and military effectiveness. It is somewhat easier to argue that if promotion policies are not based on merit—like in some autocratic regimes—then they can compromise military effectiveness. However, in democracies, it is harder to explicitly link military effectiveness with promotion policies. This is especially the case in peacetime soldiering as, ultimately, wars are the best judge of military leadership.[4] Since conventional wars are a rarity, it is difficult to assess whether officer promotion policies are properly designed to reward military competency.[5] These factors make it difficult to study military effectiveness as a function of officer promotion policies. Despite that (perhaps insurmountable) research limitation, there is still room to assess civil–military interaction on officer promotion policies. More importantly, one can judge the role that civilians play in choosing their military commanders and the manner in which it shapes organizational behavior and priorities.

This chapter examines officer promotion and selection policies in India. In keeping with the theme of this book, it does so through the prism of civil–military relations. It begins with a conceptual discussion of the role of civilians in officer promotion policies, mainly by examining the practice in other democracies. Next, it describes the historical evolution of officer promotion and selection policies. This focuses on major controversies, under the assumption that they best illuminate the interaction between politicians, bureaucrats, and military officers. Next, it presents differing perceptions on civil–military relations and promotion policies—one alleging civilian malfeasance and the other of military autonomy and parochialism. Thereafter, it explains the applicability of the absent dialogue argument to this process. The penultimate section cautions against a possible politicization of military promotions while analyzing the controversial appointment of General Bipin Rawat as chief of army staff in 2016. The conclusion summarizes some of the main observations.

There are three main arguments in this chapter. First, promotions policies in India are an almost exclusively military affair, and civilians have little to do with the processes. Like in other established democracies, senior officer promotions are subject to the approval of political authorities; but, exceptions apart, there is little

---

[4] Dan Reiter and William A. Wagstaff, "Leadership and Military Effectiveness," *Foreign Policy Analysis* 14, no. 4 (2018): 1–22.

[5] Counterinsurgency warfare, which is most in vogue these days, is largely about junior officer leadership and provides few instances or opportunities to evaluate generalship.

evidence that civilians have actively shaped promotion policies. Procedurally, civilians have the power to accept or reject the recommendations from the services; but, by and large, they have refrained from shaping the military's top leadership. To a significant extent, this is a legacy of the defeat in the 1962 war, which was partly blamed on politicization of military promotions. Second, a lack of civilian guidance exacerbates parochial divisions within the military. Sectional interests within the military bureaucracy, especially in the army, have with some success shaped policies to suit their interests. This has caused tensions within the officer community. Third, military promotion policies would be better served with greater (but informed) civilian oversight. There is a need therefore to create conditions for a dialogue on promotion, selection, and placement policies. Such a measure, however, also needs to create safeguards to prevent politicization of the military.

Conceptual Overview: Role of Civilians in Officer Promotion Policies

What is the proper role of civilians in framing officer promotion and selection policies? There are two different views on this. According to one school, it is best to leave this process to the professional military as civilian intervention may lead to politicization of the armed forces. Indeed, in most countries, officer promotion and selection policies are left to the military, under the assumption that it is most suited to select its next generation of leaders. Moreover, the experiences of some "transitioning democracies," defined as countries moving from an authoritarian to a democratic regime, serve as a cautionary tale for the dangers of ill-conceived civilian intervention in military promotions.[6]

The other school of thought argues that civilians should have more oversight over promotion policies, especially in the selection and appointment of senior officers (at the rank of brigadier and above).[7] This is justified on a number of grounds. First, selecting senior officers is an essential element in *exercising* civilian control. If the civilians are not involved in this process, then it is construed as a sign of weak institutional control. Second, leaving promotions entirely to the military may lead to sectional interests, parochialism, and favoritism. Unlike how it is commonly perceived from outside, the military is not a unitary actor, and there are different "tribes" vying for power and influence. When leadership

---

[6] For the dangers of politicization of military promotions in Thailand and Indonesia, see Zoltan Barany, "Exits from Military Rule: Lessons for Burma," *Journal of Democracy* 26, no. 2 (2015): 92–93.

[7] Douglas L. Bland, "A Unified Theory of Civil–Military Relations," *Armed Forces and Society* 26, no. 1 (1999):19; and Barany, "Exits from Military Rule," 97.

positions are captured by one tribe/sectional interest, it may engineer the rules to ensure its supremacy. To prevent this, civilians can serve a necessary function as a form of checks and balances within the system. Third, civilians should have a role in deciding what type of officers to promote—in terms of the best fit for military effectiveness and organizational purpose. This rests on the assumption that civilians should oversee promotion policies to encourage critical thinkers and innovators and to protect "military mavericks."[8] Despite these justifications, as the following discussion shows, civilian intervention in promotion policies is more an exception than a rule.

As a parliamentary democracy, the United Kingdom shares similar organizations and processes with India. However, unlike India's compartmentalized civil–military dichotomy, one of the key strengths of the British Ministry of Defence (MoD) is "the level of integration between MOD civilians and Service personnel across the organization, including in Head Office."[9] This prevents sudden changes in policy, including on parochial grounds. The services are mostly in control of their promotion policies. However, in 2011, as a result of Lord Levene's defense reforms, civilians sought a role in services promotion boards under the "joint assured model."[10] This was based on the assumption that civilians should have a role, especially in terms of evaluating joint staff experience, when selecting senior officers. As a result, the careers of senior officers are currently managed by the Senior Appointments Committee, which includes, among others, a civilian bureaucrat (the permanent undersecretary for defense) and a nonvoting private sector member. The private sector representative was introduced in order to "increase transparency, provide a wider viewpoint and spread best practices."[11]

This novel experiment was part of a larger trend wherein civilians took a greater interest in military personnel management policies. In 2016, the office of ombudsman was created by a parliamentary act, replacing the office of the service complaints commissioner.[12] The services have reluctantly given up their grievances and vigilance function primarily because of sustained political

---

[8] Barry R. Posen, *The Sources of Military Doctrine: France, Britain, and Germany Between the World Wars* (Ithaca, NY: Cornell University Press 1984), 222–36. "Mavericks" has been defined as those "officers with unconventional ideas who are willing to cooperate with civilians to reshape the military"; see Adam Grissom, "The Future of Military Innovation Studies," *Journal of Strategic Studies* 29, no. 5 (2006): 909n20.

[9] Lord Levene, et al., *Defence Reform: An Independent Report into the Structure and Management of the Ministry of Defence* (London: Ministry of Defence, 2011), 15.

[10] Levene, et al., *Defence Reform*, 57–61.

[11] Ministry of Defence, *How Defence Works*, version 4.2 (London: Ministry of Defence, 2015), 19.

[12] The service complaints system came into effect in 2008, replacing the separate single-service legislation and processes.

pressure and attention after a review of the circumstances surrounding the deaths of four soldiers between 1995 and 2002.[13] Despite these developments, some feel that civilians have not been able to adequately exercise their powers. According to Hew Strachan,

> for senior ranks in joint appointments, the single services are extraordinarily adroit at positioning only one candidate for the job and saying that it is "their" turn, so that each of the three takes joint senior jobs in rotation. Efforts have been made to unblock this at 2 star level and above but so far not much has been achieved, and it is unlikely to happen if it means conceding armed forces' control to a process dominated by civil servants. The only truly civilianised but effectively political appointment is that of Chief of the Defence Staff, which lies with the Prime Minister.[14]

These sentiments are indicative of calls for greater political attention to military promotion and selection policies.

In the United States, historically civilians have had a strong oversight over officer promotion and selection policies as these require legislative approval. In contemporary times, the US Congress has influenced this process through two major legislative initiatives—the Defense Officer Personnel Management Act, enacted in 1980, and the 1986 Goldwater-Nichols Act. The former was aimed at providing guidelines to standardize officer promotions across the services, and the latter sought to incentivize joint assignment for further promotions. Initially, the services resisted these ideas, but over time they became more convinced of their necessity. Donald Rumsfeld, defense secretary from 2001 to 2006, sought to obtain, with some success, a greater role for civilians in the promotion, placement, and selection of military officers.[15] His successor, Robert Gates, allegedly "upended the Army's promotion board and thus allowed some of the most creative colonels, whose careers had been thwarted, to advance to the rank of general."[16] Ashton Carter also undertook an initiative for reform in personnel

---

[13] Service Complaints Ombudsman for the Armed Forces, "History and Legislation," https://www.servicecomplaintsombudsman.org.uk/about-us/history-and-legislation/.

[14] Email to author, October 31, 2018.

[15] For a good analysis, see Andrew Hoehn, Albert Robbert, and Margaret Harrell, *Succession Management for Senior Military Positions: The Rumsfeld Model for Secretary of Defense Involvement* (Santa Monica, CA: Rand, 2011).

[16] Fred Kaplan, "Robert Gates' Primal Scream," Slate, January 14, 2014, https://slate.com/news-and-politics/2014/01/robert-gates-duty-the-defense-secretarys-criticisms-of-obama-and-bush.html.

policies.[17] In addition, from time to time, civilian principals have issued general guidelines for framing promotion policies. Despite these efforts, by and large, except for the placement and selection of the senior-most officers, the military retains considerable autonomy in its promotion and placement policies.[18] This arrangement has been criticized for its lack of flexibility, inability to retain talent, and practices "far removed from the best talent-management practices of the private sector."[19]

In sum, with regard to military promotions, different countries have their unique set of rules, emanating from laws, norms, and customs. There is no normatively correct answer about the level of civilian intervention in officer promotion, placement, and selection policies. However, both of the extremes—complete civilian abdication over this process and politicization of the military—are undesirable. Instead, civilians should have some oversight—mainly to provide overall guidance, as a form of checks and balances and to ensure that promotion rules are justly formulated and implemented and in keeping with overall organizational interest. Such civilian guidance needs to be carefully crafted and informed, with an understanding of the unique circumstances of military ethos and soldiering. Militaries, even those committed to the principle of democratic civilian control, would resent such civilian oversight. What is necessary, however, is to have a civil–military dialogue on the desired features of officer promotion, selection, and placement policies. In India, as the following sections show, for a long time civilians were focused on asserting strong civilian control. Under judicial pressure, however, the MoD has pushed the military to design more transparent and logical promotion policies. Despite some improvement, much more remains to be done.

[17] Andrew Tilghman, "The 4 Big Takeaways from Ash Carter's New Push for Military Personnel Reform," *Military Times*, June 9, 2016, https://www.militarytimes.com/2016/06/09/the-4-big-takeaways-from-ash-carter-s-new-push-for-military-personnel-reform/.

[18] For autonomy within the services on promotion and selection policies, see Michael C. Veneri, "The U.S. Military's Implementation of the Joint Duty Promotion Requirement," *Armed Forces & Society* 34, no. 3 (2008): 424–27.

[19] David Barno and Nora Bensahel, "Can the U.S. Military Halt Its Brain Drain?" *The Atlantic*, November 5, 2015, https://www.theatlantic.com/politics/archive/2015/11/us-military-tries-halt-brain-drain/413965/; also see Bipartisan Policy Center, *Building a F.A.S.T. Force: A Flexible Personnel System for a Modern Military. Recommendations from the Task Force on Defense Personnel* (Washington, DC: Bipartisan Policy Center, March 2017), https://bipartisanpolicy.org/wp-content/uploads/2017/03/BPC-Defense-Building-A-FAST-Force.pdf; and Kyle Byard, Ben Malisow, and Martin E. B. France, "Toward a Superior Promotion System," *Air & Space Power Journal* (July–August 2012): 24–44.

Not Attaching too Much Importance to Seniority: Nehru and Military Promotion Policies

Prime Minister Jawaharlal Nehru had the difficult job of building up the MoD and instituting civilian control over the military. He was particularly insistent on the principle of civilian supremacy over all aspects of defense policy, including military promotion policies.[20] However, this logic and alleged civilian interference in military promotions were later to be blamed for the defeat in the 1962 China war and thereby discredited.

After independence, as a result of the exit of British officers, Indian officers were rapidly promoted up the ranks. In the initial years, civilians usually let the military handle its promotion policies. All the same, procedural rules of business allowed civilians to exercise some power. For example, under the Army Act military officers could file statutory complaints to the government against adverse remarks in their Annual Confidential Reports (ACRs).[21] The MoD could then set aside these damaging reports. One such complaint was filed by Corps Commander Lieutenant General S. P. P. Thorat against the ACR written by Western Army Commander Lieutenant General Kulwant Singh on July 22, 1956.[22] It appears that his complaint was upheld as Thorat was later appointed Eastern Army commander.

In 1957, Nehru appointed General K. S. Thimayya as the chief of army staff and in the process superseded two army commanders—Lieutenant General Sant Singh and Lieutenant General Kulwant Singh. The former retired, refusing to serve under his junior, while the latter continued in service. According to Wilkinson, this was perhaps part of a strategy "to make sure that no chiefs were chosen from Punjab."[23] Thimayya, however, was popular and well regarded, within and outside the military, so this sidelining of the other two officers did not fetch that much attention.

In the years preceding the disastrous 1962 China war, there were numerous controversies centering on civilian control of the military. The fallout between

---

[20] Steven I. Wilkinson, *Army and Nation: The Military and Indian Democracy since Independence* (Cambridge, MA: Harvard University Press, 2015), 101–10.

[21] ACRs are annual performance reports that are written for every officer, usually by the immediate senior, and are instrumental in their future promotions. For more on this, see G. D. Bakshi, "Promotion System in the Army: Dealing with Peacetime Atrophy," *Journal of Defense Studies* 4, no. 4 (2010): 2.

[22] "Statutory Complaint under AA Section 27," 53–59 in Subject File 6, Thorat Papers, NMML.

[23] Wilkinson, *Army and the Nation*, 109; however, he also admits that there would be "no publicly available document" to support this claim.

Thimayya and Krishna Menon (and Nehru) has already been discussed in Chapter 2. In addition, among other incidents, Nehru and Krishna Menon were also accused of interfering in officer promotions and thereby politicizing the officer cadre. The man at the center of this drama was Lieutenant General B. M. Kaul, who in 1961 was appointed as the chief of general staff. Kaul was a controversial officer who cultivated close ties with the political leadership, especially with Nehru, and created divisions within the officer corps. As an Army Supply Corps officer, he did not have much combat or command experience, so opposition leaders criticized his appointment.[24] Addressing this controversy, Nehru defended Kaul's appointment, arguing that, "the Army would go to pieces if we lay down the rule of promotion only by seniority. I have never heard of an Army where that has been done. It might have been done in some remote and primitive army but no advanced country can do like that."[25] He further added that it was proper for the political executive to appoint senior positions by "ignoring seniority—not ignoring it, but certainly not attaching too much importance to it."[26] Kaul subsequently failed as a military commander in the 1962 war, ending his career.

The meteoric rise and dramatic fall of Kaul has since served as a cautionary tale. Kaul was blamed for a much that went wrong during this period, and this ensured that Nehru's argument—"merit over seniority"—would forever be viewed with suspicion by the military. They feared the possibility that merit would be used as an excuse to appoint politically well-connected, pliable, and possibly incompetent officers in senior ranks. The 1962 war created a narrative that civilian tinkering with the military's promotion policies leads to disasters, and for the next decade or so the military retained considerable institutional autonomy. More importantly, a precedent was set wherein seniority would emerge as the determining factor in the selection and appointment of military posts.

[24] For the divisions with the officer cadre during this period, see Shiv Kunal Verma, *1962: The War that Wasn't* (New Delhi: Aleph Books, 2016), 29–36; and for a perspective, albeit from an affected party, see S. D. Verma, *To Serve with Honour* (Pune: New Thacker's Fine Art Press, 1988), 100–26.

[25] Nehru's statement in Parliament on April 12, 1961, in *Lok Sabha Debates (Thirteenth Session)*, Second Series, 54, no. 42 (New Delhi: Lok Sabha Secretariat, 1961), 10827. In later years Lt. Gen. B. M. Kaul would cite Nehru's statement to defend his own promotion and would argue that Nehru believed that "there was no in-turn promotion in the higher ranks of the army, otherwise it would consist of a lot of dunderheads." See B. M. Kaul, Serial no. 93, Oral History Transcripts, NMML, 150.

[26] Cited in Lloyd I. Rudolph and Susanne H. Rudolph, "Generals and Politicians in India," *Pacific Affairs* 37, no. 1 (1964): 15.

All the Right Men: Indira Gandhi as the Decider

Indira Gandhi assumed power as a diffident leader and took some time to come into her own. In the initial years, therefore, she rarely intervened with the affairs of the military. However, after winning the election in 1971 and the victory in the Bangladesh war, she felt more comfortable with exerting her political power. There was the notion of the necessity for a "committed bureaucracy" and "committed judiciary"—based on the assumption that government officials should owe their primary allegiance to the elected officials. In time, this led to an authoritarian turn in Indira Gandhi's politics and her worldview—and she put a premium on personal loyalty. It was inevitable that this logic would also apply to the armed forces.

Among the first cases in the Indian Air Force, in early 1973, Indira Gandhi appointed O. P. Mehra as the chief of air staff despite the presence of two more senior officers—Shivdev Singh and M. M. Engineer. Shivdev Singh, as the vice chief of air staff during the 1971 Bangladesh war, "was credited with masterminding the entire air operations" and had the support of Defence Minister Jagjivan Ram.[27] However, P. N. Haksar, then private secretary to the prime minister, justified Mehra's selection and argued that the other two officers should not be considered as they were eligible only due to the partial extension in service that was earlier granted to them.[28] We do not know the underlying reasons for this maneuver, although there were rumors of defense deals.[29] Eventually, this did not become a major controversy as both superseded officers quietly went into retirement.

On military promotions, Indira Gandhi first courted public controversy when Lieutenant General P. S. Bhagat was not made the chief of army staff in 1974.[30] To deny him this position, Indira Gandhi granted an extension of service to the incumbent chief, General G. G. Bewoor. Some argued that Bhagat was denied this (well-deserved) post because civilians were distrustful of his views on civil–military relations and did not want a "strong Chief on their hands."[31] Bhagat was a soldier-scholar, and his experience as a member of the Henderson-Brooks

[27] R. Chandrashekhar, *Rooks and Knights: Civil–Military Relations in India* (New Delhi: Pentagon Press, 2017), 71.

[28] Top secret internal letter from P. N. Haksar to Prime Minister Indira Gandhi dated December 8, 1972, in Subject File no. 56, Instalments I and II, 18–19, P. N. Haksar papers, NMML. Also see O. P. Mehra, *Memories: Sweet and Sour* (New Delhi: Knowledge World Publishers, 2010), 153–59.

[29] Chandrashekhar, *Rooks and Knights*, 71.

[30] Mathew Thomas and Jasjit Mansingh, *Lt Gen PS Bhagat: A Biography* (New Delhi: Lancer International, 1994), 451–60.

[31] V. K. Singh, *Leadership in the Indian Army: Biographies of Twelve Soldiers* (New Delhi: Sage Publications, 2005), 288.

Committee (which investigated the 1962 India–China war) provided an opportunity to gain insight on higher defense organization. This was reflected in his book, which was informed by this effort.[32] According to P. R. Chari, who was in the MoD at that time, his strong views on civil–military relations and the "proper role" between civilian bureaucrats and the military was common knowledge and was held against him.[33] There was also speculation that Bhagat was perceived to be "pro-Sikh"—which did not sit well with the prime minister.[34] For his role in this episode, Bewoor was criticized for becoming "a party to this sordid manipulation."[35]

Indira Gandhi's most controversial decision was to supersede S. K. Sinha and instead appoint Arun Vaidya as the chief of army staff in 1983. Based on seniority, and as per practice, Sinha should have been appointed as the army chief. However, departing from the norm, Indira Gandhi consulted with the outgoing army chief general, K. V. Krishna Rao, on his possible successor, a move that the latter admitted was "not usual."[36] According to Krishna Rao, he then recommended the supersession of Sinha and backed Vaidya to be the chief.[37] On hearing the news, Sinha immediately resigned, amid allegations that the prime minister was politicizing the military. Some prominent politicians, including Jagjivan Ram, L. K. Advani, and, ironically in light of later events, George Fernandes, drafted a joint statement urging that "at least the Chief of the Army could be spared from the politics."[38] There was considerable speculation over the reasons behind Sinha's supersession: some believed Gandhi thought that he was close to her bête noire, the late Jaya Prakash Narayan, whereas others argued that the civilian bureaucracy was against him due to his strong views on higher defense organization and civil–military relations.[39]

[32] For his views on higher command of war and a critical assessment of the role of the political and bureaucratic leaders, see P. S. Bhagat, *Forging the Shield: A Study of the Defence of India and South East Asia* (New Delhi: Statesman, 1965), 28–57. This book, out of print and rarely available, has unfortunately not got the attention it deserves from India's strategic community.

[33] Interview, New Delhi, November 1, 2011.

[34] Chandrashekhar, *Rooks and Knights*, 72.

[35] S. K. Sinha, *A Soldier Recalls* (New Delhi: Lancer International, 1992), 243. He also insinuates a quid pro quo as General Bewoor after retirement was appointed as the Indian ambassador to Denmark.

[36] K. V. Krishna Rao, *In the Service of the Nation: Reminiscences* (New Delhi: Penguin India Books, 2001), 245.

[37] Krishna Rao, *In the Service of the Nation*, 245–46. In what was viewed as a quid pro quo, General Krishna Rao was appointed as a governor within a year of his retirement.

[38] Sinha, *A Soldier Recalls*, 311; for more on this episode, see 292–314.

[39] In 1980 the officer wrote a monograph on India's higher defense organization, which was somewhat critical of the civilian bureaucracy; see S. K. Sinha, "Higher Defense Organization in India" (USI paper 7; USI Publications, New Delhi, 1980); also see Singh, *Leadership in the Indian Army*, 377–78.

In all three of these cases, civilians intervened in selecting officers for the top-most position. Doing so is a political prerogative, but there were charges that this could politicize the military. It is not known, and will perhaps never be known, if these decisions were taken by Indira Gandhi because she doubted the personal loyalty of these officers or because she was acting on the advice of bureaucrats in the MoD. Or it could have been a combination of both. Perceptually, to the military community, the latter two cases were viewed as instances wherein the scholarship and views of senior officers, especially pertaining to civil–military relations, were held against them. According to P. R. Chari, who was in the MoD during both controversies, "we were aware of what these officers were saying and some of their views seemed to challenge civilian supremacy."[40] After the controversy generated by Sinha's supersession, politicians, however, resisted from interfering blatantly in officer promotion policies.

Interestingly, the trend of holding the scholarship of an officer against him continued even in recent times. In a little-known episode, members of the ruling Bharatiya Janata Party were apparently unhappy with some sentiments, pertaining to Hindutva, expressed in a book written by Lieutenant General Arjun Ray.[41] Based on his views, the government was all set to deny him the next rank. It was only after a personal appeal from senior military leaders to the prime minister's office that this decision was overturned.[42] Ray, however, denied that he faced any political opposition and instead argued "the primary opposition to *Kashmir Diary* was from bureaucrats and not politicians. It was the civil bureaucracy that created impediments as a form of asserting control."[43]

Codification, Judicial Intervention, and Coalition-Era Politics

General K. Sundarji, chief of army staff from 1985 to 1988, undertook many initiatives to shape officer promotion policies. In 1987, for the first time, the Military Secretary (MS) Branch, which deals with officer promotions, issued a set of guidelines that was circulated within the army, codifying its policies. There was also a change in the method of selection of army commanders.[44] Another

[40] Interview, New Delhi, November 1, 2011.

[41] The book that provoked this controversy was Arjun Ray, *Kashmir Diary: Psychology of Militancy* (New Delhi: Manas Publications, 1997).

[42] Interview with former chief of army staff and a former official in the prime minister's office, both of whom wish to remain unnamed.

[43] Email to author, December 19, 2011, and remarks in a follow-up telephone interview on December 29, 2011.

[44] Raj Kadyan, *The Lies that Win Army Promotions* (New Delhi: Manas Publications, 2005), 66–70.

policy of creating separate staff and command streams, called the "streaming policy," in the general cadre was also introduced. This proved to be highly controversial as there were allegations that this was used to sideline otherwise deserving officers. Later, when faced with litigation, the army walked away from the principle and, to avoid controversies, started approving all officers for both command and staff.[45] There was also an experiment, abandoned within two years, not to show officers their ACRs.[46] All these trends codified policies in the MS branch, but there were also allegations that some of the policy changes were ad hoc, personality-based, and designed to favor certain officers over others.

In 1988, Prime Minister Rajiv Gandhi appointed S. K. Mehra as the chief of air staff and in the process overlooked M. M. Singh, who had greater operational and professional experience.[47] More controversially, in 1991, "an entirely new precedent" was set as N. C. Suri was appointed chief of air staff on the day he was supposed to retire, as his predecessor left office early, thereby denying P. K. Dey.[48] In both these cases, however, it is not known on what grounds one officer was favored over the other. Was it the result of successful lobbying by politically well-connected officers? What were the deliberation and the justification made by the civilians to orchestrate these measures? These cases are illustrative examples wherein civilians intervened to select one officer over another.

The advent of coalition governments in the 1990s led to a number of controversies that shed light on civil–military relations and political interference in promotion policies. Early in his administration, Prime Minister Chandra Shekhar tried to alter the navy's chain of command but could not do so on the intervention of President R. Venkatraman.[49] The army was embroiled in a number of controversies when Mulayam Singh Yadav was the defense minister. As the leader of the Samajwadi Party, Yadav was a prominent member of the short-lived United Front coalition government. Due to his political importance, he was able to brazenly interfere in the army's promotion system.[50] Among the more public

---

[45] Interview with Lt. Gen. Amitava Mukherjee, New Delhi, December 29, 2011. The officer served as additional military secretary from 1991 to 1994.

[46] Previously under the open system, officers would be told about their reports. Under the closed system, this was denied to them, see N. N. Bhatia, "What's Wrong with Our Performance Appraisal System," *United Service Institution of India Journal* 117, no. 487 (April-June 1987): 175.

[47] Ramindar Singh, "S. K. Mehra Supersedes M.M. Singh for IAF Chief Post," *India Today*, July 15, 1988, https://www.indiatoday.in/magazine/defence/story/19880715-s.k.-mehra-supersedes-m.m.-singh-for-iaf-chief-post-797454-1988-07-15

[48] Chandrashekhar, *Rooks and Knights*, 86.

[49] R. Venkatraman, *My Presidential Years* (New Delhi: Harpercollins Publishers, 1994), 452–54.

[50] Manoj Joshi, "Playing with Fire," *India Today*, February 16, 1998. For an account of these controversies, see R. K. Anand, *Assault on Merit: The Untold Story of Civil–Military Relations* (New Delhi: Har Anand Publications, 2012).

disputes was his advocacy on behalf of Lieutenant General B. S. Malik, a dispute that forced Army Chief General V. P. Malik to approach the prime minister directly. Ultimately, however, the defense minister had his way. Criticizing Mulayam Singh Yadav's tenure, one analyst argued, "never since the fateful years preceding the humiliating defeat of India in the border war of 1962 has political interference in connection with the promotion of officers reached the level that has been achieved in the United Front's 18-month reign."[51]

In December 1998, in an unprecedented step, the chief of naval staff, Admiral Vishnu Bhagwat, was dismissed from service. Bhagwat was a divisive figure—some considered him intellectually astute, while others thought of him as self-centered. His views on civil–military relations were particularly strong, and he had long felt that the civilian bureaucracy had suppressed the military.[52] Bhagwat was dismissed due to differing interpretations of the promotion powers of the civilian government vis-à-vis the military. The controversy was over the promotion of Vice Admiral Harinder Singh, an officer who had fallen foul of his chief. Harinder Singh appealed directly to the MoD for redress of grievance and had sought to be appointed as a deputy chief of naval staff (operations). After many exchanges, his petition was accepted; and the government, via the Appointment Committee of the Cabinet (ACC), ordered his appointment as the deputy chief. However, Bhagwat dug in his heels and argued that as the ACC order violated the Naval Act, it was, in effect, "unimplementable."[53] This provided the pretext for his dismissal.

The MoD portrayed Bhagwat's actions as a challenge to civilian control. Strangely, it issued a white non-paper, perhaps for the first time in its history, justifying its decision. Alleging that this was an "extremely dangerous trend," the document argued that it was a "deliberate and systemic plan of the CNS [Chief of Naval Staff] to function beyond parliamentary/cabinet control."[54] That it had civil–military undertones was acknowledged by Prime Minister Atal Bihari Vajpayee when he argued that the admiral "was sacked because of his defiance of civilian authority."[55] While portrayed as a "deliberate and systemic plan" to

[51] Anand, *Assault on Merit*. For a description of this controversy, albeit from an affected party, see Kadyan, *Lies that Win Army Promotions*, 53–72.

[52] As a chief he encouraged officers to study the subject of civil–military relations, which resulted in two papers written by unidentified officers, titled "The Soldier and the State" and "India's Civilizational Flaw: The Isolation of the Military (The Vital need for Defence Reforms)." Both papers are included as an appendix in Vishnu Bhagwat, *Betrayal of the Defence Forces: The Inside Truth* (New Delhi: Manas Publications, 2001).

[53] This letter has been reproduced in Vishnu Bhagwat, *Betrayal of the Defense Forces*, 187–93.

[54] Untitled report, Government of India, Ministry of Defence (New Delhi: Imprint Services, undated), 12. A copy of this document is in the Library of the History Division of the MoD, R. K. Puram, New Delhi.

[55] "Bhagwat Sacked for Defiance, Says PM," *Indian Express*, January 1, 1999.

challenge civilian control, democracy and the subservience of the military to civilian authority had taken such firm roots that there was never a possibility of any other outcome than Bhagwat's departure.

After this episode, both civilians and the military closed ranks and worked toward mending the relationship. The political class also displayed greater sensitivity toward the ethos of the military. This was apparent when in 2002 the Indian Air Force was faced with a controversy over a leaked letter indicating that Air Marshal M. S. Sekhon, air officer commanding, Southern Command, had lobbied the chief minister of Punjab, Prakash Singh Badal, for help with his next appointment. Despite the fact that Badal belonged to the ruling coalition, Sekhon was forced to resign as this was perceived to be a severe offense.[56] In his defense, Sekhon argued that other officers had done the same and that he had been unfairly targeted.[57] In this case, the government did not let political compulsions interfere with the ethos of the military.[58]

These controversies reflected two issues relevant to civil–military relations. First, in the coalition era, regional political parties and their leaders could play an increasingly influential role in military promotions. The military could not entirely resist the pressure exerted by these politicians, and this increased covert politicking. At the same time, overt politicking on the part of the service officers, like that attempted by Air Marshal Sekhon, was considered a resignation-worthy offense. Senior officer promotion and selection always had a hint of politics behind it; however, the ethos of the armed forces did not tolerate lobbying politicians openly for favors. Second, civilian bureaucrats played an important role in carrying out the wishes of their political masters. Bureaucrats in the MoD handled all the files and therefore were well versed with the "rules of the game." Promoting a politically favored candidate or preventing an approved candidate therefore required a well-thought-out plan—the onus for which fell to these officials. Each case was different, but some of them must have tried to moderate the views of their political masters and perhaps paid a price. Some, on the other hand, must have acted on political directions with more alacrity than others. These stories, of political interference, bureaucratic intrigue or military injustice, however are difficult to prove and therefore mostly remain as a matter of conjecture.

In the 1990s, there was trend of officers approaching the judiciary to challenge decisions made by the services. Among the first such instances was the "supercession drama" in the navy, caused by officers given extension in service

---

[56] "Tainted Air Marshal Quits," BBC News, March 19, 2002, http://news.bbc.co.uk/2/hi/south_asia/1881145.stm.

[57] "Air Marshal Sekhon Ends Defiance, Resigns," *Mid-Day News*, March 19, 2002.

[58] Shishir Gupta, "Wings of Shame," *India Today*, April 1, 2001.

and brought to light by a 400-page writ petition filed by the future chief Bhagwat. Eventually settled by a compromise (the petition was withdrawn), this had a "salutary effect" on the navy's personnel policies, and even the MoD became "guarded in its approach."[59] Soon the courts were deluged with cases filed by officers seeking to overturn decisions made by the services. This required the attention and presence of military officers and defense ministry officials in various courts. In many cases, officers who petitioned the courts were able to change the original decision which went against them. As the number of litigants increased, the government in 2007 created the Armed Forces Tribunal through an act of Parliament.[60]

Despite this, the number of litigation cases was still high. According to one study, "around 11,000 such cases are currently pending in various High Courts and the Supreme Court, which translates to about twenty percent of the existing officer strength of the three services combined."[61] The MoD usually backed the services; however, the media attention shed light on (unfair) promotion rules and policies. This embarrassed both the military and the MoD. To prevent further litigation, the MoD gradually pushed the services to rationalize their promotion policies and make them more just and fair. Partly, as a result, in 2009, on the advice of the ministry, the army introduced the "quantification system" for appraisal, which reduced the arbitrariness in promotion boards.[62]

Divisions Within: Chiefs and Their Policies

As a result of the 1999 Kargil war and the subsequent reforms process, there were significant changes in almost all aspects of India's defense policies. Due to the experience of the war, there was an effort to reduce the age of commanding officers, and promotion policies changed accordingly. However, within a few years, the implementation of this policy deeply divided the officer cadre. More importantly, it revealed two aspects relevant to civil–military relations. First, the service chiefs had considerable power in shaping promotion policies. As discussed later, this gave rise to allegations of parochialism. Second, the MoD

---

[59] Chandrashekhar, *Rooks and Knights*, 90.

[60] Harjeet Singh, "Armed Forces Tribunal: An Appraisal," *Indian Defense Review* 26, no. 2 (2011): http://www.indiandefencereview.com/news/armed-forces-tribunals-an-appraisal/.

[61] Dinesh Kumar, "The Officer Crisis in the Indian Military," *South Asia: Journal of South Asian Studies* 33, no. 3 (2010): 460–62.

[62] Interview with General N. C. Vij, former chief of army staff, New Delhi, December 22, 2011. According to Lt. Gen. Amitava Mukherjee, who handled promotion policies in the army HQ, the MoD was "constantly badgering us to adopt the quantification system" even in the early 1990s; interview, New Delhi, December 29, 2011.

had a limited mandate and lacked the domain knowledge or expertise to shape promotion policies.

Since 1998, the Indian Army has had nine chiefs of army staff—seven from the infantry and two from the artillery. Prior to this, officers belonging to the Armored Corps and Mechanized Infantry held a disproportionately large number of senior officer posts. Ironically, infantry officers were taking the bulk of the casualties due to operations in the Siachen glacier, Sri Lanka, and numerous internal insurgencies. This gave rise to a perception that infantry officers serving in difficult field conditions were being overlooked in favor of those who served in peace stations. Part of the problem was the phenomenon of "inflated" ACRs. According to those in the infantry, armored corps officers got more points in their reports due to regimental and combat arm loyalty. In making this argument, they conveniently overlooked that such loyalty also existed in the infantry and other arms. Moreover, since the raising of a specialized counterinsurgency force, the Rashtriya Rifles in 1994, non-infantry officers were increasingly taking part in counterinsurgency operations. The point however remains that there are considerable tensions between these 'tribes' within the army.

In an effort to lower the age of commanding officers, the government set up a committee in July 2001 under Ajai Vikram Singh, then a Special Secretary in the MoD. Among other measures, this committee examined the cadre structure within the army and recommended creation of additional posts.[63] The first phase of allocation of additional posts was done in 2004, without any complaints. However, in 2009, further allocation of vacancies was undertaken under a different formula that allegedly favored infantry and artillery officers.[64] This created widespread resentment among other arms and services. Alluding to the logic of caste-based reservations, critics argued that this led to the "Mandalisation of the army" as vacancies are dictated by the logic of numbers as opposed to merit.[65] The policy was controversial even at that time and "was stoutly opposed by several senior lieutenant generals, including army commanders."[66] However, indicative of the powers of the army chief, General Bikram Singh reshuffled his top commanders, allegedly to ensure that there would not be any opposition to his "quota based" promotion policies.[67] Even though some officers approached

[63] For a good description of the assumptions of this committee, see Arun Prakash, "All Chiefs and No Indians," *Force Magazine*, November 2007, http://forceindia.net/guest-column/guest-column-arun-prakash/chiefs-no-indians/.

[64] Ajai Shukla, "All the Chief's Men," *Business Standard*, January 14, 2012.

[65] Rahul Bedi, "Is the Indian Army Losing Its Sheen?" *SP's Land Forces* no. 2 (2008): 14.

[66] Srinath Raghavan, "The Battle Within Indian Army for Promotions," NDTV.com, May 5, 2015, https://www.ndtv.com/opinion/the-battle-within-indian-army-for-promotions-760514

[67] Ajai Shukla, "Army Promotion Politics Drives Reshuffle of Top Commanders," *Business Standard*, July 2, 2013.

the courts in an effort to overturn this policy, after a lengthy battle, in 2016 the Supreme Court upheld the controversial "command exit" promotion policy. This, however, did little to mend a divided army.

Apart from these parochial battles, the Indian Army was also being riven by personal animosities. Infighting between senior officers is not uncommon, but, for the most part, officers were careful to avoid publicity, to protect the image of the institution. From 2006 onward, however, there was an unseemly row generated by the controversy over the date of birth of General V. K. Singh, chief of army staff from 2010 to 2012. General Singh claimed that in order to clear his promotion board he was "forced" to accept 1950 as his date of birth, even though he was born a year later.[68] This technicality was important as it would shape the future line of succession. Singh then approached the Supreme Court, only to be rebuffed. During this time, in "one of the messiest chapters in the history of the Indian army," a series of steps were taken against his perceived enemies.[69] This included the dismissal from service, on corruption charges, of Lieutenant General Avdesh Prakash, who held the post of military secretary—the senior-most officer dealing with military promotions and therefore considered above reproach. Later, however, for actions against other officers, General Singh would be severely criticized for his "mala fide" actions.[70] These controversies brought into open the factionalism prevalent within senior officers of the Indian Army. But it also revealed the autonomy and the powers concentrated in the office of the service chief.

There were controversies over sectional interests and the powers of the chief in other services also. In 1997–1998, the Indian Air Force faced what was characterized as a near "mutiny" due to divisions between flight and ground crew.[71] Air Chief Marshal S. Krishnaswamy's tenure as the chief of air staff from 2001 to 2004 was also marked by controversy pertaining to officer promotions. Under a newly promulgated promotion policy, Air Vice Marshal Harish Masand was denied his next rank.[72] Masand approached the High Court, and under

---

[68] For his version of events, see V. K. Singh (with Kunal Verma), *Courage and Conviction: An Autobiography* (New Delhi: Aleph Book, 2013), 265–68, 311–14, 323–30.

[69] Saikat Datta, "Why One of the Messiest Chapters in Indian Army History Refuses to Be Closed," Scroll.in, August 19, 2016, https://scroll.in/article/814386/why-one-of-the-messiest-chapters-in-indian-army-history-refuses-to-be-closed.

[70] Purnima Tripathi, "An Order and a Snub," *Frontline* 32, no. 3 (2015), https://www.frontline.in/the-nation/an-order-and-a-snub/article6848520.ece.

[71] Manoj Joshi, "Protest Over Allowances by Section of IAF Staff Snowballs into a Dangerous Development," *India Today*, December 15, 1997, https://www.indiatoday.in/magazine/defence/story/19971215-protest-over-allowances-by-section-of-iaf-staff-snowballs-into-a-dangerous-development-831084-1997-12-15.

[72] Shishir Gupta, "Government for Brake on IAF Promotions," *Indian Express*, October 6, 2003.

exceptional circumstances, he was reinstated as an air marshal. Subsequently, realizing its potential for misuse, the ministry overturned the promotion policy.[73]

As these cases illustrate, the service chiefs have considerable powers to shape officer promotion policies. Some of the chiefs chose to use these powers to serve parochial or sectional interests. Other decisions were borne out of factionalism and personal dislikes among senior echelons of the Indian military. At times, the MoD would be consulted as it had to approve major policy shifts. Acknowledging tensions within the military, according to a former defense secretary, changes in promotion policies "may be prompted by personal likes and dislikes, or 'gang wars' (if I may use the term) within a service. Sometimes, there may be a provision in a service policy regulation for approval of the MoD, sometimes not. Disagreements do arise between the Service HQ and MoD, resulting in stalemates during which some people retire without promotion, even though approved."[74] But there are also instances wherein the ministry exercised its powers to prevent major changes. For instance, under General S. Padmanabhan (an artillery officer), an attempt was made to designate artillery as a "combat arm," but this proposal was not cleared by the ministry.[75] On the other hand, there are other cases where the ministry was unable to exercise proper control. While discussing the "pro-rata" controversy, Srinath Raghavan argues that the ministry's handling of the matter "throws unflattering light on the state of civilian control over the military."[76]

Mr. Parrikar Comes to Town

In November 2014, Manohar Parrikar, chief minister of Goa, was appointed defense minister. Around this time, there was a lot of discontent among the veteran community, which felt that the MoD's attitude, on matters like pensions and disability allowances, was unhelpful and needlessly obstructive. In a bid to assuage this sentiment, Parrikar established a committee of experts for the "review of service and pension matters including potential disputes, minimizing litigation and strengthening institutional mechanisms related to redressal of grievances." The committee, comprised of legal experts and former military officers with

[73] Josy Joseph, "MoD Cuts IAF Chief's Wings," Rediff News, April 15, 2004, http://www.rediff. com/news/2004/apr/15josy.htm.

[74] Email from Ajai Vikram Singh to author, December 27, 2011.

[75] For an early reference to this proposal, see Shishir Gupta, "Faced with Ageing Profile, Upset Officers, Indian Army Considers Restructuring and VRS," India Today, May 14, 2001, https://www. indiatoday.in/magazine/defence/story/20010514-faced-with-ageing-profile-upset-officers-indian-army-considers-restructuring-and-vrs-776234-2001-05-14

[76] Raghavan, "Battle Within Indian Army for Promotions."

experience dealing with manpower and promotion policies, claimed that it "almost functioned like a Blue Ribbon Commission with proper inputs and candid insights from all concerned, including the Ministry, Services HQ, independent experts as well as employees' organizations."[77] It's report began with a startling observation that "almost 90% of the total Civil Appeals/Special Leave Petitions filed by the MoD comprised challenges to disability benefits of disabled soldiers"—justifying charges by the veterans of a callous and indifferent ministry.[78]

The report made a number of wide-ranging observations that shed light on military promotion policies. First, it criticized the military (especially the army) for sudden changes in promotion policies. The committee observed that such actions gave rise to a "feeling of favoritism or a perception that the change has been tailormade to help . . . [a] particular section of officers."[79] The report unfortunately did not list any instances but hinted at the problem of parochialism. Significantly it observed that, at times, the military does not even seek the ministry's approval while changing its policies and argued that "the non-approval of certain important aspects of policy by the MoD has also led to greater litigation . . . [and] it is therefore imperative that [the] MoD be informed about major promotion related policies before implementation."[80] That, at times, the military allegedly did not do so indicates weak civilian control and oversight.

Second, the report called for an "ombudsman"-type institution and proposed an independent Grievances Examination Committee. The report underscored the weaknesses in the system of statutory complaints. Statutory complaints can be filed by military officers raising objections to matters pertaining to promotions, ACRs, and other grievances. These are processed through the services but can only be settled by the MoD. This gives an opportunity for civilians to deliberate upon the complaint, take a considered decision, and, if necessary, overrule decisions made by the services. The Experts Committee report argued that "forwarding of the [statutory] complaint to the ministry is a mere paper formality since the Ministry has *no expertise* or way of finding out the veracity of the issues raised by the Complainant or the notes recorded on the file by all officers in the chain till the Services HQ and that in most cases the Ministry

---

[77] Ministry of Defence, *Raksha Mantri's Committee of Experts* (New Delhi: Ministry of Defence, 2015), 3, https://mod.gov.in/sites/default/files/Reportcc_0.pdf.

[78] Ministry of Defence, *Raksha Mantri's Committee of Experts*, 2; also see Navdeep Singh, "The Defence Ministry's Approach to Litigation: Misdirected, Highly Adversarial and Sadistic," *Bar and Bench*, November 1, 2018, https://barandbench.com/defence-ministry-approach-to-litigation-misdirected-highly-adversarial-and-sadistic-part-i/

[79] Ministry of Defence, *Report of Raksha Mantri's Committee of Experts*, 142.

[80] Ministry of Defence, *Raksha Mantri's Committee of Experts*, 143.

blindly accepts what is put up from below."[81] This was an admission not only of a lack of expertise within the MoD but also of an absence of domain knowledge to honestly adjudicate on the statutory complaints. The report thereafter suggested the creation of an "ombudsman"-type organization, arguing that this idea was initially suggested by Parrikar and would fit comfortably with the personnel management guidelines of the central government.[82]

Finally, the report of the Experts Committee deliberated upon the need for an "outside member" in the military selection boards as the "closed door system of conducting selection boards leads to dissatisfaction and lack of transparency giving rise to doubts and also rumor-mongering." The MoD was keen to have a civilian member of the board, but this was rejected by the Experts Committee. Instead, they proposed two observers, not members, to these selection boards— either civilians or from a different service to "truthfully record their observations on file."[83] These suggestions were remarkable, especially from a committee comprised of senior army officers who handled military promotions in their careers. They also reflected the evolution of personnel policies in other established democracies—mirroring, for instance, the creation of the ombudsman and civilian participation in promotion boards in the United Kingdom. However, in India, civilians have been less successful in enforcing new ideas, and the services are reluctant to enforce such reforms.

The story of how the report of this committee has been processed remains untold. Parrikar seemed committed to bring about change, and in February 2017 he created another committee to review the promotion policies specifically in the army.[84] However, within a month, Parrikar left the MoD to attend to a political crisis in his home state of Goa. This took the wind out of the sails of the reforms process.

The ministry claims it is still committed to promotion reforms, but many who have dealt with the subject are pessimistic. According to Navdeep Singh, a member of the Experts Committee, the implementation of the report of this committee is

> very slow and till date not even one comprehensive letter has been issued on any of the subjects, including the ones accepted by the government in principle. The reasons for this inertia are multifarious. One,

[81] Ministry of Defence, *Raksha Mantri's Committee of Experts*, 136, emphasis added.

[82] Ministry of Defence, *Raksha Mantri's Committee of Experts*, 137–39.

[83] Ministry of Defence, *Raksha Mantri's Committee of Experts*, 149.

[84] Sushant Singh, "MoD Wants 'More Objectivity, Transparency and Fairness' in Army Promotions, Sets Up a Committee," *Indian Express*, February 8, 2017, https://indianexpress.com/article/india/committee-set-up-to-review-armys-promotion-policy-4513295/.

that Mr. Manohar Parrikar is not around to chase it. He was pretty much charged about bringing reform into the system. Two, that officers in key appointments are just not bothered. Three, and very importantly, there is always this resistance to change, including from the Services HQ, since the Report, besides recommending steps to reduce litigation, also puts forth steps to improve the system of redressal of grievances and in the bargain decentralizes powers from certain few power centers within the Services and the Ministry . . . personnel related branches such as the MS Branch do not want to embrace transparency and will continue resisting ideas such as the "Grievances Examination Committee."[85]

In sum, as a result of judicial pressure and the resultant negative publicity, the MoD has, over the years, constantly nudged the services to be more transparent and fair with their promotion and selection policies. There has been some progress from the previous years. However, as the following discussion shows, there are differing perceptions on the role of civilians in this process.

Differing Perceptions: Civil–Military Interaction on Officer Promotions

Unlike other government services, the armed forces—due to the nature of their function and organization—have a steep pyramidal structure. This leads to grievances and allegations of injustice and favoritism. Comparison with the civilian services is unfair, but by most counts the promotion policies in the armed forces are among the best of all government of India services.[86] As per the rules of business, major changes in promotion policies, results of senior officer promotion boards, and statutory complaints have to be approved by the MoD. The ACRs of senior officers are also handled by civilian staff working in the services. These procedures have evolved over time and form an essential component of exercising civilian control. Perhaps inevitably, this manner of control is resented by the military and has been a constant source of friction. Currently, on this issue, there are two different narratives—one of overarching civilian dominance and the other alleging that the military has too much autonomy, leading to cronyism and abuse.

---

[85] Email to author, November 6, 2018.

[86] Statement by Defence Ministry official to the Standing Committee on Defense, *Thirty Fourth Report: Human Resources Planning, Shortage of Manpower, Infusion of Hi-Tech Training and Infrastructure for the Armed Forces* (New Delhi: Lok Sabha Secretariat, February 2009), 65; for a description of the promotion system in the Indian Army, see Kadyan, *Lies that Win Army Promotions*, 9–20.

Civilian Dominance and Malfeasance

The dominant narrative within the military on matters pertaining to promotions is that civilians have too much power, which they have often misused. Books on this subject have typically accused the political class, "backed by complaisant bureaucrats," of endangering the country's security by disregarding the military's "merit system" and encouraging "favoritism and nepotism."[87] Another strand of this narrative accuses the civilian bureaucracy of abrogating the powers of the political class, misleading them and lording over the military. This view has been informed by instances wherein civilian bureaucrats have allegedly used their proximity to political leaders to lobby for or against officers.

Civilians procedurally exercise their powers in three ways. First is to delay or refuse approval of promotion board results or changes in promotion policies.[88] Usually, this is the result of a tussle, either personal or professional, between civilians and the military. Professional disagreements are understandable as civilians may not be willing to ratify changes in promotion policies, either fearing litigation or suspecting parochialism. Unfortunately, as a result, sometimes military officers, through no fault of their own, are forced into early retirement.[89] Another manner of exercising power by the MoD is by writing the note that goes to the ACC for approval. The recommendations and promotion board results are sent by the military to the MoD for submission to the ACC. The recommendations and advice tendered by the ministry are not shared with the services. This increases the potential for abuse of power. In one such instance, threatened with contempt of court, a defense secretary tendered an "unqualified apology" and admitted to misleading the ACC.[90] Third, civilians are also able to exercise their powers while addressing statutory complaints. Created to protect officers from personal vendettas and to address grievances, the statutory complaints allegedly provide an opportunity for the ministry to play favorites. According to a former deputy chief of army staff, the "system of statutory complaints brings the bureaucrats in the decision making loop. Since the politicians generally lack continuity and do not have enough knowledge on the subject they invariably go by what the bureaucrats recommend . . . this opens a vista for unscrupulous elements in the bureaucracy."[91]

[87] Anand, *Assault on Merit*, 6; and Kadyan *Lies that Win Army Promotions*, 252.

[88] "Army Promotion Policy: MOD yet to Decide," *Asian Age*, April 14, 2011. For a previous instance of non-approval of board results, see Manvendra Singh, "MoD's Stance on Promotions Causes Army Retirements," *Indian Express*, January 31, 1998.

[89] Ajay Bannerjee, "Officers Suffer in Army–MOD Promotion Tussle," *The Tribune*, April 25, 2011.

[90] "Ex-Defence Secy Apologizes to HC," *The Tribune*, February 13, 1999, https://www.tribuneindia.com/1999/99feb13/nation.htm#1; also see Kadyan, *Lies that Win Army Promotions*, 61.

[91] Kadyan, *Lies that Win Army Promotions*, 19.

This is an overly simplistic narrative as it ignores instances, wherein civilians checked the (worst) impulses of military leaders—either in furthering parochial policies or in cronyism.

Military Autonomy and Parochialism

In contrast to allegations of civilian overreach, there is another narrative which argues that the military has too much autonomy and power and that the system is prone to misuse. The MoD therefore serves a necessary role to provide "checks and balances" and prevents an abuse of power by military officials. According to a former air officer personnel in the Indian Air Force, "The checks and balances [exercised by the MOD] are good for the military. It holds and controls that [military] commander who often takes off from the block and moderates an over enthusiastic, typically military 'can-do' spirit, which might have unintended consequences."[92] Promotion policies are shaped largely by the services, and the chiefs have significant procedural powers, which has advantages and disadvantages. On the positive side, the system has flexibility, is responsive to feedback, and can quickly implement correctives. However, there are also some disadvantages.

First, the existing system gives considerable powers to the service chiefs in framing promotion, selection, and appointment policies. This gives a service chief the advantage of selecting his team but also results in frequent and personality-driven policy changes. The chief usually selects his personal staff officers including crucial appointments handling promotions, operations, manpower, and personnel.[93] This also enables him to make policy changes, and as military culture is instinctively deferential, his orders are rarely challenged.[94] As a result, there are allegations of frequent and sudden changes in policy, as admitted by the report of the Committee of Experts.[95] According to Lieutenant General Mohinder Puri, a former military secretary (the senior-most officer handling promotions), "there is no consistency in policy—changes happen depending upon the person in the chair [chief of army staff]."[96]

[92] Interview with Air Marshal Sumit Mukherji, New Delhi, October 21, 2011.

[93] According to a former defense secretary, the personal staff appointments are made on the recommendation of the service chief but with the approval of the ACC. He did not recall any instance in which the MoD disagreed with the chief's recommendation and was unaware of any policy note on this subject; email from Ajai Vikram Singh to author, December 27, 2011.

[94] It is difficult for senior officers, even at the level of army commanders (and their equivalent in the other two services), to overturn the recommendations of the chief. One such episode was the unsuccessful attempt by Lt. Gen. H. S. Panag to rescind his transfer orders; see Manu Pubby, "Lt Gen Panag to Meet Antony over Transfer," *Indian Express,* January 5, 2008.

[95] Ministry of Defense, *Raksha Mantri's Committee of Experts,* 142–144.

[96] Telephone interview with author, December 19, 2011.

Second, a related problem, is that it is prone to serving parochial interests. Parochialism is defined as a policy which favors a particular sectional interest, usually the arm, service, or regiment that one is commissioned in. This is one of the biggest criticisms of the promotion policies in the army, although sectional interests are also prevalent in the other two services.[97] In recent times, parochial policies have divided the officer cadre and created a major rift between different arms and services.[98] According to one general officer, "regrettably, some army chiefs have acted in a parochial manner . . . tampering with policy has militated against well-established systems. Pushing up his own group or arm of service by certain army chiefs, to a position of advantage, has inflicted great damage on the service. Such lopsided policies have caused serious divide within the officer cadre."[99]

Parochialism of some sort has always been an issue in the Indian army and is possibly an inevitable consequence of what is hailed as its strength—the regimental system.[100] This refers to the system "wherein officers and soldiers spend bulk of their service in a single unit which generally is part of an umbrella regiment."[101] Over the years, regimental identities, associations and loyalties have become stronger; leading to allegations of cronyism and favoritism. Instead of addressing this as a problem, successive generations of senior army officers have embraced this as part of their tradition and identity.[102] Criticizing the rise of parochialism, one analyst argued that

[97] In the air force and the navy, promotion policy changes are relatively less frequent. Personnel management is also probably easier as they have a much smaller cadre and have billets in attractive peace stations to accommodate officers who do not "make the cut."

[98] Shishir Arya, "Rift in Army Cadres over New Promotion Policy," *Times of India*, June 25, 2012, http://timesofindia.indiatimes.com/articleshow/14378933.cms?utm_source=contentofinterest&utm_medium=text&utm_campaign=cppst.

[99] Harwant Singh, "Defence Matters: Army's Promotion Policy for Higher Ranks," *Hindustan Times*, May 8, 2015, https://www.hindustantimes.com/chandigarh/defence-matters-army-s-promotion-policy-for-higher-ranks/story-wNUgwFGDE8JCf06JkGDbEM.html; also see K. J. Singh, "Cadre Review in Indian Army," *Times of India*, March 25, 2018, https://timesofindia.indiatimes.com/blogs/generals-jottings/cadre-review-in-indian-army/

[100] For more on the strengths of the regimental system, see P. K. Gautam, *Composition and Regimental System of the Indian Army: Continuity and Change* (New Delhi: Shipra Publishers, 2008), 19–29.

[101] H. S. Panag, "Restructuring & Reorganisation of Combat Arms," *Times of India*, September 17, 2017, https://timesofindia.indiatimes.com/blogs/shooting-straight/restructuring-reorganisation-of-combat-arms/

[102] For example, the army continues with the tradition of the colonel commandant, which some argue encourages parochialism; see Mrinal Suman, "Colonel Commandants: An Archaic and Parochial Institution," *Indian Defense Review*, Net Edition, April 25, 2011, http://www.indiandefencereview.com/spotlights/colonel-commandants-an-archaic-and-parochial-institution/. Regimental identities have also strengthened over the years through association and annual social gatherings.

the [promotion] system lends itself to manipulation by smart functionaries and thus, perpetuates a regime of patronage. . . . Earlier such manipulation was done in a discrete manner. Over a period of time, the practice has become so well entrenched that Chiefs have no qualms in openly flaunting their preferences. The worst, the environment has got so used to this partisanship that it has come it accept it as a normal practice.[103]

To be fair, most chiefs-have attempted to function in a collegiate manner and have tried to build consensus among the senior leadership. Moreover, if his principal staff officers perform their job without fear or favor, then they can succeed in, according to one officer, "protecting the Chief from himself" and preventing a misuse of power. But, since the chief appoints his staff officers, the system is open to manipulation.

The MoD may be aware through informal channels of possible discrepancies in the promotion process, but it is unable to do much—as norms prevent it from interfering in the "internal affairs" of the military. Moreover, as these proposals have the concurrence of the chief, it is assumed that this reflects the views of the senior leadership. According to a former defense secretary,

> The MoD does not know in case there has been a division [difference of opinion] in arriving at a conclusion. . . . The recommendations come to the MoD as those of the [Promotion] Board and as approved by the Chief. Surely, there would be cases on which unanimity is missing, but then the Chief has the last word before the case goes to the Ministry. Informally, one might come to know of disagreements within a Service on various issues, but these cannot be taken up formally, as there is only one official "party line" at a time—depending on the Chief of the day.[104]

Both these narratives—of civilian malfeasance and of military parochialism—are informed by a selective use of anecdotes and evidence. The system unsurprisingly works on the personalities, preferences, and integrity of all three sets of actors—politicians, bureaucrats, and military officers. If any one of them has a particular agenda or a preference, then it leads to a potential abuse of power.

---

[103] Mrinal Suman, "Selecting Military's Top Brass," *Indian Defense Review*, November 19, 2010, http://www.indiandefencereview.com/news/selecting-militarys-top-brass/

[104] Email from Ajai Vikram Singh to author, December 27, 2011.

Former chief of naval staff Admiral Arun Prakash avers that civilians have rarely interfered:

> If the Service HQs play their role according to the book, there is no room either for the bureaucrat or the politician to interfere in the promotion process. From my own experience, as COP [chief of personnel], VCNS [vice chief of naval staff] and Chief [of naval staff], I can say that there were just a few occasions when MoD attempted to intercede, but once they were told the rule position and warned that any fiddle would set a wrong precedent, they backed off. However, it is on the occasions that there has been an error on the part of the Service, either genuine or through *mala fide* intent, or there has been miscarriage of justice that a window of intervention is opened for the MoD. . . . Rarely has there been an occasion (in recent times) where the MoD has blatantly tried to push through a personnel related case in the face of principled opposition from the SHQ [service headquarters].[105]

The Dialogue on Officer Promotions

Does the pattern of civil–military relations, especially the absent dialogue argument, apply to military promotions? Not completely but in parts. There are three broad characteristics of the absent dialogue as presented in this book.

First is the lack of civilian expertise. Procedurally, the MoD approves the postings and promotions of all flag-ranked officers (brigadiers and above). This is not just meant to be pro forma as they are supposed to assess "qualifications, experience and professional competence to execute responsibilities, adherence to norms, policies, regulations . . . any apparent favoritism and whether as per their records and inputs available with them, there are reasons to apprehend an inability of the officer to execute his functions freely and objectively."[106] However, officials in the ministry do not have the requisite expertise to effectively play this role. While complaining about the lack of "domain knowledge" in the MoD, the report of the Experts Committee (2015), recommended that "officers with *adequate expertise* are posted to such appointments."[107] According to an officer who handled promotions policies in the army, the MoD "is tasked to carry out diligent oversight of all promotions to select ranks as a necessary

---

[105] Email from former chief of naval staff, Admiral Arun Prakash to author, March 7, 2012.

[106] Chandrashekhar, *Rooks and Knights*, 142.

[107] Ministry of Defence, *Raksha Mantri's Committee of Experts*, 141, emphasis added.

check ... but unfortunately lacks the professional and domain knowledge of the complex functional environment of the Army, to do full justice to this oversight function."[108]

The second characteristic is an institutional design leading to strong bureaucratic control. Indeed, there are bureaucratic controls, as approval from the defense ministry is necessary for major changes in policies and approval for promotion and posting of senior officers. For the most part however the MoD has a hands-off attitude toward promotion policies, treating promotion as an internal matter for the military. To be sure, there have been instances wherein these powers have been misused, usually on political directions, to favor well-connected officers. On the other hand, the ministry has also used some of these controls judiciously, for instance, by pushing the services to have more logical and transparent promotion policies. In addition, if alerted of a blatant sectional interest or favoritism, usually informally by affected officers, it is able to delay granting approval and, in some cases, can overturn the proposals.[109] The role of institutional design therefore is mixed— the process would surely be better served with greater informed dialogue on this issue. However, it does not appear as if any of the existing bureaucracies want to engage in one.

The third characteristic—that of military autonomy—best captures promotion policies in the Indian military. This autonomy allows frequent policy changes, often at the whim of the service chiefs and to serve parochial interests. Expressing his frustration, an MoD official dealing with manpower issues complained, "as you know in the army much depends on the views of the person in charge at a particular time. Once that view is expressed nobody goes against it when somebody else comes up with a contrary view."[110] It is also easier to alter policies as personnel dealing with promotion policies are generalists who "learn on the job" without undergoing any specialized human resources training. Such policy changes are also made possible because of the absence of an overall guiding philosophy or manual on officer promotion and selection policies. According to one analyst, "the military has no promotion manual; policy exists only in a constantly revised torrent of letters from the Military Secretary's branch."[111]

[108] Email from Lt. Gen. Amitava Mukherjee to author, July 26, 2017; the officer served as additional military secretary (B), which handles all promotion policies.

[109] Ajay Bannerjee, "MoD Rejects New Promotion Policy for Maj Gen and Above," *The Tribune*, June 7, 2011.

[110] Standing Committee on Defense, *Thirty Fourth Report*, 2009, 47.

[111] Ajai Shukla, "Soldier, Heal Thyself," *Business Standard*, April 6, 2010; also see Ajai Shukla, "Promoting Crisis Within the Military," *Business Standard*, April 5, 2011. This problem was highlighted in the 1990s; see M. L. Chibber, "Career Management of Military Officers," *Indian Defense Review*, (July, 1991): 86.

Despite criticism of the system of promotion policies, there are differing views on the sources of change.[112] For some, greater *informed* civilian intervention and oversight is necessary to usher in reforms. According to Lieutenant General Anil Ahuja, member of the committee set up by the MoD to review promotion policies, "Major policy changes with large ramifications can only come from outside, as internally organizations can only get that far. Major changes in promotion policy of armed forces require external impetus and support."[113] This view is supported by a former military secretary, who argued that there is "tremendous amount of autonomy within the army on promotion policies and as a result they are largely personality based. Where the monitoring should be done by the MOD is to ensure that this autonomy is not misused."[114] However, others argue that it is best left to the military to fix its own shortcomings and not let the civilians interfere in this process.[115] This is born out of a fear that civilian intervention will create more problems.

To sum up, civilians in India have had mixed success in shaping officer promotion policies. On the one hand, they have introduced some measures, like the quantification system, to bring in more transparency. But more ambitious efforts—like the recommendations made by the Committee of Experts in 2015 and the review of promotion policies in 2017—have not come to fruition, opposed by existing civilian and military bureaucracies. Indeed, there are few politicians willing to wade into this complexity, which favors the status quo. In addition, civilians have been unable to incentivize joint staff experience, as was done in the United States and United Kingdom. Describing the ministry's overall attitude toward promotion policies, according to a former military officer, "where something does matter to them [MoD] then they intervene however where it does not they don't care what happens within the services. They are only bothered if it is an inter-service issue, has major financial implications or has a bearing on the equation between the civilians and the military."[116]

[112] For criticism of the military's promotion policies, see Philip Campose, "Senior Leadership in the Indian Army: Time for Introspection and Rebuilding," *CLAWS Journal* (Summer 2017): 54, Vinay Dalvi, "Indian Military Officer's Promotion Policies," *Fauji India* 2, no. 11 (2016): 61–63.

[113] Email to author, November 15, 2018.

[114] Interview with Lt. Gen. Mohinder Puri, Gurgaon, October 17, 2011.

[115] For such a sentiment, see Syed Ata Hasnain, "Turbulence in Officer Ranks of the Indian Army: Comprehending a Problem that Needs Immediate Resolution," Swarajya.com, October 15, 2017, https://swarajyamag.com/defence/turbulencein-officer-ranks-of-the-indian-army-comprehending-a-problem-that-needs-immediateresolution.

[116] Interview with senior officer who worked in the secretariat of a former chief of army staff, New Delhi, December 20, 2011.

A Cautionary Tale: Politicization of the Military?

In December 2016, the MoD announced that General Bipin Rawat will be the next chief of army staff, overlooking, and effectively superseding, two more senior generals. There was no official rationale for why the government set aside a norm of selecting the senior-most officer that, in the case of the army, had only been overlooked twice since independence.[117] However, MoD officials, in non-attributable remarks, claimed that "merit and suitability have been taken into account while selecting the new Army Chief . . . [Lieutenant General Rawat] had more than 10 years of experience in counter-insurgency operations and on the Line of Control, besides serving on the China border. He has the requisite experience considering the current situation."[118] That the two superseded officers did not have counterinsurgency experience echoed the rationale offered when Lieutenant General S. K. Sinha was overlooked in 1983—that he lacked "combat experience."[119] Be that as it may, this triggered a controversy, with critics arguing that the government was risking politicizing the army.[120]

Constitutionally, it is the prerogative of the government to select the service chief—an important indicator of civilian control. The government therefore was within its powers to select Rawat over the claims, based on seniority, of the other two officers. Most critics, however, took issue with the lack of transparency on how the government defined "merit and suitability." Lieutenant General H. S. Panag captured the prevailing sentiment within the military community that "though it is good to have a meritocracy, there must be clear criteria for determining merit. Otherwise, generals will start approaching politicians who can promote them to the top, and that will end the apolitical character of the army."[121] Indeed, weeks after this incident there were speculations about the political character of this maneuver, with "men in shadows" allegedly orchestrating events.[122]

[117] C. Uday Bhaskar, "A Poorly Handled Army Chief Appointment," *Live Mint*, December 22, 2016, https://www.livemint.com/Opinion/CmwltREjgvkl1DXDAQMlkI/A-poorly-handled-army-chief-appointment.html

[118] Sushant Singh, "Superseding Two Senior Lt Gens, Bipin Rawat Is New Army Chief; Dhanoa to Head Air Force," *Indian Express*, December 18, 2016, https://indianexpress.com/article/india/bipin-rawat-indian-army-chief-birender-singh-dhanoa-air-force-4432972/

[119] Singh, *Leadership in the Indian Army*, 377–78.

[120] Purnima S. Tripathi, "Farewell to Norms," *Frontline*, 34, no. 1, January 20, 2017, https://www.frontline.in/cover-story/farewell-to-norms/article9456607.ece.

[121] Quoted in Ajai Shukla, "Controversy Clouds Out-of-Turn Appointment of Next Army Chief," *Business Standard*, December 19, 2016.

[122] Sandeep Unnithan, "Malicious Campaign, Deep Rooted Conspiracy, Men in the Shadows: Lt General Praveen Bakshi," *India Today*, January 11, 2017, https://www.indiatoday.in/india/story/lt-general-praveen-bakshi-new-year-eve-eastern-army-commander-general-bipin-rawat-kolkata-

There is no clear answer on the issue of whether the government should adhere to selection via seniority or through merit. As Srinath Raghavan points out, "the choice of service chiefs is a matter of political judgment. It involves multiple trade-offs and considerations that cannot be wished away by sticking to seniority or hankering after criteria of 'merit.'"[123] The seniority principle is predictable and prevents politicians from picking favorites but may not necessarily reward merit. Moreover, there is an alleged "fixing of the processes" by senior military officers who, motivated by parochial loyalties, may "choose" their successors. On the other hand, if it is left to civilians to select a chief on the basis of merit, then it may lead to overt politicking on the part of military officers. Warning about this possibility, Richard Kohn argued that "both civilian control and military effectiveness require that the officer corps be insulated from partisan politics, particularly from the promotion and assignment of officers on the basis of partisan affiliation."[124]

According to some, the best way to deal with this conundrum is to remove the ambiguity and formalize the selection on merit process. Panag advocated creating a committee comprised of civilians and military officers to jointly deliberate upon and select senior military officers.[125] This recommendation calls for a greater dialogue between civilians and the military on the promotion and selection process. Such an effort would also examine other aspects, for instance, the necessity to create an ombudsman, incentivize joint staff experience, check on parochialism, and perhaps include an outside member as an independent observer for promotion boards. These measures would emulate the practice in other mature democracies where civilians and the military to varying degrees have come together to formalize guidelines and enact forward-looking promotion policies.

954480-2017-01-11; and Shiv Kunal Verma, "Men in Shadows Derailed Bakshi's Chances of Becoming Army Chief," *Sunday Guardian*, December 25, 2016, https://www.sundayguardianlive. com/investigation/7780-men-shadows-derailed-bakshi-s-chances-becoming-army-chief.   Also see Ali Ahmed, "So Who Are the 'Men in Shadows' Guiding Top Army Appointments?" *The Wire*, January 27, 2017, https://thewire.in/security/army-selection-bipin-rawat.

[123] Srinath Raghavan, "The Choice of Service Chiefs Is a Matter of Political Judgment," *Hindustan Times*, December 21, 2016, https://www.hindustantimes.com/columns/the-choice-of-service-chiefs-is-a-matter-of-political-judgment/story-hPOnQTOr7T92s8XgrfSYaO.html

[124] Richard Kohn, "How Democracies Control the Military," *Journal of Democracy* 8, no. 4, (1997): 150.

[125] H. S. Panag, "The COAS Controversy Shows Need for Reform in Army," Newslaundry. com, December 21, 2016, https://www.newslaundry.com/2016/12/21/the-coas-controversy-shows-need-for-reform-in-army

Conclusion

There are four main conclusions that can be drawn from this chapter. First, as a result of the narrative that emerged from the 1962 China war, politicians rarely intervene in officer promotion policies. Instead, they have left this almost entirely to the military leadership, which has over time imbibed the "seniority principle" in its promotion policies. To some, this is indicative of civilian abdication of responsibility, whereas others caution against the dangers of politicians actively shaping promotion policies. They argue that this might over time politicize the Indian military.

Second, notwithstanding this generalization, procedurally civilians have considerable powers to appoint, select, and vet changes in promotion policies. They have used these powers to, at times, veto proposals sent by the military and, on rare occasions, even overruled the "seniority principle" to select and appoint senior military officers. Such occasions cause controversy and draw attention to the state of civil–military relations.

Third, there is a need for a greater civil–military dialogue on all aspects pertaining to the military's personnel and promotion policies. Despite some efforts to usher in more transparency, the reform measures are opposed by existing bureaucracies. Therefore, the services, at times along with the MoD, have resisted proposals like creating an ombudsman-type organization or having an outside observer in the promotions boards. Military autonomy in this realm has, at times, led to parochial promotion policies, which have divided the officer cadre.

Finally, there is a need for more research on the role of civil–military relations and military promotion policies in democratic states. There is a lack of clarity on the role and the effectiveness of civilians in shaping personnel policies in military organizations. Curiously, despite the dearth of academic literature, in practice there have been a number of civilian led initiatives to reshape personnel policies in different countries. The role of civilians in shaping military promotion policies is therefore an underexplored topic and in need of further research.

7

The Best of Intentions

Defense Planning in India

Defense planning, or force development, is the "deliberate process of planning a nation's future forces, force postures, and force capabilities."[1] Distinct from operations planning (or force employment), defense planning is the process through which countries decide upon future-oriented (near, medium, and far term) defense capabilities to deal with anticipated threats and opportunities. Planners, while justifying expenditure, have to anticipate the future, including technological changes and emerging threats while worrying about unforeseen developments. Planning assumptions can be suddenly overturned by changing events and myriad developments—political, diplomatic, economic, and technological. Defense planners also have to operate under procedures and idiosyncrasies of a completely different bureaucracy—that of financial managers. Typically, soldiers operate under the impression that as guardians of society their budgetary demands should get first priority. However, absent an existential threat, political leaders have to consider larger societal interests and, in a democracy, have to be responsive to electoral demands. "The worlds of politics and of military preparation do not easily combine," writes Colin Gray, while observing that soldiers are especially "light in understanding" the responsibilities of the central government.[2] Crucially, defense planning and choice of technology and capability shape military effectiveness.[3] As a result of all these factors, defense

---

[1] Paul K. Davis, "Defense Planning When Major Changes Are Needed," *Defence Studies* 18, no. 3 (2018): 375.

[2] Colin S. Gray, *Strategy and Defence Planning: Meeting the Challenge of Uncertainty* (London: Oxford University Press, 2014), 146–47.

[3] For a collection of essays that emphasizes the importance of defense planning through historical case studies, see Imlay Talbot and Monica Duffy Toft, eds., *The Fog of Peace and War Planning: Military and Strategic Planning under Uncertainty* (New York: Routledge, 2006).

planning is probably one of the more essential but inexact processes undertaken by military organizations.

There are three main arguments in this chapter. First, effective defense planning requires a close partnership between civilians and the military. As part of this deliberative process, civilians should provide political guidance and integrate the plans of the three services. Second, defense planning in India is marked by a lack of civilian guidance and institutional discordance, creating friction in civil–military relations. To an extent, this is because of a lack of expertise and an institutional design that creates strong civil–military silos. Third, notwithstanding the above, there have been periodic attempts at reforming defense-planning structures. Progress has been achieved in some sectors; however, much more remains to be done. Specifically, there needs to be a continuous civil–military dialogue on aspects and assumptions underlying the defense-planning process.

This chapter begins with a conceptual discussion on the role of civilians in defense planning. Next, it describes the history of defense planning in India, focusing on the interaction between services and the Defence and Finance Ministries. As we shall see, there have been periodic attempts to undertake reforms, in almost every decade, in this sector, with varying results. The penultimate section analyzes the role of civil–military relations in perpetuating these problems in defense planning. It concludes with a summary of the main arguments.

Conceptual Overview: Role of Civilians in Defense Planning

Despite its importance, defense planning remains largely "underexamined not only in defense and strategic studies, but also in public administration and management literature."[4] Even so, it is widely acknowledged that "national variations in civil–military relations" significantly shape this process.[5] As defense planning involves considerable interactions between civilians and the military, it is both indicative of and shaped by civil–military relations. In most countries, defense planning is considered a military function, with the civilian role being restricted

---

[4] Jordan Tama, "Tradeoffs in Defense Strategic Planning: Lessons from the U.S. Quadrennial Defense Review," *Defence Studies* 18, no. 3 (2018): 281. Also see Magnus Håkenstad and Kristian Knus Larsen, *Long-Term Defence Planning: A Comparative Study of Seven Countries* (Oslo: Norwegian Institute for Defence Studies, 2012), 9.

[5] Henrik Breitenbauch and André Ken Jakobsson, "Defence Planning as Strategic Fact: Introduction," *Defence Studies* 18, no. 3 (2018): 257.

to overall allocation of the defense budget. This should not be surprising in countries where the military is a politically influential power, but it is also true for many democratic states with firm civilian control. However, letting the military control defense planning is neither effective nor desirable. As Imlay and Toft argue, "a balance of civilian and military input is indispensable for effective planning. One mistake is to leave planning to military planners alone: military planners are especially effective when it comes to military aspects of planning, but less skilled when it comes to working out the broader grand-strategic and political implications of war planning."[6] Indeed, the architects of long-range defense planning in the United States, which has served as a template for many countries, set out to fundamentally address the civil–military gap. According to Alain C. Enthoven and K. Wayne Smith,

> the key reason for the limited usefulness of the defense budget was the fact that defense budgeting was, in effect, conceived as being largely unrelated to military strategy. The two were treated as almost independent activities. They were carried out by different people, at different times, with different terms of reference, and without a method for integrating their activities. The strategy and forces were thought to be essentially military matters, while the budget was thought to be mainly a civilian matter. Force planning was done for several years into the future, by military men, on a mission-oriented basis, by the Services with attempts at coordination by the JCS [Joint Chiefs of Staff] organization. Financial planning was done one year at a time, largely by civilians, in terms of object classes of expenditures such as personnel and procurement. . . . This gap between strategy and forces, on the one hand, and budgets, on the other, posed a serious obstacle to rational defense planning.[7]

The importance of political guidance to ensure that future military capabilities are tailored toward grand-strategic ends cannot be understated. In some democracies, civilians have increasingly played an important role in defense planning. They are not only more hands-on and able to influence planning within the services but also more likely to give top-down planning directives. This is

---

[6] Talbot Imlay and Monica Duffy Toft, "Conclusion: Seven Lessons about the Fog of Peace," in *Fog of Peace*, 205.

[7] Alain C. Enthoven and K. Wayne Smith, *How Much Is Enough? Shaping the Defense Program, 1961–1969* (Santa Monica, CA: Rand, 2005), 13. The authors along with Charles J. Hitch, serving under Defense Secretary Robert McNamara, are widely credited with introducing the "planning, programming, budgeting, and execution system" (PPBE, often named PPBS), which largely guides defense planning in the United States.

a result of two functions, expertise and bureaucratic procedures (institutional design), that allow for a joint civil–military partnership in the planning process.

Civilian expertise in defense planning emerges from a combination of on-the-job experience and education.[8] As Colin Gray argues, the challenge of defense planning "can best be met by people and organizations educated in general strategic theory, in history, and in methods of defense analysis."[9] Defense planning would be problematic in countries where such expertise is not encouraged. One approach to overcoming this problem is to have integrated offices, comprising civilians and military officers, to jointly deliberate upon defense plans. A close partnership between civilians and the military is also more likely to deliver on "the most important task of a defense planner ... to produce *costed priorities.*"[10] Without it, one would expect piecemeal development of military capabilities as defense plans (made by the military) can be arbitrarily dealt with—accepted or rejected based on shifting financial considerations. A combination of military and financial planning expertise is therefore desirable as it is more likely to create conditions for a civil–military dialogue centering on defense plans. Both these functions, encouraging expertise and integrated offices, guard against, without completely eliminating, service parochialism.

In practice, there is wide variance in the ability of civilians to effectively guide and shape defense plans. A comparative study of the strengths and weaknesses in defense planning of different countries is beyond the scope of this book. Instead, the rest of this chapter focuses on defense planning in India.

As the following discussion shows, Indian defense planning is marked by a series of recurring and unresolved tensions between military strategy, defense budgeting, and financial outlays. As the services (army, air force, and navy) have remained dominant in framing their service-specific plans, civilians (lacking expertise) have been unable to bring unity of effort among them. In turn, the military also lacks expertise in financial planning and is unable to produce properly costed priorities for civilians to deliberate over. The lack of expertise combined with bureaucratic controls creates considerable institutional discordance in the planning function. Acknowledging this problem, every decade or so, the government has created an institution to more closely align defense plans with budgetary outlays. These represent efforts to overcome the civil–military gap, and

---

[8] For a good study linking expertise, defense planning, and civilian control, see Diana Molodilo, "The Impact of Civilian Control on Contemporary Defense Planning Systems: Challenges for South East Europe" (master's thesis, Naval Postgraduate School, 2011).

[9] Gray, *Strategy and Defence Planning*, 153.

[10] Thomas-Durell Young, "Questioning the 'Sanctity' of Long-Term Defense Planning as Practiced in Central and Eastern Europe," *Defence Studies* 18, no. 3 (2018): 366, emphasis in the original. Costed priorities refers to the process of prioritizing weapons purchases based on an awareness of their full life cycle costs. This activity is closely linked to a nation's defense plans.

there has been a gradual professionalization. However, much more remains to be done.

There are two caveats to keep in mind while reading the rest of this chapter. First, there is a structural research limitation due to the lack of primary documents. Due to the Indian government's immature approach to declassification, I have not been able to access any of the defense plans (apart from some in the 1970s).[11] As a result, much of this discussion emerges from interviews, and with selective access to some primary material and secondary literature. Second, defense planning is a notoriously nebulous activity. As Colin Gray points out, "it can be exceedingly difficult to provide convincing evidence of error in defense planning."[12] Despite these limitations, as a process which converts economic into military power, defense planning is an important activity and, moreover, gives an insight into the depth of civil–military relations in the country under discussion.

"Nobody Really Knew What Was Happening": 1947–1962

At the time of independence there was very little capability, competence, or guidance to undertake defense planning. Indicative of the conditions at the time, Brigadier J. N. Chaudhuri, later chief of army staff, was posted to army headquarters as director of planning in 1947, but this post was soon abolished as "there was very little planning to do in the sense that nobody really knew what was happening."[13] Realizing this problem, Prime Minister Jawaharlal Nehru engaged British Nobel laureate and physicist P. M. S. Blackett to draw up plans to "Indianize the military" and recommend a broad defense plan.[14] After submitting his report, Blackett continued to work as a military consultant and had some influence on defense planning, though he was more interested in the development of defense science. However, as one study noted, it is "difficult to give a measure of Blackett's influence in India."[15]

---

[11] For an appeal for a rational policy leading to a declassification of defense plans, see Amit Cowshish, "A Perspective on Defense Planning in India," *Strategic Analysis* 36, no. 4 (2012): 680–81.

[12] Gray, *Strategy and Defence Planning*, 142.

[13] Oral History Transcript, General J. N. Chaudhuri, no. 426, p. 19, Nehru Memorial Library and Museum (hereafter NMML), New Delhi.

[14] Chris Smith, *India's Ad Hoc Arsenal: Direction or Drift in Defense Policy* (New York: Oxford University Press, 1994), 48–56.

[15] Robert S. Anderson, "Patrick Blackett in India: Military Consultant and Scientific Intervenor, 1947–72, Part I," *Notes and Records of the Royal Society of London* 53, no. 2 (1999): 255.

Force development during this period was not according to any plan per se but was shaped by Nehru's attempts to contain defense expenditure. Accordingly, in the early 1950s a committee was set up under a Ministry of Defence (MoD) official, B. B. Ghosh, to "examine the armed forces development plans to see how they could best be meshed with the National plan."[16] Among other measures, this committee recommended reducing the size of the army; but after border tensions with Pakistan, this suggestion and "its work seemed to dissolve into a blur."[17] From then until the 1962 war, there is no evidence that integrated plans were formulated at the MoD. Instead, individual services episodically and erratically formulated service-specific plans.[18] While assessing this period, P. V. R. Rao, defense secretary from 1962 to 1965, admitted that defense planning was amateurish and ad hoc.[19] However, we should be charitable when we look back upon this period as even in other militaries, defense planning as a formal activity only emerged in the 1960s.

A major development during this period, with probably unintended consequences, was a decision to categorize the defense budget as a non-plan expenditure. In 1950, the government set up the Planning Commission, entrusted to create plans for economic growth and to decide on resource allocation. Government expenses were thereby categorized as planned (under the purview of the Planning Commission) or unplanned. As the defense budget was categorized under the latter, its plans were formally excluded from the purview of the Planning Commission. This led to complaints about the "non-integration of defense and economic planning."[20] This arrangement ill-suited both defense planners and the Planning Commission as the latter was criticized for not fully taking into account the defense expenditure.[21] More importantly, even as the defense budget constituted a major share of the central government expenditure, the Planning Commission did not feel the need to build up expertise to examine

---

[16] According to Vice Admiral Vivian Barboza, cited in Satyindra Singh, *Blueprint to Bluewater: The Indian Navy 1951–65* (New Delhi: Lancer International, 1992), 88.

[17] Singh, *Blueprint to Bluewater*, 88.

[18] For details of the air force plans during this period, see Jasjit Singh, *Defence from the Skies: Indian Air Force Through 75 years* (New Delhi: Knowledge World Publishers 2007), 62–69; and for a personalized account, see M. S. Chaturvedi, *History of the Indian Air Force* (New Delhi: Vikas Publishers, 1978), 94–148. On naval plans see Singh, *Blueprint to Bluewater*, 41–92; and for the army's experience just before the 1962 war, see D. K. Palit, *War in the High Himalayas: The Indian Army in Crisis, 1962* (London: Hurst 1991), 83.

[19] P. V. R. Rao, *Defence Without Drift* (Bombay: Popular Prakashan, 1970), 307–9.

[20] V. P. Malik, "Defence Planning System in India," *Strategic Analysis* 13, no. 1 (1990): 36.

[21] Medha Kudaisya, "'A Mighty Adventure': Institutionalizing the Idea of Planning in Post-Colonial India, 1947–60," *Modern Asian Studies* 45, no. 4 (2009): 969.

defense plans. This created problems in subsequent years when attempts were made to involve the commission in defense-planning efforts.

1962–1972: The First Plans Take Shape

The defeat of the Indian Army in the 1962 China war led to a number of far-reaching changes including in defense planning. During the war, in a clear departure from its non-aligned policy, India requested military aid from the United States. To understand India's security needs, a number of American defense delegations came to India and toured different military installations. One of its preconditions for military aid was that India needed to formulate a proper defense plan.[22] As a result, a five thousand–crore five-year defense plan was formulated in 1964.[23] However, the first defense plan was not properly deliberated and was just a compilation of the annual projections made by the three services.[24]

In 1965, a planning cell was established in the MoD to be headed by an additional secretary (equivalent to a three-star general).[25] According to K. Subrahmanyam, this was done at the behest of Prime Minister Lal Bahadur Shastri, who was of the view that defense planning was a neglected subject.[26] This office was meant to coordinate the plan with the "wider aspects of development planning . . . maintain constant liaison with the Planning Commission and other ministries and to ensure that such of the constituents of the development plan as have a bearing on the defense effort are given appropriate priorities."[27] Designating an additional secretary exclusively for defense planning was indicative of the importance that was purportedly given to this issue. However, although the organizational chart incorporated this position, no official was

[22] According to K. Subrahmanyam, who was then in the Defence Ministry, the first defense plan was made at the behest of US military advisers; interview, New Delhi, October 1, 2010. Even the term "Five-Year Defense Plan" was borrowed from US literature on defense planning at that time. Also see Tanvi Madan, "With an Eye to the East: The China Factor and The U.S.–India Relationship, 1949–1979" (PhD diss., University of Texas at Austin, 2012), 351–52.

[23] For a good description of the implementation of this defense plan, see K. Subrahmanyam, "Five Years of Indian Defense Effort in Perspective," *International Studies Quarterly* 13, no. 2 (1969): 159–89.

[24] In 1970, the Defence Ministry noted that the first plan "was no more than a sum total of estimated yearly budgets over a 5-year span." See *Ministry of Defence: Annual Report, 1969–70* (New Delhi: Government of India Press, 1970), 6.

[25] *Ministry of Defence: Annual Report, 1963–64* (New Delhi: Government of India Press, 1964), annexure I. The post of deputy secretary (planning) under this additional secretary was also established.

[26] Interview, New Delhi, October 1, 2010.

[27] *Ministry of Defence: Annual Report, 1965–66* (New Delhi: Government of India Press, 1966), 6.

appointed; and in 1968, the additional secretary post was abolished.[28] It is not clear what transpired, but they may have found it difficult to find a person with the necessary expertise to perform this function. Alternatively, the military might have opposed this measure. Ironically, even while abolishing the post, the ministry went on to claim that "the planning machinery in the Ministry of Defence is being strengthened."[29] In retrospect, it was a lost opportunity as the ministry did not invest in the building in-house planning capabilities. Instead, the planning function was left entirely to the uniformed personnel.

The next planning effort, for the second defense plan, covered the period from 1969 to 1974; and, according to the MoD, this was much more organized effort. The plan was resource-based, and "an assurance was obtained that the financial resources and foreign exchange would be made available as laid down in the plan."[30] It was also decided that it would be a "roll-on" plan—a concept according to which after an annual review "the first year of the 5-Year Plan is dropped and an additional year added at the end so that the Services have, at all times, before them a fully updated 5-Year-Plan."[31] Despite the MoD's claims of professionalism, however, according to a former secretary of defense finance, the plan was "a statistical projection of current level expenditure escalated marginally."[32]

1973–1985: The Planning Commission and the Committee for Defence Planning

The defeat of the Pakistan Army in the Bangladesh war and India's regional preeminence resurrected the debate between defense and development.[33] To settle this issue and to formulate the third defense plan, a committee, called the Apex Planning Group I, was set up in early 1973 under D. P. Dhar, then deputy chairman of the Planning Commission.[34] The report assessed the likely threats

---

[28] Interview with K. Subrahmanyam, New Delhi, October 1, 2010; also see Annexure I which, in comparison to the report of the previous years, shows that the post was abolished, *Ministry of Defence: Annual Report, 1968–69* (New Delhi: Government of India Press, 1969).

[29] *Ministry of Defence: Annual Report, 1968–69*, 2.

[30] *Ministry of Defence: Annual Report, 1970–71* (New Delhi: Government of India Press, 1971), 7.

[31] *Ministry of Defence: Annual Report, 1969–70*, 7–8.

[32] D. S. Nakra, "Defense Budgeting in India," *USI Papers*, no. 5 (1979): 26–27.

[33] For more on the defense versus development debate, see Chapter 3. For a classic essay, see K. Subrahmanyam, *Defence and Development* (Delhi: Minerva Associates, 1972); and *Ministry of Defence: Annual Report, 1972–73* (New Delhi: Government of India Press, 1969), 10–13.

[34] The other members of this committee were Defense Secretary K. B. Lall; chairman, Chiefs of Staff Committee and army chief General G. G. Bewoor; cabinet secretary B. D. Pande; Finance Secretary M. R. Yardi; and Foreign Secretary Kewal Singh. For a copy of this report, see Cabinet

and recommended defense outlays and acquisitions. The Cabinet Committee on Political Affairs adopted this plan in a meeting held in May 1973. However, even after its approval, there were "serious differences of approach and assessment between the Ministries of Finance and Defence and it was thought that it would be desirable to constitute another committee to make fresh recommendations to the [Cabinet Committee on Political Affairs]."[35]

Accordingly, another committee, called the Apex Group II, headed by the newly appointed deputy chairman of the Planning Commission P. N. Haksar, was created to study the issue and make a new set of recommendations.[36] The services were invited to present their plans and instructed to set up internal expert committees "to improve fighting capacity as cost effectively as possible."[37] However, there was a variance in the reports of the army and the navy experts committees.[38] The army experts committee, while seemingly tasked by Chief of Army Staff General T. N. Raina to "bringing about greater cost effectiveness and a more rational 'tooth to tail' ratio," also took on the task of deliberating upon future threat environment and force levels.[39] Contrary to expectations, the report of the army's expert committee provided the intellectual justification for the large-scale mechanization and the subsequent ballooning of the defense budget in the 1980s.[40] The navy's expert committee, on the other hand, took a hard look

Secretariat (Military Wing), *The Defense Plan: Report of the Apex Planning Group*, Copy no. 2, Subject File no. 299, III Instalment, P. N. Haksar Papers, NMML, New Delhi. For a description about this committee, see *Ministry of Defence: Annual Report, 1973–74* (New Delhi: Government of India Press, 1974), 7.

[35] Top secret letter from Govind Narain to P. N. Haksar dated April 3, 1975, explaining why a new committee needs to be formed. This letter also lists ten problems with the Apex I plan, Subject File no. 297, III Instalment, P. N. Haksar Papers, NMML.

[36] The other members of this committee were S. Chakravarthi (member, planning commission), G. Parthasarthi (chairman, Policy Planning Division, Ministry of External Affairs), cabinet secretary, defense secretary, foreign secretary, finance secretary, P. N. Dhar (secretary to the prime minister), secretary (expenditure), the three service chiefs, and the scientific adviser to the defense minister.

[37] G. M. Hiranandani, *Transition to Guardianship: The Indian Navy, 1991–2000* (New Delhi: Lancer Publishers, 2009), 158.

[38] There is not much literature on whether the air force set up an expert committee, although there is a reference to a perspective plan that was apparently created in 1975; see George Tanham and Marcy Agmon, *The Indian Air Force: Trends and Prospects* (Santa Monica, CA: Rand, 1995), 60.

[39] Secret letter no. 92660/EC dated December 3, 1975, from General T. N. Raina, chief of army staff, to P. N. Haksar, Sub File 298, part 2, III Instalment, P. N. Haksar Papers, NMML, New Delhi. This committee was comprised of the following: Lieutenant General K. V. Krishna Rao, Major Generals K. Sundarji and M. L. Chibber, and Brigadier A. J. M. Homji.

[40] For a description of the mandate, functioning, and implementation of the army's first Expert Committee, see K. V. Krishna Rao, *In the Service of the Nation: Reminiscences* (New Delhi: Penguin India Books, 2001), 143–57. Also see Vivek Chadha, *Even If It Ain't Broke Yet, Do Fix It: Enhancing Effectiveness Through Military Change* (New Delhi: Pentagon Press, 2016), 38–40; and Amit Gupta,

at cost-cutting measures in maintenance, logistics, and training, and while the "brutal frankness and objectivity" of the report caused some controversy within the navy, it was able to usher in reforms.[41] This variance in the approach and the report of the two expert committees, despite a similar mandate, raises an interesting counterfactual—would it have been better to have a civilian member as a part of the expert committee? However, this would have gone against the canon of Indian civil–military relations, which assumes that military threats and force structures are in the domain of military experts.

The armed forces presented their plans to the Apex II committee, which, after a few months of deliberation, submitted its final report to the defense minister on July 9, 1975.[42] This plan formed the bedrock for the fourth defense plan, 1974–1979, and was approved by the cabinet. However, the financial demands accruing from the Apex II committee shocked the Finance Ministry and set off extensive rounds of deliberations. The most persistent objection was from secretary (expenditure) in the Finance Ministry, Ajit Mazoomdar. In a top secret note he questioned the strategic assumptions of the military and complained that the Apex II group "as a whole never discussed the threat assessment or the deployment of the army."[43] Some of his observations were valid, but others transgressed into matters of foreign and strategic policies. For instance, in an earlier note vis-à-vis Pakistan, he had called for a "token reduction unilaterally" in the size of the Indian Army and limitations on acquisition of offensive weapons including tanks and aircraft.[44]

Despite the Finance Ministry's objections and the mandate of the Apex Committee to reduce defense expenditure to attain cost-effectiveness, over the next decade the military was able to obtain its highest share of the central government expenditure. To a significant extent, this is because Prime Minister Indira Gandhi was partial toward military expenditure. The political context of the time, with the merger of Sikkim and the imposition of Emergency (both in 1975), ensured that the military had the full support of its political leaders. Indeed, for the short time that Indira Gandhi held the position of defense

Building an Arsenal: The Evolution of Regional Power Force Structures (Westport, CT: Praeger Publishers, 1997), 49.

[41] Hiranandani, *Transition to Guardianship*, 159–65.

[42] Top secret letter no. 53/DC/75/S-J, from P. N. Haksar to Defence Minister Swaran Singh, July 9, 1975, Sub File 298 (part 2), III Instalment, P. N. Haksar Papers, NMML. For parts of the presentation made by the services to this committee, see Subject File 297, III Instalment, P. N. Haksar Papers.

[43] Top secret Ministry of Finance (Department of Expenditure) internal note dated March 29, 1976, from Ajit Mozoomdar, in Subject File no. 298 (Part II), P. N. Haksar Papers, III Instalment, NMML.

[44] Top secret letter titled "Defense Review" from Ajit Mozoomdar to P. N. Haksar on April 28, 1975, in Subject File no. 298 (Part II), P. N. Haksar Papers, III Instalment, NMML.

minister she made "major departures from the approved Defense Plan for 1974–79."[45] This trend continued when, despite the Finance Ministry's objections, the MoD was soon lobbying for funds in addition to what was allocated in the defense plan.[46]

The Janata Party government, comprising a coalition of opposition parties, came to power in 1977 and undertook the next initiative in defense planning. They created the Committee on Defence Planning (CDP) "to provide for a standing forum where periodical assessments relevant to defense planning can be undertaken in the light of all relevant factors ... [including] the needs of Economic development as well as defense."[47] There are few primary documents that shed light on the functioning of this committee, but in later years it was heavily criticized. Military officers questioned the credentials and ability of the committee to scrutinize defense plans.[48] Others argued that the CDP was dominated by civilian bureaucrats and "sought to limit interaction between military and government leaders."[49] The CDP functioned erratically and episodically, and while the government claimed that it functioned as late as 1996, there is little evidence or account of it.[50] According to a former joint secretary (planning) in the MoD, "the CDP lost its validity and was defunct long ago but the date of its exact demise is hard to say. It's like a river running dry, at what point it ran dry never really mattered."[51]

In 1979, another forum, the Defence Plan Coordination and Implementation Committee, was created to "review the formulation, coordination and implementation of plans" and to provide necessary linkages between defense, defense production, and research and development programs.[52] This committee, however,

---

[45] Top Secret D.O. letter no. 35/SE/76/TS dated April 12, 1976, from Ajit Mozoomdar to P. N. Haksar, in Subject File no. 298 (Part II), P. N. Haksar Papers, III Instalment, NMML.

[46] Top secret note from Defense Secretary D. R. Kohli, "Additional Resources Required for Defense During 1974–79" in Subject File no. 298 (Part II), P. N. Haksar Papers, III Instalment, NMML. Although this letter is not dated, it was written in the latter half of 1976.

[47] Ministry of Defense: Annual Report, 1978–79 (New Delhi: Government of India Press, 1979), 4; this committee was convened by the cabinet secretary and comprised of the three service chiefs, foreign secretary, secretary to the prime minister, defense secretary, finance secretary, planning secretary, and secretary for defense production.

[48] Malik, "Defence Planning System in India," 37.

[49] Jerrold F. Elkin and W. Andrew Ritezel, "The Debate on Restructuring India's Higher Defense Organization," Asian Survey 24, no. 10 (1984): 1075–76.

[50] Standing Committee on Defense, Defense Policy, Planning and Management 1995–96 (New Delhi: Lok Sabha Secretariat, 1996), 14.

[51] Telephone interview with official who wishes to remain unnamed, January 29, 2011. This officer served as a joint secretary (planning) in the 1980s.

[52] Ministry of Defense: Annual Report, 1979–80 (New Delhi: Government of India Press, 1980), 6. It was headed by the defense secretary and consisted of the secretary defense production, scientific adviser to defense minister, financial adviser (defense services), and joint secretary (planning and coordination).

excluded military officers as it focused on defense production. However, the assumption that the military need not bother with production plans was itself problematic and indicative of the absence of links between the defense plans and that of other departments including research, production, and ordnance and defense public sector units.[53]

Over time, the military gradually developed its capability to formulate defense plans. In the initial years, most plans made by the services had little correlation with the financial outlay and were often unrealistic. For instance, after the 1962 China war, the J. R. D. Tata committee recommended expansion of the Indian Air Force to sixty-four squadrons, a figure that air power proponents would frequently cite.[54] However, the actual strength of the air force only increased to a maximum of forty-five squadrons. Army headquarters did not even have an office of planning until 1974.[55] Due to its historical importance and long shipbuilding timelines, the navy had the most developed planning structures. Gradually, financial-planning sections were located alongside the planning directorates. Despite these efforts, however, the planning process has been characterized by one participant as a "haphazard process . . . in which plans were made without comprehensive discussion and were just a collection of ongoing operational and force structuring schemes."[56]

Table 7.1 describes the status of the first six defense plans. In broad terms, there were three major trends pertaining to defense planning during this period.[57] First, the civilian side of the planning function reflected a fair bit of confusion stemming from a lack of expertise and divided responsibilities among numerous stakeholders. Integrating the civilian and military aspects of the defense plan was one of the biggest challenges faced by policymakers. There were recurring disagreements between the Ministries of Defence and Finance.[58] Second, to overcome problems stemming from a lack of expertise and

[53] T. R. Sivasubramanian, "Defence Budget and the Planning Process," in *Defence Planning: Problems and Prospects*, ed. V. P. Malik and Vinod Anand, 47 (New Delhi: Manas Publications, 2006).

[54] Singh, *Defence from the Skies*, 68–69.

[55] *Ministry of Defense: Annual Report, 1974–75* (New Delhi: Government of India Press, 1975), 8. The Perspective Planning Department was formed a decade later in 1984 in army headquarters.

[56] Interview with Lt. Gen. K. K. Hazari, Gurgaon, October 19, 2010.

[57] There is a lack of clarity on the precise dates of the five-year plans, primarily due to the concept of the roll-on plan. This table relies on interviews with defense planners and data from the Standing Committee on Defense; *Defense Policy, Planning and Management 1995–96* (New Delhi: Lok Sabha Secretariat, 1996), 14. For a good analysis of defense planning during this period, see Raju Thomas, "Defense Planning in India," in *Defense Planning in Less-Industrialized States: The Middle East and South Asia*, ed. Stephanie Neuman, 249–52 (Lexington, MA: Lexington Books, 1984).

[58] Jerrold F. Elkin and W. Andrew Ritezel, "The Debate on Restructuring India's Higher Defense Organization," *Asian Survey* 24, no. 10 (1984), 1075.

Table 7.1 **Status of Defense Plans, 1964–1985**

Year and Plan	Status	Remarks
First defense plan, 1964–1969	It was a simple compilation of annual projections of the services.	Fairly successful as it prepared the military for the 1971 Bangladesh war.
Second defense plan, 1969–1974	Focused on army expansion and catered to problems due to embargo imposed by the West after the 1965 war.	According to the Ministry of Defence, for the first time it took into account the changes in strategic needs and tactical concepts and made 10-year forecasts.
Third defense plan, 1970–1975	Planning assumptions disrupted by the 1971 war and the 1973 oil crisis.	Was the first roll-on plan.
Fourth defense plan, 1974–1979	This plan was informed by the reports of the Apex Group I and II.	This plan was modified after the oil crisis triggered by the 1973 Yom Kippur war.
Fifth defense plan, 1979–84	The plan was made coterminous with the National Plan in 1980 and reviewed in 1981–1982.	Informed by deliberations of the Committee on Defense Planning.
Sixth defense plan, 1980–1985	Approved by cabinet in April 1982.	Reviewed after the Soviet invasion of Afghanistan and massive US military aid to Pakistan.

institutional discordance, civilians tried to nest defense planning in other ad hoc forums—the two Apex committees and the CDP—and these functioned erratically (the former was considered to be more successful than the latter). Third, despite strengthening their offices of planning, the services focused mainly upon simple force structuring plans. Moreover, "due to a lack of clear directions at the higher level and each service planning for itself primarily, joint planning as well as coordination of service and department plans remained a very weak area."[59] These attempts at refining the defense-planning process led to one of the most important, though ultimately unsuccessful, measures—the creation of the Defence Planning Staff (DPS) in 1986.

[59] Malik, "Defence Planning System in India," 33.

1985–2001: The Defence Planning Staff

In September 1985, Arun Singh was appointed minister of state for defense. A close confidant of Prime Minister Rajiv Gandhi (who also held charge of the defense minister's portfolio), Arun Singh partnered with military officers to transform the Indian military. In the realm of defense planning, he pushed through the idea of a DPS, formed in May 1986, as an interservice organization comprising both civilian and military officials. This organization not only was "responsible for preparation of coordinated perspective defense plan"[60] but, more ambitiously, was tasked to evolve military aims, encourage joint and combined operations, recommend balanced force levels, and carry out threat analyses.[61] It was therefore created as an "integrated office," comprising all three services and with civilian officials from the Ministries of External Affairs, Finance, and Defence. Such a joint civil–military approach, enjoying full political support, addressed most prior shortcomings in the defense-planning process; and there were great expectations from this experiment.

Upon its founding, the DPS was able to obtain the full cooperation of the services as it went about drafting a perspective document called Defence Plan 2000.[62] In order to prepare a holistic plan, members of the DPS undertook countrywide tours and were given advance copies of the service perspective plans, called Army Plan 2000, Air Force Plan 2000, and Navy Plan 2000. True to their mandate, the DPS gave a realistic costing estimate, questioned many of the assumptions made by the services, and recommended a joint, integrated plan. These questions raised the hackles of those in the services, who were unhappy with (and not used to having) their assumptions challenged, that too on operational grounds. Despite these problems, a planning document (described as "unsatisfactory" by one of the staff members) was created by the DPS. This was signed—with reservations—by the Chiefs of Staff Committee (COSC) and forwarded to the political authorities for approval. This plan was presented to the cabinet, but it never got the necessary financial sanction as the country was facing a tightening economic situation.[63] Moreover, in July 1987, after a falling out with Rajiv Gandhi, Arun Singh resigned from his position; and this effectively took the wind out of this initiative.

---

[60] *Ministry of Defense: Annual Report, 1986–87* (New Delhi: Government of India Press, 1987), 6.

[61] Hiranandani, *Transition to Guardianship*, 215.

[62] This account of the DPS is based on interviews with two of its founding members, Lt. Gen. Amitava Mukherjee, Pune, April 27, 2008, and Major General Ashok Mehta, New Delhi, November 16, 2010.

[63] Smith, *India's Ad Hoc Arsenal*, 134–39.

In later years, both civilians and the military opposed the DPS. As the DPS was under the COSC, civilians perceived it to be beholden to the military and "did not pay much attention to it. The Ministry of External Affairs . . . did not even send a representative."[64] The ministry reportedly tried to shift the DPS under its control, but this was opposed by the services.[65] Ironically, the more consequential opposition to the DPS came from its own fraternity—the military. The services resented the mandate of the DPS (which was to create a joint plan) as it meant that their plans were open to questioning. They therefore treated the DPS with suspicion and gradually marginalized it as they preferred directly engaging with the MoD.[66] Though the DPS continued to create five-year plans, it was merely a compilation of the respective service plans, and they were not subject to analytical or fiscal rigor.[67] By 1996, problems in the DPS were widely known as the Standing Committee on Defence pointed out that it was "impossible for the Directorate [DPS] to provide coherent and coordinated assessment for perspective planning, achieve positive results and generate the desired level of involvement in the planning process."[68] According to Lieutenant General Mohinder Puri, who served in the DPS in 1997, it had "become a defunct organization as there was no follow up on its papers and it had lost its importance . . . the main opposition came from the services."[69]

High rates of defense expenditure in the 1980s and the financial crisis in 1991 forced the government to dramatically scale down defense expenditure. Thus, for the next decade the emphasis was on cost-cutting measures, and accordingly, there was a "plan holiday" in 1991–1992, "marking it as the worst years for defense allocations."[70] Despite that, there were some efforts to deal with the financial uncertainty and still have the semblance of a plan.[71] In reality, the resources crunch and the inability to align services and Finance Ministry projections meant that the eighth defense plan, from 1992 to 1997, was not formally approved.

---

[64] Malik, "Defence Planning System in India," 40.

[65] Ashok Mehta, "An Emasculated Defense Planning Staff," *Indian Defense Review* 11, no. 1 (1996): 38.

[66] The DPS had six heads in the first six years and gradually lost its importance; see Jasjit Singh, "Defense Doctrine and Policy Planning in India," *Strategic Analysis* 16, no. 6 (1993): 646.

[67] Rahul Roy-Chaudhury, "Higher Defense Planning in India: Critical Need for Reassessment," *Strategic Analysis* 16, no. 7 (1993): 830.

[68] Cited in Laxman Kumar Behera, "Defense Planning in India," *Journal of Defense Studies* 4, no. 3 (2010): 128.

[69] Interview, Gurgaon, May 25, 2010.

[70] Hiranandani, *Transition to Guardianship*, 217.

[71] A. K. Ghosh, *Defense Budgeting and Planning in India: The Way Forward* (New Delhi: Knowledge World Publishers, 2006), 222–86.

The next plan, the ninth defense plan, 1997–2002, represents the only instance when the cabinet approved the plan early in the planning cycle. This was primarily due to the personal equation and efforts of senior military officers at that time and the concurrence of the political leadership. According to then vice chief of army staff General V. P. Malik, after the experience with the non-approval of the eighth defense plan, senior military leaders lobbied Prime Minister I. K. Gujral, Defense Minister Mulayam Singh Yadav, and Finance Minister P. Chidambaram and insisted upon obtaining plan approval.[72] Because of their efforts, this plan was approved in time; however, Finance Ministry officials were able to add a crucial caveat. They insisted that "the Ministry of Defence should approach the Ministry of Finance with an integrated defense plan."[73] "Integrated defense plan" meant that the plan not only had the concurrence of all three services but also the approval of other departments, like Defense Production and the Department of Research. Finance Ministry officials were certain that, as interservice prioritization was problematic, such an "integrated defense plan" would not come about. Indeed, within a few years, with a change in government and developments following the 1998 nuclear tests and the 1999 Kargil war, the assumptions made in this plan fell by the wayside.

In sum, during this period there were a number of developments pertaining to defense planning. The most innovative, and promising, experiment was the creation of the DPS that, at least on paper, addressed the "civil–military problem" by incorporating both military expertise and financial planners under the same roof. However, upon the departure of Arun Singh, this organization lost its importance and was sidelined. The overriding lesson from this experiment was the necessity for continued political support for reform initiatives. In 1996, the Standing Committee on Defence scathingly observed that "ad hocism" in defense planning was "amply evident from the fact that in the period of 20 years, 6 Defense Five-Year Plans were prepared but none could be completed for one reason or the other and had either been deferred or reframed midway."[74] In light of the financial difficulties that India faced at this time, the alleged "ad hocism" in defense planning was perhaps understandable, but the attitude of the civilians (whether in the MoD or the Finance Ministry) embittered military officers and added to the tensions in civil–military relations. In 1993, Rahul Roy-Chaudhury, while analyzing the defense-planning process, would warn that, as defense plans are subject to "much arbitrary reductions" by civilians, this could "gravely affect

---

[72] Interview, New Delhi, November 2, 2010.

[73] Interview with Lt. Gen. V. K. Chopra, who served for seven years in the Financial Planning Directorate in army headquarters, New Delhi, December 15, 2010.

[74] Standing Committee on Defense, *Sixth Report: Defense Policy, Planning and Management 1995–96* (New Delhi: Lok Sabha Secretariat, 1996). 21.

the combat capability of the services to a disastrous extent in war-time."[75] There were others giving similar warnings of problems in India's approach to national security, but it would take a war, as they usually do, to focus political attention. The 1999 Kargil war therefore proved to be a mixed blessing.

2001–2015: The Integrated Defence Staff

As discussed elsewhere, the Kargil war triggered wide-ranging defense reforms.[76] Problems in defense planning were acknowledged by one of the reform committees, which argued, "the defense planning process is greatly handicapped by the absence of a national security doctrine, and commitment of funds beyond the financial year. It also suffers from a lack of inter-service prioritization, as well as the requisite flexibility."[77] Because of its recommendations, the government undertook a number of reforms.

First, within the MoD, new organizations like the Defence Acquisition Council, the Defence Procurement Board, and the Director General Acquisitions were established. These have provided for greater political involvement and, along with frequent iterations of the Defense Procurement Procedure, have helped in streamlining the planning process.[78] Emphasizing this development, Dhirendra Singh, a former joint secretary (planning) in the MoD, observed that "earlier the MoD and Finance Ministry mainly questioned the military on two issues relating to acquisition of new systems: quantity and necessity. This created considerable tensions between civilians and the military and was a source of problems but now that it has been referred to the Defense Acquisition Council, it allows for a better interaction between all stakeholders and faster decision-making."[79]

Second, at the level of the services, the office of the DPS was incorporated into the newly constituted Integrated Defence Staff (IDS). Over the years, the staff and functions of the IDS have evolved, and the planning process has become more systematic. The services have now been tasked to create fifteen-year

[75] Roy-Chaudhury, "Higher Defense Planning in India," 828.

[76] Anit Mukherjee, "Failing to Deliver: The Post Crises Defence Reforms in India, 1998–2010" (IDSA occasional paper 18, Institute for Defence Studies and Analyses, New Delhi, March 2011).

[77] *Report of the Group of Ministers on National Security* (New Delhi: Government of India, 2001), 98.

[78] For a recent iteration of the procurement procedure and a description of the planning processes, see Ministry of Defence, *Defence Procurement Procedure 2016: Capital Procurement* (New Delhi: Ministry of Defence, March 2016), 3–4, https://mod.gov.in/sites/default/files/dppm.pdf_0.pdf

[79] Interview, New Delhi, November 4, 2009.

Long Term Integrated Perspective Plans (LTIPPs), five-year Service Capital Acquisition Plans, and Annual Acquisition Plans. These plans are deliberated upon by the IDS, and in case the services intend to acquire a common platform, they are collated under a common acquisition strategy.[80]

The centerpiece of this reform initiative hinged on the creation of the Chief of Defence Staff (CDS), with the assumption that an empowered office would be best placed to carry out interservice and intraservice prioritization, work with financial planners, and implement a holistic plan. However, as described in Chapter 2, the government demurred from appointing a CDS. Lacking bureaucratic heft, the IDS is unable to "integrate" the plan—in terms of intraservice or interservice prioritization—and (like its predecessor, the DPS) merely adds "up the 'wish lists' of the three Services" and forwards them to the MoD.[81] As a result, despite some procedural improvement, defense planning remains problematic, with strong silos between the civilian and military bureaucracies.

Table 7.2 lists the status and emphasis of the five-year defense plans made between 1985 and 2018. As seen from Tables 7.1 and 7.2, out of twelve plans, only three (the sixth, seventh, and ninth plans) were approved by the cabinet committee. But does cabinet approval even matter? According to a former MoD official who handled planning and acquisitions, "empirically, approval or non-approval of the FYPs [five-year plans] by the CCS [Cabinet Committee on Security] does not really have a direct bearing on capital acquisition programs."[82]

In 2018, the MoD supported this assessment and, in a written statement to the parliamentary standing committee, argued, "non-approval of the Defense Plan does not act as hindrance in implementation of Defense projects. Activities planned are likely to proceed according to available annual budget allocations. The Defense Plan serves only as a guide for formulating annual budgetary projections even without the formal approval of the Ministry of Finance." In the same statement, the MoD argued that hereinafter defense plans "may be sent to the Ministry of Finance only for information and not for its approval."[83] Historically, the non-approval of defense

[80] Shekhar Sinha, "Role of Integrated Defence Staff in Defence Procurement," *Bharat Shakti*, December 13, 2015, https://bharatshakti.in/role-of-integrated-defence-staff-in-defence-procurement/

[81] Arun Prakash, "India's Higher Defense Organization: Implications for National Security and Jointness," *Journal of Defence Studies* 1, no. 1 (2007): 28. Also see Behera, "Defense Planning in India," 131–33; and V. P. Malik and Gurmeet Kanwal, "Defense Planning in India" (ORF working paper, Observer Research Foundation, New Delhi, 2005), 8–9. https://www.orfonline.org/wp-content/uploads/2005/01/Defence.pdf.

[82] Amit Cowshish, "Distortions in the Discourse on Modernization of Armed Forces," *Journal of Defence Studies* 8, no. 3 (2014): 13.

[83] Standing Committee for Defense, *Forty Second Report: Capital Outlay on Defense Services, Procurement Policy and Defense Planning* (New Delhi: Lok Sabha Secretariat, March 2018), 52.

Table 7.2 **Status of Defense Plans, 1985–2023**

Year and Plan	Status	Remarks
Seventh defense plan, 1985–1990	This plan was approved by the cabinet only in its fourth year (August 1988).	Defense Planning Staff was formed during this plan period.
Eighth defense plan, 1992–1997	The plan was not approved due to disagreement between the Ministry of Finance and services.	There was a two-year plan holiday (1992–1994) preceding this due to an acute financial crunch.
Ninth defense plan, 1997–2002	The plan was approved early (December 1997), but the Finance Ministry was able to stymie implementation.	Planning assumptions were overcome by the 1998 nuclear tests and the 1999 Kargil war.
Tenth defense plan, 2002-2007	Tentatively approved at the end of its specified period.[a]	Basic thrust of last three years of this plan was on infantry modernization.
Eleventh defense plan, 2007–2012	Due to a difference of opinion between the Defence and Finance Ministries, this plan was not approved by the cabinet.[b]	The Defence Ministry claimed a shift from equipment- to capability-based planning.
Twelfth defense plan, 2013–2018	Plan approved by the Defence Acquisitions Committee but not approved by the Ministry of Finance.	Emphasis on offsets, capabilities for power projection, and out-of-area contingencies.
Thirteenth defense plan, 2018–2023	Still in progress, but military assumptions about the budget seem unrealistic.	The Ministry of Defence has made a policy decision that henceforth defense plans may be sent to the Ministry of Finance for information only and not for approval.

[a]Standing Committee on Defence, *Sixteenth Report: Demand for Grants, 2007–2008* (New Delhi: Lok Sabha Secretariat, 2007), 18.

[b]Standing Committee on Defence, *Sixth Report: Demand for Grants* (New Delhi: Lok Sabha Secretariat, 2010), 25–27.

plans has been a constant complaint, one made repeatedly by analysts, military officers, and especially the parliamentary standing committee on defense.[84] By claiming that defense plans need not have cabinet or finance ministry approval and that, in any case, such approvals are not necessary for effective implementation of the plan, the ministry is perhaps trying to preempt this criticism. However, a closer look at the budgetary figures underlying recent plans indicates that "allocations in all the years have been substantially less than the projections."[85] Inevitably, this has had an adverse impact on capability-building and military modernization.

Regardless of this issue, defense planning remains problematic. In 2011, the government appointed a committee headed by prominent bureaucrat Naresh Chandra to revisit the defense-reforms process. The report of this committee identified problems in defense planning, and while arguing that "a long term solution to the travails of planning and funding of plans may take some time to emerge," it recommended the creation of a defense planning board.[86] A similar recommendation had been made in 2009 by another reform committee, the Defence Expenditure Reform Committee, which had suggested that such a board could function like a "planning commission" to deal with defense plans. However, this recommendation was not accepted, and planning procedures remained unchanged. Subsequently, analysts argued not only that defense planning was "ad hoc" and "silo driven" but also that the "services as well as the civilian and defense agencies are often seen to be working at cross purposes."[87]

2018: The Return of the Defence Planning Committee

In April 2018, the government announced the formation of the Defence Planning Committee (DPC). In the 1970s the cabinet secretary headed a

[84] Reports of the Standing Committee on Defence which discussed defense planning inevitably focused on the issue of non-approval of plans. Also see Amiya Kumar Ghosh, *Defence Budgeting and Planning in India: The Way Forward* (New Delhi: Knowledge World, 2006), 224; Narender Kumar, "Defense Planning: A Review," in *Defense Reforms: A National Imperative*, ed. Gurmeet Kanwal and Neha Kohli, (New Delhi: Pentagon Press, 2018), 84–86 .

[85] Vinay Kaushal, "Defense Planning and Budget Dilemma" (IDSA occasional paper 48, Institute for Defense Studies and Analyses, New Delhi, 2018), 6.

[86] National Security Council Secretariat (NSCS), *Report of the Task Force on National Security* (New Delhi: NSCS, 2012), Section 3.57, 37 (otherwise known as the Naresh Chandra Committee Report).

[87] Harsh V. Pant, "Reforming Defence Planning in India," *Live Mint*, April 24, 2018, https://www.livemint.com/Opinion/YXsvzqyHhK6IoFqAK7MntO/Reforming-defence-planning-in-India.html.

committee with a similar nomenclature, but this time the DPC would function under the national security adviser (a position that was created in 2001). The committee consists of senior civilian and military officials, including the three service chiefs, the defense and foreign secretaries, and the secretary (expenditure) of the Ministry of Finance, among others. It has a wide-ranging remit, including creating "prioritized capability development plans for the armed forces over different time-frames in consonance with the overall priorities, strategies and likely resource flows."[88]

The DPC is too recent a development to assess properly. To its credit, it has been set up as a "supercommittee" that comprises key decision-makers across different sectors including foreign, defense, and financial planners. It has the potential therefore to address many of the existing lacunae in the defense-planning process. However, that it was formed just a year before national elections (slated for summer 2019) has prompted critics to argue that it is merely an "attempt by the government to refurbish its image."[89] Indeed, it is hard to deny that this "step has been taken four years too late."[90]

In sum, defense planning in India has been a difficult exercise. That it has been problematic is borne out by a number of factors. First, there have been periodic attempts (almost once every decade) to set up committees or institutions to address existing shortcomings. The formation of the Apex group and the DPC in the 1970s, the DPS in the 1980s, the IDS in 2001, and, once again, the DPC in 2018 is indicative of recurring efforts to revisit the defense-planning process. Second, the non-approval of defense plans by the cabinet or the Finance Ministry has been a constant complaint. It is questionable whether this has had any real effect, but perceptually this sends a dispiriting signal about the value of the planning processes. Third, various reports of the Standing Committee on Defence and other reform committees (like the 2009 Defense Expenditure Review Committee and the 2012 Naresh Chandra Committee) have time and again criticized defense planning. Fourth, as discussed later, intraservices and interservices prioritization remains highly problematic.

[88] Laxman Kumar Behera, "Creation of Defence Planning Committee: A Step Towards Credible Defence Preparedness," *IDSA Comment*, April 19, 2018, https://idsa.in/idsacomments/creation-of-defence-planning-committee-lkbehera-190418.

[89] Pravin Sawhney, "Some Home Truths for the Ajit Doval–Led Defence Planning Committee," *The Wire*, April 23, 2018, https://thewire.in/security/some-home-truths-for-the-ajit-doval-led-defence-planning-committee.

[90] Amit Cowshish, "A Blunt Instrument," *Indian Express*, May 24, 2018, https://indianexpress.com/article/opinion/columns/narendra-modi-government-defence-planning-committee-nsa-general-elections-5188758/.

It is important to note that not all problems in defense planning are due to civil–military relations. Often, other issues, like delays in acquisition or in domestic research, development, and production, create redundancies in planning assumptions. To a significant extent however, as we shall see in the following section, India's unique civil–military relations exacerbate these problems.

Civil–Military Relations and Defense Planning

India's pattern of civil–military relations create problems in both the formulation and implementation of plans. As admitted by a former official in the MoD, the "decision making with regard to defense plans can sometimes become a test of civil–military relationship between the armed forces, and the civilian bureaucracy in the ministries of defence and finance."[91] In the following, we analyze how the three characteristics of civil–military relations (lack of civilian expertise, institutional design, and military autonomy) shapes the defense-planning process.

Civilian Expertise

The absence of civilian expertise is a significant problem in defense planning. The MoD is staffed with generalist civilian bureaucrats, whose job is to question and vet the plans made by the military. Carrying out such a function is inherently difficult, if not impossible, without the benefit of expertise. As a result, according to a narrative common within the military, they usually focus on procedural matters. While analyzing the role of the MoD in the planning process, a former chief of naval staff argued that, "Because of the staffing pattern, its competence lies in procedural matters, but as 'examiner', it feels obliged to raise numerous, supposedly searching queries that are often based on superficial information."[92] In turn, this lack of civilian expertise creates a number of problems in the defense-planning process.

First, civilians are unable to provide strategic guidance that should ideally inform military capability and plans. The framing of the Defense Minister's Directives (known as the Raksha Mantri Directives), which is meant to guide

---

[91] N. S. Sisodia, "Planning for Sound Defense Budget," *Journal of Defense Studies* 3, no. 2 (2009): 21.

[92] V. S. Shekhawat, "Challenges in Defense Planning," *Strategic Analysis* 30, no. 4 (2006): 699–700.

defense plans, is indicative of this problem. The first directive, framed in 1983, was allegedly too generic in nature. Subsequently, there were a number of attempts to update it.[93] Reportedly, in 2008, the MoD adopted a version of this document.[94] However, reflecting the lack of capability on the civilian side, this was prepared by the services and the IDS.[95] Similarly, the services frame other planning documents like the LTIPPs with minimal civilian guidance.[96] The military preparing its own planning guidelines upends the normative civil–military relationship. Acknowledging this problem, Admiral Arun Prakash argues that the defense planner starts "with a handicap and tends to grope a bit for direction."[97]

Second, a lack of expertise results in an inability on the part of the civilians to professionally integrate the service plans and take considered decisions on intraservices and interservices prioritization. The three services lobby for their respective platforms and, as they are usually unable to come to a consensus, look towards the ministry for adjudication and direction. According to General V. P. Malik, "inter-service prioritization was done entirely by the civil bureaucracy in the Ministry of Defence."[98] In practice, lacking expertise, civilian bureaucrats in the ministry have passed on this function to the office of defence (finance).[99] Some of these officials have a comparatively longer experience of working with the military; however, their experience is mainly restricted to dealing with finances and accounts. Ultimately, interservices prioritization is more a function of financial planning than making careful trade-offs in capability accretion.

In 2012, while expressing its unhappiness with the defense-planning process, the Naresh Chandra Committee observed that the MoD "does not have the in-house expertise nor does it seek independent professional advice regarding force architecture and force-planning. In such a system, little or no critical examination or cost-benefit analysis can possibly take shape. All wish-lists from the Services become sacrosanct and, eventually, receive MoD approval."[100] The lack

[93] Vinod Anand, "Integrating the Indian Military: Retrospect and Prospect," *Journal of Defence Studies* 2 no. 2 (2008): 20–24.

[94] Sandeep Unnithan, "The ChiPak Threat," *India Today*, October 23, 2010, https://www.indiatoday.in/magazine/the-big-story/story/20101101-the-chipak-threat-744556-2010-10-23.

[95] B. M. Kapur, "Integrated Tri Services Perspective Planning," in *Defence Planning: Problems and Prospects*, ed. V. P. Malik and Vinod Anand, 114–15 (New Delhi: Manas Publications, 2006).

[96] R. Sivasubramanian, "Defence Budget and the Planning Process," in *Defence Planning: Problems and Prospects*, 44.

[97] Arun Prakash, "Challenges of Defense Planning," in *From the Crow's Nest* (New Delhi: Lancer Publications, 2007), 28; also see Behera, "Defense Planning in India," 130.

[98] Email to author, November 20, 2010.

[99] Prakash, "Challenges of Defense Planning," 29.

[100] *Report of the Task Force on National Security*, 37.

of civilian expertise also results in handing over agenda-setting powers to the military. As defined by Srinath Raghavan, the term "agenda-setting powers" refers to "the way issues are defined before they are decided; how certain outcomes tend to be institutionalized in the routines of organizations."[101] Civilians therefore face a fait accompli with regard to choosing future capabilities. Indeed, the inability of the ministry to shape and professionally deliberate upon defense plans makes the entire exercise somewhat ad hoc, and, according to a former MoD official, it "has ceased to have any operational meaning."[102]

Institutional Design

Institutional design in this case refers to the bureaucratic structures and offices involved in the defense planning process. In India, the institutional design creates strong silos between civilians and the military while giving procedural control to the former. This tends to lead to a "depthless interaction" and recurring impasse between the civilians and the military.

Like in any other democracy, civilians have the authority to decide upon budget appropriations. India's defense-planning processes are such that it "allows the Finance Ministry to control the Defence Ministry and the Defence Ministry to control the armed service headquarters."[103] Ordinarily this would not be an issue however many within the military believe that civilians (hindered in any case by a lack of expertise) have focused more on procedural control rather than defense planning. Military officers therefore frequently complain that the government does not provide in-principle sanction for its plans and that it deliberately applies "brakes" on its modernization projects for covering the deficit in its finance budget.[104]

In addition, military officers also argue that there is a lack of fiscal guidance and an absence of long-term commitment of funds. According to Jasjit Singh, "service headquarters keep planning for future force development, essentially in a vacuum, since they are not part of the process examining/planning resource

---

[101] Srinath Raghavan, "Soldiers, Statesmen, and India's Security Policy," *India Review* 11, no. 2 (2012): 118.

[102] Amiya Kumar Ghosh, "Defence Planning in India at Crossroads," in *Core Concerns in Indian Defense and Imperatives for Reforms*, ed. Vinod Misra, 91 (New Delhi: Pentagon Press, 2015).

[103] Thomas, "Defense Planning in India," 251.

[104] See "Army Chief General V.K. Singh Advocates for Defense Planning Commission," *DNA: Daily News and Analysis*, May 1, 2011, https://www.dnaindia.com/india/report-army-chief-general-v-k-singh-advocates-for-defence-planning-commission-1538318; Anjan Mukherjee, "Defense Budget: Optimizing Planning and Utilization—I," in *Defense Reforms: A National Imperative*, 152.

allocation."[105] In 2001, the Group of Ministers Report highlighted this problem and recommended that the Ministry of Finance "should give a firm indication of the availability of financial resources, for a period of 5 years, at least 6 months before the commencement of the ensuing Five Year Plan."[106] In order to obtain assured budgetary support, some have argued for a "non-lapsable Defense Modernization Fund."[107]

These perceptions feed a narrative within the military of strong bureaucratic control. However, this is not entirely the case. In recent times, the Finance Ministry has been more forthcoming with expected outlays for the budget.[108] The problem is that the military's plans rely on financial projections that are "not realistic."[109] Ultimately, the institutional design in such that it creates frequent back and forth. It is not surprising therefore that the government periodically feels the needs to create a "super committee," like the current experiment with the DPC.

Military Autonomy

The third characteristic of the absent dialogue framework is that of considerable military autonomy. Military officers formulate defense plans , from the LTIPPs to the five-year plans to the annual acquisition plans. They have to seek approval from the MoD, but in conceptualizing the preferred force structure, they enjoy considerable autonomy. This, creates a number of problems in the defense-planning process.

First, due to the prevailing culture within the military, plans can change frequently depending on changes in personnel. To be sure, defense plans should not be rigid, and there is a tension between adhering to a plan and retaining the capability to respond to emerging threats and unforeseen situations. However, as military officers, without specialist knowledge, draft defense plans, their priorities can change with a change in leadership. "The culture of service headquarters is that of a field command and not that of a service staff headquarters," K. Subrahmanyam wrote while analyzing defense planning; "consequently, recommendations as to the choice of equipment, with a few exceptions, are not

[105] Singh, "Defense Doctrine and Policy Planning in India," 649. Also see Prakash, "Challenges of Defense Planning," 29.

[106] Reforming the National Security System: Report of the Group of Ministers on National Security (New Delhi: Government of India, 2001), 108.

[107] See discussion on this in Standing Committee on Defence, Forty Second Report, 20–21.

[108] Kaushal, "Defense Planning and Budget Dilemma," 34–38.

[109] Amit Cowshish, "Defense Budget: Optimizing Planning and Utilisation—II," in Defense Reforms: A National Imperative, 166; also see Kaushal, "Defense Planning and Budget Dilemma," 39–40.

vigorously debated within the service headquarters . . . [and] in a number of cases, these recommendations are highly personalized, with the result that one Chief of Staff may repudiate his predecessor's recommendations."[110] Agreeing with this contention, according to Jasjit Singh, "the present process also permits frequent changes in force development plans due to changes in personalities in the service headquarters, reducing the sanctity of the plans."[111] A related problem with frequent change in personnel is the lack of expertise in financial planning. Officers in the planning directorates serve on a rotational basis, leading to charges that these are "ad hoc un-trained appointments in the Finance Divisions of the three services."[112] This quality makes it even more difficult to have a well-informed dialogue on budgeting, costing, life cycle costs, and financial planning.

Second, military autonomy in framing defense plans contributes to problems in the development of joint capabilities. The services (army, navy, and air force) have been successful at resisting attempts to curb their autonomy in the realm of planning—whether it was in the form of the DPS or its current avatar the IDS. The dominance of the single-service approach has resulted in problems of joint capability development.[113] According to Lieutenant General Prakash Menon, "for the most part, the Armed Forces, bereft of adequate political guidance, have been formulating their own schemes and plans based on their service-specific interpretations to shape themselves."[114] Perhaps as important is to take into consideration other organizations which have a stake in the outcome of the plans, including the Coast Guard, the Border Roads Organization, ordnance factories, defense public sector units, and the Defence Research and Development Organization. Not doing so makes the plan somewhat unrealistic.

Finally, the military has considerable agenda-setting power. According to some, the services frame their single-service plans without, for the most part, taking into consideration the expected fiscal outlays. The most important document for long-term planning, the LTIPP, is framed by the military and is considered by them to be a "mother document" whose "sanctity . . . needs to be maintained."[115] However, this document does not factor into the expected

---

[110] K. Subrahmanyam, "Commentary: Evolution of Defense Planning in India," in *Defense Planning in Less-Industrialized States*, 269.

[111] Jasjit Singh, *India's Defence Spending: Assessing Future Needs* (New Delhi: Knowledge World, 2000),,, 76.

[112] Mukherjee, "Defense Budget—I," 161.

[113] Laxman Kumar Behera, "Examining the US Defence Acquisition Apparatus: What Can India Learn?" *Journal of Defence Studies* 11, no. 4 (2017): 90.

[114] Prakash Menon, "The Problems of Defence Planning," *Pragati*, May 16, 2018, https://www.thinkpragati.com/opinion/4527/the-problems-of-defence-planning/.

[115] Anil Ahuja, "Budgeting for Defence: Beyond Mere 'Apportioning' of Financial Resources," *India Foundation Journal* 6, no. 4 (2018): 38.

budget. Complaining about this, according to a former official dealing with the subject, the finance division "has to be associated with the process right from the beginning. There is no use having a plan that is unachievable because of it being based on unrealistic financial assumptions."[116] Indeed, one analysis of the Thirteenth Defense Plan, slated from 2017 to 2022, pithily argued that it "appears to be an illusion."[117] The military's power to set the agenda predetermines the choices presented to the civilians. As a result, there is a constant impasse between the two, leading to repeated calls for "deep restructuring and reform."[118]

Conclusion

Defense planning is a critical and difficult exercise that shapes future capabilities. It also requires extensive interaction between civilians and the military to discuss issues pertaining to political objectives and financial outlays. As described in this chapter, there are problems in India's defense planning due to its civil–military relations and the institutional design, creating strong silos between civilians and the military. To be sure, there have been improvements over time. Most notably, the creation of new organizations like the Defense Acquisition Council, the Defense Procurement Board and the IDS has made planning more systematic. Nevertheless, as pointed out by the Naresh Chandra Committee in 2012, problems remain. The committee's recommendation was clear: a "permanent Chairman COSC backed by an Integrated Defence Staff which will include Finance representatives will be able to provide the needed expertise to MoD."[119]

However, it is a question not just of expertise within the MoD but also of bringing civilians deep within the planning process. According to an official who used to handle the plans in the MoD and was deeply involved in the planning process,

> The problem seems to be that (a) the civilians are *ipso facto* viewed by the military brass as being incapable of making any contribution and (b) it is wrongly presumed that the civilians will interfere in the purely military aspect of planning. The understanding is wrong on both these counts. For one thing, the association of civilians is not to be at the level of the clerical staff and at the higher-levels things are not really as bad as

---

[116] Cowshish, "Perspective on Defense Planning in India," 684

[117] Kaushal, "Defense Planning and Budget Dilemma," 40.

[118] Manoj Joshi, *Scraping the Bottom of the Barrel: Budgets, Organisation and Leadership in the Indian Defence System*, ORF Special Report 74 (New Delhi: Observer Research Foundation, 2018), 9.

[119] *Report of the Task Force on National Security*, 37.

they are made out to be [in terms of lack of expertise/competency]. In any case, it is better to be challenged by the civilians before the plans are made rather than being questioned by them afterwards. I have a feeling that the association of civilians especially those of the MoD, will ensure collective ownership of the plans, rather than their being seen as unrealistic wish lists.[120]

As described in this chapter, there are many different bureaucracies involved in planning: the services, the IDS, defense finance (in the MoD), domestic defense research and production units, and the Ministries of Defence and Finance. Unfortunately, the MoD has an "institutional incapacity" to bring together all the stakeholders.[121] The proffered solution to this problem is to create an "empowered independent entity" which can then make and implement difficult decisions.[122] The current effort (the DPC created in 2018) appears to be just another example, in a long list of examples, of such an effort. The jury is still out on whether it will be successful. However, instead of these episodic attempts, there is a need to maintain a "permanent civil–military dialogue in defense planning."[123] In order to do so, more political attention and ownership of defense plans can also help in resolving the perennial dispute between the Ministries of Finance and Defence. Equally importantly, there is a need to examine the staffing pattern and planning processes within the three services, IDS, and the MoD. Without such structural changes, any fresh efforts at improving the planning process, however well intentioned, are unlikely to succeed.

[120] Email from Amit Cowshish to author, December 12, 2018.

[121] Cowshish, "Distortions in the Discourse," 19.

[122] Mrinal Suman, "Modernisation of the Armed Forces: Reforming the Defence Procurement Regime," *India Foundation Journal* 6, no. 4 (2018): 31–34. For a similar recommendation, see Cowshish, "Perspective on Defense Planning in India," 683.

[123] George Cristian Maior and Mihaela Matei, "Bridging the Gap in Civil–Military Relations in Southeastern Europe," *Mediterranean Quarterly* 14, no. 2 (2003): 74.

8

Tumultuous Times

The Contemporary Discourse on Civil–Military Relations

Civil–military relations in contemporary India have been in the news for all the wrong reasons. The tumultuous tenure of General V. K. Singh, chief of army staff from 2010 to 2012, placed enormous strain on civil–military relations and created many controversies including allegations that the military was "snooping" on its political masters and rumors of undisclosed troop movement that unnerved the government.[1] These controversies forced the prime minister, Manmohan Singh, perhaps for the first time, to speak on the issue of civil–military relations while addressing top military commanders in November 2013. He affirmed that the political leadership "has the highest faith in its military and its institutional rectitude within the democratic framework."[2] Perceived as an attempt "to apply a healing touch to the frustration that is evident within the military establishment,"[3] this, however, did little to build trust between civilians and the military.[4]

Tensions between civilians and the military, while not as virulent as before, have continued under Prime Minister Narendra Modi. As discussed later in the chapter, the controversies over one rank, one pension (OROP), status equivalence between civilian and military officials and other issues—some seemingly trivial (like the opening of cantonment roads)—have caused civil–military friction. Why are there recurring problems and controversies between civilians and

---

[1] For a description of some of these events, see Shashank Joshi, "India's Civil–Military Dysfunction," *The Interpreter*, December 9, 2013, http://www.lowyinterpreter.org/the-interpreter/indias-civil-military-dysfunction.

[2] Hemant Abhishek, "Prime Minister Addresses Combined Commanders' Conference: Full Speech," *Zee News*, November 23, 2013.

[3] B. D. Jayal, "Heed the Timely Message," *The Telegraph*, January 25, 2014; also see "Former Navy Chief Calls for 'Less Adversarial' Civil–Military Ties," *Business Standard*, January 20, 2014.

[4] Vishal Thapar, "Undermined Chiefs Unhappy with Antony," *Sunday Guardian*, March 2, 2014; also see "Gone Adrift," *Indian Express*, February 28, 2014; and C. Uday Bhaskar, "Civil–Military Relation in India Need Holistic Review," *Salute: To the Indian Soldier* (February–March 2014).

the military? One of the main causes is the structure of civil–military relations, which not only inhibits a free and frank dialogue but also creates bitterness and mistrust. To be sure, some conflicts are the result of a clash of personalities, and no "structure," however sophisticated, can obviate that. However, the nature of India's civil–military interaction amplifies the differences between the two and creates an inherently, and unnecessarily, tense relationship.

This chapter contextualizes the current discourse in India's civil–military relations. It also engages with and occasionally refutes a number of narratives that have emerged on this topic. Examining controversies in civil–military relations is useful as it reveals the functioning of and tensions in the triangular relationship between politicians, civilian bureaucrats, and military officers. It also analyzes the defense reforms process and argues that unless the issues of institutional design, a lack of civilian expertise, and military autonomy are addressed, civil–military relations will continue to be problematic.

The chapter proceeds as follows. It begins with an overview of the main controversies pertaining to civil–military relations since 2004. This aims to illuminate the dissonance between the civilians and the military. Next, it briefly discusses civil–military relations under the Modi government. Thereafter, it examines the issue of defense reforms. This is followed by an analysis of the divergence in the positions typically taken by political, bureaucratic, and military leaders.

The Controversies

What follows is an analysis of four main controversies pertaining to contemporary civil–military relations in India: the dispute about withdrawal of troops from the Siachen glacier, the discontent over withdrawal of the Armed Forces Special Powers Act (AFSPA), the tenure of General V. K. Singh, and issues arising from reports of the pay commission and the equivalence between civilians and the military. I discuss these controversies not only because I provide a fresh perspective on them but also because, read together, they encapsulate the tense and fragile state of civil–military relations.

Siachen: Mountains of Misperception

The conflict in the Siachen glacier between India and Pakistan began when India, in what it claimed to be a preemptive move, inserted its troops into the region in 1984. Since then this localized conflict has claimed thousands of lives. There have been numerous rounds of talks aimed at resolving this dispute, but they have failed to break the impasse. The two countries came closest to some sort of an agreement on four occasions—in 1989, 1992, 1994, and 2005–2006.[5] However, it was only after the failure of the 2005–2006 initiative that questions were raised about India's civil–military relations. It is a commonly held view that opposition from the Indian Army *alone* stymied the civilian government's efforts to find a solution.[6] As Srinath Raghavan points out, this militates against the idea of democratic civil–military relations as "the military, in effect, exercises a veto on a critical foreign policy issue."[7] If the army's intransigence blocks a deal that politicians had agreed upon, then, indeed, it undermines civilian control. However, a closer examination reveals that this was not a case of a conflict in civil–military relations.

Prime Minister Manmohan Singh invested heavily in the peace process with Pakistan despite periodic setbacks, usually in the form of terror attacks in India. He believed the Siachen dispute could be solved relatively easily. Anticipating opposition from the army, the prime minister invited almost all of the general officers who commanded troops in Siachen and sought their views on demilitarization of the Siachen glacier. Thereafter, the government went ahead with its diplomatic initiative to resolve the dispute. It is then, critics allege, that the chief of army staff, General J. J. Singh, publicly aired his opposition and "successfully thwarted the government's policy on a sensitive issue."[8]

There are three reasons to support the contention that it was not just the army's opposition which led to the failure of the prime minister's Siachen initiative. First, the prime minister was not able to overcome opposition from within his own cabinet and senior advisers, including senior ministers Pranab Mukherjee and A. K. Antony and National Security Adviser M. K. Narayanan.[9] General J. J. Singh was initially amenable to such an initiative, but later, when others in the cabinet opposed it, he reversed his stance. According to then foreign secretary Shyam Saran, General Singh had "happily gone along with the proposal in its earlier iterations, [but] now decided to join Narayanan in rubbishing it."[10] Therefore, it was not the army but other senior members of the

---

[5] A. G. Noorani, "Settle the Siachen Dispute Now," *The Hindu*, June 14, 2012.

[6] Srinath Raghavan, "Siachen and Civil–Military Relations," *Economic and Political Weekly* 42, no. 35 (2007): 3531–33; and Siddharth Srivastava "India's Army Digs in over Siachen," *Asia Times*, November 16, 2006.

[7] Srinath Raghavan, "Soldiers, Statesmen, and India's Security Policy," *India Review*, 11, no. 2 (2012): 128.

[8] A. G. Noorani, "Talkative Generals," *Frontline*, 27, no. 16 (2010): 85–86.

[9] Sanjaya Baru, *The Accidental Prime Minister: The Making and Unmaking of Manmohan Singh* (New Delhi: Viking Press, 2014), 188–89; this was confirmed by a senior official who wishes to remain unnamed, interview, New Delhi, July 3, 2013.

[10] Shyam Saran, *Kautilya to the 21st Century: How India Sees the World* (New Delhi: Juggernaut Books, 2017), 91.

government who killed this initiative. According to a former senior official, who wished to remain unnamed,

> At the CCS [Cabinet Committee on Security] meeting there was op-position from political leaders, which they had not raised earlier. Once General JJ Singh saw which way the wind was blowing, he also then opposed it . . . [it is] absolutely wrong to say that it was opposition from the army alone that killed this initiative.[11]

The other two reasons are circumstantial. On November 12, 2006, on the eve of a meeting between the foreign secretaries of India and Pakistan, the Indian Army held a press conference at Siachen glacier and, in front of domestic and international reporters, declared its opposition to "demilitarizing Siachen."[12] A press conference at this location would have required clearance from the Ministry of Defence (MoD), suggesting that the army obviously had got the po-litical approval to do so. Indeed, a few days later Defence Minister A. K. Antony publicly supported the army's position—confirming divisions within the cab-inet.[13] Finally, soon after retirement, General J. J. Singh was appointed as gov-ernor of Arunachal Pradesh. It is inconceivable that he could have obtained such a generous post-retirement benefit if he had, as the critics allege, opposed and single-handedly thwarted the prime minister's peace initiative.

If this was the case, then why did the government allow the belief to persist that the army's opposition alone stymied this diplomatic initiative and not re-fute the allegation that there had been a loss of civilian control? Simply because this narrative suited all stakeholders. As we know now, Manmohan Singh was politically a weakprime minister, but early in what was his first term he would not have wanted to advertise the fact that his cabinet colleagues could over-rule him. Instead, the army's opposition provided a better cover—that security considerations did not allow him to do so. This narrative was also convenient for diplomats as they expressed their inability to overcome the army's opposi-tion. For instance, in a meeting with a US diplomat, then joint secretary T. C. A. Raghavan expressed the difficulty in pulling back troops from Siachen as the "Indian Army has drawn a line with its political leadership."[14] The army too went

---

[11] Interview, the official was present at this CCS meeting, New Delhi, July 3, 2013.

[12] Sandeep Dikshit, "Army Once Again Sets Its Face Against Demilitarizing Siachen," *The Hindu*, November 12, 2006.

[13] "Siachen Is Safe, Says Antony," *The Hindu*, November 16, 2006, https://www.thehindu.com/todays-paper/tp-national/siachen-is-safe-says-antony/article3048326.ece.

[14] Cable report of their meeting held on August 27, 2008, released by Wikileaks: https://www.wikileaks.org/plusd/cables/08NEWDELHI2401_a.html. Ironically, this excuse was readily embraced in Pakistan; see "Indian Army Hurdle in Way of Siachen Solution," *Dawn*, June 2, 2011.

along with this story as it was perceived to be "standing up to the civilians" and defending its "legitimate" interests.

To reiterate, the issue of troop withdrawal from Siachen was not a matter of civil–military relations but more a lack of political consensus and divisions within the cabinet. This is not to suggest that the Indian military, like other bureaucracies, has not been assertive at all.[15] Its stand opposing the AFSPA has been especially strident.

The AFSPA: Standing by the Unpopular

The AFSPA, enacted in 1958, is an enabling legislation that provides legal cover to the military in carrying out internal security operations.[16] According to this act, once a state, or a district within a state, is declared a "disturbed area," the armed forces are conferred special powers to restore order. These special powers include the authority to "shoot, kill and arrest without warrant" and have been a source of long-standing controversy. It was only in the late 1990s, with increasing awareness about human rights, that a movement grew to repeal or, failing that, amend this act. The military tried to preempt this criticism by claiming to spread awareness about human rights within its ranks and appointing officers to engage with this issue. However, responding to allegations of human rights abuses in Manipur in November 2004, the government set up what is popularly known as the Jeevan Reddy Committee to "review the provisions of the Act" and advise whether to "replace the Act by a more humane Act."[17] To include the army's point of view, one of the committee members was former Lieutenant General V. R. Raghavan, a respected member of India's strategic community. After seeking the views of a cross section of Indian society and from the security forces, the committee recommended that the act be repealed.[18] According to Sanjay Hazarika,

---

[15] Bureaucracies are assertive especially when faced with a weak polity. For instance, under Prime Minister Manmohan Singh, the chairman of the Atomic Energy Commission and a government employee, Dr. Anil Kakodar, in an interview publicly disagreed with the government's initiative toward concluding a nuclear deal with the United States and thereby seriously undermined the prime minister; see Praful Bidwai, "Snags Surface in India–US Nuclear Deal," *Antiwar Online*, February 13, 2006, http://antiwar.com/horton/?articleid=8525.

[16] For a good historical overview, see Pushpita Das, "The History of Armed Forces Special Powers Act," in *Armed Forces Special Powers Act: The Debate*, IDSA Monograph Series 7, ed. Vivek Chadha, 10–21 (New Delhi: Lancer Publications, 2012).

[17] For terms of reference of this committee, see *Report of the Committee to Review the Armed Forces (Special Powers) Act*, 1958 (New Delhi: Government of India, Ministry of Home Affairs, 2005), 5.

[18] See *Report of the Committee to Review the Armed Forces*, 74.

one of its members, this surprised the government as it had not expected such a drastic recommendation.[19]

Even before the Jeevan Reddy Committee submitted its report, the army had been making its position very clear—it was opposed to the withdrawal of the act.[20] When the government circulated the report internally, the army expressed its opposition. General J. J. Singh, then chief of army staff, wrote a particularly strong note on file opposing any tinkering with the act, arguing that it would curtail the effectiveness of the military in counterinsurgency operations.[21] This argument had the tacit support of other agencies including the police, intelligence, and the paramilitary.[22] The views of Defence Minister Pranab Mukherjee and, later, A. K. Antony on the AFSPA are not entirely clear. Were they personally in favor of amending or repealing the AFSPA but reluctant to take on the military, or did they agree with the military's contention? Nevertheless, some accounts suggest that they were sympathetic to the security forces' point of view but did not publicly comment on it.[23]

The matter did not go away amid periodic reports that, because of the internal deliberations flowing from the report of the Jeevan Reddy Committee, the government was considering amending the AFSPA.[24] In December 2006, while addressing a public rally in Manipur—a state where this act is especially unpopular—Prime Minister Manmohan Singh openly called for amending it.[25] However, mirroring his predicament over the Siachen dispute, he did not have the political power to implement his vision. Years later, in 2010, because of unrest in Kashmir, the AFSPA once again gained public attention,

[19] Video interview, September 28, 2014. Lt. Gen. Raghavan deserves mention for dissenting from the army's institutional stand on this issue, an unpopular decision that fetched him some opprobrium from within the service.

[20] For instance, in February 2005, during a press conference in Assam (a state where this act is especially unpopular) General J. J. Singh publicly opposed overturning it; see "Army Chief in Favor of AFSPA," *Sangai Express*, February 6, 2005; also see "Ulfa Lashes Out at Army Chief on Act," *The Telegraph*, February 16, 2005.

[21] Telephone interview with Major General Nilendra Kumar, who was the judge advocate general of the army from 2001 to 2008, February 7, 2015. For General J. J. Singh's views on AFSPA, see J. J. Singh, *A Soldier's General: An Autobiography* (New Delhi: Harpercollins India, 2012), 226–27.

[22] According to Major General Nilendra Kumar, a briefing was held in 2004, which was attended by the National Security Adviser J. N. Dixit and senior Ministry of Home Affairs (MHA) and Ministry of Defence officials, during which he successfully impressed upon all the importance of obtaining legal cover when deployed for counterinsurgency operations; telephone interview, February 7, 2015.

[23] According to Major General Nilendra Kumar, Defence Minister Pranab Mukherjee and A. K. Antony were convinced by the army's arguments and therefore supported them; telephone interview, February 7, 2015.

[24] Sudhi Ranjan Sen, "AFSPA to Be Watered Down," *Indian Express*, January 4, 2006.

[25] "Armed Forces Special Powers Act Must Be Amended: Manmohan," *Daily News and Analysis*, December 2, 2006.

with Chief Minister Omar Abdullah calling for its withdrawal.[26] By this time, P. Chidambaram had taken over as home minister and was in favor of amending the act but failed to convince other members of the cabinet.[27] During this time the army expressed its opposition to amending the act. Perhaps out of exasperation, Chidambaram publicly blamed the army, arguing "if the Army takes a very strong stand against any dilution or any amendment to AFSPA, it is difficult for a civil government to move forward."[28] After 2014, all talk of even amending the act, let alone withdrawing, ended when in the first meeting of the Cabinet Committee of Security the Bharatiya Janata Party (BJP)–led coalition government " 'thoroughly' rejected the recommendations seeking dilution in the stringent provisions of the Act."[29]

Successive army chiefs have held the same institutional position as General J. J. Singh for not repealing, or even amending, the AFSPA claiming that this is the view of the majority of the security forces. Those in favor of the status quo argue that the army needs the legal protection to operate effectively in a difficult counterinsurgency environment. In addition, they further argue that, in any case, the army takes cognizance of and action against officers found guilty of human rights abuses. Those in opposition offer their own counterarguments. First, the insurgencies both in the northeast and in Kashmir are no longer as virulent as before and should be the responsibility of local police forces. Second, the army has been notoriously opaque on the issues relating to human rights abuses. General V. P. Malik, a staunch defender of the AFSPA, admitted this and argued that there is "a need for the Army to become more transparent on human rights violation cases and where necessary, expedite sanction from the central government to prosecute personnel guilty of deliberate human rights violations."[30] The problem is that the army

---

[26] "Kashmir Burning: Cabinet Committee on Security Mum on AFSPA, to Call All-Party Meeting," *Daily News and Analysis*, September 13, 2010.

[27] "I Am Trying to Revisit AFSPA: Chidambaram," *Livemint*, September 1, 2011, https://www.livemint.com/Politics/notZnPvGZybkTbB7KXt0IM/I-am-trying-to-revisit-AFSPA-Chidambaram.html; and "Amendments to AFSPA Pending: Chidambaram," *News 18*, April 10, 2012 https://www.news18.com/news/india/amendments-to-afspa-pending-chidambaram-463990.html. After leaving government, he came out more strongly against this act; see "P. Chidambaram Calls AFSPA 'Obnoxious'; Calls for Amendments to the Act," *Daily News and Analysis*, November 14, 2014.

[28] "Army Is not Ready for a More Humane Law: Chidambaram on AFSPA," *NDTV News*, February 6, 2013.

[29] Rakesh K. Singh, "NDA Shoots Down Diluted AFSPA Idea," *The Pioneer*, August 3, 2014.

[30] V. P. Malik, "Raging Debate on Armed Forces Special Powers Act in J&K," *SP's MAI*, http://www.spsmai.com/experts-speak/?id=26&q=Raging-Debate-on-Armed-Forces-Special-Powers-Act-in-Jammu-and-Kashmir.

rarely sanctions prosecution of its officials in civilian courts, even in the case of egregious violation of human rights.[31]

From the perspective of democratic civil–military relations, it is disturbing if the army can scuttle initiatives, like amendments or repeal of the AFSPA, as it is a civilian prerogative to decide on policy. However, like Siachen, this too is a case of a weak and divided political establishment. While Chidambaram may have blamed the army, he did not have the support of his cabinet colleagues. Indeed, Sanjoy Hazarika castigates the government for using the army's opposition as an excuse for not acting on this issue.[32]

Fratricide: General V. K. Singh and the War Within South Block

In times of peace, the chief of army staff should rarely be in the news. General V. K. Singh broke that tradition and was frequently in the news, making headlines amid numerous controversies. An in-depth analysis of his time in office is beyond the scope of this book, but it is important to note that his tenure, effectively, laid to rest any hopes of defense reforms. General V. K. Singh's actions, conduct, and legacy have polarized the Indian strategic community. On the one hand are his supporters who perceive him to be an honest and outspoken officer, unfairly targeted by a corrupt cabal of politicians, bureaucrats, and "compromised" military officers.[33] They supported his stance of taking on the MoD as "an opportunity to put 'an end to the civilian bureaucracy's meddling in service matters' . . . [and as] someone who was finally taking 'them' head on."[34]

On the other hand, General V. K. Singh has been criticized as a "self-obsessed officer" who took on the system for a mere "personal redress."[35] A widely shared perception is that he devoted too much time and energy to furthering his personal ambitions instead of working for the good of the organization. His efforts to block the promotion of his successors, General Bikram Singh and General Dalbir Singh Suhag, made him out to be a vindictive person prone to indulging

---

[31] Wajahat Habibullah, "Armed Forces Special Powers Act, Jammu and Kashmir," in *Armed Forces Special Powers Act: The Debate*, 28.

[32] Sanjoy Hazarika, "An Abomination Called AFSPA," *The Hindu*, February 12, 2013.

[33] For instance, see M. D. Nalapat, "General Singh Pays for Integrity," *The Diplomat*, April 4, 2012; and Prakash Katoch, "Indian Army: Whose Personal Fiefdom?" *Outlook India*, January 25, 2012.

[34] Chandra Suta Dogra, "The Creeping Barrage," *Outlook India*, March 12, 2012; also see G. D. Bakshi, "The Age of Differences . . . Wasn't It Born Before 1962?" *Outlook India*, October 3, 2011.

[35] Pravin Sawhney, "The Good, the Bad and the Ugly," *Daily Pioneer*, November 21, 2003; also see Ali Ahmed, "Civil–Military Relations: Questioning the VK Singh Thesis" (IPCS Brief 3638, Institute of Peace and Conflict Studies, New Delhi, June 13, 2012).

in "shenanigans."[36] After he retired, a secret board of officers investigated alleged irregularities conducted by a unit that, unusually, he had directly commanded. The report of this board was too sensitive, and the government preferred not to take any action.[37] Perhaps more damagingly, in a television interview V. K. Singh alleged that to maintain stability the army transfers money to Kashmiri politicians and has done so since independence.[38] This statement, according to a top official, caused "enormous damage" to the country's interests and set off a political firestorm.[39]

When controversies involving General V. K. Singh dominated television news, there were a number of people calling for action against him. Former national security adviser, the late Brijesh Mishra argued that he should be sent on "compulsory leave."[40] So why did the government not take action against V. K. Singh's alleged transgressions? According to a senior official who served in the MoD at that time, the matter of "disciplinary action" against the chief was brought to the level of the prime minister on two occasions.[41] However, on both occasions the prime minister demurred as he did not want to tarnish the office of the chief of army staff. Perhaps another explanation could be that it was not politically feasible as the Congress Party did not want to face charges of compromising national security by mishandling the armed forces. Politics came into play more prominently later when, after retirement, General V. K. Singh gravitated toward the opposition. A report highly critical of the general was then leaked shortly thereafter, an act that one commentator termed "appallingly irresponsible."[42]

Among the bigger irony was that this deterioration in civil–military relations effectively put paid to efforts to ameliorate problems in higher defense management. During V. K. Singh's tenure, as discussed later, the Naresh Chandra Committee was concomitantly suggesting measures to address institutional

[36] Ajai Shukla, "Thank God That's Over . . . " *Business Standard*, May 29, 2012. Years later the Ministry of Defence publicly disavowed General V. K. Singh's actions; see Sujan Dutta, "General Fires 'Illegal Ban' Salvo at VK," *The Telegraph*, June 19, 2016, https://www.telegraphindia.com/india/general-fires-illegal-ban-salvo-at-vk/cid/1517281.

[37] Ritu Sarin, "Unit Set Up by V K Singh Used Secret Funds to Try and Topple J&K Govt, Block Bikram Singh: Army Probe," *Indian Express*, September 20, 2013.

[38] A. G. Noorani, "Bribes and Spies," *Frontline* 30, no. 22 (2013), https://frontline.thehindu.com/the-nation/bribes-and-spies/article5281422.ece.

[39] Siddharth Varadarajan, "V.K. Singh's Claims Damaged India's Interests, Officials Say," *The Hindu*, September 26, 2013.

[40] See transcript of his interview with Karan Thapar, "General VK Singh Is the Worst Army Chief So Far: Brajesh Mishra," *IBN News*, April 1, 2012, https://www.news18.com/videos/india/devils-advocate-217-461175; also see Sandeep Unnithan, "General Singh's War on India," *India Today*, April 9, 2012.

[41] Interview, February 15, 2015; to speak frankly, the official requested anonymity.

[42] Srinath Raghavan, "The General and His Stink Bombs," *The Hindu*, September 30, 2013.

shortcomings. But its recommendations were scuttled by the numerous controversies surrounding General V.K. Singh's alleged defiance of civilian authority. His actions came to represent an "out of control" military and was a cautionary tale on the dangers of empowering the military—be it institutionally or politically.[43] Military reformists were defensive after these upheavals in civil–military relations, while it strengthened the arguments made by those in favor of the status quo.

The Pay Commissions, Equivalence, and "Callous" Civilians: A Ritualistic Crisis

The Pay Commission is a committee periodically appointed by the government to make recommendations on the pay and allowances of all its employees. Its reports from the time of the Third Pay Commission in 1973 have perhaps inadvertently shaped the equivalence between civilian and military ranks. This is because pay and allowances are both a formal and an informal barometer of seniority in the government of India. Over successive pay commissions, the military felt that many of its concerns, especially with regard to equivalence with civilian ranks, were overlooked, triggering discontent.[44]

Civil–military relations were especially aflame after the Sixth Pay Commission in 2008, which was accused of "cherry picking" data and thereby throwing the "entire equation [between civilians and the military] into disarray."[45] The military raised a number of objections to this report, and to allay them the government appointed a Committee of Secretaries.[46] Officers from the Indian Administrative Service (IAS) dominated this committee, but after the experience of previous pay commissions, the military had no faith in them.[47] True to

---

[43] "*Babus* Now Oppose General Singh's Vision for MoD," Rediff News, April 5, 2012, http://www.rediff.com/news/special/babus-now-oppose-general-singhs-vision-for-mod/20120405.htm.

[44] For more on the history of the pay commissions and the grievances within the military, see G. M. Hiranandani, *Transition to Triumph: History of the Indian Navy: 1965–1975* (New Delhi: Lancer Publishers, 2000), 353–56; and G. M. Hiranandani, *Transition to Guardianship: The Indian Navy, 1991–2000* (New Delhi: Lancer Publishers, 2009), 310–11.

[45] Navdeep Singh, "Sitharaman Restores 'Sheen' to Military Ranks after 2016 Uproar," *The Quint*, January 5, 2018, https://www.thequint.com/voices/opinion/civil-military-ranks-7th-pay-commission-controversy.

[46] According to Admiral Sureesh Mehta, the military raised thirty-two objections "in writing"; interview, Goa, March 19, 2014.

[47] For a perspective on the IAS and the committee of secretaries, see Sharad Savur, "A Matter of Confidence," LiveFist (blog), October 15, 2008, http://www.livefistdefence.com/2008/10/livefist-column.html.

the apprehensions of the military, according to Admiral Sureesh Mehta, then chief of naval staff and chairman of the Chiefs of Staff Committee, "the implementation orders that emerged [from the Committee of Secretaries] were even worse. Then we took up cudgels very strongly."[48] The objection was not on financial grounds as the military had "initially welcomed the revised pay deal for the forces."[49] The problem was regarding equivalence between civilian and military officers that, due to the differences in pay, effectively meant that junior civilian director-level officers would outrank their more senior (by years of service) military counterparts.[50] To press the military's demands, Admiral Mehta took some controversial steps. Besides directly approaching the prime minister, and thereby indicating a loss of faith in the defense minister, he decided to delay the implementation of the pay commission report.[51] This was criticized as an alleged defiance of civilian authority.[52] Eventually, some, but not all, of the anomalies raised by the military were resolved.[53] Like clockwork, there were problems again after the Seventh Pay Commission, which submitted its report in 2015. According to one account, once again, "at the heart of the civil–military dispute lies a battle for parity between the civilian bureaucracy and the armed forces. The military sees the not-so-hidden hand of the civilian bureaucracy behind a gradual attempt to whittle down the military's status."[54]

The issue of equivalence between military and civilian ranks creates problems in the functioning of organizations in which both have to work together. For instance, in organizations like the National Technical Research Organisation, the Research and Analysis Wing, the National Security Guard, the Coast Guard, and the National Security Council Secretariat, there is a variance in the pay, allowances, and associated benefits of officers of the military and other services.

---

[48] Personal interview, Goa, March 19, 2014.

[49] "Defence Chiefs Take Their Pay Grudge to PM," *IBNlive*, September 5, 2008.

[50] "It Is about Status and Equality, not Money: Navy Chief," *Indian Express*, October 4, 2008.

[51] Nitin Gokhale, "Higher Defence Management in India: Need for Urgent Reappraisal," *CLAWS Journal* (Summer 2013): 30n11; also see 23–26.

[52] Shekhar Gupta, "Chain of Command, Demand," *Indian Express*, October 4, 2008 http://archive.indianexpress.com/news/chain-of-command-demand/369248; for a similar view, see Sushant K. Singh and Nitin Pai, "The Service Chiefs Protest," *LiveMint*, October 12, 2008 https://www.livemint.com/Opinion/5FJAijp1WZKTOU9mAJ6y3H/The-service-chiefs8217-protest.html.

[53] According to one report, "46 odd anomalies of the 6th Pay Commission remain unresolved"; see Vinod Bhatia, "Civil–Military Status Equivalence and Pay-Parity Need for Urgent Intervention" (CENJOWS Occasional Paper 2, Center for Joint Warfare Studies, New Delhi, November 2017), 1.

[54] Sandeep Unnithan, "Simmering Discontent," *India Today*, September 14, 2016, https://www.indiatoday.in/magazine/nation/story/20160926-orop-central-pay-commission-indian-army-indian-navy-indian-air-force-manohar-parrikar-829574-2016-09-14; also see Pragya Singh, "Achchey Din for Retired Faujis," *Outlook India*, February 17, 2015; and Yogendra Narain, *Born to Serve: Power Games in Bureaucracy* (New Delhi: Manas Publications, 2017), 138.

This further reinforces the military's perception that over the years its status vis-à-vis civilian officers has been progressively downgraded.

Apart from pay and equivalence, there are other issues that have aggravated the military's resentment toward civilians. For instance, there have been frequent complaints of "callous" civilian bureaucrats routinely opposing the requests of disabled or aggrieved soldiers and veterans and resorting to litigation.[55] Further, as noted by Admiral Arun Prakash, a widely respected former chief of the navy, much of the anger among veterans arises from the "indifference of politicians and the hostile manner in which the MoD bureaucracy" handles their problems.[56]

New Regime, Old Problems

In the run-up to the 2014 general elections in India, a large number of former servicemen came out in support of the BJP. Notably the first public rally addressed by Narendra Modi, after the announcement that he was the party's prime ministerial candidate, was a massive former servicemen's rally held in Rewari, Haryana, in September 2013. Sharing the dais with a large number of distinguished exservicemen, including the most recent (and controversial) army chief General V. K. Singh, Modi made a speech promising support to the veteran community and its long-pending demand for OROP.[57] This rally, widely covered by the media, strengthened perceptions that the BJP was the "natural party" for veterans. Shortly thereafter General V. K. Singh, accompanied by over thirty other retired officers, joined the BJP, calling it the only "nationalist party."[58] The BJP's election manifesto mentioned subjects dear to the military community—construction of a war memorial, implementation of OROP, organizational reform, and, curiously, ensuring "greater participation of Armed Forces in the decision-making process of the Ministry of Defence."[59] Later, when the BJP won

---

[55] See, for instance, Navdeep Singh, "The Defence Ministry's Approach to Litigation: Misdirected, Highly Adversarial and Sadistic (Parts 1 and 2)," *Bar and Bench*, November 1, 2018, https://barandbench.com/defence-ministry-approach-to-litigation-misdirected-highly-adversarial-and-sadistic-part-i/; and Purnima S. Tripathi, "A Soldier's Worth," *Frontline*, 30, no. 19 (2013), https://frontline.thehindu.com/the-nation/a-soldiers-worth/article5128006.ece

[56] Arun Prakash, "Failing India's Veterans," *Times of India*, September 24, 2013.

[57] For more on this issue, see Sushant Singh, "OROP Explained: Emotive Issue for Veterans and Soldiers, but Reasons for Caution," *Indian Express*, June 1, 2015; and Srinath Raghavan, "Decoding OROP and the Politics at Play," NDTV, June 2, 2015, https://www.ndtv.com/opinion/decoding-orop-and-the-politics-at-play-768052.

[58] "VK Singh Joins BJP, Says It Is Only Nationalist Party," *Hindustan Times*, March 2, 2014. Also see Christophe Jaffrelot, "Soldiers of the Party," *Indian Express*, March 6, 2014.

[59] BJP Election Manifesto, *Ek Bharat, Shreshtha Bharat: Sabka Saath, Sabke Vikas*, 2014, 38–39. https://www.thehinducentre.com/multimedia/archive/01831/BJP_Manifesto_1831221a.pdf

an unprecedented mandate, there were expectations that it would move quickly and address the military's grievances.

However, within a couple of years, the wheel had turned full circle. Veterans organizations, which had previously backed the BJP, now publicly supported the opposition Congress Party, expressing its unhappiness over the manner of implementation of OROP, among other issues.[60] To be sure, there has been an improvement in the tenor of civil–military relations under the Modi government. Also, he has fulfilled the pre-election promise of constructing a war memorial. However, several more substantive issues have remained unaddressed.

Shortly after assuming office, in December 2015, Prime Minister Modi made a forward-looking speech at the Combined Commanders Conference on board the INS *Vikramaditya* in favor of defense reforms.[61] This sentiment was supported by his defense minister, Manohar Parrikar, when in March 2015 he asserted that a "Chief of Defense Staff (CDS) is a must . . . because the three forces' integration does not exist in the present structure."[62] However, even after five years in power, there were no substantive organizational reforms. The BJP was learning that making promises was easier than delivering on them.

During its tenure, the Modi government had to deal with the same problems as its predecessor—military complaints about equivalence vis-à-vis civilians and charges about an apathetic MoD.[63] While criticizing its defense policies, Srinath Raghavan argued that "the government has yet to undertake serious reforms of

[60] Aurangzeb Naqshbandi, "Ex-Servicemen Protesting OROP to Back Congress in Poll-Bound States," *Hindustan Times*, January 5, 2017, https://www.hindustantimes.com/india-news/ex-servicemen-protesting-orop-to-back-congress-in-poll-bound-states/story-8gz6kQSIX18UJYI7uB1qHJ.html.

[61] Press Information Bureau, "PM Chairs Combined Commanders Conference on Board INS Vikramaditya at Sea," Prime Minister's Office, December 15, 2015, http://pib.nic.in/newsite/PrintRelease.aspx?relid=133265.

[62] "Manohar Parrikar for Integration of Three Services, Creation of CDS," *Zee News*, March 13, 2015.

[63] For instance, see Arun Prakash, "There Is Growing Civil–Military Dissonance and Acrimony in India's Defence Ministry," *The Print*, October 20, 2018, https://theprint.in/opinion/there-is-growing-civil-military-dissonance-and-acrimony-in-indias-defence-ministry/141359/; Navdeep Singh, "Civil–Military Rank Parity: Can a Defence Board Address Wage Woes?" *The Quint*, October 27, 2016, https://www.thequint.com/voices/opinion/civil-military-rank-parity-can-a-defence-board-address-wage-woes-indian-army-manohar-parrikar-one-rank-one-pension; and D. S. Hooda, "Gap in Civil–Military Relations Will Only Grow with Creation of Defence Planning Committee," *News 18*, November 13, 2018, https://www.news18.com/news/opinion/gap-in-civil-military-relations-will-only-grow-with-creation-of-defence-planning-committee-writes-lt-gen-ds-hooda-1937513.html.

the structures of national security management. What's worse, it has weakened and complicated the existing ones."[64]

Why did a so-called nationalist party with a self-professed strong affiliation with and appreciation of the military fail to undertake reforms to ameliorate problems in civil–military relations? As recent history, this question requires more research, and at this stage one can only offer conjectures. Nonetheless, interviews with officials who worked closely within this government do offer some perspectives.[65] First, frequent leadership changes in the MoD took away some of the impetus for reforms, dissipating "the concentrated focus this specialist ministry demands."[66] Since 2014, there have been three defense ministers—Arun Jaitley (two truncated tenures of around six months each), Manohar Parrikar (twenty-eight months), and Nirmala Sitharaman (twenty months as of May 2019). Parrikar, who was probably best placed to undertake reforms, focused more on procurement reform and the "Make in India" campaign and not so much on organizational reform. There are many who hold the opinion that he intended to undertake more substantive defense reforms but unfortunately was sent to deal with local politics in his home state of Goa. Sitharaman's tenure coincided with the furor over the Rafale aircraft deal, which consumed most of her attention. Second, and perhaps more importantly, there is a lack of consensus between civilians and the military and even within the military over the proposed reforms. As discussed in the next section, the Modi government preferred to go with minor reforms rather than transformative changes.

Finally, Prime Minister Modi himself was ambivalent about defense reforms. Early in his tenure, Modi claimed that this was an "area of priority" for him; however, according to some officials who worked closely with him, he was unable to find agents to transform his vision into a reality. To some this was a failure of senior leadership—both civilian and military—to deliver on the prime minister's vision. Others argue that Modi's ties with the senior military leadership soured after the OROP agitation. In September 2015, the government unveiled its proposals for meeting the long-pending demands for OROP. These proposals, however, did not satisfy all of the veteran groups. Modi expected his senior officers to publicly support these proposals, but once they refused to do

[64] Srinath Raghavan, "Why Modi Govt Only Boasts about Surgical Strikes on National Security Front," *The Print*, December 25, 2018, https://theprint.in/opinion/why-modi-govt-only-boasts-about-surgical-strikes-on-national-security-front/168582/.

[65] This section relies on interviews with six senior officials, conducted in New Delhi, Kolkata, and Singapore, who worked under Prime Minister Modi. To speak frankly, they requested anonymity.

[66] Sandeep Unnithan, "A Work in Progress," *India Today*, June 2, 2018, https://www.indiatoday.in/magazine/cover-story/story/20180611-a-work-in-progress-1246595-2018-06-02.

so, he was reportedly very upset.[67] Even if we disregard such speculations, it is amply clear that Modi was unable to fulfill his own vision, as he stated in his speech at the Combined Commanders Conference in December 2015.

Dust in the Wind: The Defense Reforms Process

Defense reforms in India have been episodic—usually occurring after a crisis. As described in Chapter 2, the most consequential effort was after the 1999 Kargil war that led to the creation of many new institutions. A decade or so after this initiative, members of the strategic community were calling for "structural reform of its higher defence set-up."[68] Responding to these demands, in 2011 the government set up the Naresh Chandra Committee to revisit the defense reforms process. This triggered a debate on restructuring India's higher defense management and its civil–military relations.[69] Unfortunately, around the time that the Naresh Chandra Committee (NRC) submitted its report, there was considerable turmoil in civil–military relations on account of various controversies surrounding General V. K. Singh. This served as a pretext for those opposing changes in the status quo, especially if it even remotely empowered the military. The General V. K. Singh saga, effectively, set back defense reforms by years.

After the Modi government came to power, it created another committee (called the Shekatkar Committee), which submitted its report to the government in December 2016. The report of this committee is not in the public domain, although there are a number of journalistic accounts describing its major recommendations. The 561-page report allegedly contained 218 recommendations including appointing a four-star chief of defense staff (or a permanent chairman of the Chiefs of Staff Committee [PCOSC]), reducing the tooth to tail ratio, and the selective closure of redundant organizations like

---

[67] For another take supporting this version of events and based on interviews with officials close to the Modi government, see Bharat Karnad, *Staggering Forward: Narendra Modi and India's Global Ambition* (New Delhi: Penguin Random House, 2018), 354–56.

[68] Sushant Singh and Rohit Pradhan, "For a New Civil–Military Order," *LiveMint*, November 26, 2008; also see Anit Mukherjee, "Failing to Deliver: Post-Crisis Reforms 1998–2010" (IDSA occasional paper 18, Institute for Defence Studies and Analyses, New Delhi, 2011).

[69] See, for instance, B. D. Jayal, V. P. Malik, Anit Mukherjee, and Arun Prakash, eds., *A Call for Change: Higher Defence Management in India*, IDSA Monograph Series 6 (New Delhi: Institute for Defence Studies and Analyses, 2012); Srinath Raghavan, "Integrating Defence into Strategic Thinking," *Seminar* no. 668 (April 2015); Happymon Jacob, "Civilian Supremacy and Defence Reforms," *The Hindu*, October 28, 2014; Anit Mukherjee "Facing Future Challenges: Defense Reforms in India," *RUSI Journal*, 156, no. 5 (2011): 30–37; and various articles in the special issue of *CLAWS Journal* (Summer 2013) and *Synergy* (December 2012).

military farms, postal services, and other cost-cutting measures.[70] Out of all these, according to the government, "a total of 99 recommendations, including the 65 recommendations pertaining to the Indian Army were forwarded for implementation to concerned agencies."[71] However, the recommendations that the government chose to implement mostly pertained to cost-cutting measures within the army, and there were no major institutional reforms.

From the perspective of civil–military relations, there were three important issues that emerged from the deliberations of these committees. First, both committees recommended creation of the post of PCOSC. This was a change in nomenclature from the historical demand, made from the 1960s, to appoint a Chief of Defence Staff (CDS). Encouragingly, in 2013, for the first time the three services unanimously and publicly accepted such a recommendation and, according to one report, admitted this as "an interim measure towards appointing a CDS."[72] The support for a PCOSC was reaffirmed by Admiral Sunil Lanba, chief of naval staff, in December 2018.[73] However, there is little clarity on the powers of such a newly created post. According to the Naresh Chandra Committee, the PCOSC will coordinate the Long Term Integrated Perspective Plan and the five-year and annual acquisition plans of the services; administer tri-services institutions including Andaman and Nicobar Command, a newly created Special Forces Command, and forces for out-of-area contingencies (when tasked to do so); plan and conduct major joint services exercises; and integrate common functions in logistics, training, and administrative areas.[74] This also appears to be the thrust of the recommendations made by the Shekatkar Committee.[75] According to the proposals made by both committees, the service chiefs will retain their powers of both staff and command responsibilities, effectively making the PCOSC "toothless"[76] and creating an institutional design which is "deeply

[70] Nitin A. Gokhale, "All You Wanted to Know about the Shekatkar Committee Report," *Bharat Shakti*, January 11, 2017, http://bharatshakti.in/all-you-wanted-to-know-about-the-shekatkar-committee-report/; also see panel discussion including a member of the committee in "Security Scan—Defence Reforms: Shekatkar Committee Report," Rajya Sabha TV, August 4, 2017, https://www.youtube.com/watch?v=WnM6q8851LY; Sushant Singh, "Defence Reforms: Shekatkar Panel Recommends Four-Star Rank for Top Military Adviser," *Indian Express*, January 11, 2017;

[71] See reply to unstarred question no. 1376, July 25, 2018, Lok Sabha, New Delhi, http://164.100.47.190/loksabhaquestions/annex/15/AU1376.pdf.

[72] Ajai Shukla, "Tri-Service Chief to Be Chosen Soon," *Business Standard*, December 2, 2013.

[73] Sujan Datta, "Indian Military Divided on Integration, but Air Force Chiefs are Learning from Navy School," *The Print*, December 3, 2018, https://theprint.in/security/indian-military-divided-on-integration-but-air-force-chiefs-are-learning-from-navy-school/157978/.

[74] National Security Council Secretariat, *Report of the Task Force on National Security*, 2012, sect. 3.19, 25 (otherwise known as the Naresh Chandra Committee Report).

[75] Gokhale, "All You Wanted to Know about the Shekatkar Committee Report."

[76] Syed Ata Hasnain, "India's Chief of the Defence Staff: An Imperative in the Making," *Synergy: Journal of the Center for Joint Warfare Studies* (February 2017): 13.

problematic."[77] This vision is at variance with the model followed in other democracies where the service chiefs are responsible only for staff functions like training, equipping, and preparing the forces for deployment. However, to be charitable, perhaps both committees thought that it would be best to recommend incremental rather than revolutionary changes.

Second, the Naresh Chandra Committee devoted a section to analyzing "Synergy in Civil–Military Functioning" and, among other measures, recommended posting military officers in civilian billets in the MoD and vice versa to promote better understanding between the services and the ministry.[78] It is unclear if the Shekatkar Committee examined this issue or suggested similar measures. This problem of institutional design remains a significant fault line in India's civil–military relations. As a consequence of this, an almost completely civilian-staffed ministry adjudicates over military-dominant services, which creates considerable resentment and perpetuates an "us versus them" narrative.

Third, these committees focused on the absence of expertise among civilians on defense and military-specific issues. The Naresh Chandra Committee specifically recommended that "a special cadre of Defence specialists should be introduced in the civil service to ensure knowledge build up among the civilian staff."[79] Without such expertise, the military largely perceives civilian interventions as unwanted, uninformed, and unprofessional; and this has been a constant source of tension.[80] Former defense and cabinet secretary N. N. Vohra acknowledged this problem and recommended "the establishment of a dedicated security administration cadre," which would allow bureaucrats "to develop specialization in dealing with security related matters."[81] However, perhaps because this issue concerns the entire system of administration in India—without political impetus—such recommendations are difficult to implement.

These measures have the potential to significantly alter not just higher defense management but the overall tenor of civil–military relations. However, even such long-standing institutional reforms proved to be a bridge too far.

---

[77] Srinath Raghavan, "Not Fully Empowered Chief of Defence Staff Is a Bad Idea," *Hindustan Times*, January 18, 2017, https://www.hindustantimes.com/analysis/not-fully-empowered-chief-of-defence-staff-is-a-bad-idea/story-4TzdNbq2XXddQXKsQcfoJJ.html.

[78] National Security Council Secretariat, *Report of the Task Force on National Security*, 23.

[79] National Security Council Secretariat, *Report of the Task Force on National Security*, 23. It is again unclear if the Shekatkar Committee examined this issue.

[80] For more on problems in the MoD due to a lack of expertise, see Stephen P. Cohen and Sunil Dasgupta, *Arming Without Aiming: India's Military Modernization* (Washington, DC: Brookings Institution Press, 2010), 144–49.

[81] N. N. Vohra, "Civil–Military Relations: Opportunities and Challenges," *Air Power Journal* 8 no. 4 (2013): 15. Such a measure mirrors the recommendations for "domain expertise" among civil servants which have been made by both the Administrative Reforms Committees.

Instead, as we shall see in the next section, there are differing motivations across the political, bureaucratic, and military levels.

Working at Cross Purposes: Political, Bureaucratic, and Military Motivations

What are the typical motivations of politicians, bureaucrats, and the military officers on the subject of civil–military relations? The following is a conjectural analysis of these three disparate actors in contemporary India.

Political Control

For the most part, it appears that politicians are largely content with exercising control over the military without attempting to reshape it from the perspective of effectiveness or efficiency. To be sure, the enormous defense outlays, as a proportion of central government expenditure (12% in financial year 2018–2019), evoke their interest in reducing the budget; however, without dramatically reshaping the military, this cannot be done. Instead, it appears that politicians are content with the formal exercise of civilian control and preventing allegations of corruption in the defense sector.

The prominent politician A. K Antony earned the distinction of being India's longest-serving defense minister, holding the office for eight years between 2006 and 2014. His main qualification was seemingly his clean image—an important consideration for the Congress Party still haunted by the ghosts of the Bofors scandal. Unfortunately, toward the end of his tenure, he faced the ignominy of being termed the "worst defence minister ever."[82] His indecisive leadership and overreliance on advice from civil servants were criticized, and according to some, he depended "excessively on the advice of IAS officers inexperienced in strategic policy and defence."[83] In addition, throughout the periodic crises in civil–military relations, Antony was criticized for his apparent inability to act decisively. "The defence ministry," Pratap Bhanu Mehta observed, "seems to have lost control of every issue."[84] All accounts indicate that Antony failed to take ownership of the ministry and was driven from one crisis to another.

---

[82] Sandeep Unnithan, "The Worst Defence Minister Ever," *India Today*, March 17, 2014; also see Hakeem Irfan, "The Mixed Legacy of Defence Minister AK Antony," *DNA News*, December 12, 2013.

[83] Baru, *Accidental Prime Minister*, 188.

[84] Pratap Bhanu Mehta, "Cabinet Is Bare," *Indian Express*, February 28, 2014.

Antony's tenure also coincided with the Naresh Chandra Committee, and he played a critical role in the way it was processed. Despite the military being amendable to the post of a PCOSC, why did Antony not push for creating this position? Like a true and experienced politician, perhaps Antony was responding to signals from elsewhere. Reportedly, Sonia Gandhi, the head of the Congress Party, was not convinced about the need to appoint a CDS or even a PCOSC. According to Manoj Joshi, a member of the Naresh Chandra Committee, "the principal opposition to the CDS in the UPA [United Progressive Alliance] government came from Ms. Sonia Gandhi, who raised worries about the possibility of a coup were a CDS-like figure be appointed."[85] Perhaps taking a cue from her, Antony dragged his feet and thereby "outmanoeuvred the military reformists."[86] Therefore, despite Prime Minister Manmohan Singh's public support for defense reforms, he was, like on many other issues, unable to implement his vision.[87]

By comparison, defense ministers under the Modi government—Jaitley, Parrikar, and Sitharaman—had an easier time as they did not have to deal with the vicious infighting that characterized General V. K. Singh's tenure. Despite that, they all had to deal with civil–military friction caused by the report of the Seventh Pay Commission, problems of equivalence between civilians and the military, OROP, the "deep selection" of General Bipin Rawat as chief of army staff, controversy over the opening of cantonment roads, and allegations of bypassing procedures while buying the French Rafale aircraft. On matters pertaining to civil–military relations, none of them pushed through any major reforms. Prime Minister Modi's personal views on higher defense management are not known; however, since no transformative reforms were undertaken during his tenure, we can assume that he was unconvinced about their necessity.

In sum, a cursory examination of political leadership of the military indicates a deep aversion to changes in the current arrangement of civil–military relations. Politicians instead are seemingly content with the ritualistic exercise of civilian control and are unwilling to implement substantive defense reforms.

Bureaucratic Control

The civilian bureaucracy in India has been an important element in the exercise of civilian control. They not only uphold their constitutional duties but also are

---

[85] Manoj Joshi, *The Unending Quest to Reform India's National Security System*, RSIS Policy Brief (Singapore: S. Rajaratnam School of International Studies, March 2014), 8n18.

[86] Anit Mukherjee, "Cleaning the Augean Stables," *Seminar* no. 658 (June 2014): 44.

[87] For Manmohan Singh's support for restructuring higher defense management, see Hemant Abhishek, "Prime Minister Addresses Combined Commanders' Conference: Full Speech," *Zee News*, November 22, 2013.

an important source of checks and balances by providing advice to politicians on various proposals emanating from the military. However, civilian control has become a goal in itself and is used as a pretext to avoid "second-order" discussions on effectiveness and efficiency. A former defense secretary justified strong procedural control on the military as, in his opinion, in the coalition era, the polity is weak. "If we [civilian bureaucrats] do not do so," he argued, "the military will gradually defy civilian control."[88] Those sympathetic to such views dismiss comparisons with Western democracies and instead cite the experience of the "near neighborhood"—Pakistan, Bangladesh, Myanmar, Thailand, among others, all of which have struggled to control their military. Such sentiments also explain the hesitation in creating the post of a CDS (or PCOSC) as they are fearful that this will diminish the institutional powers of the civilians. These fears resonate to an extent within India's polity and some sections of Indian bureaucracy including intelligence agencies, police forces, etc.

Critics, however, dismiss such apprehensions and blame the bureaucrats for molding "the political leadership's thought process according to their own perceptions on governance and administration."[89] This is the crux of the civil–military problem—while bureaucrats argue that they deliver professional advice, the military perceives this both as an unwanted intrusion and as unprofessional.

Civilian bureaucrats have also been the traditional bugbear for many in the Indian military. According to former defense secretary Vijay Singh, any decision that does not go the military's way "is attributed to bureaucratic intrigue . . . [leading to] much acrimony."[90] Indeed, some of this narrative within the military against civilian bureacrats (disparagingly referred to as *babus*) is ill-informed and downright toxic. It is also convenient for some to deflect blame on the bureaucracy for organizational shortcomings. According to former deputy chief of army staff Lieutenant General Subrata Saha, "the narrative of a hostile [civilian] bureaucracy is being fed from generation to generation to cover our own [military's] inadequacies."[91]

At the same time, the bureaucracy has been complacent and has allowed a trust deficit to creep into its relationship with the military. It should have been more attuned to the bitterness that had crept into the military due to the disputes arising from successive pay commissions and a seemingly callous attitude toward veterans, including those with disabilities. As noted by a defense journalist, the armed forces "do not have faith in the civilian dispensation—largely

---

[88] Personal interview, New Delhi, December 23, 2014; to speak freely, the official requested anonymity.

[89] Gokhale, "Higher Defence Management in India," 14.

[90] Chandra Suta Dogra, "The Creeping Barrage," *Outlook India*, March 12, 2012.

[91] Interview, December 13, 2017, New Delhi.

the bureaucracy."[92] To a significant extent, this is because of the rotational nature of the job—bureaucrats may assume important posts with no experience in the MoD and therefore little knowledge of underlying issues.

Some also argue that civilian bureaucrats oppose any changes in the status quo.[93] After his resignation, former naval chief Admiral D. K. Joshi hinted at this when he argued that "vested interests" have stalled defense reforms. When pressed further, he added, "vested interests . . . are the ones who wield the authority without accountability."[94] For members of the strategic community this was an indication that the opposition had come from civilians in the MoD.[95]

Military's Quest for Autonomy

The military most often complains about the kind of civilian control exercised in India but paradoxically enjoys the autonomy afforded under this model. Civilian intervention or joint civilian and military deliberation upon the minutiae of defense policy would make most members of the military uncomfortable. The fact is that the military finds the current single-service approach convenient. It is not surprising therefore that the service chiefs oppose the creation of an *empowered* CDS or PCOSC. In addition, the services are bitterly divided over the model of jointness that they would like to follow—disagreeing over the need to establish theater and functional commands.[96]

[92] Rajat Pandit, "India's Civil–Military Ties Worsening?" *Times of India*, October 7, 2013.

[93] Manoj Joshi, "Shutting His Ears to Change," *India Today*, November 22, 2013.

[94] See "Vested Interests Have Stalled Reforms: Former Navy Chief Admiral D.K. Joshi Tells NDTV," https://aamjanata.com/politics/media/vested-interests-have-stalled-reforms-former-navy-chief-admiral-dk-joshi-tells-ndtv-full-transcript/; in an interview the late K. Subrahmanyam had once argued that in India civilian "bureaucrats wield power without any accountability"; see Anit Mukherjee, "The Absent Dialogue," *Seminar* no. 599 (July 2009). Since then this phrase has been adapted by the strategic community to describe the role of civilian bureaucrats and was even discussed in a section titled "Authority, Accountability and Responsibility" by the Naresh Chandra Committee; see National Security Council Secretariat, *Report of the Task Force on National Security*, 23.

[95] C. Uday Bhaskar, "Reforming India's Higher Defence Management: Will Modi Bite the Bullet?" *Economic Times*, October 16, 2014; also see P. K. Vasudeva, "MoD Scuttled the Proposal for a Permanent Chairman of Chiefs of Staff Committee," *Indian Defence Review*, June 19, 2013, http://www.indiandefencereview.com/spotlights/mod-scuttled-the-proposal-for-a-permanent-chairman-of-chiefs-of-staff-committee/.

[96] For differing viewpoints, see Monty Khanna, "The Indian Air Force and Theaterisation: Misplaced Apprehension" (Synodos Paper 12, no. 11, Centre for Joint Warfare Studies, New Delhi, July 2018); S. Krishnaswamy, "Why Theatre Commands Is an Unnecessary Idea," *Indian Express*, August 16, 2018; Gurmeet Kanwal, "Where Is India's Chief of Defence Staff?" *Economic Times*, September 27, 2018; and Arjun Subramaniam, "The Roadmap to Military Reform," *The Hindu*, August 16, 2018.

The military's preference for autonomy comes across clearly in its Joint Doctrine, which was unveiled in April 2017. Curiously for a doctrine, publicly released by the three service chiefs, it had a short section on civil–military relations, which crisply captured the military's perspectives. Making clear its preference for autonomy, the doctrine argues that civilians (in consultation with the military) should decide upon the military objective "and then leave it to the military professionals to decide upon the best way of achieving the objective."[97] This is a classic exposition of Huntington's "objective control" model, which presupposes that military autonomy maximizes effectiveness. However, as the academic literature readily admits, this not only is false and overly simplistic but misunderstands the purpose and nature of warfare. As pointed out by Srinath Raghavan, "On one hand the military wants greater say in policy matters, but on the other it wants to keep the civilians out of its domain."[98]

Conclusion

Tensions between civilians and the military are not new in India. However, like in many other fields, the proliferation and reach of social media have only served to amplify differences. Instant opinions, traditional and non-traditional news media, and the emergence of the veteran community as a semi-organized lobby have exacerbated tensions and added to the pressure—on both civilians and the military. The underlying reason for these crises is that the military had lost faith in the bureaucracy's role as an honest interlocutor. Embittered by past experiences and a feeling that their grievances have been ignored, the military has increasingly adopted an uncharacteristically strong stance. As a result, one would expect continuing tensions and crises between the two.

The contemporary trend in India's civil–military relations is clear—politicians, largely, refuse to intervene in those matters which are considered to be in the military's domain. Civilian bureaucrats in the MoD lack expertise and therefore by norm do not engage with the military on professional matters. This arrangement leaves the "army, navy and air force chiefs the unfettered right to run their services as they deem fit; while the ministry controls the money and procures military equipment . . . [indicating] abdication of ministerial responsibility."[99]

---

[97] Integrated Defense Staff, *JP-01/2017 Joint Doctrine: Indian Armed Forces* (New Delhi: Ministry of Defense, 2017), 60.

[98] Srinath Raghavan, "Defence Policy Has to Be a Joint Effort Between Civilians and the Military," *Hindustan Times*, May 11, 2017, https://www.hindustantimes.com/columns/defence-policy-has-to-be-a-joint-effort-between-civilians-and-the-military/story-55KtLiHsr63M1buTG7li3N.html.

[99] Ajai Shukla, "A Full Time Job in South Block," *Business Standard*, November 11, 2014.

At the same time, as the military functions as "attached offices" to the ministry, all proposals have to be cleared by the latter. This bestows considerable decision-making powers on the bureaucrats. In addition, while careful not to interfere in the military's domain, civilians are vigilant to any perceived threat to civilian control. Such an arrangement "keeps the armed forces headquarters separate from the Ministry of Defence [and] has encouraged an adversarial relationship between the military leadership and the bureaucrats in the Ministry of Defence."[100] As this chapter describes, there are structural problems causing constant civil–military tensions, which cannot be wished away without changes in institutional design. However, such reforms are unlikely as political leaders are sanguine about the current model and would prefer strong civilian control over effectiveness. Moreover, this arrangement—despite occasional complaints—is convenient for all the stakeholders, and there is little appetite for change.

[100] Raghavan, "General and His Stink Bombs."

Conclusion

It would not be exaggeration to say that civil–military relations have shaped the politics—and by extension the society and development—of most countries in Asia, Africa, and South America. Civilian control therefore is not an issue to be taken lightly or for granted. Fortunately, India has been the exception in this regard and holds many lessons for the theory and practice of democratic civil–military relations. Much of the current literature on India's civil–military relations focuses on the reasons for civilian success in maintaining control. However, as argued in this book, this success has come at the cost of military effectiveness. This is not to suggest that there is a trade-off between the two. Instead, one can argue the opposite—certain steps taken to increase military effectiveness can, in fact, *consolidate* civilian control. For instance, altering the institutional design of existing bureaucracies to enable joint civil–military deliberation over the granular aspects of defense policies—pertaining to force structures and employment, jointness, promotion policies, doctrine and education—enhances civilian control. Such institutional redesigning should be accompanied by encouraging the growth of civilian expertise, the importance of which has been made amply clear across the book.

This chapter begins by re-examining the absent dialogue framework, which I argue best describes India's civil–military relations. Thereafter, it discusses whether the conditions resembling an absent dialogue are unique to India. Next, relying on the insights from India, it revisits the problems associated with the theory and practice of civil–military relations. The penultimate section discusses avenues for further research, and the chapter concludes by discussing the possible triggers for change.

Revisiting the Absent Dialogue

As argued through this book, India's pattern of civil–military relations is best described as resembling an "absent dialogue." This consists of three factors: lack of civilian expertise on military issues, an institutional design which leads to strong bureaucratic controls, and military autonomy over its own domain. I subsequently analyzed how these factors shaped the variables most closely associated with military effectiveness—weapons procurement, jointness, officer education, promotion policies, and defense planning. Does the argument apply fully across all cases?

The lack of civilian expertise has been a constant and applies fully across all of the variables. Undoubtedly, greater civilian expertise within the Ministry of Defense (MoD) will enhance both the degree of civilian control and the efficiency of defense policymaking.

The second factor is that of an institutional design characterized by strong bureaucratic control. Like in other democracies, the military has to seek the concurrence of the MoD for major policy initiatives. In India's case, however, the MoD is a civilian-dominated one (worse, one without much expertise)— which bestows it with significant decision-making powers. This factor plays an important role in weapons procurement, in defense planning, and, to a lesser extent, in shaping promotion policies. It, however, does not apply as much in the case of jointness and in professional military education. On the contrary, both are examples of weak civilian control as the services have successfully resisted reforms which would have curtailed their autonomy.

The third factor is that of military autonomy. In India the military retains considerable agenda-setting powers, especially over activities which it considers to be within its domain. This applies to a large extent to issues like jointness, education, and, to a lesser degree, military promotion policies and defense planning.

Admittedly, it is difficult to disentangle the messiness surrounding the interrelated concepts of institutional design (and bureaucratic control) with military autonomy. Where does the military have too much autonomy, and where do civilians exercise their discretionary powers? There is no normative or even academic consensus surrounding the delineation of roles between civilians and the military on all of these variables. Instead, one has to examine the empirical evidence—which may vary over time. Perhaps one manner to overcome this messiness is to accept the fundamental notion that civilians and the military should engage in a well-informed dialogue on all aspects of defense policy. Such a dialogue should be permanent and iterative without arguments of separate domains.

To be sure, in India's case, there has been considerable improvement in defense policymaking. As described in the preceding chapters, there have been improvements in all of the processes: weapons procurement, jointness, military education, promotion policies, and defense planning. The Indian military and the entire defense apparatus are therefore on the cusp of a major paradigm shift—this transformation, however, would require overcoming the civil–military silos, which have prioritized civilian control over effectiveness. To achieve such a transformation, the three main actors—politicians, bureaucrats, and the military—will have to come together and be willing to share and sometimes shed some of their institutional powers.

The Problem of Democratic Civilian Control and Military (In)Effectiveness

Is India, like the United States, an exceptional case; and is the absent dialogue sui generis? This requires further research, but some of the aspects of the absent dialogue argument—for instance, the lack of expertise and strong bureaucratic controls—resonate in other countries. In postwar Japan, for instance, civilian bureaucrats in the MoD have wielded considerable powers even, at times, without possessing relevant expertise.[1] Similarly, in Canada, civil–military relations are characterized by "political inattention, a significant degree of independence and discretion on the part of senior officers and officials, and disharmony followed by surprise."[2] Mirroring the "absent dialogue" argument, according to one study, the "absence of strategy and strategic dialogue are at the heart of the problem of civil–military relations in Canada."[3]

The situation is somewhat different in the United States as it is unique in many respects. First, civilians in the United States—especially from the 1960s onward—increasingly had an opportunity to gain expertise in military affairs. They did this through a variety of ways. The flourishing of strategic studies as a subfield in American academia provided a pathway for students and academics to learn about the military. Not only were they routinely employed in the vast Pentagon bureaucracy, but the system of embedded political appointees and the growth of military-focused think tanks facilitated a "revolving door" of civilian experts. In addition, many of the "civilians" hired by the Defense Department

---

[1] Richard J. Samuels, *Securing Japan: Tokyo's Grand Strategy and the Future of East Asia* (Ithaca, NY: Cornell University Press, 2007), 57. Also see Takao Sebata, *Japan's Defense Policy and Bureaucratic Politics, 1976–2007* (Lanham, MD: University Press of America, 2010), 83; and Takako Hikotani, "The Paradox of Antimilitarism: Civil–Military Relations in Post World War II Japan" (PhD diss., Columbia University, 2014), 32–34.

[2] Douglas L. Bland, "Who Decides What? Civil–Military Relations in Canada and the United States," *Canadian–American Public Policy* no. 41 (February 2000): 38; also see Douglas L. Bland, *National Defence Headquarters: Centre for Decision*, study prepared for the Commission of Inquiry into the Deployment of Canadian Forces to Somalia (Ottawa: Minister of Public Works and Government Services, 1997), 47–48.

[3] M. L. Roi and Gregory Smolynec, "Canadian Civil–Military Relations: International Leadership, Military Capacity, and Overreach," *International Journal* 65, no. 3 (2010): 705.

may actually have prior experience of serving in the military—which helps bridge the expertise gap. Second, the Department of Defense is deeply integrated with the services, and civilian and military officials work closely together—enmeshed in different bureaucracies. This helps build collegiality between civilians and the military, without entirely overcoming their cultural differences and disagreements. Moreover, civilian bureaucrats serving in the Defense Department usually do not rotate to other "ministries" and vice versa. The United Kingdom is also fortunate because one of its strengths is an institutional design with enmeshed civil–military bureaucracies.[4] An emphasis on longer tenures and professional education also helps develops expertise among civilian officials.

This is not to suggest that these countries do not have their share of controversies or problems in civil–military relations.[5] Despite considerable civilian expertise, an integrated Department of Defense and, arguably, "balanced" military autonomy, the US military has faced significant problems in Iraq and Afghanistan amid complaints that its civil–military relations are akin to a "broken dialogue."[6] Moreover, the diplomatic community has long complained about the pernicious role of the Pentagon in "militarizing foreign policy."[7] Even in a well-integrated and institutionalized country like Britain, there are arguments that strategy-making has been neglected due, in part, to "the professional emasculation of the chiefs of staff as a strategic advisory body and the elevation of financial management over military thought."[8] Clearly, there is no fail-safe arrangement or insurance mechanism against bad strategy and poor leadership—whether political, bureaucratic, or military.

To sum up, there is considerable variation in civilian control within the small universe of mature democracies, and some of them can suffer from *pathologies* in civil–military relations. The characteristics of an absent dialogue therefore may resonate in other countries.

---

[4] Lord Levene, et al. *Defence Reform: An Independent Report into the Structure and Management of the Ministry of Defence* (London: Ministry of Defence, June 2011), 15.

[5] Hew Strachan, *The Direction of War: Contemporary Strategy in Historical Perspective* (Cambridge: Cambridge University Press, 2014), 64–97.

[6] Janine Davidson, "Civil–Military Friction and Presidential Decision Making: Explaining the Broken Dialogue," *Presidential Studies Quarterly* 43, no. 1 (2013): 129–45.

[7] Gordon Adams and Shoon Murray, eds., *Mission Creep: The Militarization of US Foreign Policy?* (Washington, DC: Georgetown University Press, 2014).

[8] Strachan, *Direction of War*, 74; see pp. 64–97 for a critique of the inability of the United States and the United Kingdom to formulate strategy primarily due to problematic civil–military relations. Also see Timothy Edmunds, "British Civil–Military Relations and the Problem of Risk," *International Affairs* 88, no. 2 (2012): 265–82.

Professional and Civilian Supremacist: India and the Theories of Civil–Military Relations

The main theoretical debate surrounding civil–military relations in democracies is the one between, what Peter Feaver calls, the professional supremacist vis-à-vis the civilian supremacist.[9] In very simplistic terms, proponents of the former, leaning on Huntington's notion of "objective control," argue that civilians should not "interfere" in military activities. Instead, militaries, left to themselves, will respond professionally, which would maximize their effectiveness. Civilian supremacists, however, citing Eliot Cohen's idea of an "unequal dialogue," argue that civilians should critically interrogate the military's plans and assumptions and, if need be, overrule them.

As pointed out in this book, civil–military relations in India—which more closely resemble Huntington's model of objective control—have, contrary to its prediction, not maximized military effectiveness. This is because civilians need to integrate military advice in framing national security policies, and military professionalism, in turn, requires civilian intervention. Instead of attempting to fix an artificial boundary around civilian and military domains, as Huntington's model does, a better approach is to create conditions that allow for a continuous, even if contentious, dialogue.

This, however, is not a wholehearted embrace of civilian meddling; instead, *informed* civilian intervention is key. Indeed, ill-informed or, worse, politically motivated civilian intervention, which is made possible under the civilian supremacist model, could lead to disaster. Politicians, therefore, by virtue of their own intellectual study and interest, rely on advisers in exercising civilian control. Indeed, Cohen's analysis of successful wartime leaders highlights the importance of "skilled assistants to translate their [leaders] wishes into directives, orders, requests, and suggestions."[10] Interestingly, these assistants were outside the military's chain of command, and, as noted by Cohen, "modern civil–military command systems do not allow for such a role."[11] The importance of such "skilled assistants" in fostering healthy civil–military relations and enhancing military effectiveness, however, needs further research.

One must, however, admit that the idea of objective control will probably continue to resonate. Indeed, the objective control model has been criticized almost since it was first presented, but it still finds devotees in both academic

---

[9] Peter D. Feaver, "The Right to Be Right: Civil–Military Relations and the Iraq Surge Decision," *International Security* 35, no. 4 (2011): 89–97.

[10] Cohen, *Supreme Command*, 214.

[11] Cohen, *Supreme Command*, 215.

and policy circles. In part, this is because of its elegant simplicity but also because there is a strong affinity for this model among members of the military. They like its underlying assumption—that politicians should set the strategic goals and grant maximum autonomy to the military to achieve these goals. The continuing resurrection of the objective control model therefore usually follows from a botched military campaign, which can be blamed, whether rightly or wrongly, on civilian interference and/or on pliant senior military leaders.

India and the Practice of Civil–Military Relations

There are three main insights for the practice of civil–military relations emerging from this book. First, attempts at creating distinct "civilian" and "military" domains have ill-served the state and the military. In India's case, due to the narrative surrounding the 1962 war, there are strong silos between the civilian and military domains, which has been inimical to complex civil–military tasks like strategy and doctrine formulation, defense planning, weapons procurement, and jointness, among others. This calls to attention the importance of the institutional design that is most conducive to what has been called the "necessary dialogue" between civilians and the military on matters pertaining to defense policy—from formulation to implementation.[12] As pointed out by Suzanne Nielsen and Don Snider, "policy choices must be informed by military expertise, while military operations must be aimed towards and infused with political purpose, or they make no strategic sense. This reality . . . requires close and constant interaction between political and military leaders."[13] An institutional design which creates distinct silos between them will certainly create problems and strengthen the "us and them" characteristic peculiar to civil–military relations. An integrated MoD—one that allows for civilians and military officials to work as colleagues—offers the best model for healthy civil–military relations. According to Douglas Bland, "the institution best suited to serve the minister's multifaceted duties is the integrated defense ministry. This type of ministry combines the [defense] minister's office, the civil service bureaucracy, and the military high command and their separate but linked responsibilities in one

---

[12] Suzanne Nielsen, "American Civil–Military Relations Today: The Continuing Relevance of Samuel P. Huntington's *The Soldier and the State*," *International Affairs* 88, no. 2 (2012): 376.

[13] Suzanne Nielsen and Don Snider, "Conclusions," in *American Civil–Military Relations: The Soldier and the State in a New Era*, ed. Suzanne C. Nielsen and Don M. Snider, 292 (Baltimore, MD: Johns Hopkins University Press, 2009).

establishment."[14] Such a measure goes a long way toward creating the conditions for a healthy dialogue.

Another insight emerging from this book is the importance of civilian bureaucrats in managing the routine, procedural matters that comprise the practice of everyday civil–military relations. This issue has not fetched the attention it deserves, but bureaucrats play an important role in managing the "expert problem" in civil–military relations.[15] The "expert problem" refers to the "information asymmetry" dilemma of "how are ministers to control the armed forces when they (usually) lack the necessary knowledge and experience to do this effectively?"[16] Put another way, how can civilians exercise control when they are dependent upon the military for information and advice?[17] This is an agency problem, but in practice, politicians try to overcome this dilemma by relying on bureaucrats who emerge as advisers, and provide assistance, to the defense minister. They are therefore the crucial pivot connecting politicians to the military and helping both in implementing defense policies.[18] India's experience in this regard has been mixed; bureaucrats have played an important role in exercising civilian control, but some of their actions, by both commission and omission, have hampered military effectiveness. It is axiomatic to say so, but considering the importance of their role, personnel who man these bureaucracies play a critical role in the conduct of civil–military relations.

Finally, this book highlights the importance of expertise in the practice of civil–military relations. Framing and implementing defense policies require experience and knowledge, as highlighted by all of the chapters in this book. Without such expertise, civilians struggle to understand the complexities and overcome information asymmetries. Bureaucratic expertise therefore strengthens the quality of civilian control and improves the "dialogue" between civilians and the military. In India, problems due to a lack of such expertise have been long acknowledged. In 2012, the Naresh Chandra Committee recommended that a "special cadre of Defence specialists should be introduced in the civil service to ensure knowledge build up among the civilian staff."[19] However, no steps have

[14] Douglas Bland, "Managing the 'Expert Problem' in Civil–Military Relations," *European Security* 8, no. 3 (1999): 38.

[15] Samuel Huntington, *The Soldier and the State: The Theory and Politics of Civil–Military Relations* (New York: Vintage Books 1957), 20.

[16] Douglas Bland, "A Unified Theory of Civil–Military Relations," *Armed Forces & Society* 26, no. 1 (1999): 13.

[17] For more on this, see Peter Feaver, *Armed Servants: Agency, Oversight, and Civil–Military Relations* (Cambridge, MA: Harvard University Press, 2003), 68–72.

[18] For more on the role of civilian bureaucrats, see Bland, "Managing the 'Expert Problem,'" 25–43.

[19] National Security Council Secretariat, *Report of the Task Force on National Security* (New Delhi: National Security Council Secretariat, 2012), 23. For a similar recommendation of a

been taken in this direction so far. The importance of civilian expertise is increasingly being acknowledged as an important element in civil–military relations. For instance, in Latin America, experts have identified the problem of a "defense wisdom deficit," arguing that "there are too few civilians who can call themselves experts—knowledgeable about the military organization and its inner workings and knowledgeable about defense policy, strategy, planning, and implementation. . . . The challenge is to get many more civilians educated in defense-related topics, creating programs and career tracks that can facilitate their entrance into government positions in the defense orbit."[20]

In addition, it is important to draw attention to the expertise of military officers themselves. It is often assumed that military officers, by virtue of their experience and training, would automatically possess relevant expertise. However, this would be a mistake. Most militaries emphasize and incentivize professional soldiering, but they need not educate their soldiers for handling complex defense-policy processes like weapons procurement, military education, and defense planning. Moreover, officers usually serve on a rotational basis, calling into question their expertise. Overcoming this problem would require sophisticated career planning and creating opportunities for developing sector-specific skills within the military. In sum, the expertise of both civilians and military officers is important in shaping civil–military relations.

These measures will go a long way toward creating conditions for healthier civil–military relations; however, there are also some caveats. First, there is no perfect institutional structure or system of civil–military relations that mitigates all of the problems in the relationship. Some tension between civilians and the military, what Eliot Cohen describes as a "deep undercurrent of mutual mistrust," is inevitable and cannot be wished away.[21] Moreover a fundamental principle of democratic civilian control—that "civilians have the right to be wrong"—by definition, creates resentment within the military. All the same, some practices are more conducive to healthier civil–military relations than others. Second, regardless of the institutional structure, personalities play an important role in civil–military relations. This is an understudied topic, perhaps because it does not lend itself to theorizing and generalizing; however, the psychological profile (and cognitive biases) of different actors—politicians, bureaucrats, and military officers—has an important role in the practice of civil–military relations.

"dedicated security administration cadre," see N. N. Vohra, "Civil–Military Relations: Opportunities and Challenges," *Air Power Journal* 8, no. 4 (2013): 15.

[20] David Pion-Berlin and Rafael Martínez, *Soldiers, Politicians, and Civilians: Reforming Civil–Military Relations in Democratic Latin America* (Cambridge: Cambridge University Press, 2017), 211.

[21] Eliot Cohen, *Supreme Command: Soldiers, Statesmen, and Leadership in Wartime* (New York: Free Press, 2002), 10.

Avenues for Future Research

There are three broad avenues for future research stemming from this book. First, there is a need for more comparative studies of civil–military relations to investigate aspects pertaining to institutional design, civilian expertise, and military autonomy. Such an approach can reveal insights pertaining to all three. For instance, how does the institutional design—the degree of integration between the MoD and the military headquarters—shape civil–military relations? Does greater integration necessarily lead to a greater degree of civilian control and healthier civil–military relations? Or does it instead institutionally empower the military and threaten civilian control? Should military officers at all serve in the MoD? If yes, how can this ensure firm civilian control while guarding against a potential conflict of interest? Despite its crucial role, ministries of defense, institutions that have been established relatively recently, are surprisingly understudied.[22] One promising area of scholarship is that pertaining to defense reforms, with its stated aim of addressing problems of institutional design and civil–military relations. Understanding what measures can enhance both civilian control and military effectiveness therefore should be of some interest.

The importance of civilian expertise has been highlighted throughout this book, but this aspect also requires further research. Does expertise among civilian bureaucrats strengthen civilian control and create conditions conducive to healthy civil–military relations? Or will such expertise create tensions with the military, which may resent its claims being challenged? How does one create and sustain such expertise? Is a seemingly mundane process like declassification of official papers the sine qua non for generating civilian expertise?

The extent of military autonomy is also fiercely debated. Should civilian faculty be involved in military education? Is this conducive to healthier civil–military relations? And does it enhance military effectiveness? How much oversight should civilians have in the framing and implementation of the military's promotion policies? What is the desired role for the military in weapons acquisition and development processes? There are no normative answers to these questions; however, an empirical study of how these processes play out in different countries would be enormously useful.

The second avenue for further research pertains specifically to the Indian military. One line of research could more explicitly show causation, or lack thereof, between the five variables and military effectiveness. For instance, have problems

---

[22] Thomas C. Bruneau and Richard B. Goetze, Jr., "Ministries of Defense and Democratic Control," in *Who Guards the Guardians and How: Democratic Civil–Military Relations*, ed. Thomas Bruneau and Scott Tollefson, 71–98 (Austin: University of Texas Press, 2006).

in weapons procurement, jointness, and defense planning adversely shaped combat and military effectiveness? There is some evidence that supports this claim; however, it requires some systematic investigation, ideally based on primary documents. There are also other possible lines of inquiry. Unlike the United States, why is it that in India nuclear weapons did not generate the rise of a civilian expertise on defense matters? Did the civil–military divide play any role in the development and robustness of India's nuclear weapons and its delivery systems? There is some evidence that in the early years India's nuclear scientists zealously guarded their autonomy and kept the military at the margins, but has this situation changed?[23] In short, even without primary documents, there are many issues worthy of investigation pertaining to the nuts and bolts of India's defense policy.

Finally, there is a need to undertake more research pertaining to state capacity and institutional effectiveness in India. One of the major findings of this book is that problems in India's military effectiveness can be blamed, in part, on a generalist civil service, which retains considerable decision-making powers. Logically, if lack of domain expertise creates problems in the defense sector, then shared administrative structures and procedures should create problems in other ministries and departments too. However, such broad generalization requires further research, which can then contribute to the current debate on state capacity, institutional effectiveness, and civil services performance and reform.[24] Interestingly, both administrative reform committees recommended some form of "domain specialization."[25] But the generalist versus specialist debate in public administration is an ongoing one. Yet, the experience of the Indian military suggests a need for a reform of administrative structures. Sadly this hasn't received the political attention that it deserves.

Looking to the Future

A constant theme of this book is for greater civilian dialogue with the military on various matters pertaining to defense policy. However, can this be a

---

[23] Anit Mukherjee, "Correspondence: Secrecy, Civil–Military Relations, and India's Nuclear Weapons Program," *International Security* 39, no. 3 (2015): 202–7.

[24] Devesh Kapur and Pratap Bhanu Mehta, eds., *Public Institutions in India: Performance and Design* (New Delhi: Oxford University Press, 2005); S. K. Das, *Building a World-Class Civil Service for Twenty-First Century India* (New Delhi: Oxford University Press, 2010); Prabhu Ghate, "Reforming the Civil Service: Meeting Crucial Need for Expertise," *Economic and Political Weekly* 33, no. 7 (1998): 359–65; and Vithal Rajan, "A System in Decay," *Economic and Political Weekly* 43, no. 14 (2008): 31.

[25] Second Administrative Reforms Committee, *Tenth Report: Refurbishing of Personnel Administration: Scaling New Heights* (New Delhi: Government of India, 2008), 14–18.

double-edged sword? In India's case, especially, is there a case to be made that greater political interest may politicize the armed forces and thereby weaken and divide it? Indeed, the fate of other institutions, like the judiciary, the Central Bureau of Investigation, the police and administrative services may serve as a cautionary tale.[26] The question then arises of whether the Indian people and its military can trust the judgment of its politicians. Democratic theory would suggest that has to be the case, but it is something that the people have to be vigilant about.

Apart from the potential danger of politicization of the military, perhaps a more probable scenario is that of recurring crises in civil–military relations. Without institutional reforms and a change in the adversarial nature surrounding civil–military relations, there may be more friction. It is not inconceivable that military officers, influenced by a toxic narrative of civilian mismanagement and hostility, will push back against perceived civilian intervention, thereby creating further controversies. Indeed, among the more worrying (and relatively recent) developments is the potential role of the Indian military as a pressure group.[27] For instance, In 2012, a track-two dialogue initiative had suggested some measures to demilitarize and eventually resolve the dispute in the Siachen glacier between India and Pakistan. However, the military and the veteran community acted as a pressure group to effectively kill this initiative.[28]

Some believe that in a democracy crises are necessary for change and, without it, bureaucracies are content with the status quo. The burden of proof lies with the reformers, who have to show that the system is ineffective or inefficient. A crisis, however, creates the opportunity for reformist officials to step in with their policy solutions. In India's case, such an argument applies for the 1991 economic liberalization, post-Kargil defense reforms, and the internal security reforms after the 2008 Mumbai attacks. Going by this logic, unfortunately, India might require an external crisis to bring about organizational change.

---

[26] Pratap Bhanu Mehta, "Whom do You Trust?" *Indian Express*, October 16, 2015, https://indianexpress.com/article/opinion/columns/whom-do-you-trust/; Ritu Sarin, "A Lower Low," *Indian Express*, October 26, 2018, https://indianexpress.com/article/opinion/a-lower-low-5418861/.

[27] Srinath Raghavan, "First OROP, Now Cantonment Roads: India Sees Rise of Military as Political Pressure Group," *The Print*, June 12, 2018, https://theprint.in/opinion/orop-cantonment-roads-india-sees-emergence-of-military-as-political-pressure-group/68976/

[28] Shiv Aroor and Gaurav C. Sawant, "Siachen Demilitarisation: Could PM Gift Away to Pakistan What Army Has Won?" *India Today*, May 14, 2012, https://www.indiatoday.in/magazine/cover-story/story/20120514-siachen-glacier-demilitarisation-indian-army-pakistan-758307-2012-05-05; Karan Kharb, "'Siachen Track II Forum' on a Treacherous Trek," *India Defence Review*, June 7, 2014, http://www.indiandefencereview.com/siachen-track-ii-forum-on-a-treacherous-trek/.

As discussed in the first chapter of this book, the absent dialogue persists because of three main factors. First, Indian politicians feel that as there is no dire existential threat, they can afford to have a system that muddles along. Historically, this is because they have feared a loss of civilian control, perhaps not in a manner that threatens the state (although some politicians may still harbor that fear); but apprehensions exist of a politically powerful military. Second, there are no electoral incentives for politicians to take an active interest in reshaping the military, especially when there is no consensus on defense reforms. Third, the existing institutional structure is convenient for all stakeholders as civilians are comfortable with this time-tested model, and the military is unwilling to discard the idea of strong civil–military domains. Politicians, by and large, are more comfortable and have familiarity with working with civilian bureaucrats than with military officers. Bureaucrats therefore became the face of civilian control, giving rise to a narrative, within the military, that they are under "bureaucratic control and not political control." Such a sentiment, whether justified or not, overlooks the considerable constraints under which bureaucrats operate within the government.[29] Moreover, "a pliant bureaucracy serves the purpose" of the political authorities.[30]

In sum, the weaknesses in the Indian military should not be blamed on civilian bureaucrats or on senior military officers but on the political leadership and its management of the military. A few years before his death, K. Subrahmanyam, having spent a lifetime in dealing with national security, had come to the conclusion that India's political class was "not in a position to tackle the national security issues with the seriousness they deserve."[31] That unfortunate reality is perhaps the single biggest takeaway of this book—that the absent dialogue is primarily because the politicians are unwilling to engage in one.

---

[29] See, for instance, "Battling the Baburaj," *The Economist*, March 6, 2008; and Sanjoy Bagchi, *The Changing Face of Bureaucracy: Fifty Years of the Indian Administrative Service* (New Delhi: Rupa Publishers, 2007).

[30] Editorial, "Perform or Perish?" *Economic and Political Weekly* 43, no. 52 (2008): 6.

[31] See "Report of the Kargil Review Committee: An Appraisal," *CLAWS Journal* (Summer 2009): 19.

POSTSCRIPT

Even while this book was going into print, a number of events pertaining to civil–military relations and military effectiveness came in for public discussion. This section analyzes three of these recent developments and their future implications.

First was the India–Pakistan crisis which occurred after a terrorist attack on an Indian paramilitary convoy in Pulwama in Kashmir on February 14, 2019.[1] The attack was carried out by a local Kashmiri; however, it was almost immediately claimed by the Pakistan-based terrorist group Jaish-e-Mohammed (JeM). Two weeks later, on February 26, the Indian Air Force (IAF) launched a targeted air strike at a JeM seminary in Balakot, Pakistan. Whether the bombs hit the intended target is still contested, but it was the first time that the Indian military had responded in this manner. The very next day, the Pakistan Air Force launched what it claimed was a retaliatory action in Indian Kashmir. There are conflicting reports of the aerial action, but on the Indian side a Mig-21 was shot down, its pilot captured by Pakistan (he was later repatriated), and an Mi-17 helicopter was brought down, in a friendly fire incident, killing six crew members and a civilian on the ground. The IAF claimed that it brought down a Pakistani F-16 fighter aircraft but could not present convincing evidence.[2] Most Indian commentators were supportive of the government's decision to launch air strikes

---

[1] This attack resulted in the death of forty-four security forces personnel and was the single largest loss of life in the entire Kashmiri insurgency since 1987; see Shaswati Das, "44 CRPF Jawans Killed, 70 Injured in Pulwama Terror Attack in J&K," Live Mint, February 18, 2019, https://www.livemint.com/news/india/pulwama-terror-attack-death-toll-rises-to-40-jem-claims-responsibility-1550143395449.html

[2] Sameer Lalwani and Emily Tallo, "Did India Shoot Down a Pakistani F-16 in February? This Just Became a Big Deal," *Washington Post*, April 17, 2019, https://www.washingtonpost.com/politics/2019/04/17/did-india-shoot-down-pakistani-f-back-february-this-just-became-big-deal/?utm_term=.b6bae93c9d13

but critical of the performance of the IAF. One analyst argued that the IAF "failed to deliver a deterrent punishment" on the Pakistan Air Force, blaming it on years of civilian neglect and slothful bureaucracies.[3] There were other accounts that supported this argument—that a lack of civilian responsiveness and urgency had created structural weaknesses within the IAF.[4] It may be misleading to read too much into a couple of tactical engagements; however, for critics, this was evidence of problems with military capability.[5] As pointed out by others, India's pattern of civil–military relations, therefore, has "hurt military effectiveness."[6] Despite Prime Minister Narendra Modi's rhetoric on being strong on national security, many were calling attention to declining budgetary allocations and a lack of substantive defense reforms, especially pertaining to civil–military relations and higher defense management.[7] Ironically, a few months later, Modi successfully used national security as one of his main election planks.

India held national parliamentary elections in the summer of 2019. In the beginning of the year, it appeared as if the opposition parties were ascendant as they won a number of state-level elections. However, after the Pulwama terrorist attack and the Balakot air strikes, there was a significant change in the public narrative and the tenor of the elections. Hereinafter, the elections effectively

---

[3] Shekhar Gupta, "Wing Commander Abhinandan Being Shot Down Is the Real Rafale Scandal," The Print, March 27, 2019, https://theprint.in/opinion/the-factivist/wing-commander-abhinandan-being-shot-down-is-the-real-rafale-scandal/212399/. For other critiques of the IAF, see Bharat Karnad, "IAF's Goofs and Delhi's Post-Pulwama Debacle: A Post-Mortem," Security Wise Blog (blog), March 19, 2019, https://bharatkarnad.com/2019/03/19/iafs-goofs-and-delhis-post-pulwama-debacle-a-post-mortem/, and Pravin Sawhney, "Fighting Tactical Battles for One-Upmanship," Tribune, April 18, 2019, https://www.tribuneindia.com/news/comment/fighting-tactical-battles-for-one-upmanship/760082.html. For a contrary view, see Rohit Vats, "The Print Article by Shekhar Gupta on Air Battle after Balakot Airstrikes Peddles Faulty Analysis, Half-Truths and Whole Lies," Opindia.com, March 31, 2019, https://www.opindia.com/2019/03/the-print-article-by-shekhar-gupta-on-air-battle-after-balakot-airstrikes-peddles-faulty-analysis-half-truths-and-whole-lies/, and Arjun Subramaniam, "Balakot and after: IAF Demonstrates Full Spectrum Capability," Firstpost.com, March 11, 2019, https://www.firstpost.com/world/balakot-and-after-iaf-demonstrates-full-spectrum-capability-6236391.html

[4] Snehesh Alex Philip, "Never Mind Balakot, IAF Is Worse Off than Pakistan Air Force on Pilot Strength," The Print, May 7, 2019, https://theprint.in/defence/never-mind-balakot-iaf-is-worse-off-than-pakistan-air-force-on-pilot-strength/231826/

[5] Sumit Ganguly and Rajan Menon, "What the India–Pakistan Crisis Taught China," The National Interest, March 7, 2019, https://nationalinterest.org/feature/what-india-pakistan-crisis-taught-china-46377

[6] Steven I. Wilkinson, Army and Nation: The Military and Indian Democracy since Independence (Cambridge, MA: Harvard University Press, 2015), 28.

[7] Manoj Joshi, "Why Modi Has Chosen Not to Side with the Indian Military," Daily O, March 26, 2018, https://www.dailyo.in/politics/defence-budget-narendra-modi-bjp-china-pakistan/story/1/23090.html

were about national security.[8] The Bharatiya Janata Party (BJP), led by Modi, telegraphed its national security credentials—through not just its "tough on terror" talk but also its support for the armed forces. Sensing the mood of the electorate, the opposition Congress Party also got into the act and, for the first time, released a "Plan on National Security."[9] In a press conference, the party further added that, "it would transform the Ministry of Defence into a fully integrated headquarters with the posting of service officers and appoint a Chief of Defence Staff."[10] This was an unprecedented development as in its forty-nine years in power; the Congress had always been reluctant to appoint a chief of defense staff. However, this became a moot point, and of an academic interest, as the BJP returned to power in an impressive electoral victory. While voting patterns and preferences require further research, it appears as if Modi's national security credentials paid off to a significant extent.

Finally, in the run-up to the polls, there were growing concerns about a possible politicization of the armed forces. This was perhaps inevitable for an election that focused on national security, but after the Balakot air strikes, the Election Commission of India sent a letter to all political parties instructing them to desist from using military photographs or symbols during their campaigns. Despite this advisory, there were transgressions, both minor and major—as the electoral spotlight turned to the military.[11] Alarmed by this development over 150 veterans, including some very senior officers, wrote an open letter to the president. However, BJP leaders dismissed this complaint as an instance of "fake news" as some of the listed officers subsequently denied supporting such an initiative.[12] A week later, the defense minister publicly welcomed seven retired military officers to join the

[8] Rahul Verma and Pranav Gupta, "Research Shows It Makes Sense for Narendra Modi & BJP to Focus on National Security in 2019," The Print, April 10, 2019, https://theprint.in/opinion/research-shows-it-makes-sense-for-narendra-modi-bjp-to-focus-on-national-security-in-2019/219143/; also see Rohan Venkataramakrishnan and Nithya Subramanian, "The Election Fix: Kargil to Balakot, Do Indians Vote with National Security in Mind?" Scroll.in, March 19, 2019, https://scroll.in/article/916860/the-election-fix-kargil-to-balakot-do-indians-vote-with-national-security-in-mind

[9] The Congress claimed that its plan was inspired by a report prepared by Lieutenant General D. S. Hooda; see India's National Security Strategy, March 2019, https://manifesto.inc.in/pdf/national_security_strategy_gen_hooda.pdf

[10] "Lok Sabha Elections: Congress Releases National Security Plan, Promises One Border, One Force," Indian Express, April 22, 2019, https://indianexpress.com/elections/congress-releases-national-security-plan-promises-one-border-one-force-lok-sabha-elections-5687490/

[11] Among the more controversial episodes was a reference by a prominent BJP politician to the armed forces as Modi ki Sena ("Modi's army").

[12] "Veterans Split over 'Politicisation of Armed Forces' Letter," The Quint, April 12, 2019, https://www.bloombergquint.com/politics/army-veterans-write-to-president-kovind-politicisation-of-forces

BJP.[13] When considered together, all these developments indicate that the military is in uncharted territory—wooed by political parties, while its actions and symbols are appropriated for political purposes. This had happened even earlier, in 2016, when the BJP had prominently played up the Uri "surgical strikes" ahead of crucial assembly elections.[14] For a number of observers, this close embrace of the military by political parties and their potential dalliance is a cause for alarm.[15] Indeed, if the military is identified too strongly with one political party, then it has the potential to cause turbulence in civil–military relations. There is a need therefore to enact policies to safeguard the apolitical image of the armed forces. For instance, there could be rules regarding cooling-off periods for all government employees (of a certain rank) who wish to join politics.

There is, however, a potential upside to these recent developments and political interest in the military. As explained in the introductory chapter, the absent dialogue in India persists because of three main factors: lack of existential threat, low salience in electoral politics, and a reluctance to change the status quo. If the takeaway after the Balakot air strikes is that the Indian military is in need of a radical overhaul and modernization or that India faces a deteriorating security scenario, then it might spur political leaders to pay attention to defense reforms. Alternatively, in light of the 2019 elections, if politicians no longer consider defense as an issue with low salience, then again it might lead to significant changes. In some ways, changes are already occurring, in admittedly minor ways, within the military. Even in the administrative structures, acknowledging problems with a lack of expertise, the government has recently allowed for lateral entry, even if on a limited scale.[16] Arguably, therefore, India and its military are at the cusp of transformative reforms. Whether India's political and military leaders are up for this task is still a matter of debate.

[13] Ajai Shukla, "Generals, Step Back," *Business Standard*, April 30, 2019, https://www.business-standard.com/article/opinion/generals-step-back-119042901144_1.html

[14] Ashok K. Mehta, "The Many Dangers of Politicising India's Army," The Wire, February 7, 2017, https://thewire.in/politics/politicising-military-dangers

[15] Sanjiv Krishan Sood, "India's Armed Forces Are Losing Their Political Neutrality – Putting National Security at Risk," Scroll.in, May 25, 2019, https://scroll.in/article/924409/indias-armed-forces-are-losing-their-political-neutrality-putting-national-security-at-risk; Harsha Kakar, "Politicising the Indian Army Is Destroying Its Internal Fabric," The Quint, November 9, 2017, https://www.thequint.com/voices/opinion/opinion-politicising-indian-army-could-ruin-its-internal-fabric, and Manoj Joshi, "Dividing to Conquer," *Tribune*, April 16, 2019, https://www.tribuneindia.com/news/comment/dividing-to-conquer/759056.html#disqus_thread

[16] Yamini Aiyar, "Can Lateral Entrants Save the Day?" *Hindustan Times*, April 24, 2019, https://www.hindustantimes.com/columns/can-lateral-entrants-save-the-day/story-EvwiueTA60XXhXKFGfDo6J.html. However, this is as yet not allowed for the Ministry of Defence; see P. C. Katoch, "Lateral Entry in Govt Service—and MoD Dumped," *SP's MAI*, April 19, 2019, http://www.spsmai.com/experts-speak/?id=682&q=Lateral-Entry-in-Govt-Service-and-MoD-Dumped

Appendix A

ARCHIVAL AND PRIMARY SOURCES

Hartley Library, University of Southampton: Louis Mountbatten Papers

MB1/D 139: Defence Committee: the establishment of committees and the military secretariat of the Indian 7 cabinet Dec 1947–Feb 1948

MB1/I-225: First Sea Lord (all three folders), 1955–1959

MB1/I 341: Admiral Sir Charles Thomas Mark Pizey: commander-in-chief Indian Navy, 1955–1956; commander-in-chief, Plymouth, 1956–1958, 1955–1959

MB1/J235: India: Politics and defense, 1959–1965.

MB1/J236: India 1959–1965

MB1/J302: Pandit Jawaharlal Nehru

MB1/J325: Srimati Vijaya Lakshmi Pandit, high commissioner for India in London; governor of Maharashtra 1960–1965

MB1/J341: Sir Richard Royle Powell: Ministry of Defence, 1959; permanent secretary, Board of Trade, 1960, 1959–1960

MB1/J599: Tour Far East 1964, India (1 of 2)

MB1/K 146: India: correspondents include Prime Ministers Moraji Desai and Indira Gandhi and President Dr. Sarvepalli Radhakrishnan, 1966–1977

The National Archives, London

DO 164/84: Communist China seen as main enemy against India and critical report into 1962 defeat by Chinese

DO 196/209: Krishna Menon

PREM/11, 3838: China/India frontier dispute

PREM 11/3876: Prime minister commented on visit of former US Treasury secretary to Kuwait to advise on investment policy

PREM 11/4865: Political situation in India

DEFE 11/ 845: India: senior defense appointments include Foreign and Commonwealth Office correspondence on arrest of Indira Gandhi

National Army Museum, London

Bucher Papers
Royal Society, London
PMS Blackett papers

Nehru Memorial Library and Museum (NMML), New Delhi

Oral History Transcripts: Lieutenant General B. M. Kaul, General J. N. Chaudhuri, Govind Narain, K. B. Lall, and P. M. S. Blackett
Personal Papers: P. N. Haksar papers, Thimayya papers, Thorat papers

Private Collection

Interview notes, Stephen Cohen papers

Appendix B

SELECTED GOVERNMENT DOCUMENTS

(Arranged Chronologically)

Reforming the National Security System: Report of the Group of Ministers on National Security. Group of Ministers Report. New Delhi: Government of India, 2001

Report of the Committee on National Defence University (CONDU), Vol. 1, 2002

Towards Strengthening Self Reliance in Defense Preparedness. New Delhi: Ministry of Defense, April 2005

Report of the Committee to Review the Armed Forces (Special Powers) Act, 1958. New Delhi: Ministry of Home Affairs, Government of India, 2005

Report of the Committee on Improving Defense Acquisition Structures in MoD, July 2007

Defence Expenditure Review Committee. New Delhi: Government of India, Ministry of Defence, 2009

Report of the Task Force on National Security. New Delhi: National Security Council Secretariat, 2012

Report of Raksha Mantri's Committee of Experts. New Delhi: Ministry of Defence, 2015

Defence Procurement Procedure 2016: Capital Procurement. New Delhi: Ministry of Defence, March 2016

Report on the Task Force of Selection of Partners. New Delhi: Government of India, Ministry of Defence, 2016

JP-01/2017 Joint Doctrine: Indian Armed Forces. New Delhi: Ministry of Defence, Integrated Defence Staff, 2017

Appendix C

INTERVIEW LIST

(Alphabetized By First Name)

1. A. K. Ghosh, financial adviser (Defence Services), Ministry of Defence
2. Air Marshal A. K. Nagalia, deputy chief of air staff, Air HQ
3. Lieutenant General A. S. Kalkat, Indian Peace Keeping Forces commander, Sri Lanka, 1987–1990
4. Lieutenant General Aditya Singh, commander-in-chief, Andaman and Nicobar Command (CINCAN)
5. Colonel Ajai Shukla, columnist, *Business Standard*
6. Lieutenant General Ajai Singh, director general, combat vehicles, Army HQ
7. Ajai Vikram Singh, defence secretary
8. Lieutenant General A. K. Singh, army commander
9. Amit Cowshish, financial adviser (acquisitions), Ministry of Defence
10. Lieutenant General Amitava Mukherjee, director general, air defense artillery
11. Lieutenant General Anil Ahuja, deputy chief of Integrated Defence Staff
12. Lieutenant General Anil Chait, chief of Integrated Defence Staff
13. Vice Admiral Anil Chopra, flag officer commanding, Western Naval Command
14. Vice Admiral Anup Singh, flag officer commanding, Eastern Naval Command
15. Archana Rai, principal director (Military Secretariat)
16. Lieutenant General Arjun Ray, army HQ
17. Lieutenant General Arun Kumar Sahni, army commander
18. Admiral Arun Prakash, chief of naval staff
19. Major General Arun Roye, Centre for Eastern and North Eastern Regional Studies Kolkata
20. Brigadier Arun Sahgal, Integrated Defence Studies

21. Arun Singh, minister of state for defense
22. Air Chief Marshal Arup Raha, chief of air staff
23. Arvind Gupta, deputy national security adviser, National Security Council Secretariat (NSCS)
24. Arvind Kadyan, Institute of Defense Studies and Analyses
25. Major General Ashok Mehta, Defense Planning Staff
26. Air Marshal Tej Mohan Asthana, commander-in-chief, Strategic Forces Command
27. Lieutenant General Ata Hasnain, military secretary
28. B. G.Verghese, member, Kargil Review Committee
29. Lieutenant General B. S. Malik, army HQ
30. Lieutenant General B. S. Nagal, Centre for Land Warfare Studies
31. Vice Admiral Barin Ghosh, Integrated Defence Staff
32. Bharat Karnad, National Security Advisory Board
33. General Bikram Singh, chief of army staff
34. Air Marshal B. D. Jayal, air officer commanding-in-chief, South Western Air Command
35. Brijesh Mishra, principal secretary and national security adviser
36. Lieutenant General Daljit Singh, army commander
37. General Deepak Kapoor, chief of army staff
38. Dhirendra Singh, home secretary
39. Major General Dipankar Bannerjee, Institute for Peace and Conflict Studies
40. G. K. Pillai, home secretary
41. G. Parthasarthy, Indian Foreign Service
42. Brigadier Gurmeet Kanwal, Centre for Land Warfare Studies
43. Lieutenant General H. S. Bagga, director general, manpower planning
44. Lieutenant General H. S. Panag, army commander
45. Major General Harkirat Singh, Indian Peace Keeping Forces
46. I. K. Gujral, prime minister
47. Air Commodore Jasjit Singh, director, Centre for Air Power Studies
48. Jaswant Singh, defense minister
49. Lieutenant General J. S. Bajwa, director general of infantry
50. K. C. Pant, defense minister
51. Lieutenant General K. K. Hazari, member, Kargil Review Committee
52. Major General K. S. Sethi, army HQ
53. K. Santhanam, Defence Research and Development Organisation
54. Lieutenant General Kamal Davar, Defense Intelligence Agency
55. Air Vice Marshal Kapil Kak, Center for Air Power Studies
56. Air Chief Marshal Srinivasapuram Krishnaswamy, chief of air staff
57. K. Subrahmanyam, chairman of the Kargil Review Committee
58. Laxman Kumar Behera, Institute for Defense Studies and Analyses

59. M. K. Narayanan, national security adviser
60. Air Vice Marshal Manmohan Bahadur, Centre for Air Power Studies
61. Air Marshal M. Matheswaran, deputy chief of the Integrated Defence Staff
62. Lieutenant General Mohinder Puri, deputy chief of army staff, army HQ
63. Rear Admiral Monty Khanna, commandant, Naval War College, Goa
64. Major General Mrinal Suman, army HQ
65. Lieutenant General N. C. Marwah, commander-in-chief, Andaman and Nicobar Command, (CINCAN)
66. General N. C. Vij, chief of army staff
67. N. S. Sisodia, Institute for Defense and Security Analyses
68. Air Vice Marshal Narayan Menon, air HQ
69. Lieutenant General S. L. Narasimhan, National Security Advisory Board
70. Naresh Chandra, cabinet and defense secretary
71. Major General Nilendra Kumar, judge advocate general, Indian Army
72. Vice Admiral P. K. Chatterjee, commander-in-chief, Andaman and Nicobar Command, (CINCAN)
73. Air Marshal P. K. Mehra, Centre for Air Power Studies
74. Lieutenant General P. K. Singh, director, United Service Institution of India
75. Lieutenant General P. R. Kumar, director general military operations
76. Vice Admiral Pradeep Chauhan, National Maritime Foundation
77. Vice Admiral Pradeep Kaushiva, National Maritime Foundation
78. Pradeep Kumar, defense secretary
79. Lieutenant General Prakash Menon, National Security Council Secretariat
80. Pramit Pal Chaudhuri, National Security Advisory Board
81. P. R. Chari, Institute for Defense Studies and Analyses
82. R. Chandrashekhar, Centre for Joint Warfare Studies
83. Major General R. K. Malhotra, National Security Council Secretariat
84. R. K. Mathur, defense secretary
85. Lieutenant General R. Nannavatty, army commander
86. Air Commodore R. V. Phadke, Institute for Defense and Security Analyses
87. Rear Admiral Raja Menon, assistant chief of naval staff (operations)
88. Lieutenant General Rakesh Sharma, adjutant general
89. Vice Admiral Raman Puri, chief of Integrated Defense Staff
90. Ronen Sen, prime minister's office
91. Brigadier Rumel Dahiya, Institute for Defense Studies and Analyses
92. Sanjoy Hazarika, member, Jeevan Reddy Committee
93. S. K. Sharma, defense secretary
94. Lieutenant General S. K. Sinha, vice chief of army staff
95. Air Chief Marshal S. P. Tyagi, chief of air staff
96. Lieutenant General S. S. Mehta, deputy chief of army staff
97. Rear Admiral Samir Chakraborty, Integrated Defence Staff

98. Sanjaya Baru, media advisor, prime minister's office
99. Lieutenant General Sanjay Kulkarni, Centre for Joint Warfare Studies
100. Rear Admiral Sanjeev Kapoor, Integrated Defence Staff
101. Satish Chandra, National Security Council Secretariat
102. Air Marshal Satish Inamdar, deputy chief of air staff
103. Lieutenant General Satish Nambiar, deputy chief of army staff
104. Vice Admiral P. S. Das, commander-in-chief, Eastern Naval Command
105. Shakti Sinha, secretary, government of India
106. Lieutenant General Shankar Ghosh, army commander
107. General Shankar Roychoudhary, chief of the army staff
108. Lieutenant General Shantonu Choudhary, vice chief of army staff
109. Shekhar Dutt, defense secretary
110. Vice Admiral Shekhar Sinha, chief of Integrated Defence Staff
111. Shilabhadra Bannerjee, director general, acquisition, Ministry of Defence
112. Shiv Shankar Menon, national security adviser
113. Shyam Saran, foreign secretary
114. Lieutenant General Subrata Saha, deputy chief of army staff (planning and systems)
115. Air Marshal Sumit Mukherjee, air officer personnel, air HQ
116. Admiral Sureesh Mehta, chief of naval staff
117. Admiral Sushil Kumar, chief of naval staff
118. Admiral R. H. Tahiliani, chief of naval staff
119. Commodore Uday Bhaskar, Institute for Defense Studies and Analyses
120. V. K. Misra, financial adviser (Defense Services), Ministry of Defence
121. General V. N. Sharma, chief of army staff
122. General V. P. Malik, chief of army staff
123. Lieutenant General V. Patankar, army HQ
124. Lieutenant General V. R. Raghavan, director general military operations
125. Lieutenant General Vijay Oberoi, army commander
126. Lieutenant General Vinod Bhatia, director general of military operations
127. Air Marshal Vinod Patney, vice chief of air force
128. Colonel Vivek Chadha, Institute for Defense Studies and Analyses
129. Lieutenant General V. K. Chopra, army HQ

INDEX